P O W E R

LEARNING AND YOUR LIFE
Essentials of Student Success

Robert S. Feldman
University of Massachusetts, Amherst

CUSTOM EDITION FOR SUFFOLK COMMUNITY COLLEGE
WITH STUDENT ACTIVITIES BY NANCY GERLI AND KRISTEN CONSENTINO

D1363797

 Learning Solutions

Boston   Burr Ridge, IL   Dubuque, IA   New York   San Francisco   St. Louis
Bangkok   Bogotá   Caracas   Lisbon   London   Madrid
Mexico City   Milan   New Delhi   Seoul   Singapore   Sydney   Taipei   Toronto

P.O.W.E.R. Learning and Your Life
Essentials of Student Success

This book is a McGraw-Hill Learning Solutions textbook and contains select material from *P.O.W.E.R. Learning and Your Life: Essentials of Student Success* by Robert S. Feldman. Copyright © 2011 by The McGraw-Hill Companies, Inc. Reprinted with permission of the publisher. Many custom published texts are modified versions or adaptations of our best-selling textbooks. Some adaptations are printed in black and white to keep prices at a minimum, while others are in color.

1 2 3 4 5 6 7 8 9 0 BRP BRP 13 12 11

ISBN-13: 978-0-07-751946-9
ISBN-10: 0-07-751946-9

Learning Solutions Manager: Domenic DiNardo
Production Editor: Nina Meyer
Printer/Binder: BR Printing

Research Your Major Objective

Purpose: Many college students choose a major without careful consideration. This assignment will help you to understand the importance of a college education in relation to your future. Upon completion, you should have more insight concerning your major field of study and be able to explore the various job opportunities available to you through your major.

Content: This is a 2 page written assignment that requires some researching. Answering the questions below will allow you to complete this project in an effective and efficient manner.

Discuss you major and why you chose it.
How do you personal interests translate into a college major?

Discuss the types of courses required.
What are the types of projects, papers and assignments involved?

Discuss the difficulty of your major.
Give three examples of the Pros and Cons of your major.
Does your field of study require more than a bachelor degree?

What types of jobs are available in your major?
How can one get a job in your field of study?
Approximately how many careers are in your major?
Are there other areas of work not directly related to your major?

Is you major not at Suffolk? What school would you be likely to transfer to to find your perfect major? What can you do at Suffolk now that will help you reach this goal?

Reports must be typed, double-spaced and have 1" margins. All research and information must be properly cited.
  Suggested Sources:
  1. **College websites and other internet sources**
  2. **Teachers, parents and friends**
  3. **College guide books and magazines**

Cite your sources using endnotes. To cite people include the name of the person, their position and when you talked to them. When using the internet, be careful to use reliable websites. Include the full web address and title of article used. When possible include author and page number. College guide books and magazines can be cited by giving their title, date of publication, title of article and page number(s).

Campus Resource Project

Name: _____

In order to complete the following project, you may need to speak to staff or faculty on the campus. The college catalog and the student handbook will also be useful.

1. In what office can you get your blood pressure taken? _____

What is the room number? _____

2. Your car has a flat tire and until your student loan check come in you don't have money to buy

a new one. Where can you get the money in the interim? _____

_____

3. What is the Compass? _____

(ATTACH A COPY)

4. List three campus clubs:

a. _____

b. _____

c. _____

5. What does G.P.A. mean? _____

6. Where is the Writing Center? _____

7. Is smoking permitted in any classroom? _____

8. What is the speed limit on campus? _____

9. Where so you get information on transferring to another college? _____

_____

10. How do you drop or add a class? _____

_____

Where is the Bookstore? _____

12. From what building can you observe the stars? _____

13. Where do you go to change your emphasis? _____

14. What is the name of the President of the College? _____

15. Who is the Executive Dean and where is he/she located? _____

_____

16. Where is the Art Gallery? _____

17. Where are part-time and full-time jobs listed? _____

18. List two jobs currently posted:

     a. _____

     b. _____

19. Where do you find a CLEP test? _____

20. Name four requirements for Graduation:

     a. _____

     b. _____

     c. _____

     d. _____

21. What is Evolution? _____

22. How much is a student ticket to a performance in Shea Theatre? _____

23. Phi Alpha Sigma is the _____

24. If you do not own a word processor, where can you type your papers on campus?

_____

CAMPUS ACTIVITY REPORT

The Campus Activity report should be a one page types report consisting of three parts: A description of the activity, the audience and your reaction to it. The following are guidelines to aid you in the report.

Name:
Campus Activity:
When: (time, date)
Where:
Participants:

The Activity:

The report should include at least one paragraph describing the activity you attended. If you attend a lecture, indicate the purpose of the main idea of the presentation and some of the issues raised. If you attend a club meeting, indicate the club name, type of club, purpose of the meeting, the issues discussed and the outcome (if any). If you attend a concert, indicate the specific type of performance, the length of the performance, and the types and variety of selections presented. If you attend a theater performance, summarize the plot of the production, and descried the setting and the performances.

The Audience:

Describe the reaction of others attending the activity. Indicate the size of the audience. Did people ask questions? How did people participate?

You:

Write a discovery statement about the activity you attended. What did you learn about the activity that you did not know before? What did you learn about yourself? Would you do this again?

Dedication

To my students, who make teaching a joy.

ROBERT S. FELDMAN

Robert S. Feldman still remembers those moments of being overwhelmed when he started college at Wesleyan University. "I wondered whether I was up to the challenges that faced me," he recalls, "and—although I never would have admitted it at the time—I really had no idea what it took to be successful at college."

That experience, along with his encounters with many students during his own teaching career, led to a life-long interest in helping students navigate the critical transition that they face at the start of their own college careers. Professor Feldman, who went on to receive a doctorate in psychology from the University of Wisconsin–Madison, teaches at the University of Massachusetts at Amherst, where he is the Dean of the College of Social and Behavioral Sciences. He directs POWER Up for Student Success, the UMass first-year experience course for incoming students.

Professor Feldman's proudest professional accomplishment is winning the College Outstanding Teaching Award at UMass. He also has been named a Hewlett Teaching Fellow and was Senior Online Instruction Fellow. He has taught courses at Mount Holyoke College, Wesleyan University, and Virginia Commonwealth University.

Professor Feldman is a Fellow of both the American Psychological Association and the Association for Psychological Science. He is a winner of a Fulbright Senior Research Scholar and Lecturer award and has written some 100 scientific articles, book chapters, and books. His books, some of which have been translated into Spanish, French, Portuguese, and Chinese, include *Improving the First Year of College: Research and Practice, Understanding Psychology*, 9/e, and *Development Across the Life Span,* 5/e. One of his most recent publications, *Psychology and Your Life,* afforded Professor Feldman an opportunity to work closely with returning and commuter students. It was through that experience that he devoted research and development to applying the P.O.W.E.R. Plan to a text devoted to this underserved and highly career-motivated student population. The result was this text. Professor Feldman's research interests encompass the study of honesty and truthfulness in everyday life, development of nonverbal behavior in children, and the social psychology of education. His research has been supported by grants from the National Institute of Mental Health and the National Institute on Disabilities and Rehabilitation Research.

With the last of his three children completing college, Professor Feldman occupies his spare time with serious cooking and earnest, but admittedly unpolished, piano playing. He also loves to travel. He lives with his wife, who is an educational psychologist, in a home overlooking the Holyoke mountain range in western Massachusetts.

Brief

Table of Contents

3 Taking Notes

4 Taking Tests

5 Reading and Remembering

6 Careers

9 Diversity and Relationships 212

10 Juggling: Stress, Money, Family, and Work   *235*

Robert S. Feldman

P O W E R

LEARNING AND YOUR LIFE

Essentials of Student Success

www.mhhe.com/power

The P.O.W.E.R. to Evolve

More so than ever before, the concept of "student" is changing. The idea that a student encompasses a cross-section of 18-year-olds attending a four-year university no longer applies as universally as it once did.

Students are also:

Employees
Employers
Co-workers
Parents
Friends
Siblings
Little League coaches
"Taxi drivers"
Overworked
Overcommitted
Overwhelmed

The list can probably go on from there. What else are you?

The purpose of this text is to take the P.O.W.E.R. framework, which has been proven effective, and apply it to a different type of student. While understanding your own study habits is important, how to study in a dorm is not information that every student needs. Just as our ideas of students are evolving, so can the texts that serve them.

We want all students to understand what it takes to be successful in school, life, and career. By providing a context that applies to students in a variety of educational models, we can better foster connections between the classroom and the professional arena. The educational conversation this text facilitates should speak to students that are more than just . . . students.

Succeed Now
School + Career + Life

Text Features:
Achieving the Goals of

P.O.W.E.R. Learning

P.O.W.E.R. Learning provides a systematic framework for organizing the strategies that lead to success

Each chapter utilizes the principles of the **P.O.W.E.R. system (Prepare, Organize, Work, Evaluate, and Rethink),** so students can clearly see how easy it is to incorporate this effective process into their everyday routine. The P.O.W.E.R. plan illustration highlights the key steps for the corresponding chapter material.

P Prepare

O Organize

W Work

E Evaluate

R Rethink

P.O.W.E.R. Plan

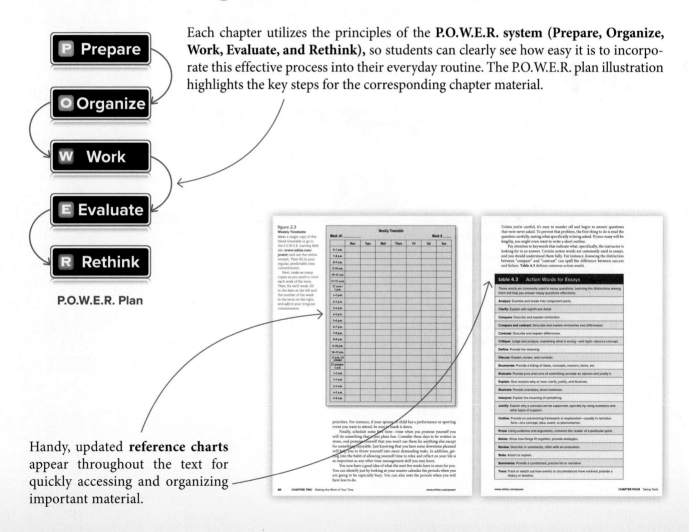

Handy, updated **reference charts** appear throughout the text for quickly accessing and organizing important material.

P.O.W.E.R. *Learning* offers a wide range of skill-building opportunities

Every chapter offers numerous **Try It** activities for gaining hands-on experience with the material covered in the chapter. These include questionnaires, self-assessments, and group exercises to do with classmates. The **Try It** activities, along with other assessment opportunities, are also available on the text's Web site at **www.mhhe.com/power.**

Try It!

Determine the Diversity of Your Community

Try to assess the degree of diversity that exists in your community. *Community* can be a loosely defined term, but for this **Try It** think of it as the group of people you encounter and interact with on a regular basis. When thinking of diversity, remember to include the many different ways in which people can be different from one another, including race, ethnicity, culture, sexual orientation, physical challenges, and so on.

Overall, how diverse would you say your community is?

Are there organizations in your community that promote diversity? Are there organizations that work to raise the visibility and understanding of particular groups within your community?

What is the nature of your college's *student* diversity in terms of statistics regarding membership in different racial, ethnic, or cultural groups? (You may be able to find these statistics on your college's website.)

Is your college community more or less diverse than your community at large? Why do you think this might be?

How does the diversity on your community compare to the following statistics on diversity in the United States as of the 2006 census: white, 74 percent; Hispanic or Latino, 15 percent; Black or African American, 13 percent; Asian, 4 percent; two or more races, 2 percent; American Indian and Alaska Native, .7 percent; Native Hawaiian and other Pacific Islander, .1 percent; other race, 6 percent? (Note: Percentages add up to more than 100 percent because Hispanics may be of any race and are therefore counted under more than one category.)

To Try It online, go to **www.mhhe.com/power.**

[RESOURCES]

AT SCHOOL

Some colleges offer courses in critical thinking, and they are a good b
decision-making and problem-solving skills. In addition, courses in log
will help improve critical thinking skills.

If you are having a personal problem that is difficult to solve, don't
staff at the counseling center or mental health center. Trained counsel
can help sort through the different options in an objective manner. They
sibilities for solutions that you didn't even know existed. Even if the pers
speak initially is not the right one, he or she can direct you to someone

Every chapter includes an updated list of the three types of **resources** that are useful in finding and utilizing information relevant to the chapter: a list of on-campus resources; books; and Web sites. There are also exercises in using the Web, called **Taking It to the Net.** This material helps students study and retain important concepts presented in the chapter, as well as guide future inquiry.

TAKING IT TO THE NET

1 Making good decisions can depend on distinguishing legitimate appeals (good reasons) from fallacious appeals (bad reasons). Go to San Jose State University's "Mission: Critical," an interactive tutorial in critical thinking (**www.sjsu.edu/depts/itl/graphics/adhom/appeal.html**). After reading the description of the different kinds of fallacious appeals, do the related exercises.

2 Locate three problem-solving strategies on the Internet. Possible strategy: Go to Yahoo! (**www.yahoo.com**) or AltaVista (**www.altavista.com**), and enter the key phrase "problem solving." Search the results until you find at least three different problem-solving strategies. Are these strategies similar to the ones described in the book? If not, how are they different?

Every chapter includes a **Course Connections** box that shows students how to use the chapter's content to maximize their success in particular classes.

The goals of *P.O.W.E.R. Learning and Your Life: Essentials of Student Success* are achieved through a consistent, carefully devised set of features common to every chapter. Students and faculty endorsed each of these elements.

Course Connections

Special Techniques for Dealing with Math Anxiety

For many students, the greatest test anxiety comes when they're taking a test involving math. Math seems to bring out the worst fears in some people, perhaps because it's seen as a discipline in which answers are either totally right or totally wrong, or because they've felt they've "hit the wall" and they'll never be able to understand a new concept, no matter how hard they try.

Such feelings about math can be devastating, because they can prevent you from doing well even if you know the material. If you suffer from math anxiety, keep these things in mind:

* Math is like any other subject: the greatest component of success is the effort you put in, not whether you have a "math gene" that makes you naturally good at math. It's not true that you either are born "good at math" or not and that there's some "secret" about math that some people know and others don't.

* It's also not true that there's only one way to solve a math problem. Sometimes there are a variety of routes to coming up with a solution. And keep in mind that the solution to math problems often calls for creativity, not just sheer logic.

* It's a false stereotype that women are not as good at math as men, but it's a stereotype that many women buy into. Research has shown that when men do badly on a math test, they're most likely to think that they haven't put in enough effort. But when women don't do well on a math test, they're three times more likely than men to feel that they don't have enough ability to be successful.[1] That's an erroneous view of the world. Don't become a prisoner of stereotypes.

Use these special strategies to deal with math problems on exams:

BEFORE TESTS:

1. Math is cumulative, building on prior concepts and knowledge. Make sure you review math fundamentals before moving on to more advanced topics.
2. Ask questions in class. Don't be afraid that you'll ask the wrong question in the wrong way. Instructors want you to understand their subject.
3. Make use of review sessions and other study resources.
4. Practice, practice, practice. The more experience you have completing math problems under pressure, the better you'll do. Practice math problems using a timer in order to simulate an actual test.

DURING TESTS:

1. Analyze math problems carefully. What are the known quantities or constants, and what pieces of information are missing? What formula(s) or theorem(s) apply?
2. Consider drawing a diagram, graph, or probability tree.
3. Break down calculations into their component parts.
4. Check your math carefully.
5. Be neat and logical in your presentation, and show every step as you solve problems. Your instructor may give you partial credit if you lay out every step you're going through. In addition, some instructors may require you to show your work.

P.O.W.E.R. Learning demonstrates the connection between academic success and success beyond the classroom

The **Career Connections** feature links the material in the chapter to the world of work, demonstrating how the strategies discussed in the chapter are related to career choices and success in the workplace.

speaking of **success**

NAME: Gustavus Dampier

SCHOOL: Hinds Community College, Jackson, Mississippi; Mississippi College, Clinton, Mississippi

HOME: Atlanta, Georgia

Many new **Speaking of Success** articles have been added that profile real-life success stories. Some of these people are well-known individuals, whereas others are current students or recent graduates who have overcome academic difficulties to achieve success.

When Gustavus Dampier first started classes he was confronted with two of the most challenging aspects of going to college: getting organized and managing his time. It wasn't long before he realized he needed to do something.

"I found it difficult to study my notes, primarily because they weren't organized. I wouldn't date my notes and would tend to lose them," he said. "I started getting a folder for each of my courses and used them to keep my notes. I would label the notes with the chapters they covered and dated them. Once I did that I started doing much better."

As his notes became more organized, Dampier often rewrote them. By rewriting his notes, he was able to better remember and retain the material, and this in turn made him prepared for exams.

At the same time he was organizing his notes, Dampier, who belonged to the track team, realized he needed to better manage his time between his studies and athletic activities.

"I found running track and studying was difficult. I just wasn't managing my time," he said. "So I just started studying earlier in the day instead of waiting until the last minute. And when I had time, I would take advantage of it."

Dampier improved his grades as well as his study habits, eventually moving on to a four-year college.

"But the transition was difficult for me," he explained, "because it took me out of my comfort zone at Hinds. There I knew the instructors, knew the school, and had friends. When I entered Mississippi College, it was like starting over again.

"But I made an effort to visit my professors in their office and whenever I would see them I would greet them with 'good morning' or 'good afternoon,' so after awhile they remembered me just by being polite to them."

258   CHAPTER TEN   Juggling: Stress, Money, Family, and Work   www.mhhe.com/power

From the perspective of . . .

A STUDENT To truly retain what you are reading, you must give your reading your undivided attention. Make a list of your biggest distractions and consider strategies for avoiding those distractions when you read.

From the Perspective of . . . . This feature highlights how the lessons learned in this course impact you both now and in your future career. Created to show the correlation between academic and professional life, these features answer the question of why this course matters and how it will impact student growth long after graduation.

P.O.W.E.R. *Learning* helps you develop critical thinking skills

Chapter 1 features a **P.O.W.E.R. Profile Assessment tool** that gives students a sense of where they stand—both numerically and graphically—in relation to the key topics addressed in the book. The **"P.O.W.E.R. Profile"** helps students identify their strengths and weaknesses and determine how they want to improve. Students can return to the **P.O.W.E.R. Profile** at the end of the course to assess and chart their progress.

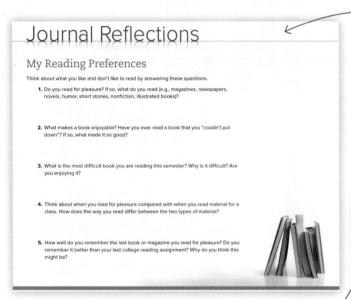

The **Journal Reflections** feature provides students with the opportunity to keep an ongoing journal, making entries relevant to the chapter content. Students are asked to reflect and think critically about related prior experiences. These conclude with questions designed to elicit critical thinking and exploration.

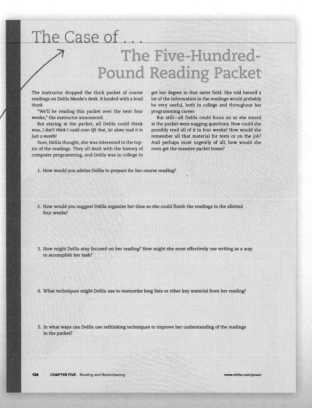

Each chapter ends with a **case study (The Case of . . .)** to which the principles described in the chapter can be applied. Case studies are based on situations that students might themselves encounter. Each case provides a series of questions that encourage students to consider what they've learned and to use critical thinking skills in responding to these questions.

P.O.W.E.R. Learning provides an engaging, accessible, and meaningful presentation

An appealing design and visual presentation highlight large, clear photos carefully selected to show the diversity of students as well as the latest in technological aids and devices.

Chapter-opening scenarios describe an individual grappling with a situation that is relevant to the subject matter of the chapter. Readers will be able to relate to these vignettes, which feature students running behind schedule, figuring out a way to keep up with reading assignments, or facing a long list of vocabulary words to memorize.

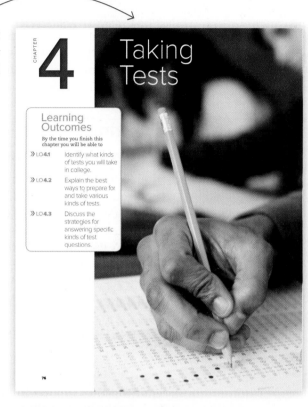

Key terms appear in boldface in the text and are defined in the margins. In addition, they are listed in a **Key Terms and Concepts** section at the end of the chapter, with accompanying page references.

CHAPTER 4 — Taking Tests

Learning Outcomes
By the time you will finish this chapter you will be able to

» LO 4.1 — Identify what kinds of tests you will take in college.

» LO 4.2 — Explain the best ways to prepare for and take various kinds of tests.

» LO 4.3 — Discuss the strategies for answering specific kinds of test questions.

76

Months of study and classes and reading and commuting to and from his college . . . now it all came down to a test.

That was the thought that ran through Eddie Penn's head as he sat down to take the final exam in his computer programming course. Eddie knew the test would end up counting for 65 percent of his final grade. If he passed, he would have enough credits to get the graphic design degree he'd been working toward for years. If he failed . . . Eddie tried not to think about that.

He'd taken tests before, but the stakes had never seemed so high for a single exam. Although he was fairly confident—he had studied hard—he couldn't relax altogether. He told himself that he had always done well on tests in the past; he wasn't going to fail now. But still—Eddie couldn't help but feel like his entire career, maybe his entire future, was on the line.

Looking Ahead

Although many tests are not as critical as Eddie Penn's computer programming final, tests do play a significant role in everyone's academic life. Students typically experience more anxiety over tests than over anything else in their college careers. If you're returning to college after a long break, or perhaps struggled with tests earlier in your academic career, you may find the prospect of taking a test especially intimidating.

But tests don't have to be so anxiety-producing. There are strategies and techniques you can learn to reduce your fear of test-taking. In fact, learning how to take tests is in some ways as important as learning the content that they cover. Taking tests effectively does not just involve mastering information; it also requires mastering specific test-taking skills.

One of the most important goals of this chapter is to take the mystery out of the whole process of taking tests. To do that, you'll learn about the different types of tests and strategies you can start using even before you take a test. You'll gain insight into how different kinds of tests work and how best to approach them, and you'll also learn about the various types of test questions and strategies for responding most effectively to each type.

This chapter also explores two aspects of test-taking that may affect your performance: test anxiety and cramming. You will learn ways to deal with your anxiety and keep cramming to a minimum—but you will also learn how to make the most of cramming, if you do have to resort to it.

The chapter ends with suggestions for evaluating your performance toward the end of a test and for using what you learn to improve your performance the next time around.

» LO 4.1 — Getting Ready

Tests may be the most unpopular part of college life. Students hate them because they produce fear, anxiety, apprehension about being evaluated, and a focus on grades instead of learning for learning's sake. Instructors often don't like them very much either, because they produce fear, anxiety, apprehension about being evaluated, and a focus on grades instead of learning for learning's sake. That's right: Students and instructors dislike tests for the very same reasons.

But tests are also valuable. A well-constructed test identifies what you know and what you still need to learn. Tests help you see how your performance compares with that of others. And knowing that you'll be tested on a body of material is certainly likely to motivate you to learn material more thoroughly.

However, there's another reason you might dislike tests: You may assume that tests have the power to define your worth as a person. If you do badly on a test, you may be tempted to believe that you've received some fundamental information about yourself from the instructor and the college, information that says you're a failure in some significant way.

$$\Big[\ \text{KEY TERMS AND CONCEPTS}\ \Big]$$

Advance organizers (p. 106)	Mnemonics (p. 118)	Overlearning (p. 120)
Frontmatter (p. 107)	Acronym (p. 118)	Learning disabilities (p. 121)
Attention span (p. 110)	Acrostic (p. 118)	
Rehearsal (p. 118)	Visualization (p. 120)	

All of these reviewed and tested features are designed not only to help understand, practice, and master the core concepts presented in this text, but also to collectively support the main goals and vision of this text, as demonstrated on the following pages.

The P.O.W.E.R. Resources

The same philosophy and goals that guided the writing of *P.O.W.E.R. Learning and Your Life: Essentials of Student Success* led to the development of a comprehensive teaching package. Through a series of focus groups, questionnaires, and surveys, we asked instructors what they needed to optimize their courses. We also analyzed what other publishers provided to make sure that the ancillary materials accompanying *P.O.W.E.R. Learning and Your Life* would surpass the level of support to which instructors are accustomed. As a result of the extensive research that went into devising the teaching resources, we are confident that whether you are an instructor with years of experience or are teaching the course for the first time, this book's instructional package will enhance classroom instruction and provide guidance as you prepare for and teach the course.

Print Resources

INSTRUCTOR'S EDITION

(0-07-737539-4): The Instructor's Edition (IE), prepared by Joni Webb Petschauer and Cindy Wallace of Appalachian State University, contains the full text of the student edition of the book with the addition of notes that provide a rich variety of teaching strategies, discussion prompts, and helpful cross-references to the Instructor's Resource Manual. The IE has been completely redesigned in an effort to provide more frontline teaching assistance. Notes are easily laid out in the back of the text and include myriad additional class activities, teaching advice, and guidance toward a successful classroom.

INSTRUCTOR'S RESOURCE MANUAL

(0-07-730123-4): Written by Joni Webb Petschauer and Cindy Wallace of Appalachian State University with additional contributions from experienced instructors across the country, this manual provides specific suggestions for teaching each topic, tips on implementing a first-year experience program, handouts to generate creative classroom activities, audiovisual resources, sample syllabi, and tips on incorporating the Internet into the course.

CUSTOMIZE YOUR TEXT

P.O.W.E.R. Learning and Your Life: Essentials of Student Success can be customized to suit your needs. The text can be abbreviated for shorter courses and can be expanded to include semester schedules, campus maps, additional essays, activities, or exercises, along with other materials specific to your curriculum or situation. Chapters designed for student athletes, transferring students, and career preparation are also available.

STUDENT PLANNER

Updated annually, this convenient organizational tool is available as a standalone or with the student text. The planner provides daily tips for success, time-management techniques, a daily calendar, and contact information.

Human Resources

WORKSHOPS WITH AUTHOR AND AUTHOR TEAM

Are you faced with the challenge of launching a first-year experience course on your campus? Would you like to invigorate your college success program, incorporating the most recent pedagogical and technological innovations? Is faculty recruitment an obstacle to the success of your program? Are you interested in learning more about the P.O.W.E.R. system?

Workshops are available on these and many other subjects for anyone conducting or even just considering a first-year experience program. Led by author Robert Feldman, *P.O.W.E.R. Learning and Your Life* Instructor's Resource Manual authors Joni Webb Petschauer and Cindy Wallace, or one of the McGraw-Hill P.O.W.E.R. Learning consultants, each workshop is tailored to the needs of individual campuses or programs. For more information, contact your local representative, or e-mail us at **fye@mcgraw-hill.com.**

Digital Resources

LASSI: LEARNING AND STUDY STRATEGIES INVENTORY

The LASSI is a 10-scale, 80-item assessment of students' awareness about and use of learning and study strategies related to skill, will, and self-regulation components of strategic learning. The focus is on both covert and overt thoughts, behaviors, attitudes, and beliefs that relate to successful learning and that can be altered through educational interventions. Research has repeatedly demonstrated that these factors contribute significantly to success in college and that they can be learned or enhanced through educational interventions such as learning and study skills courses.

The LASSI provides standardized scores and national norms for 10 different scales. The LASSI is both diagnostic and prescriptive. It provides students with a diagnosis of their strengths and weaknesses compared to other college students in the areas covered by the 10 scales, and it is prescriptive in that it provides feedback about areas where students may be weak and need to improve their knowledge, attitudes, beliefs, and skills.

The LASSI is available in print or online at **www.hhpublishing.com.** Ask your McGraw-Hill sales representative for more details.

IMPLEMENTING A STUDENT SUCCESS COURSE

This innovative Web content (available on the OLC) assists you in developing and sustaining your Student Success course. Features include a "how to" guide for designing and proposing a new course, with easy-to-use templates for determining budget needs and resources. Examples of model programs are provided from two-year, four-year, and career schools. The site explores course goals, such as orientation and retention, and provides research data to support your proposal. Also included are materials to help sustain your course, such as faculty development programs and online resources.

COURSE CONTENT FOR YOUR LEARNING MANAGEMENT SYSTEM

The online content of *P.O.W.E.R. Learning and Your Life: Essentials of Student Success* is supported by WebCT, eCollege.com, and Blackboard. Additionally, our PageOut service, free to qualified adopters, is available to get you and your course up and running online in a matter of hours! To find out more contact your local McGraw-Hill representative or visit **www.pageout.net.**

P.O.W.E.R. LEARNING AND YOUR LIFE: ESSENTIALS OF STUDENT SUCCESS ONLINE LEARNING CENTER WEB SITE

(**www.mhhe.com/power**): Instructors and students will find materials such as downloadable resources, self-quizzes, online journal activities and assessments, case study assignments, Web exercises, and a rich bank of links for college success. Instructor's resources also include an EZ Test computerized test bank and chapter-by-chapter PowerPoint presentations. There is also the inclusion of an Asset Map that identifies ancillary material for instructors and is broken down by Learning Outcome.

connect™ plus+

LESS MANAGING.

MORE TEACHING.

GREATER LEARNING.

What Is Connect *Plus*+?

McGraw-Hill Connect *Plus*+ is a revolutionary online assignment and assessment solution providing instructors and students with tools and resources to maximize their success.

Through Connect *Plus*+, instructors enjoy simplified course setup and assignment creation. Robust, media-rich tools and activities, **all tied to the textbook's learning outcomes**, ensure you'll create classes geared toward achievement. You'll have more time with your students and less time agonizing over course planning.

Connect *Plus*+ Features

McGraw-Hill Connect *Plus*+ includes powerful tools and features that allow students to access their coursework anytime and anywhere, while you control the assignments. Connect *Plus*+ provides students with their textbook and homework, **all in one accessible place.**

▶ *Simple Assignment Management*
Creating assignments takes just a few clicks, and with Connect *Plus*+, you can choose not only which chapter to assign but also specific learning outcomes. **Videos, animations, quizzes**, and many other activities bring **active learning** to the forefront.

▶ *Smart Grading*
Study time is precious and Connect *Plus*+ assignments **automatically provide feedback** to you and your students. You'll be able to conveniently review class or individual student knowledge in an online environment.

▶ *Connect Plus+ eBooks*
McGraw-Hill has seamlessly **integrated eBooks** into their Connect *Plus*+ solution with **direct links to the homework, activities, and tools**—students no longer have to search for content, allowing them more time for learning.

McGraw-Hill provides live instructor orientations for Connect *Plus*+ to guarantee you will have a worry-free experience.

The POWER to Succeed!

→ The POWER of Support!

Let the McGraw-Hill Student Success Team support your course with our workshop program.

> ▸ Planning to develop a First-Year Experience course from scratch?
> ▸ Reenergizing your First-Year Experience course?
> ▸ Trying to integrate technology in your class?
> ▸ Exploring the concept of learning communities?

We offer a range of author- and consultant-led workshops that can be tailored to meet the needs of your institution.

Our team of experts, led by *P.O.W.E.R. Learning and Your Life: Essentials of Student Success* author Robert Feldman, can address issues of course management, assessment, organization, and implementation. How do you get students to commit to your program? How do you achieve support from your institution? How can you evaluate and demonstrate the effectiveness of your first-year experience course? These are questions that every program faces. Let us help you to find an answer that works for you.

Other workshop topics may include:

> ▸ Classroom Strategies for Enhancing Cultural Competence: The P.O.W.E.R. of Diversity
> ▸ Using Learning Styles in the Classroom
> ▸ Creating Student Success Courses Online
> ▸ Motivating Your Students

To schedule a workshop, please contact your local McGraw-Hill representative. Alternately, contact us directly at **fye@mcgraw-hill.com** to begin the process of bringing a P.O.W.E.R. Learning workshop to you.

The POWER to Create Your Own Text!

Do you want to:

> ▸ Cover only select chapters?
> ▸ Personalize your book with campus information (maps, schedules, registration materials, etc.)?
> ▸ Add your own materials including exercises or assignments?
> ▸ Address specific student populations, such as student athletes and transferring students?

P.O.W.E.R. Learning and Your Life: Essentials of Student Success can be customized to suit your needs.[1]

WHY CUSTOMIZE?

Perhaps your course focuses on study skills and you prefer that your text not cover life issues such as money matters, health and wellness, or information on choosing a major. Whatever the reason, we can make it happen, easily. McGraw-Hill Custom Publishing can deliver a book that perfectly meets your needs.

[1]Orders must meet our minimum sales unit requirements.

WHAT WILL MY CUSTOM BOOK LOOK LIKE?

Any chapters from the *P.O.W.E.R. Learning and Your Life* book that you include will be in full color. Additional materials can be added between chapters or at the beginning or end of the book in black and white. Binding (paperback, three-hole punch, you name it) is up to you. You can even add your own custom cover to reflect your school image.

WHAT CAN I ADD?

Anything! Here are some ideas to get you started:

▸ **Campus map** or anything specific to your school: academic regulations or requirements, syllabi, important phone numbers or dates, library hours.

▸ **Calendars** for the school year, for local theater groups, for a concert series.

▸ **Interviews** with local businesspeople or your school's graduates in which they describe their own challenges and successes.

▸ **Your course syllabus or homework assignments** so your students have everything they need for your course under one cover and you don't have to make copies to hand out.

SPECIAL CHAPTERS DESIGNED FOR THE UNIQUE NEEDS OF YOUR STUDENTS!

Three additional chapters are available for your customized text and have been designed to address the needs of specific student populations.

▸ Strategies for Success for Student Athletes. This chapter discusses the unique challenges of student athletes, such as managing school and team pressures, using resources and understanding eligibility, and knowing when and how to ask for help. It also addresses special concerns such as burnout, dealing with injury, and hazing.

▸ Taking Charge of Your Career. This chapter helps students determine the best career choices that fit personal goals. It provides important tips on how to develop a career portfolio, prepare a résumé and cover letters, and have a successful interview, including follow-up strategies.

▸ Transfer Strategies: Making the Leap from Community College to a Four-Year School. Designed for the potential transfer student, this chapter looks at the pros and cons of moving beyond a two-year degree and what personal decisions to make. It guides students through the transfer process, including applications, credit transfer, financial assistance, and transfer shock.

HOW DO I CREATE A CUSTOM BOOK?

The secret to custom publishing is this: Custom Publishing Is Simple!
Here are the basic steps:

▸ You select the chapters you would like to use from P.O.W.E.R. Learning with your McGraw-Hill sales representative.

▸ Together, we discuss your preferences for the binding, the cover, etc., and provide you with information on costs.

▸ We assign your customized text an ISBN and your project goes into production. A custom text will typically publish within 6–8 weeks of the order.

▸ Your book is manufactured and it is put into inventory in the McGraw-Hill distribution center.

➤ You are sent a free desk copy of your custom publication.

➤ Your bookstore calls McGraw-Hill's customer service department and orders the text.

You select what you want—we handle the details!
Contact us:

www.mhhe.com/power
Canada: 1-905-430-5034
United States: 1-800-446-8979
E-mail: fye@mcgraw-hill.com

I am indebted to the many reviewers of *P.O.W.E.R. Learning and Your Life* who provided input at every step of development of the book and the ancillary package. These dedicated instructors and administrators provided thoughtful, detailed advice, and I am very grateful for their help and insight. They include the following:

Overall P.O.W.E.R. Plan–Miriam Frances Abety, Miami Dade College; Peg Adams, Northern Kentucky University; Angela Alexander, Nicholls State University; Mary Asher-Fitzpatrick, Cuyamaca College; Brenda Atchison, McLennan Community College; Rebecca Barr, Palomar College; Michelle Bates, Southeastern Louisiana University; Linda Blair, Pellissippi State Technical Community College; Judith Chaplain, Ozarks Technical Community College; Lisa Christman, University of Central Arkansas; Emily Cowdrick, Georgia Perimeter College–Lawrenceville; Margo Eden-Camann, Georgia Perimeter College; Louise Ericson, University of South Carolina–Upstate; Jo Ella Fields, Oklahoma State University–Oklahoma City; Connie Gulick, Central New Mexico Community College; Linda Hasty, Motlow State Community College; Bob Holdeman, University of South Carolina; Lois Darlene Hurd, Jefferson Community and Technical College, Southwest; Ann Iseda, Jackson Community College; Joel Jessen, Eastfield College; Cathi Kadow, Purdue University–Calumet; Linda Cooper Knight, College of the Albemarle; Judith Lynch, Kansas State University; Judith Miller, Blue Ridge Community College; David Neis, Southern Illinois University–Carbondale; Maria Parnell, Brevard Community College; Joanne Pinkston-McDuffie, Daytona Beach Community College; Angela Reeves, Mott Community College; Janice Reilly, Mesa Community College; Sherry Rhoden, Grand Rapids Community College; Dwight Rinehart, Reading Area Community College; Brieana Roumeliotis, California State University–Fullerton and Golden West College; Ryan Ruda, Garden City Community College; Dawn Shaffer, Central Piedmont Community College; Sharon Snyders, Ivy Tech Community College; Bruce Tucker, Santa Fe Community College; Douglas Watson, Weber State University; Kathie Wentworth, Tri-State University; Stephanie Foote, University of South Carolina, Aiken; Linda Burdsall, Jackson State Community College; Cheryl Burk, Wake Technical Community College; Terry Rafter Carles, Valencia Community College–East; Stephanie Crecca, Institute of Business and Medical Careers; Melanie Deffendall, Delgado Community College; Rebecca Ellison, Jefferson College; Charles Frederick, Jr., Indiana University; Jo Ann Jenkins, Moraine Valley Community College; Elvira Johnson, Central Piedmont Community College; Mahalia Johnson, Greenville Technical College; Elizabeth Kennedy, Florida Atlantic University; Kimberly Little, Southern Illinois University–Carbondale; Candace Maher, Central New Mexico Community College; Lucy Marrero, Santa Fe Community College; Al Matthews, North Lake College; Richard McMullen, Western Michigan University; Beryl Odom, Gadsden State Community College; Jody Owen, South Dakota State University; Mia Pierre, Valencia Community College–West; Karen Sumner, University of Sioux Falls; Francisca Uvah, University of West Florida.

Student Success and Your Life–Dr. P.C. Baytop, The Community College of Baltimore County; Sharon R. Vriend-Robinette, Davenport University; Christine M. Gaiser, Bryant & Stratton College; John Luukkonen, Ph.D., TCI College of

Technology; Deborah A. Herzog, BA, Lewis and Clark Community College; Alfred Ebert, Brown Mackie College; Ryan B. Weaver, Brown Mackie College; Kathy Hipp, Brown Mackie College; Jean Fennema, Pima Medical Institute; D. Jeanne Ross, Monroe College; Laura Ristrom Goodman, Pima Medical Institute; Charlene Latimer, Daytona State College; Linda Denniston, Brown Mackie College; Dr. Wayne C. Smith, Community College of Spokane.

P.O.W.E.R. *Learning and Your Life* author Bob Feldman and some of his first-year experience program participants.

The students in my own first-year experience courses (some of whom are shown here) provided thoughtful and wise advice. I thank them for their enthusiasm and eager willingness to provide constructive feedback.

Professors Cindy Wallace and Joni Webb Petschauer of Appalachian State University wrote the Instructor's Resource Manual and provided notes and tips for the Instructor's Edition. I thank both of them for their enthusiasm, good ideas, dedication, and friendship.

Edward Murphy, Ed.D, an educational testing expert, helped develop the exercises in the book, and I'm grateful for his excellent work.

John Graiff and Tolley Jones were a great help on every level in putting this book together, and I thank them for their willingness to go the extra mile. I could not have written this book without their unflagging support.

I am proud to be part of an extraordinary McGraw-Hill editorial, marketing, and sales team. My sponsoring editor, Alice Harra, has brought enthusiasm and intelligence to the project, and I welcome her good work.

I am especially grateful to Kristin Bradley, development editor, whose keen editorial eye, creativity, and wealth of good ideas has improved this book significantly. She is truly a delight to work with.

There are several folks who, while no longer officially working on the project, still patiently answer my queries and offer their advice, for which I am extremely grateful. Andy Watts made superb contributions in extending the reach of *P.O.W.E.R. Learning and Your Life,* and I'm very grateful for his work and even more for his friendship. Phil Butcher, Thalia Dorwick, David Patterson, Allison McNamara, and Alexis Walker were part of the team that developed the book, and I'm ever thankful for their efforts. Above all, I'm grateful to Rhona Robbin, first development editor on the project, and sponsoring editor Sarah Touborg, who provided the impetus for the book. Certainly, the pages of *P.O.W.E.R. Learning and Your Life* continue to reflect their many contributions.

Without a doubt, there is no better publishing group in the business than the one that worked on *P.O.W.E.R. Learning and Your Life.* I count myself extremely lucky not only to have found myself a part of this world-class team, but to count each of them as friends.

In the end, I am eternally indebted to my family, both extended and immediate. Sarah, Josh, Julie, Jon, Leigh, Alex, and of course Kathy, thank you for everything.

Robert S. Feldman

Congratulations! You are at the beginning of an academic journey that has the potential to impact your future in ways you can only imagine. This text and this course are designed to help make that journey as meaningful and enriching as possible. As you begin this chapter of your life, remember that you are not alone.

Every first-year student (as well as many returning students) encounters challenges. Whether it be juggling family, work, and school or preparing for a test, the challenges you face are winnable. This is where *P.O.W.E.R. Learning and Your Life: Essentials of Student Success* comes in. It is designed to help you to master the challenges you'll face in school as well as in life after graduation. The P.O.W.E.R. Learning system—which is based on five key steps embodied in the word P.O.W.E.R. (Prepare, Organize, Work, Evaluate, and Rethink)—teaches strategies that will help you become a more successful student and that will give you an edge in attaining what you want to accomplish in life.

But it's up to you to make use of the book. By familiarizing yourself with its features and using the built-in learning aids, you'll maximize its usefulness and be more likely to get the most out of it.

Familiarize Yourself with the Scope of *P.O.W.E.R. Learning and Your Life*

Begin by skimming the Table of Contents, which provides an overview of the book. By reading the chapter titles, you'll get a sense of the topics that are covered and the logic of the sequence of chapters.

Then, Take Some Time to Flip through the Book

Choose a chapter that sounds interesting to you, skim a few pages, and see for yourself the kinds of practical information the book provides. Note that every chapter has the same diamond-shaped pattern:

Opening Prologue
Looking Ahead
The Main Body of the Chapter
Looking Back/Resources
Case Study

Get in Touch

I welcome your comments and suggestions about *P.O.W.E.R. Learning and Your Life,* as well as the Web site that accompanies the book. You can write me at the College of Social and Behavioral Sciences at the University of Massachusetts, Amherst, Massachusetts 01003. Even easier, send me an e-mail message at **feldman@sbs. umass.edu.** I will write back!

A final word: *P.O.W.E.R. Learning and Your Life* presents the tools that can maximize your chances for academic and life success. But remember that they're only tools, and their effectiveness depends on the way in which they are used. Ultimately, you are the one who is in charge of your future.

Make the journey a rewarding, exciting, and enlightening one!

Robert S. Feldman

CHAPTER 1

Learning Outcomes

By the time you finish this chapter you will be able to

▶ LO**1.1** Discuss the benefits of a college education.

▶ LO**1.2** Identify the basic principles of P.O.W.E.R. Learning.

▶ LO**1.3** Explain how expert students use P.O.W.E.R. Learning.

▶ LO**1.4** Compare and contrast learning styles and identify your own.

P.O.W.E.R.
Learning:
Becoming
an Expert
Student

The day has started off with a bang. Literally. As Abbie Suarez struggles sleepily to turn off her clock radio's continual buzzing at 6:35 a.m., she knocks it off the table next to her bed. The loud bang it makes as it hits the floor not only wakes her fully, but rouses her daughters sleeping in the next room, who grumble resentfully.

Struggling out of bed, Abbie reflects on the day ahead. It's one of her most intense days—two shifts at two different part-time jobs on different sides of town. She also must get her children ready for school and then take them to swimming lessons in the afternoon. And on top of all that, she has an exam that morning at the college she attends.

After a quick shower, Abbie manages to get her daughters off to school, and then joins her fellow paralegal students on campus. She glances at her paralegal textbook and feels a wave of anxiety flood over her: Will I do well enough on my exam? How will I manage to hold down two jobs, take care of my family, and have enough time to study? Will I find a job as a paralegal after graduation? Will I make my children proud? . . . *And underlying them all is a single challenge: Will I be successful in college and in my career?*

Looking Ahead

Whether academic pursuits are a struggle or come easily to you . . . whether you are returning to college or attending for the first time . . . whether you are gaining new skills for your current job or are starting on a whole new career path—college is a challenge. Every one of us has concerns about our capabilities and motivation, and new situations—like starting college—make us wonder how well we'll succeed.

That's where this book comes in. It is designed to help you learn the most effective ways to approach the challenges you encounter, not just in college, but in your career, too. It will teach you practical strategies, hints, and tips that can lead you to success, all centered around an approach to achieving classroom and career success: P.O.W.E.R. Learning.

This book is designed to be useful in a way that is different from other college texts. It presents information in a hands-on format. It's meant to be used—not just read. Write on it, underline words and sentences, use a highlighter, circle key points, and complete the questionnaires right in the book. The more exercises you do, the more you'll get from the book. Remember, this is a book to help you throughout college and throughout your career, so it's a good idea to invest your time here and now. If the learning techniques you master here become second nature, the payoff will be enormous.

This first chapter lays out the basics of P.O.W.E.R. Learning. It will also help you determine the way in which you learn best and how you can use your personal learning style to study more effectively.

» LO 1.1 Why Go to College?

Congratulations. You're in college.

But why? Although it seems as if it should be easy to answer why you're continuing your education, for most people it's not so simple. The reasons that people go to college vary from the practical ("I need new skills for my job"), to the lofty ("I want to build a better life for my family"), to the vague ("Why not?—I don't have anything better to do"). Consider your own reasons for attending college, as you complete **Try It 1.**

It's likely that one of your primary motivations for attending college is to further your career. In fact, surveys of first-year college students at all types of institutions show that almost three-quarters say they want to learn about things that interest them, get training for a specific career, land a better job, and make more money

Why Am I Going to College?

Place a 1, 2, and 3 by the three most important reasons that you have for attending college:

1 I want to get a good job when I graduate.

1 I want to make my family proud.

3 I couldn't find a job.

3 I want to try something new.

3 I want to get ahead at my current job.

1 I want to pursue my dream job.

2 I want to improve my reading and critical thinking skills.

2 I want to become a more cultured person.

1 I want to make more money.

2 I want to learn more about things that interest me.

3 A mentor or role model encouraged me to go.

2 I want to prove to others that I can succeed.

Now consider the following:

- What do your answers tell you about yourself?
- What reasons besides these did you think about when you were applying to college?
- How do you think your reasons compare with those of other students who are starting college with you?

To Try It online, go to www.mhhe.com/power.

(see **Figure 1.1** on page 4). Statistics clearly demonstrate that a college education helps people find better jobs. On average, college graduates earn about 75 percent more than high school graduates over their working lifetime. That difference adds up: Over the course of their working lifetimes, college graduates earn close to a million dollars more than those with only a high school degree. Furthermore, as jobs become increasingly complex and technologically sophisticated, college will become more and more of a necessity.

But even if you feel the only reason you're in college is to help your career prospects, remember that the value of college extends far beyond dollars and cents. Consider these added reasons for pursuing a college education:

> **You'll learn to think critically and communicate better.** Here's what one student said about his college experience after he graduated: "It's not about what you major in or which classes you take. . . . It's really about learning to think and to communicate. Wherever you end up, you'll need to be able to analyze and solve problems—to figure out what needs to be done and do it."[1]

> Education improves your ability to understand the world—to understand it as it now is, and to prepare to understand it as it will be.

> **You'll be able to better deal with advances in knowledge and technology that are changing the world.** Genetic engineering . . . drugs to reduce forgetfulness . . . computers that respond to our voices. . . . No one knows what the future will hold, but you can prepare for it through a college education. Education can provide you with the intellectual tools that you can apply regardless of the specific situation in which you find yourself.

figure 1.1
Choosing College

These are the most frequently cited reasons that first-year college students gave for why they enrolled in college when asked in a national survey.[2]

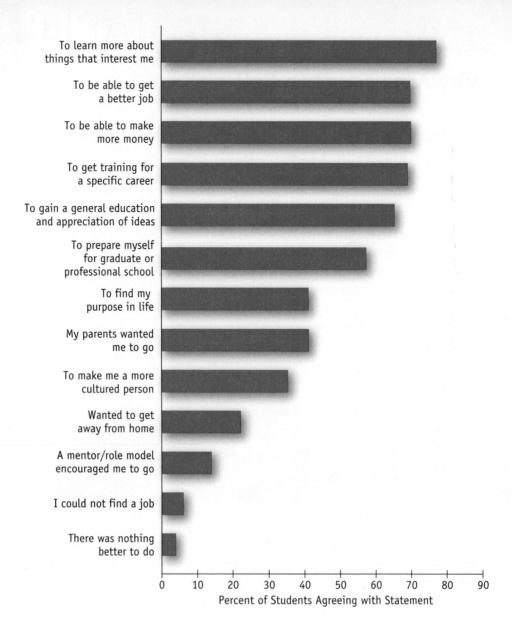

Percent of Students Agreeing with Statement

- To learn more about things that interest me
- To be able to get a better job
- To be able to make more money
- To get training for a specific career
- To gain a general education and appreciation of ideas
- To prepare myself for graduate or professional school
- To find my purpose in life
- My parents wanted me to go
- To make me a more cultured person
- Wanted to get away from home
- A mentor/role model encouraged me to go
- I could not find a job
- There was nothing better to do

> **You'll learn to adapt to new situations.** College is a different world from high school or the workplace. It presents new experiences and new challenges. Your adjustment to the college culture will prepare you for future encounters with new situations.

> **You'll be better prepared to live in a world of diversity.** The racial and ethnic composition of the United States is changing rapidly. Whatever your ethnicity, chances are you'll be working and living with people whose backgrounds, lifestyles, and ways of thinking may be entirely different from your own.

> You won't be prepared for the future unless you understand others and their cultural backgrounds—as well as how your own cultural background affects you.

> **You'll make learning a lifelong habit.** Higher education isn't the end of your education. Education will build upon your natural curiosity about the world, and it will make you aware that learning is a rewarding and never-ending journey.

To help you attain these benefits, it's time to introduce you to a process that will help you achieve success, both in college and in life beyond: P.O.W.E.R. Learning.

Journal Reflections

My School Experiences

Throughout this book, you will be given opportunities to write out your thoughts. These opportunities—called Journal Reflections—offer a chance to think critically about the chapter topics and record your personal reactions to them. As you create your reflections, be honest, to yourself and to your instructor.

Completing these Journal Reflections provides a variety of benefits. Not only will you be able to mull over your past and present academic experiences, you'll begin to see patterns in the kind of difficulties—and successes!—you encounter. You'll be able to apply solutions that worked in one situation to others. And one added benefit: You'll get practice in writing.

If you save these entries and return to them later, you may be surprised at the changes they record over the course of the term. You can either write them out and keep an actual journal, or create your journal electronically at the *P.O.W.E.R. Learning* Web site at **www.mhhe.com/power.**

1. Think of one of the successful experiences you've had during your previous years in school or on the job. What was it?

2. What made the experience successful? What did you learn from your success?

3. Think of an experience you had in school or on the job that you could have handled more successfully and briefly describe it. Why did it occur?

4. What could you have done differently to make it successful? What did you learn from it?

5. Based on these experiences of success and failure, what general lessons did you learn that could help you to be more successful in the future, in the classroom and in your career?

» LO 1.2 P.O.W.E.R. Learning: The Five Key Steps to Achieving Success

P.O.W.E.R. Learning itself is merely an acronym—a word formed from the first letters of a series of steps—that will help you take in, process, and make use of the information you'll acquire in college. It will help you to achieve your goals, both while you are in college and later after you graduate.

Prepare, **O**rganize, **W**ork, **E**valuate, and **R**ethink. That's it. It's a simple framework, but an effective one. Using the systematic framework that P.O.W.E.R. Learning provides (and which is illustrated in the P.O.W.E.R. Plan diagram on page 6) will increase your chances of success at any task, from writing a college paper to buying the weekly groceries to filling out a purchase order.

Keep this in mind: P.O.W.E.R. Learning isn't a product that you can simply pull down off the bookshelf and use without thinking. P.O.W.E.R. Learning is a process, and you are the only one who can make it succeed. Without your personal investment in the process, P.O.W.E.R. Learning consists of just words on paper.

P.O.W.E.R. Learning

A system designed to help people achieve their goals, based on five steps: *Prepare, Organize, Work, Evaluate,* and *Rethink*

Everyone goes to school for their own reasons. Gwen recently visited a friend in the hospital and was struck by how much she wanted to be a part of the health-care community. John has survived several rounds of layoffs at his job and wants to make himself more marketable.

P.O.W.E.R. Plan

Relax, though. You already know each of the elements of P.O.W.E.R. Learning, and you may discover that you are already putting this process, or parts of it, to work for you. You've applied and been accepted into college. You may have also held down a job, started a family, and paid your monthly bills. Each of these accomplishments required that you use P.O.W.E.R. Learning. What you'll be doing throughout this book is becoming more aware of these methods and how they can be used to help you in situations you will encounter in college and your career.

P Prepare

Chinese philosopher Lao Tzu said that travelers taking a long journey must begin with a single step.

But before they even take that first step, travelers need to know several things: what their destination is, how they're going to get there, how they'll know when they reach the destination, and what they'll do if they have trouble along the way. In the same way, you need to know where you're headed as you embark on the academic journeys involved in college. Whether it be a major, long-term task, such as landing a new and better job, or a more limited activity, such as getting ready to complete a paper due in the near future, you'll need to prepare for the journey.

Setting Goals

Before we seek to accomplish any task, all of us do some form of planning. The trouble is that most of the time such planning is done without conscious thinking, as if we are on autopilot. However, the key to success is to make sure that planning is systematic.

The best way to plan systematically is to use goal-setting strategies. In many cases, goals are clear and direct. It's obvious that our goal in washing dishes is to have the dishes end up clean. We know that our goal at the gas station is to fill the car's tank with gas. We go to the post office to buy stamps and mail letters.

Other goals are not so clear-cut. In fact, often the more important the task—such as going to college—the more complicated may be our goals.

From the perspective of . . .

A STUDENT What goals did you set when you decided to go school? What can you do to ensure that you meet these goals?

What's the best way to set appropriate goals? Here are some guidelines:

> **Set both long-term and short-term goals. Long-term goals** are aims relating to major accomplishments that take some time to achieve. **Short-term goals** are relatively limited steps you would take on the road to accomplishing your long-term goals. For example, one of the primary reasons you're in college is to achieve the long-term goal of helping your career. But in order to reach that goal, you have to accomplish a series of short-term goals, such as completing a set of required courses and earning your degree. Even these short-term goals can be broken down into shorter-term goals. In order to complete a required course, for instance, you have to accomplish short-term goals, such as completing a paper, taking several tests, and so on. For practice in setting long- and short-term goals, complete **Try It 2** on page 8, "What Are Your Goals?"

> **Make goals realistic and attainable.** Someone once said, "A goal without a plan is but a dream." We'd all like to win gold medals at the Olympics or star in rock videos or write best-selling novels. Few of us are likely to achieve such goals.

Be honest with yourself. There is nothing wrong with having big dreams. But it is important to be realistically aware of all that it takes to achieve them. If our long-term goals are unrealistic and we don't achieve them, the big danger is that we may wrongly reason that we are inept and lack ability and use this as an excuse for giving up. If goals are realistic, we can develop a plan to attain them, spurring us on to attain more.

> **State goals in terms of behavior that can be measured against current accomplishments.** Goals should represent some measurable change from a current set of circumstances. We want our behavior to change in some way that can usually be expressed in terms of numbers—to show an increase ("raise my grade point average 10 percent") or a decrease ("reduce wasted time by two hours each week"); or to be maintained ("keep in touch with my out-of-town

Long-term goals
Aims relating to major accomplishments that take some time to achieve

Short-term goals
Relatively limited steps toward the accomplishment of long-term goals

"Goal setting, as far as I can see it, is simply a state of mind, a way of thinking about things. A goal setter makes sure he accomplishes what he needs to accomplish."
Greg Gottesman, Stanford University[3]

What Are Your Goals?

Before you begin any journey, you need to know where you are going. To plan your academic journey—and your later career—you first need to set goals. *Short-term goals* are relatively limited objectives that bring you closer to your ultimate goal. *Long-term goals* are aims relating to major accomplishments that take more time to achieve.

In this **Try It,** think about your short- and long-term academic and career goals for a few minutes, and then list them. Because short-term goals are based on what you want to accomplish in the long term, first identify your long-term goals. Then list the short-term goals that will help you reach your long-term goals. An example is provided for each kind of goal:

Long-Term Goal #1 Get a college degree _____

  Related Short-Term Goals:

  - Complete four courses with a grade of B or above each term
  - _____
  - _____
  - _____
  - _____

Long-Term Goal #2: _____

  Related Short-Term Goals:

  - _____
  - _____
  - _____
  - _____
  - _____

Long-Term Goal #3: _____

  Related Short-Term Goals:

  - _____
  - _____
  - _____
  - _____
  - _____

Long-Term Goal #4: _____

  Related Short-Term Goals:

  - _____
  - _____
  - _____
  - _____
  - _____

Long-Term Goal #5: _____

  Related Short-Term Goals:

  - _____
  - _____
  - _____
  - _____
  - _____

After you complete the chart, consider how easy or difficult it was to identify your long-term goals. How many of your long-term goals relate to college, and how many to your future career? Do any of your short-term goals relate to more than one long-term goal?

To Try It online, go to **www.mhhe.com/power.**

friends by writing four e-mail messages each month"), developed ("participate in one workshop on critical thinking"), or restricted ("reduce my phone expenses 10 percent by speaking and texting less").

> **Goals should involve behavior over which you have control.** We all want world peace and an end to poverty. Few of us have the resources or capabilities to bring either about. On the other hand, it is realistic to want to work in small ways to help others, such as by becoming a Big Brother or Big Sister or by volunteering at a local food bank.

> **Identify how your short-term goals fit with your long-term goals.** Your goals should not be independent of one another. Instead, they should fit together into a larger dream of who you want to be. Every once in a while step back and consider what you're doing today relates to the kind of career that you would ultimately want to have.

● Organize

By determining where you want to go and expressing your goals in terms that can be measured, you have already made a lot of progress. But there's another step you must take on the road to success.

The second step in P.O.W.E.R. Learning is to organize the tools you'll need to accomplish your goals. Building upon the goal-setting work you've undertaken in the preparation stage, it's time to determine the best way to accomplish the goals you've identified.

How do you do this? Suppose you've decided to build a set of bookshelves for one room in your house. Let's say that you've already determined the kind of bookshelves you like and figured out the basic characteristics of the ones you will build (the preparation step in P.O.W.E.R. Learning). The next stage involves gathering the necessary tools, buying the wood and other building materials, sorting the construction supplies, and preparing the room for the shelving project—all aspects of organizing for the task.

Similarly, your academic success will hinge to a large degree on the thoroughness of your organization for each academic task that you face. In fact, one of the biggest mistakes that students make in college is plunging into an academic project—studying for a test, writing a paper, completing an in-class assignment—without being organized.

The Two Kinds of Organization: Physical and Mental

On a basic level is *physical organization,* involving the mechanical aspects of task completion. For instance, you need to ask yourself if you have the appropriate tools, such as pens, paper, and a calculator. If you're using a computer, do you have access to a printer? Do you have a way to back up your files? Do you have the books and other materials you'll need to complete the assignment? Will the campus bookstore be open if you need anything else? Will the library be open when you need it? Do you have a comfortable place to work?

Mental organization is even more critical. Mental organization is accomplished by considering and reviewing the academic skills that you'll need to successfully complete the task at hand. You are an academic general in command of considerable forces; you will need to make sure your forces—the basic skills you have at your command—are at their peak of readiness.

Looking at the Big Picture

It's natural to view college as a series of small tasks—classes to attend, a certain number of pages to read each week, a few papers due during the term, quizzes and final exams to study for, and so on.

But such a perspective may lead you to miss what college, as a whole, is all about. Using the P.O.W.E.R. Learning framework can help you to take the long view of your education, considering how it helps you achieve your long- and short-term goals for your professional and personal life (the *Prepare* step) and what you'll need to do to maximize your success (the *Organize* step). By preparing and organizing even before you step foot in the classroom for the first time, you'll be able to consider what it is that you want to get out of college and how it fits into your life as a whole.

For example, if you're working on a math assignment, you'll want to consider the basic math skills that you'll need and brush up on them. Just actively thinking about this will help you organize mentally. Similarly, you'd want to mentally review your knowledge of engine parts before beginning repair work (either in class or on the side of the road!). Why does producing mental organization matter? The answer is because it provides a context for when you actually begin to work. Organizing paves the way for better subsequent performance.

Too often students or workers on the job are in a hurry to meet a deadline and figure they had better just dive in and get it done. Organizing can actually *save* you time, because you're less likely to be anxious and end up losing your way as you work to complete your task.

Much of this book is devoted to strategies for determining—*before* you begin work on a task—how to develop the mental tools for completing an assignment. However, as you'll see, all of these strategies share a common theme: that success comes not from a trial-and-error approach, but from following a systematic plan for achievement. Of course, this does not mean that there will be no surprises along the way, nor that simple luck is never a factor in great accomplishments. But it does mean that we often can make our own luck through careful preparation and organization.

W Work

You're ready. The preliminaries are out of the way. You've prepared and you've organized. Now it's time to get started actually doing the work.

In some ways work is the easy part, because—if you conscientiously carried out the preparation and organization stage—you should know exactly where you're headed and what you need to do to get there.

It's not quite so easy, of course. How effectively you'll get down to the business at hand depends on many factors. Some may be out of your control. There may be a power outage that closes down the library or a massive traffic jam that delays your getting to the office. But most factors are—or should be—under your control. Instead of getting down to work, you may find yourself thinking up "useful" things to do—like finally cleaning underneath the couch—or simply sitting captive in front of the TV. This kind of obstacle to work relates to motivation.

Finding the Motivation to Work

"If only I could get more motivated, I'd do so much better with my _____" (insert *schoolwork, job, diet, exercising,* or the like—you fill in the blank).

All of us have said something like this at one time or another. We use the concept of **motivation**—or its lack—to explain why we just don't work hard at a task. But when we do that, we're fooling ourselves. We all have some motivation, that inner power and psychological energy that directs and fuels our behavior. Without any motivation, we'd never get out of bed in the morning.

We've also seen evidence of how strong our motivation can be. Perhaps you're an avid runner and you love to jog in the morning and compete in weekend races. Or maybe your love of music helped you learn to play the guitar, making practicing for hours a pleasure rather than a chore. Or perhaps you're a single parent, juggling work, school, and family, and you get up early every morning to make breakfast for your kids before they go off to school.

All of us are motivated. The key to success in the classroom and on the job is to tap into, harness, and direct that motivation.

If we assume that we already have all the motivation we need, P.O.W.E.R. Learning becomes a matter of turning the skills we already possess into a habit. It becomes a matter of redirecting our psychological energies toward the work we wish to accomplish.

In a sense, everything you'll encounter in this book will help you to improve your use of the motivation that you already have. But there's a key concept that underlies the control of motivation—viewing success as a consequence of effort:

Effort produces success.

Suppose, for example, you've gotten a good performance review from your new supervisor. The boss beams at you as she discusses your results. How do you feel?

You will undoubtedly be pleased, of course. But at the same time you might think to yourself, "Better not get a swollen head about it. It was just luck." Or perhaps you explain your success by thinking, "The new boss just doesn't know me very well."

If you often think this way, you're cheating yourself. Using this kind of reasoning when you succeed, instead of patting yourself on the back and thinking with satisfaction, "All my hard work really paid off," is sure to undermine your future success.

A great deal of psychological research has shown that thinking you have no control over what happens to you sends a powerful and damaging message to your self-esteem—that you are powerless to change things. Just think of how different it feels to say to yourself, "Wow, I worked at it and did it," as compared with "I lucked out" or "It was so easy that anybody could have done it."

In the same way, we can delude ourselves when we try to explain our failures. People who see themselves as the victims of circumstance may tell themselves, "I'm just not smart enough," when they don't do well on an academic task. Or they might say, "My coworkers don't have children to take care of."

The way in which we view the causes of success and failure is, in fact, directly related to our success. Students who generally see effort and hard work as the reason behind their performance usually do better in college. Workers who see their job performance in this way usually do better in their careers. It's not hard to see why: When such individuals are working on a task, they feel that the greater the effort they put forth, the greater

> "The function of the university is not simply to teach breadwinning, or to furnish teachers for the public schools or to be a center of polite society: it is, above all, to be the organ of that fine adjustment between real life and the growing knowledge of life, an adjustment which forms the secret of civilization."
>
> **W.E.B. DuBois, author, *The Souls of Black Folk*, 1903**

their chances of success. So they work harder. They believe that they have control over their success, and if they fail, they believe they can do better in the future.

Here are some tips for keeping your motivation alive, so you can work with your full energy behind you:

> **Take responsibility for your failures—and successes.** When you do poorly on a test, don't blame the teacher, the textbook, or a job that kept you from studying. When you miss a work deadline, don't blame your boss or your incompetent coworkers. Analyze the situation, and see how you could have changed what you did to be more successful in the future. At the same time, when you're successful, think of the things you did to bring about that success.

> **Think positively.** Assume that the strengths that you have will allow you to succeed and that, if you have difficulty, you can figure out what to do.

> **Accept that you can't control everything.** Seek to understand which things can be changed and which cannot. You might be able to get an extension on a paper due date, but you are probably not going to be excused from a college-wide requirement.

To further explore the causes of academic success, consider the questions in **Try It 3,** discussing them with your classmates.

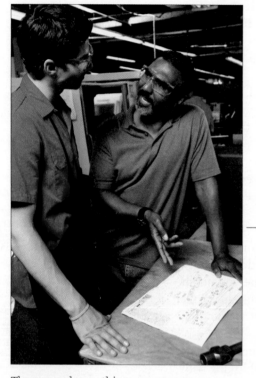

There are always things we can use as excuses for our own failures. Can you think of a time when you shifted blame away from yourself for a failure? Was it a reasonable course of action? Why or why not?

Evaluation

An assessment of the match between a product or activity and the goals it was intended to meet

E Evaluate

"Great, I'm done with the work. Now I can move on."

It's natural to feel relief when you've finished the work necessary to fulfill the basic requirements of a task. After all, if you've written the five double-spaced pages required for an assignment or balanced a complicated office budget, why shouldn't you heave a sigh of relief and just hand in your work?

The answer is that if you stop at this point, you'll almost be guaranteed a mediocre result. Did Shakespeare dash off the first draft of *Hamlet* and, without another glance, send it off to the Globe Theater for production? Do professional athletes just put in the bare minimum of practice to get ready for a big game? Think of one of your favorite songs. Do you think the composer wrote it in one sitting and then performed it in a concert?

In every case, the answer is no. Even the greatest creation does not emerge in perfect form, immediately meeting all the goals of its producer. Consequently, the fourth step in the P.O.W.E.R. process is **evaluation,** which consists of determining how well the product or activity we have created matches our goals for it. Let's consider some steps to follow in evaluating what you've accomplished:

> **Take a moment to congratulate yourself and feel some satisfaction.** Whether it's been studying for a test, writing a paper, completing a report, or drafting a memo, you've done something important. You've moved from ground zero to a spot that's closer to your goal.

> **Compare what you've accomplished with the goals you're seeking to achieve.** Think back to the goals, both short-term and long-term, that you're seeking to achieve. How closely does what you've done match what you're aiming to do? For instance, if your short-term goal is to complete a math problem set with

Try It! POWER

Examining the Causes of Success and Failure

3

Complete this Try It while working in a group. First, consider the following situations:

1. Although he made a few more sales calls than normal, Jack is told by his boss that he has failed to bring in any new business. Jack is disgusted with himself and says, "I'll never be good at attracting new clients. I'd better just give up and concentrate on the clients I already have."

2. Anne goes on a sales call and lands a major piece of new business. She is happy, but when her boss tells her the company as a whole has brought in lots of new business that month, she decides she only succeeded because the task was so easy.

3. Sales in Chen's division are slow. Because he isn't doing as well as he expected, he vows to perform better. He spends extra time researching and talking with potential clients, but sales only increase slightly. Distressed, he considers quitting his job because he thinks that he'll never be successful in sales.

Now consider the following questions about each of the situations:

1. What did each salesperson conclude was the main cause of his or her performance?
2. What effect does this conclusion seem to have on the salesperson?
3. Taking an outsider's point of view, what would *you* think was probably the main cause of the salespeople's performance?
4. What advice would you give each salesperson?

Now consider these broader questions:

1. What are the most important reasons why some people are more professionally successful than others?
2. How much does ability determine success? How much does luck determine success? How much do circumstances determine success?
3. If someone performs poorly at a job, what are the possible reasons for his or her performance? If someone performs well, what are the possible reasons for his or her performance? Is it harder to find reasons for good compared with poor performance? Why?

To Try It online, go to www.mhhe.com/power.

---

no errors, you'll need to check over the work carefully to make sure you've made no mistakes.

› **Have an out-of-body experience: Evaluate your accomplishments as if you were a respected mentor from your past.** If you've written a paper, reread it from the perspective of a favorite teacher. If you've prepared a report, imagine you're presenting it to a boss who taught you a lot. Think about the comments you'd give if you were this person.

› **Evaluate what you've done as if you were your current instructor or supervisor.** Now exchange bodies and minds again. This time, consider what you're doing from the perspective of the person who gave you the assignment. How would he or she react to what you've done? Have you followed the assignment to the letter? Is there anything you've missed?

› **Based on your evaluation, revise your work.** If you're honest with yourself, it's unlikely that your first work will satisfy you. So go back to *Work* and revise what you've done. But don't think of it as a step back: Revisions you make as a consequence of your evaluation bring you closer to your final goal. This is a case where going back moves you forward.

They thought they had it perfect. But they were wrong.

In fact, it was a $1.5 billion mistake—a blunder on a grand scale. The finely ground mirror of the Hubble space telescope, designed to provide an unprecedented glimpse into the vast reaches of the universe, was not so finely ground after all.

Despite an elaborate system of evaluation designed to catch any flaws, there was a tiny blemish in the mirror that was not detected until the telescope had been launched into space and started to send back blurry photographs. By then, it seemed too late to fix the mirror.

Or was it? NASA engineers rethought the problem for months, devising, and then discarding, one potential fix after another. Finally, after bringing a fresh eye to the situation, they formulated a daring solution that involved sending a team of astronauts into space. Once there, a space-walking Mr. Goodwrench would install several new mirrors in the telescope, which could refocus the light and compensate for the original flawed mirror.

Although the engineers could not be certain that the $629 million plan would work, it seemed like a good solution, at least on paper. It was not until the first photos were beamed back to Earth, though, that NASA knew their solution was A-OK. These photos were spectacular.

It took months of reconsideration before NASA scientists could figure out what went wrong and devise a solution to the problem they faced. Their approach exemplifies—on a grand scale—the final step in P.O.W.E.R. Learning: rethinking.

To *rethink* what you've accomplished earlier means bringing a fresh—and clear—eye to what you've done. It involves using **critical thinking,** thinking that involves reanalyzing, questioning, and challenging our underlying assumptions. While evaluation means considering how well what we have done matches our initial goals, rethinking means reconsidering not only the outcome of our efforts, but also reconsidering our goals and the ideas and the process we've used to reach them. Critically rethinking what you've done involves analyzing and synthesizing ideas, and seeing the connections between different concepts.

Rethinking involves considering whether our initial goals are practical and realistic or if they require modification. It also entails asking yourself what you would do differently if you could do it over again.

We'll be considering critical thinking throughout this book, examining specific strategies in every chapter. For the moment, the following steps provide a general framework for using critical thinking to rethink what you've accomplished:

> **Reanalyze, reviewing how you've accomplished the task.** Consider the approach and strategies you've used. What seemed to work best? Do they suggest any alternatives that might work better the next time?

> **Question the outcome.** Take a "big picture" look at what you have accomplished. Are you pleased and satisfied? Is there something you've somehow missed?

> **Identify your underlying assumptions; then challenge them.** Consider the assumptions you made in initially approaching the task. Are these underlying assumptions reasonable? If you had used different assumptions, would the result have been similar or different?

> **Consider alternatives rejected earlier.** You've likely discarded possible strategies and approaches prior to completing your task. Now's the time to think

Critical thinking
A process involving reanalysis, questioning, and challenge of underlying assumptions

P.O.W.E.R. Learning and the World of Work

As we've discussed, the P.O.W.E.R. Learning process has applications in both the classroom and on the job. In **Career Connections** boxes we'll highlight ways in which the principles we're discussing can help you excel in the workplace. Take a look at these "help wanted" advertisements and online postings. They illustrate the importance of the components of P.O.W.E.R. Learning in a wide variety of fields.

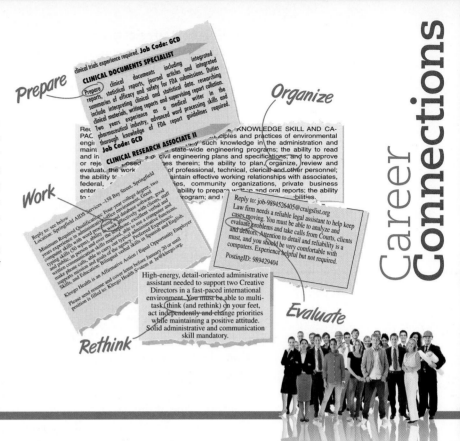

about those approaches once more and determine if they might have been more appropriate than the road you've followed.

> **What would you do differently if you had the opportunity to try things again?** It's not too late to change course.

> **Finally, reconsider your initial goals.** Are they achievable and realistic? Do your goals, and the strategies you used to attain them, need to be modified? Critically rethinking the objectives and goals that underlie your efforts is often the most effective route to success.

≫ LO 1.3   Completing the Process

The rethinking step of P.O.W.E.R. Learning is meant to help you understand your process of work and to improve the final product if necessary. But mostly it is meant to help you grow, to become better at whatever it is you've been doing. Like a painter looking at his or her finished work, you may see a spot here or there to touch up, but don't destroy the canvas. Perfectionism can be as paralyzing as laziness. Keep in mind these key points:

> **Know that there's always another day.** Your future success does not depend on any single assignment, paper, or test. Don't fall victim to self-defeating thoughts such as "If I don't do well, I'll never graduate" or "Everything is riding on this one project." Nonsense. In school, on the job, and in life, there is almost always an opportunity to recover from a failure.

> **Realize that deciding when to stop work is often as hard as getting started.** Knowing when you have put in enough time studying for a test, have revised a paper sufficiently, or have reviewed your figures adequately on an estimate is as much a key to success as properly preparing. If you've carefully evaluated what you've done and seen that there's a close fit between your goals and your work, it's time to stop work and move on.

> ► **Use the strategies that already work for you.** Although the P.O.W.E.R. Learning framework provides a proven approach to attaining success, employing it does not mean that you should abandon strategies that have brought you success in the past. Using multiple approaches, and personalizing them, is the surest road to success.

As much as anything else, doing well in college and on the job depends on an awareness *of yourself.* What are your strengths? What are your weaknesses? What do you do better than most people, and what are your areas for improvement? If you can answer such questions, you'll be able to harness the best of your talents and to anticipate challenges you might face. The next section will aid you in understanding yourself better by helping you identify your personal learning styles.

≫LO1.4 Discovering Your Learning Styles

Consider what it would be like to be a member of the Trukese people, a small group of islanders in the South Pacific.

Trukese sailors often sail hundreds of miles on the open sea. They manage this feat with none of the navigational equipment used by Western sailors. No compass. No chronometer. No sextant. They don't even sail in a straight line. Instead, they zigzag back and forth, at the mercy of the winds and tides. Yet they make few mistakes. Almost always they are able to reach their destination with precision. How do they do it?

They can't really explain it. They say it has to do with following the rising and setting of the stars at night. During the day, they take in the appearance, sound, and feel of the waves against the side of the boat. But they don't really have any idea of where they are at any given moment, nor do they care. They just know that ultimately they'll reach their final destination.

It would be foolhardy to suggest that the Trukese don't have what it takes to be successful sailors. The fact that they don't use traditional Western navigational equipment when they're sailing does not mean that they are any less able than Western navigators.

What about academic or career success? Isn't it reasonable to assume that there are different ways to reach academic goals and professional goals? Wouldn't it be surprising if everyone learned in exactly the same way?

Each of us has preferred ways of learning, approaches that work best for us either in the classroom or on the job. And our success is not just dependent on how well we learn, but on how we learn.

Learning style

One's preferred manner of acquiring, using, and thinking about knowledge

A **learning style** reflects a person's preferred manner of acquiring, using, and thinking about knowledge. We don't have just one learning style, but a variety of styles. Some involve our preferences regarding the way information is presented to us, some relate to how we think and learn most readily, and some relate to how our personality traits affect our performance. An awareness of your learning styles will help you in college by allowing you to study and learn course materials more effectively. On the job, knowing your learning styles will help you master new skills and techniques, ensuring you can keep up with changing office practices or an evolving industry.

We'll start by considering the preferences we have for how we initially perceive information.

What Is Your Preferred Receptive Learning Style?

One of the most basic aspects of learning styles concerns the way in which we initially receive information from our sense organs—our **receptive learning style.** People have different strengths in terms of how they most effectively process information and which of their senses they prefer to use in learning. Specifically, there are four different types of receptive learning styles:

▸ **Read/write learning style.** If you have a **read/write learning style,** you prefer information that is presented visually in a written format. You feel most comfortable reading, and you may recall the spelling of a word by thinking of how the word looks. You probably learn best when you have the opportunity to read about a concept rather than listening to a teacher explain it.

▸ **Visual/graphic learning style.** Those with a **visual/graphic learning style** learn most effectively when material is presented visually in a diagram or picture. You might recall the structure of an engine or a part of the human body by reviewing a picture in your mind, and you benefit from instructors who make frequent use of visual aids in class such as videos, maps, and models. Students with visual learning styles find it easier to see things in their mind's eye—to visualize a task or concept—than to be lectured about them.

▸ **Auditory/verbal learning style.** Have you ever asked a friend to help you put something together by having her read the directions to you while you worked? If you did, you may have an auditory/verbal learning style. People with **auditory/verbal learning styles** prefer listening to explanations rather than reading them. They love class lectures and discussions, because they can easily take in the information that is being talked about.

▸ **Tactile/kinesthetic learning style.** Those with a **tactile/kinesthetic learning style** prefer to learn by doing—touching, manipulating objects, and doing things. For instance, some people enjoy the act of writing because of the

Receptive learning style
The way in which we initially receive information

Read/write learning style
A style that involves a preference for written material, favoring reading over hearing and touching

Visual/graphic learning style
A style that favors material presented visually in a diagram or picture

Auditory/verbal learning style
A style that favors listening as the best approach to learning

Tactile/kinesthetic learning style
A style that involves learning by touching, manipulating objects, and doing things

Steven Spielberg is a self-admitted visual learner. How can you use your own learning style to influence your career decisions?

feel of a pencil or a computer keyboard—the tactile equivalent of thinking out loud. Or they may find that it helps them to make a three-dimensional model to understand a new idea.

To get a sense of your own receptive learning style, complete **Try It 4** on page 20. But remember, having a particular receptive learning style simply means that it will be easier to learn material that is presented in that style. It does not mean you cannot learn any other way!

From the perspective of . . .

A NURSING ASSISTANT You shouldn't see your learning style as a limitation. Repeating instructions aloud as a nursing assistant is one way for auditory learners to ensure they are comprehending instructions. How can you adapt your learning style in multiple career settings?

Receptive learning styles have implications for effective studying in class or learning new skills on the job:

If you have a read/write style, consider writing out summaries of information, highlighting and underlining written material, and using flash cards. Transform diagrams and math formulas into words.

If you have a visual/graphic style, devise diagrams and charts. Translate words into symbols and figures.

If you have an auditory/verbal style, recite material out loud when trying to learn it. Work with others in a group, talking through the material, and consider tape-recording lectures.

If you have a tactile/kinesthetic style, incorporate movement into your study. Trace diagrams, build models, arrange flash cards and move them around. Keep yourself active when learning, taking notes, drawing charts, and jotting down key concepts.

Multiple Intelligences: Showing Strength in Different Domains

Do you feel much more comfortable walking through the woods than navigating city streets? Are you an especially talented musician? Is reading and using a complicated map second nature to you?

If so, in each case you may be demonstrating a special and specific kind of intelligence. According to psychologist Howard Gardner, rather than asking "How smart are you?" we should be asking a different question: "How are you smart?" To answer the latter question, Gardner has developed a *theory of multiple intelligences* that offers a unique approach to understanding learning styles and preferences.

The multiple intelligences view says that we have eight different forms of intelligence, each relatively independent of the others and linked to a specific kind of information processing in our brains:

> *Logical-mathematical intelligence* involves skills in problem solving and scientific thinking.

> *Linguistic intelligence* is linked to the production and use of language.

> *Spatial intelligence* relates to skills involving spatial configurations, such as those used by artists and architects.

> *Interpersonal intelligence* is found in learners with particularly strong skills involving interacting with others, such as sensitivity to the moods, temperaments, motivations, and intentions of others.

> *Intrapersonal intelligence* relates to a particularly strong understanding of the internal aspects of oneself and having access to one's own feelings and emotions.

> *Musical intelligence* involves skills relating to music.

> *Bodily kinesthetic intelligence* relates to skills in using the whole body or portions of it in the solution of problems or in the construction of products or displays, exemplified by dancers, athletes, actor, and surgeons.

> *Naturalist intelligence* involves exceptional abilities in identifying and classifying patterns in nature.

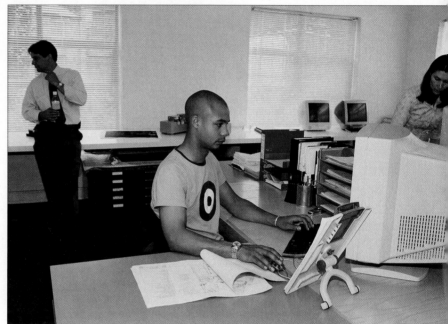

In any given day, graphic designers must be able to create amazing visuals and also do the requisite paperwork to accompany their projects. Which types of intelligence would be most important to succeed in this career?

All of us have the same eight kinds of intelligence, although in different degrees, and they form the core of our learning styles and preferences. These separate intelligences do not operate in isolation. Instead, any activity involves several kinds of intelligence working together.

Personality Styles

Our learning styles are also influenced by our personality. Are you likely to perform at an open mic night at a café? Or is the idea of getting on a stage totally lacking in appeal (if not completely terrifying)? Do you relate to the world around you primarily through careful planning or by spontaneously reacting?

According to the rationale of the *Myers-Briggs Type Indicator,* a questionnaire frequently used in business and organizational settings to place people in 1 of 16 categories, personality type plays a key role in determining how we react to different situations. Specifically, we work best in situations in which others—students, instructors, or coworkers—share our preferences and in which our personality is most suited to the particular task on which we are working. Four major personality dimensions are critical. Although we'll describe the extremes of each dimension, keep in mind that most of us fall somewhere between the end points of each dimension.

Try It!

What's Your Receptive Learning Style?

Read each of the following statements and rank them in terms of their usefulness to you as learning approaches. Base your ratings on your personal experiences and preferences, using the following scale:

1 = Not at all useful
2 = Not very useful
3 = Neutral
4 = Somewhat useful
5 = Very useful

	1	2	3	4	5
1. Studying alone					
2. Studying pictures and diagrams to understand complex ideas					
3. Listening to class lectures					
4. Performing a process myself rather than reading or hearing about it					
5. Learning a complex procedure by reading written directions					
6. Watching and listening to film, computer, or video presentations					
7. Listening to a book or lecture on tape					
8. Doing lab work					
9. Studying teachers' handouts and lecture notes					
10. Studying in a quiet room					
11. Taking part in group discussions					
12. Taking part in hands-on demonstrations					
13. Taking notes and studying them later					
14. Creating flash cards and using them as a study and review tool					
15. Memorizing and recalling how words are spelled by spelling them "out loud" in my head					

> **Introverts versus extraverts.** A key difference between introverts and extraverts is whether they enjoy working with others. Independence is a key characteristic of introverted learners. They enjoy working alone and they are less affected by how others think and behave. In contrast, extraverts are outgoing and more affected by the behavior and thinking of others. They enjoy working with others, and they are energized by having other people around.

> **Intuitors versus sensors.** Intuitors enjoy solving problems and being creative. They get impatient with details, preferring to make leaps of judgment, and they enjoy the challenge of solving problems and taking a

	1	2	3	4	5
16. Writing down key facts and important points as a tool for remembering them					
17. Recalling how to spell a word by seeing it in my head					
18. Underlining or highlighting important facts or passages in my reading					
19. Saying things out loud when I'm studying					
20. Recalling how to spell a word by "writing" it invisibly in the air or on a surface					
21. Learning new information by reading about it in a book					
22. Using a map to find an unknown place					
23. Working in a study group					
24. Finding a place I've been to once by just going there without directions					

Scoring: The statements cycle through the four receptive learning styles in this order: (1) read/write; (2) visual/graphic; (3) auditory/verbal; and (4) tactile/kinesthetic.

To find your primary learning style, disregard your 1, 2, and 3 ratings. Add up your 4 and 5 ratings for each learning style (i.e., a "4" equals 4 points and a "5" equals 5 points). Use the following chart to link the statements to the learning styles and to write down your summed ratings:

Learning Style	Statements	Total (Sum) of Rating Points
Read/write	1, 5, 9, 13, 17, and 21	
Visual/graphic	2, 6, 10, 14, 18, and 22	
Auditory/verbal	3, 7, 11, 15, 19, and 23	
Tactile/kinesthetic	4, 8, 12, 16, 20, and 24	

The total of your rating points for any given style will range from a low of 0 to a high of 30. The highest total indicates your main receptive learning style. Don't be surprised if you have a mixed style, in which two or more styles receive similar ratings.

To Try It online, go to www.mhhe.com/power.

big-picture approach. People categorized as sensors, on the other hand, prefer a concrete, logical approach in which they can carefully analyze the facts of the situation. Although they are good with details, they sometimes miss the big picture.

➤ **Thinkers versus feelers.** Thinkers prefer logic over emotion. They reach decisions and solve problems by systematically analyzing a situation. In contrast, feeling types rely more on their emotional responses. They are aware of others and their feelings, and they are influenced by their personal values and attachments to others.

> **Perceivers and judgers.** Before drawing a conclusion, perceivers attempt to gather as much information as they can. Because they are open to multiple perspectives and appreciate all sides of an issue, they sometimes have difficulty completing a task. Judgers, in comparison, are quick and decisive. They like to set goals, accomplish them, and then move on to the next task.

The Origins of Our Learning Styles

Left-brain processing

Information processing primarily performed by the left hemisphere of the brain, focusing on tasks requiring verbal competence, such as speaking, reading, thinking, and reasoning; information is processed sequentially, one bit at a time

Right-brain processing

Information processing primarily performed by the right hemisphere of the brain, focusing on information in nonverbal domains, such as the understanding of spatial relationships and recognition of patterns, drawings, music, and emotional expression

For many of us, our learning style preferences result from the kind of processing our brain "specializes" in. **Left-brain processing** concentrates more on tasks requiring verbal competence, such as speaking, reading, thinking, and reasoning. Information is processed sequentially, one bit at a time.

On the other hand, **right-brain processing** tends to concentrate more on the processing of information in nonverbal domains, such as the understanding of spatial relationships, recognition of patterns and drawings, music, and emotional expression. Furthermore, the right hemisphere tends to process information globally, considering it as a whole. Consequently, people who naturally tend toward right-brain processing might prefer visual/graphic learning styles.

Here are some key facts to remember about learning, personality, and processing styles:

> **You have a variety of styles.** As you can see in the summary of different categories of styles in **Table 1.1,** there are several types of styles. For any given task or challenge, some types of styles may be more relevant than others. Furthermore, success is possible even when there is a mismatch between what you need to accomplish and your own pattern of preferred styles. It may take more work, but learning to deal with situations that require you to use less-preferred styles is important for college and your career.

> **Your style reflects your preferences regarding which abilities you like to use—not the abilities themselves.** Styles are related to our preferences and the mental approaches we like to use. You may prefer to learn tactilely, but that in itself doesn't guarantee that the products that you create tactilely will be good. You still have to put in work!

> **Your style will change over the course of your life.** You can learn new styles and expand the range of learning experiences in which you feel perfectly comfortable. In fact, you can conceive of this book as one long lesson in learning styles because it provides you with strategies for learning more effectively in a variety of ways.

> **You should work on improving your less-preferred styles.** Although it may be tempting, don't always make choices that increase your exposure to preferred styles and decrease your practice with less-preferred styles. The more you use approaches for which you have less of a preference, the better you'll be at developing the skills associated with those styles.

> **Work cooperatively with others who have different styles.** If your instructor or supervisor asks you to work cooperatively, seek out classmates or coworkers who have styles that are different from yours. Not only will your working with people with differing styles help you to achieve collective success, but you can also learn from observing others' approaches to tackling tasks.

table 1.1   Learning, Personality, and Processing Styles

All of us have particular learning, personality, and processing styles that we tend to rely on. At the same time, we also have capabilities in less-preferred styles. So, for example, although you may be primarily a read/write learner, you have the capacity to use auditory/verbal and tactile/kinesthetic approaches. Note in particular that the four categories of personality styles are considered independent of each other. For instance, you may be an extravert and at the same time a sensor, a feeler, and a judger. Furthermore, although the "Using the Style" column suggests ways that those with a particular style can make the most of that style, you should also try strategies that work for styles different from your own.

Category	Type	Description	Using the Style[4]
Receptive Learning Styles	Read/write	A style that involves a preference for material in a written format, favoring reading over hearing and touching.	Read and rewrite material, take notes and rewrite them; organize material into tables; transform diagrams and math formulas into words.
	Visual/graphic	A style that favors material presented visually in a diagram or picture.	Use figures and drawings; replay classes and discussions in your mind's eye; visualize material; translate words into symbols and figures.
	Auditory/verbal	A style in which the learner favors listening as the best approach.	Recite material out loud; consider how words sound; study different languages; tape-record lectures or training sessions; work with others, talking through the material.
	Tactile/ kinesthetic	A style that involves learning by touching, manipulating objects, and doing things.	Incorporate movement into studying; trace figures and drawings with your finger; create models; make flash cards and move them around; keep active during class and meetings, taking notes, drawing charts, jotting down key concepts.
Multiple Intelligences	Logical- mathematical	Strengths in problem solving and scientific thinking.	Express information mathematically or in formulas.
	Linguistic	Strengths in the production and use of language.	Write out notes and summarize information in words; construct stories about material.
	Spatial	Strengths involving spatial configurations, such as those used by artists and architects.	Build charts, graphs, and flowcharts.
	Interpersonal	Found in learners with particularly strong skills involving interacting with others, such as sensitivity to the moods, temperaments, motivations, and intentions of others.	Work with others in groups.
	Intrapersonal	Strengths in understanding the internal aspects of oneself and having access to one's own feelings and emotions.	Build on your prior experiences and feelings about the world; use your originality.

(continued)

| table 1.1 | Learning, Personality, and Processing Styles *(concluded)* |

	Musical	Strengths relating to music.	Write a song or lyrics to help remember material.
	Bodily kinesthetic	Strengths in using the whole body or portions of it in the solution of problems or in the construction of products or displays, exemplified by dancers, athletes, actors, and surgeons.	Use movement in studying; build models.
	Naturalist	Exceptional strengths in identifying and classifying patterns in nature.	Use analogies based on nature.
Personality Styles	Introvert versus extravert	Independence is a key characteristic of introverted learners, who enjoy working alone and are less affected by how others think and behave. In contrast, extraverts are outgoing and more affected by the behavior and thinking of others. They enjoy working with others.	Experiment with studying or working in groups compared with by yourself; consider your performance collaborating compared with working on your own.
	Intuitor versus sensor	Intuitive people enjoy solving problems and being creative, often taking a big-picture approach. Sensors, on the other hand, prefer a concrete, logical approach in which they can carefully analyze the facts of the situation.	For intuitors, reflect on the personal meaning of material and seek out tasks that involve creativity. For sensors, seek out concrete tasks that involve the application of logical principles.
	Thinker versus feeler	Thinkers prefer logic over emotion, reaching decisions through rational analysis. In contrast, feelers rely more on their emotions and are influenced by their personal values and attachments to others.	Thinkers should seek to systematically analyze situations, attempting to identify patterns. For feelers, use emotional responses to reflect on material.
	Perceiver versus judger	Before drawing a conclusion, perceivers attempt to gather as much information as they can and are open to multiple perspectives. Judgers, in comparison, are quick and decisive, enjoying setting goals and accomplishing them.	Perceivers organize material sequentially and into component parts; for judgers, goal setting facilitates learning.
Brain Processing Styles	Left-brain processing	Information processing that focuses on tasks requiring verbal competence, such as speaking, reading, thinking, and reasoning; information is processed sequentially, one bit at a time.	Organize material logically; identify patterns; make tables of key information; break material into component parts.
	Right-brain processing	Information processing that focuses on information in nonverbal domains, such as the understanding of spatial relationships, recognition of patterns and drawings, music, and emotional expression.	Identify patterns; use graphs and drawings; read aloud; create models.

Speaking of Success

NAME: **C'Ardiss Gardner**

SCHOOL: **South Seattle Community College**

HOME: **Seattle, Washington**

When C'Ardiss Gardner began college, she was already familiar with challenge. She became a mother at age 16 and chose to finish high school while working two jobs to support her infant.

Despite the challenges, Gardner not only finished her high school requirements early but also had enough credits to start at the local community college. When she started at South Seattle Community College, not only was she taking classes, but she was working two part-time jobs. But eventually, she was forced to delay her college plans to take a third job to support herself. For three years she juggled work and child rearing.

But Gardner also had plans. She got married and reenrolled at South Seattle. After graduating with her associate's degree, she was accepted to four-year colleges around the country. She decided to move her family to the East Coast to attend Yale University. Gardner graduated from Yale with a B.A. in African-American Studies. She and her family returned to Seattle, where she now is raising three children, working as the registrar of a prep school, and studying for a master's degree in education at Seattle University.

"Attending school as an African-American student with a small child was very challenging. I did not come from a community that supported or encouraged kids like me to go to college," said Gardner.

"Even something as simple as writing was enough to set me apart from the other students, who had spent years learning how to write at a college level. I had to learn those things, and it was very difficult," she noted. "One of the most important things I learned was to access as many resources as I could to help learn skills I was lacking. Professors offered help by reading my drafts before I turned essays or papers in. By accepting help, I was able to improve my writing skills and improve my grades."

The skills Gardner developed while at South Seattle Community College laid the groundwork for her future academic success and became the foundation upon which she has been able to build the rest of her life. Not only has she been able to continue her education, but she plans to use her skills to help pave the way for other students to access education.

Looking Back

What are the benefits of a college education?

▸ The reason first-year college students most often cite for attending college is to get a better job, and college graduates do earn more on average than nongraduates.

▸ College also provides many other benefits. These include becoming well-educated, learning to think critically and communicate effectively, understanding the interconnections between different areas of knowledge and our place in history and the world, and understanding diversity.

What are the basic principles of P.O.W.E.R. Learning?

▸ P.O.W.E.R. Learning is a systematic approach people can easily learn, using abilities they already possess, to acquire successful habits for learning and achieving personal goals.

▸ P.O.W.E.R. Learning involves **p**reparation, **o**rganization, **w**ork, **e**valuation, and **r**ethinking.

How do expert students use P.O.W.E.R. Learning?

▸ To *prepare,* learners set both long-term and short-term goals, making sure that their goals are realistic, measurable, and under their control—and will lead to their final destination.

▸ They *organize* the tools they will need to accomplish those goals.

▸ They get down to *work* on the task at hand. Using their goals as motivation, expert learners also understand that success depends on effort.

▸ They *evaluate* the work they've done, considering what they have accomplished in comparison with the goals they set for themselves during the preparation stage.

▸ Finally, they *rethink,* reflecting on the process they've used, taking a fresh look at what they have done, and critically rethinking their goals.

What are my learning styles, and how can I employ them to be more successful?

▸ People have patterns of diverse learning styles—characteristic ways of acquiring and using knowledge.

▸ Learning styles include read/write, visual/graphic, auditory/verbal, and tactile/kinesthetic styles (the receptive learning styles).

▸ The multiple intelligences view says that we have eight different forms of intelligence, each relatively independent of the others.

▸ Personality styles that influence learning are classified along dimensions of introversion/extraversion, intuition/sensing, thinking/feeling, and perceiving/judging.

▸ Knowing your learning styles can help you identify the specific techniques that will allow you to master most effectively material in class and on the job.

[KEY TERMS AND CONCEPTS]

[RESOURCES]

ON CAMPUS

Every college provides a significant number of resources to help its students succeed and thrive, ranging from the activities coordination office to a multicultural center to writing labs to career centers. You can check them out on your college's Web site, catalog, or phone directory.

For example, here's a list of some typical campus resources, many of which we'll be discussing in future chapters:

- Activities/Clubs Office
- Adult and reentry center
- Advising center
- Alumni Office
- Art gallery
- Bookstore
- Career center
- Chaplain/religious services
- Child care center
- Cinema/theater
- Computing center/ computer labs
- Continuing education
- Disability center (learning or physical disabilities)

- Financial aid
- Fitness center/ gymnasium
- Health center
- Honors program
- Housing center
- Information center
- Intramural sports
- Language lab
- Lost and found
- Math lab
- Multicultural center
- Museum
- Online Education (distance learning) Office
- Off-campus housing and services
- Ombudsman/conflict resolution

- Photography lab
- Police/campus security
- Post Office
- Printing center
- Registration Office
- Residential Life Office
- School newspaper
- Student Government Office
- Student Affairs Office
- Study abroad/ exchange programs
- Testing center
- Volunteer services
- Work-study center
- Writing lab

If you are commuting to school, your first "official" encounters on campus are likely to be with representatives of the college's Student Affairs Office or its equivalent. The Student Affairs Office has the goal of maintaining the quality of student life, helping to ensure that students receive the help they need. Student Affairs personnel often are in charge of student orientation programs that help new students familiarize themselves with their new institution.

Whatever college representatives you deal with during your first days of college, remember that their job is to help you. Don't be shy about asking questions about what you may expect, how to find things, and what you should be doing.

Above all, if you are experiencing any difficulties, be certain to make use of your college's resources. College success does not come easily for anyone, particularly when it demands juggling responsibilities of work and family. You should make use of whatever support your college offers.

IN PRINT

To learn more about who your first-year classmates are across the United States, take a look at John Pryor and collegues' *The American Freshman: National Norms for Fall 2008* (Higher Education Research Institute, 2009). The book provides a comprehensive look at the attitudes and opinions of first-year college students, based on the results of a national survey.

Gail Wood's book *How to Study: Use Your Personal Learning Style to Help You Succeed When It Counts* (Learning Express Press, 2000) provides an introduction to learning styles, offering tips and suggestions for making use of the way that you learn.

ON THE WEB

The following sites on the Web provide the opportunity to extend your learning about the material in this chapter. Although the Web addresses were accurate at the time the book was printed, check the *P.O.W.E.R. Learning* Web site (**www.mhhe.com/power**) for any changes that may have occurred.

➤ The University of Buffalo (**http://ub-counseling.buffalo.edu/adjusting.shtml**) Counseling Services offers this site on adjusting to campus life that includes links to relationships, health, and study skills.

➤ The U.S. Department of Education offers *Preparing Your Child for College: A Resource Guide for Parents* (**www.ed.gov/pubs/Prepare/index.html**). Though geared toward parents' concerns, the publication offers answers to a host of valuable questions such as "Why attend college?" and "What kinds of jobs are available to college graduates?"

➤ The Learn More Resource Center (**www.learnmoreindiana.org**) provides information on a variety of useful topics regarding adjustment to college life, including comments by students on their experiences. It covers such topics as where to live, how to select classes, how to study and learn, and much more.

➤ The University of Arizona's Learning Center site (**www.ulc.arizona.edu/selfassessments.php**) offers a number of self-assessments including a Learning Style Profile Generator and a Learning Style Assessment.

TAKING IT TO THE NET

1 Find out what percentage of the population of the United States has received an undergraduate degree, using search engines such as Google to identify U.S. Census information. (If you're unfamiliar with search engines on the Web, see Chapter 7 for suggestions that will get you started.) The Census Bureau site provides information about the level of education achieved by people over 25 years of age. How many men have received a bachelor's degree? How many women?

2 Consider the reasons for going to college. The U.S. Department of Education's "Think College" site (**www.ed.gov/students/prep/college/thinkcollege/edlite-index.html**) offers various rationales for continuing your education beyond high school. Were you aware of them prior to your enrollment in college?

The Case of . . .
Doubting in Denver

It was during the second week of classes that the questioning started. Until then, Jesse had been fairly confident in his decision to enroll at a college in the Denver suburbs to gain training to be a medical technician. He had been excited to try something new and to start a new career, but more and more he was wondering if he'd made the right choice.

To get to campus, Jesse had to take a forty-five-minute bus ride, because his wife needed the car to get to her office in downtown Denver. Jesse was also keeping his part-time job as an executive assistant at a doctor's office, a job that meant another long commute. And on top of that, Jesse needed to find time among work, classes, and studying to help care for his five-year-old son.

Maybe, Jesse was beginning to think, college hadn't been such a good idea. True, he could earn more money as a medical technician and begin a more promising career. But was it really worth all this added time and stress? Plus, Jesse had never done very well academically. Why would college be any different? If he wanted to make more money, he could just add more shifts at his current job.

Why bother with college? Jesse thought to himself. What an expense, and what a hassle. For what?

1. What arguments could you provide Jesse as to the value of a college education?

2. Do you think that Jesse's doubts are common?

3. What might you suggest that Jesse do to help deal with his doubts about the value of college?

4. Why might a student's doubts about the value of college be especially strong during the beginning weeks of college?

5. Do you share any of Jesse's concerns about the value of a college education? Do you have additional ones?

2

Making the Most of Your Time

Learning Outcomes

By the time you finish this chapter you will be able to

>> LO**2.1**   Explain how to manage time more effectively.

>> LO**2.2**   Analyze how do deal with competing priorities.

>> LO**2.3**   Identify strategies for dealing with surprises and distractions.

As Vicky Marks waits in line for her morning cup of coffee, she mentally goes over the things she needs to get done during the day: *Get to the gym at 8:00 A.M. to teach her morning yoga classes . . . study for her anatomy quiz over lunch at 12:30 . . . from 1:30 to 4:30 go to classes at the college where she's studying for her physical therapist's degree . . . meet her husband at 5:00 to watch her son's soccer game . . . go home, make dinner, put her son to bed by 8:00.* She has the nagging feeling that there's something else she needs to do, but she can't put her finger on it.

She finally gets to the head of the line to pay for her coffee, which she starts drinking even before she pays for it. Glancing at a clock as she leaves the coffee shop, she gives up the thought of getting in some last-minute studying for her anatomy quiz before teaching her yoga class. It will be a minor miracle if she even makes it to the gym on time.

She's been up less than an hour, and already Vicky is running behind schedule.

Looking Ahead

Are your days like Vicky's? Are you constantly trying to cram more activities into less time? Do you feel as if you never have enough time?

You're not alone: Most of us wish we had more time to accomplish the things we need to do. However, some people are a lot better at juggling their time than others. What's their secret?

There is no secret. No one has more than 24 hours a day and 168 hours a week. The key to success lies in figuring out our priorities and better using the time we do have.

Time management is like juggling a bunch of tennis balls: for most of us, juggling doesn't come naturally, but it is a skill that can be learned. Not all of us will end up perfect jugglers (whether we are juggling tennis balls or time), but, with practice, we can become a lot better at it.

This chapter will give you strategies for improving your time management skills. After first helping you learn to account for the ways you currently use—and misuse—time, it gives you strategies for planning your time, including some ways to deal with the inevitable interruptions and counterproductive personal habits that can sabotage your best intentions. It will provide you with skills that are not only important for success in college and on the job, but for your personal life as well.

We also consider techniques for dealing with competing goals. There are special challenges involved in juggling the priorities of college and work with other aspects of life, such as child rearing or hobbies.

» LO 2.1 Time for Success

Without looking up from the page, answer this question: What time is it?

Most people are pretty accurate in their answer. And if you don't know for sure, it's very likely that you can find out. Your cell phone may display the time; there may be a clock on the wall, desk, or computer screen; or maybe you're riding in a car that shows the time in the instrument panel.

Even if you don't have a timepiece of some sort nearby, your body keeps its own beat. Humans have an internal clock that regulates the beating of our heart, the pace of our breathing, the discharge of chemicals within our bloodstream, and myriad other bodily functions.

Time is something from which we can't escape. Even if we ignore it, it's still going by, ticking away, second by second, minute by minute, hour by hour. So the main issue in using your time well is, "Who's in charge?" We can allow time to slip by and let it be our enemy. Or we can take control of it and make it our ally.

Prepare

Learn where
time is going

Organize

Use a master calendar,
weekly timetable, and
daily to-do list

Work

Follow the schedules
you've put together

Evaluate

Keep track of your
short-term and long-term
accomplishments

Rethink

Reflect on your personal
style of time management

P.O.W.E.R. Plan

Time log

A record of how one spends
one's time

> "You may delay, but time will not."
>
> Benjamin Franklin

By taking control of how you spend your time, you'll increase your chances of becoming more successful in college and in your career. Perhaps more important, the better you are at managing the time you devote to your studies and your job, the more time you will have to spend on your outside interests. (You can get a sense of your own personal time style by completing **Try It 1** on page 33.)

The goal of time management is not to schedule every moment so we become pawns of a timetable that governs every waking moment of the day. Instead, the goal is to permit us to make informed choices as to how we use our time. Rather than letting the day slip by, largely without our awareness, the time management procedures we'll discuss can make us better able to harness time for our own ends. In short, time management doesn't confine us. On the contrary, it frees us to do the things we want and need to do.

Prepare

Learning Where Time Is Going and Where It Should Go

Before you get somewhere, you need to know where you're starting from and where you want to go. So the first step in improving your time management skills is figuring out how you're managing your time now.

Create a Time Log

"Where did the day go?" If you've ever said this to yourself, one way of figuring out where you've spent your time is to create a time log. A time log is the most essential tool for improving your use of time.

A **time log** is simply a record of how you actually have spent your time—including interruptions. It doesn't have to be a second-by-second record of every waking moment. But it should account for blocks of time in increments as short as 15 minutes.

Look at the blank time log in **Try It 2** on page 34. As you fill out the log, be specific, indicating not only what you were doing at a given time (for example, "studying for economics quiz") but also the interruptions that occurred (such as "answered cell phone twice" or "switched to Internet for 10 minutes").

By looking at how much time you spend doing various activities, you now know where your time goes. How does it match with your perceptions of how you spend your time? Be prepared to be surprised, because most people find that they're spending time on a lot of activities that just don't matter very much.

From the perspective of . . .

A STUDENT Time logs can be helpful tools when determining how you spend your time; they can also help you find more time for the activities you enjoy doing. What areas of your life do you wish you had more time to spend in?

Try It!

Find Your Time Style

Rate how well each of the statements below describes you.   Use this rating scale:

1 = Doesn't describe me at all

2 = Describes me only slightly

3 = Describes me fairly well

4 = Describes me very well

	1	2	3	4
1. I often wake up later than I should.				
2. I am usually late for classes and appointments.				
3. I am always in a rush getting places.				
4. I put off big tasks and assignments until the last minute.				
5. My friends often comment on my lateness.				
6. I am easily interrupted, putting aside what I'm doing for something new.				
7. When I look at a clock, I'm often surprised at how late it is.				
8. I often forget appointments and have to reschedule them.				
9. When faced with a big task, I feel overwhelmed and turn my mind away from it until later.				
10. At the end of the day, I have no idea where the time went.				

Rate yourself by adding up the points you assigned. Use this scale to assess your time style:

10–15 = Very efficient time user

16–20 = Efficient time user

21–30 = Time use needs work

31–40 = Victim of time

To Try It online, go to www.mhhe.com/power.

≫ LO 2.2 Set Your Priorities

By this point you should have a good idea of what's taking up your time. But you may not know what you should be doing instead.

To figure out the best use of your time, you need to determine your priorities. **Priorities** are the tasks and activities you need and want to do, rank-ordered from most important to least important. There are no right or wrong priorities; you have to decide for yourself what you wish to accomplish. Maybe spending time on your studies is most important to you, or working to earn more money, or maybe your top priority is spending time with your family. Only you can decide. Furthermore, what's important to you at this moment may be less of a priority to you next month, next year, or five years from now.

Priorities

The tasks and activities that one needs and wants to do, rank-ordered from most important to least important

Try It!

Create a Time Log

Keep track of the way you spend your time across seven days on time logs. Insert the amount of time you spend on each activity during each one-hour period for a single day. Do the same thing for every day of the week on separate time logs. *Be sure to make copies of this log before you fill it in for the first day.* You can print out copies at the *P.O.W.E.R. Learning* Web site at **www.mhhe.com/power.**

Analyze your log: After you complete your log for a week, analyze how you spend your time according to the major categories on the log. Add up the amount of time you spend on each category. You can also create other broad categories that eat up significant amounts of time.

Now consider the following:

1. What do you spend most of your time on?

2. Are you satisfied with the way that you are using your time? Are there any areas that seem to use up excessive amounts of time?

3. Do you see some simple fixes that will allow you to use time more effectively?

 WORKING IN A GROUP

Compare your use of time during an average week with those of your classmates. What are the major differences and similarities in the use of time?

To Try It online, go to www.mhhe.com/power.

For the purpose of effective time management in college, the best procedure is to start off by identifying priorities for an entire term. What do you need to accomplish? Don't just choose obvious, general goals, such as "passing all my classes." Instead, think about your priorities in terms of specific, measurable activities, such as "studying ten hours before each exam"—*not* "studying harder" which is too vague. (Look at the example of a priority list in **Figure 2.1** on page 36 and also the **Course Connections** feature.)

Write your priorities on the chart in **Try It 3** on pages 36 and 37. After you've filled out the chart, organize it by giving each priority a ranking from 1 to 3.

Time Log

Day: _____   Date: _____

	personal care	food	classes	studies	work	recreation	sleep	other
6–7 a.m.								
7–8 a.m.								
8–9 a.m.								
9–10 a.m.								
10–11 a.m.								
11–12 (noon)								
12 (noon)– 1 p.m.								
1–2 p.m.								
2–3 p.m.								
3–4 p.m.								
4–5 p.m.								
5–6 p.m.								
6–7 p.m.								
7–8 p.m.								
8–9 p.m.								
9–10 p.m.								
10–11 p.m.								
11 p.m.–12 (midnight)								
12 (midnight)– 1 a.m.								
1–2 a.m.								
2–3 a.m.								
3–4 a.m.								
4–5 a.m.								
5–6 a.m.								

A "1" represents a priority that absolutely must be done; without it you'll suffer a major setback. For instance, showing up for work should receive a "1" for a priority ranking; carving out time to take those guitar lessons you always wanted to take might be ranked a "3" in terms of priority. The important point is to rank-order your priorities to reveal what is and is not important to accomplish during the term.

Setting priorities will help you to determine how to make best use of your time. No one has enough time to complete everything; prioritizing will help you make informed decisions about what you can do to maximize your success.

Try It!

Set Priorities

Set your priorities for the term. They may include getting to class on time, finishing papers and assignments by their due dates, maintaining a good reputation with your boss, or spending time with your family. To get started, list priorities in any order. Be sure to consider priorities relating to your classes, work, family, social obligations, and health. After you list them, assign a number to each one indicating its level—giving a "1" to the highest priority items, a "2" to medium priority items, and a "3" to the items with the lowest priority.

List of Priorities	
Priority	Priority Index

Now redo your list, putting your number 1s first, followed by as many of your number 2s and 3s to which you feel you can reasonably commit.

figure 2.1
Sample List of Priorities

Priority	Ranking
Study for each class at least 30 minutes/day	1
Start each major paper 1 week in advance of due date	2
Hand in each paper on time	1
Review for test starting a week before test date	2
Be on time for job	1
Check in with Mom once a week	3
Work out 3x/week	3

Final List of Priorities	
Priority	
1.	
2.	
3.	
4.	
5.	
6.	
7.	
8.	
9.	
10.	
11.	
12.	

Now consider the following:

- What does this list tell you about your greatest priorities? Are they centered around school, your career, friends and family, or some other aspect of your life?
- Do you have so many "1" priorities that they will be difficult or impossible to accomplish successfully? How could you go back to your list and trim it down even more?
- What does this listing of priorities suggest about how successful you'll be during the upcoming term?

To Try It online, go to www.mhhe.com/power.

Study Time: How Much Is Enough?

What would you guess is the average number of hours instructors think you should be studying each week? In the view of instructors queried in a national survey, students should spend, on average, 6 hours per week preparing for *each* class in which they're enrolled. And if they're taking courses in the sciences and engineering, instructors expect their students to put in even more hours.[1]

Keep in mind that study time does not include actual class time. If you add that in, someone taking four classes would need 24 hours of outside class preparation and would be in class for 16 hours—for a total of 40 hours, or the equivalent of full-time employment.

If you've underestimated the amount of time instructors believe is necessary to devote to class preparation, you may need to rethink the amount of time you'll need to allocate to studying. You might also speak to your individual instructors to see what they believe is an appropriate amount of preparation. Although they may not be able to give exact figures, their estimates will help you to prioritize what you need to do to be a successful student.

Course
Connections

Journal Reflections

Where Does My Time Go?

1. On the typical weekday, what time do you wake up? When would you prefer to wake up if you had the choice?

2. When do you typically go to bed on a typical weekday night? When would you prefer to go to bed if you had the choice?

3. Would you characterize yourself as a "morning person," who accomplishes the most in the early morning, or more as a "night person," who is most comfortable doing work in the evenings? What implications does this have for your scheduling of classes and work shifts?

4. Generally speaking, how would you characterize your time management skills? What would be the benefit to you personally if you could manage time more effectively? What goals might you accomplish if you had more time at your disposal?

Master calendar

A schedule showing the weeks of a longer time period, such as a college term, with all assignments and important activities noted on it

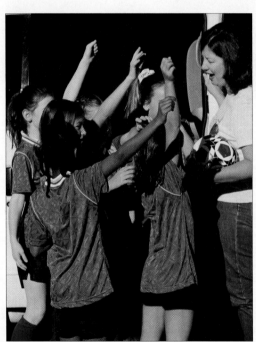

Short- and long-term priorities may not always match. What would you do if a class you needed to graduate conflicted with your daughter's weekly soccer game?

» ⊙ **Organize**

Mastering the Moment

You now know where you've lost time in the past, and your priority list is telling you where you need to head in the future.

Now for the present. You've reached the point where you can organize yourself to take control of your time. Here's what you'll need:

> A **master calendar** that shows all the weeks of the term on one page. You don't need to buy one; you can make it easily enough yourself. It need not be great art; a rough version will do. The important point is that it must include every week of the term and seven days per week. (See the example of a master calendar in **Figure 2.2** on page 39.)

> A weekly timetable. The **weekly timetable** is a master grid with the days of the week across the top and the hours along the side. This will permit you to write in all your regularly scheduled activities, as well as one-time appointments when they arise. (A blank weekly timetable is provided in **Figure 2.3** on page 40. You can also find it online at **www.mhhe.com/power.**)

> A daily to-do list. Finally, you'll need a **daily to-do list.** The daily to-do list can be written on a small, portable calendar that includes a separate page for each day of the week. Or it can simply be a small notebook, with a separate sheet of paper for every day of the week. Whatever form your daily to-do list takes, make sure it's portable, because you'll need to keep it with you all the time.

figure 2.2
Master Calendar Sample

figure 2.2 Master Calendar Sample

Writing

M	T	W	TH	F	SA	S
Sept. 7	8	9 Classes Start	10	11	12 Camping →	13
14	Add/ drop 15 ends	16	English 17 short paper due	18	19	20
21	Work 22	23	English 24 short paper due	Work 25	26	27
28	29	30 Math exam	OCT 1 English short paper due	Legal 2 Studies quiz	3	4
5	Legal Studies 6 paper due	7	English 8 short paper due	Work 9	10	11
12	Work 13	14	English short 15 paper due	Legal 16 Studies quiz	17	18
First-yr 19 seminar journal due	20	Math 21 exam	English 22 short paper due Dad's bd—call	Work 23	Bartending 24 job	25
Work 26	English 27 midterm exam	28	Eng-short 29 paper due	Legal Studies 30 quiz	31	NOV 1
2	3	4	English 5 short paper due	Work 6	7	Darcey's 8 Wedding!
9	Work 10	Holiday— 11 Veteran's Day	Eng-short 12 paper due	Legal 13 Studies quiz Math exam	14	15
First-yr 16 seminar group project due	17	Preregistration 18 for next semester	English 19 short paper due	20	21	22
23	Work 24	25	Thanksgiving 26	No Classes! 27	28	29
30	DEC 1 Legal Studies paper due	2	English 3 short paper due	Work 4	5	6
First-yr 7 seminar final journal due	Work 8	9	Legal 10 studies quiz	Math exam 11 Last day of class!!	12	13
English 14 final exam	Legal 15 Studies final exam	16	Math 17 final exam	Legal 18 Studies exam MY birthday!	19	20
21	22	23	24	Xmas 25	26	27

The basic organizational task you face is filling in these three schedules. You'll need at least an hour to do this, so set the time aside. In addition, there will be some repetition across the three schedules, and the task may seem a bit tedious. *But every minute you invest now in organizing your time will pay off in hours that you will save in the future.*

Follow these steps in completing your schedule:

> **Start with the master calendar, which shows all the weeks of the term on one page.** Write on the master calendar every class assignment you have for the entire term, noting it on the date that it is due. Also include major events at work, such as days when you might need to work overtime. In addition, include important activities from your personal life, drawn from your list of

Weekly timetable

A schedule showing all regular, prescheduled activities due to occur in the week, together with one-time events and commitments

Daily to-do list

A schedule showing the tasks, activities, and appointments due to occur during the day

figure 2.3

Weekly Timetable

Make a single copy of this blank timetable or go to the *P.O.W.E.R. Learning* Web site (**www.mhhe.com/power**) and use the online version. Then fill in your regular, predictable time commitments.

Next, make as many copies as you need to cover each week of the term. Then, for each week, fill in the date on the left and the number of the week in the term on the right, and add in your irregular commitments.

Weekly Timetable

Week of: _____   Week # _____

	Mon	Tues	Wed	Thurs	Fri	Sat	Sun
6–7 a.m.							
7–8 a.m.							
8–9 a.m.							
9–10 a.m.							
10–11 a.m.							
11–12 (noon)							
12 (noon)– 1 p.m.							
1–2 p.m.							
2–3 p.m.							
3–4 p.m.							
4–5 p.m.							
5–6 p.m.							
6–7 p.m.							
7–8 p.m.							
8–9 p.m.							
9–10 p.m.							
10–11 p.m.							
11 p.m.–12 (midnight)							
12 (midnight)– 1 a.m.							
1–2 a.m.							
2–3 a.m.							
3–4 a.m.							
4–5 a.m.							
5–6 a.m.							

priorities. For instance, if your spouse or child has a performance or sporting event you want to attend, be sure to mark it down.

Finally, schedule some free time—time when you promise yourself you will do something that is just plain fun. Consider these days to be written in stone, and promise yourself that you won't use them for anything else except for something enjoyable. Just knowing that you have some downtime planned will help you to throw yourself into more demanding tasks. In addition, getting into the habit of allowing yourself time to relax and reflect on your life is as important as any other time management skill you may learn.

You now have a good idea of what the next few weeks have in store for you. You can identify just by looking at your master calendar the periods when you are going to be especially busy. You can also note the periods when you will have less to do.

Use the off-peak periods to get a head start on future assignments!

In this way, your master schedule can help you head off disaster before it occurs.

➤ **Now move to the weekly timetable provided in Figure 2.3** on page 40. Fill in the times of all your fixed, prescheduled activities—the times that your classes meet, when you have to be at work, the times you have to pick up your child at day care, and any other recurring appointments.

Once you've filled in the weekly timetable, as in the one on page 40, you get a bare-bones picture of the average week. You will still need to take into account the specific activities that are required to complete the assignments on the master calendar.

To move from your "average" week to specific weeks, make photocopies of the weekly timetable

Sometimes it is okay (and even necessary) to simply relax. Make sure that you make time to unwind!

that now contains your fixed appointments. Make enough copies for every week of the term. On each copy write the week number of the term and the specific dates it covers. (See a sample in **Figure 2.4** on page 42.)

Using your master calendar, add assignment due dates, tests, and any other activities on the appropriate days of the week. Then pencil in blocks of time necessary to prepare for those events.

How much time should you allocate for schoolwork? One very rough rule of thumb holds that every one hour that you spend in class requires, on average, two hours of study outside of class to earn a B and three hours of study outside of class to earn an A. Do the arithmetic: If you are taking 15 credits (with each credit equivalent to an hour of class per week), you'll need to plan for 30 hours of studying each week to earn a B average—an intimidating amount of time. Of course, the amount of time you must allocate to a specific class will vary from week to week, depending on what is happening in the class.

For example, if you estimate that you'll need five hours of study for a midterm exam in a certain class, pencil in those hours. Don't set up a single block of five hours. People remember best when their studying is spread out over shorter periods rather than attempted in one long block of time. Besides, it will probably be hard to find a block of five straight hours on your weekly calendar.

Keep in mind that estimates are just that: estimates. Don't think of them as set in stone. Mark them on your weekly calendar in pencil, not pen, so you can adjust them if necessary.

But remember: It's also crucial not to overschedule yourself. You'll still need time to eat, to talk with your friends, to spend time with your family, and to enjoy yourself in general. If you find that your life is completely filled with things that you feel you must do in order to survive and that there is no room for fun, then take a step back and cut out something to make some time

figure 2.4
A Sample Weekly
Timetable

Weekly Timetable

Week of: _9/28_   Week # _3_

	Mon	Tues	Wed	Thurs	Fri	Sat	Sun
6–7 a.m.							
7–8 a.m.							
8–9 a.m.							
9–10 a.m.	9:05 Math	9:05 Legal Studies	9:05 Math	9:05 Math	9:05 Legal Studies		
10–11 a.m.		⇓		⇓			
11–12 (noon)		11:15 Writing I		11:15 Writing I			
12 (noon)–1 p.m.	12:20 First Year Seminar	⇓		⇓			
1–2 p.m.	⇓	Work	Work	Work	Work		
2–3 p.m.							
3–4 p.m.							
4–5 p.m.							
5–6 p.m.		⇓	⇓	⇓	⇓		
6–7 p.m.							
7–8 p.m.							
8–9 p.m.							
9–10 p.m.							
10–11 p.m.							
11 p.m.–12 (midnight)							
12 (midnight)–1 a.m.							
1–2 a.m.							
2–3 a.m.							
3–4 a.m.							
4–5 a.m.							
5–6 a.m.							

for yourself in your daily schedule. Finding time for yourself is as important as carving out time for what others want you to do. Besides, if you are over-worked, you're likely to "find" the time by guiltily goofing off without really setting aside the time and enjoying it.

> **If you've taken each of the previous steps, you're now in a position to work on the final step of organization for successful time management: completing your daily to-do list.** Unlike the master calendar and weekly timetable—both of which you develop at weeks or even months advance—complete your daily to-do list just one day ahead of time, preferably at the end of the day.

List all the things that you intend to do during the next day, and their priority. Start with the things you know you *must* do and which have fixed times, such as classes, work schedules, and appointments. These are your first priority

figure 2.5
Sample Daily To-Do List

Item	Priority	Completed
To-Do List for _____ (date)		
Call Chris to get econ notes	1	✗
Meet with Prof. Hernandez	1	✗
Finish budget reports at work	1	✗
Work on outline for legal studies paper	2	✗
Return books to library	2	
Pick up Nettie at school	1	✗
Call Deena about Saturday	2	
Do laundry	3	

items. Then add in the other things that you *should* accomplish, such as an hour of study for an upcoming test or a trip to the garage to have your oil changed. Finally, list things that are lower priority but enjoyable, setting aside time for a run or a walk, for example.

Don't schedule every single minute of the day. That would be counterproductive, and you'd end up feeling like you'd failed if you deviated from your schedule. Instead, think of your daily to-do list as a path through a forest. If you were hiking, you

From the perspective of . . .

A WORKING PARENT The balancing act between work and family can be a challenge. How can a weekly timetable help you ensure all areas of your life are getting the attention they deserve?

would allow yourself to deviate from the path, occasionally venturing onto side tracks when they looked interesting. But you'd also be keeping tabs on your direction so you end up where you need to be at the end and not miles away from your car or home.

Like the sample daily to-do list in **Figure 2.5**, include a column to check or cross off after you've completed an activity. There's something very satisfying in acknowledging what you have accomplished.

≫ LO 2.3 | w Work | Controlling Time

You're in luck: There is no work to time management—or at least not much more than you've already done. The work of time management is to follow the schedules that you've prepared and organized. But that doesn't mean it will be easy. Our lives are filled with surprises: Things take longer than we've planned. A friend we haven't spoken to in a while calls to chat, and it seems rude to say that we don't have time to talk. A crisis occurs; buses are late; computers break down; kids get sick.

The difference between effective time management and time management that doesn't work lies in how well you deal with the inevitable surprises.

There are several ways to take control of your days and permit yourself to follow your intended schedule:

> **Just say no.** You don't have to agree to every request and every favor that others ask of you. You're not a bad person if you refuse to do something that will eat up your time and prevent you from accomplishing your goals. And if you do decide to do someone else a time-consuming favor, try to come up with the most efficient way of accomplishing it. Don't let all your time get taken up by the priorities of others.

> **Get away from it all.** Go to the library. Lock yourself into your bedroom. Find a quiet, out-of-the-way coffee shop. Any of these places can serve to isolate you from everyday distractions and thereby permit you to work on the tasks that you wish to complete. Try to adopt a particular spot as your own, such as a corner desk in a secluded nook in the library. If you use it enough, your body and mind will automatically get into study mode as soon as you seat yourself at it.

> **Enjoy the sounds of silence.** Although many people insist they accomplish most while a television, radio, or CD is playing, scientific studies suggest otherwise: We are able to concentrate most when our environment is silent. So even if you're sure you work best with a soundtrack playing, experiment and work in silence for a few days. You may find that you get more done in less time than you would in a more distracting environment.

> **Take an e-break.** Text messages, phone calls, Facebook status updates, instant messages, e-mail. Who doesn't love to hear from others?
>
> We may not control when communications arrive, but we can make the message wait until we are ready to receive it. Take an e-break and shut down your communication sources for a period of time.

> **Expect the unexpected.** Interruptions and crises, minor and major, can't be eliminated. However, they can be prepared for.
>
> How is it possible to plan for surprises? Though it may still be too early in the term to get a clear picture of what sorts of unanticipated events you'll encounter, you should keep an eye out for patterns. Perhaps one instructor routinely gives surprise assignments. Maybe you're asked to work extra hours on the weekends because someone doesn't show up and you have to work overtime.
>
> You'll never be able to escape from unexpected interruptions and surprises that require your attention. But by trying to anticipate them in advance, and thinking about how you'll react to them, you'll be positioning yourself to react more effectively when they do occur.

Procrastination
The habit of putting off and delaying tasks that need to be accomplished

> **Combat procrastination. Procrastination,** the habit of putting off and delaying tasks that need to be accomplished, is like a microscopic parasite. It is invisible to the naked eye, but it eats up your time nonetheless.
>
> You can't control interruptions and crises that are imposed upon you by others. But even when no one else is throwing interruptions at us, we make up our own. Procrastination is a problem that many of us face. To identify

whether you are a procrastinator, find your "Procrastination Quotient" (see **Try It 4,** page 46).

If you find yourself procrastinating, several steps can help you:

Break large tasks into small ones. People often procrastinate because a task they're seeking to accomplish appears overwhelming. If writing a 15-page paper seems nearly impossible, think about writing a series of five 3-page papers. If reading a 750-page book seems impossible, think of it as reading several 250-page books.

Start with the easiest and simplest part of a task, and then do the harder parts. Succeeding initially on the easy parts can make the harder parts of a task less daunting—and make you less apt to procrastinate in completing the task.

Just begin! Sometimes the hardest part of an activity is simply getting started. So take the leap and begin the task, and the rest may follow more easily.

Work with others. Just being in the same physical location with others can motivate you sufficiently to accomplish tasks that you consider unpleasant and on which you might be tempted to procrastinate. For instance, filling out tedious order forms can be made easier if you collaborate with coworkers. Beware, though—if you spend too much time socializing, you lower the likelihood of success.

Keep the costs of procrastination in mind. Procrastination doesn't just result in delay; it may also make the task harder than it would have been if you hadn't procrastinated. Not only will you ultimately have less time to complete the task, but you may have to do it so quickly that its quality may be diminished. In the worst scenario, you won't even be able to finish it at all.

> **Balance school and work obligations with family demands.** If you have a job and are a student and also have caregiver responsibilities for children or other family members such as aging parents, time management is especially challenging. Not only does your family demand—and deserve—substantial quantities of time, but juggling school and work and family obligations can prove to be exhausting. However, there are some specific strategies that can help.

Dealing with child-care demands:

Provide activities for your children. Kids enjoy doing things on their own for part of the day. Plan activities that will keep them happily occupied while you're doing work.

Make spending time with your children a priority. Carve out "free play" time for your kids. Even 20 minutes of good time devoted to your children will give all of you—you and them—a lift. No matter how busy you are, you owe it to your children—and yourself—to spend time as a family.

Enlist your child's help. Children love to play adult and, if they're old enough, ask them to help you study. Maybe they can help you clear a space to study. Perhaps you can give them "assignments" that they can work on while you're working on your assignments.

Encourage your child to invite friends over to play. Some children can remain occupied for hours if they have a playmate.

Use television appropriately. Television viewing is not all bad, and some shows and DVDs can be not just engaging, but educational. The trick is to pick and choose what your children watch.

Try It!

Find Your Procrastination Quotient

Do you procrastinate?[2] To find out, circle the number that best applies for each question using the following scale:

| **Strongly agree** | **4** | **3** | **2** | **1** | **Strongly disagree** |

1. I invent reasons and look for excuses for not acting on a problem.

| **Strongly agree** | **4** | **3** | **2** | **1** | **Strongly disagree** |

2. It takes pressure to get me to work on difficult assignments.

| **Strongly agree** | **4** | **3** | **2** | **1** | **Strongly disagree** |

3. I take half measures that will avoid or delay unpleasant or difficult tasks.

| **Strongly agree** | **4** | **3** | **2** | **1** | **Strongly disagree** |

4. I face too many interruptions and crises that interfere with accomplishing my major goals.

| **Strongly agree** | **4** | **3** | **2** | **1** | **Strongly disagree** |

5. I sometimes neglect to carry out important tasks.

| **Strongly agree** | **4** | **3** | **2** | **1** | **Strongly disagree** |

6. I schedule big assignments too late to get them done as well as I know I could.

| **Strongly agree** | **4** | **3** | **2** | **1** | **Strongly disagree** |

7. I'm sometimes too tired to do the work I need to do.

| **Strongly agree** | **4** | **3** | **2** | **1** | **Strongly disagree** |

8. I start new tasks before I finish old ones.

| **Strongly agree** | **4** | **3** | **2** | **1** | **Strongly disagree** |

9. When I work in groups, I try to get other people to finish what I don't.

| **Strongly agree** | **4** | **3** | **2** | **1** | **Strongly disagree** |

10. I put off tasks that I really don't want to do but know that I must do.

| **Strongly agree** | **4** | **3** | **2** | **1** | **Strongly disagree** |

Scoring: Total the numbers you have circled. If the score is below 15, you are not a chronic procrastinator and you probably have only an occasional problem. If your score is 16–25, you have a minor problem with procrastination. If your score is above 25, you procrastinate quite often and should work on breaking the habit.

Now, consider the following:

- If you do procrastinate often, why do you think you do it?
- Are there particular kinds of assignments that you are more likely to procrastinate on?
- Is there something that you are putting off doing right now? How might you get started on it?

 WORKING IN A GROUP

Think about the last time you procrastinated. Describe it as completely as you can. What was the task? What did you do rather than doing what needed to be done? What could you have done to avoid procrastinating in this situation? Ask others what strategy they might suggest for avoiding procrastinating.

To Try It online, go to www.mhhe.com/power.

Find the best child care or babysitters that you can. The better the care your children are getting, the better you'll be able to concentrate on your classes or your job. You may still feel guilty that you're not with your children as much as you'd like, but accept that guilt. Remember, your attendance in college and good performance at work builds a better future for your children.

Use your children's "downtime" effectively. If your children are young, use their nap time as a chance to catch up on work or chores. Or consider getting up early, before your children wake up, for a period in which you will have fewer interruptions than later in the day.

Dealing with the elder-care demands:

Encourage as much independence as possible on the part of older adults for whom you are responsible. Not only will it take some of the pressure off you, but it will be helpful to the older adult.

Ask for support from your siblings and other family members. Caring for an ill or aging parent should be a family affair, not a burden that falls on any one individual.

Determine what community resources are available. Local centers for aging may provide assistance not only to the elderly but also to their caregivers.

Respect your own needs. Remember that your own priorities are important. Elders for whom you are responsible will understand that you will sometimes need to put yourself first.

> **Balance school and work demands.** Juggling school and a job can be a real challenge. Not only must you manage your time to complete your schoolwork, but in many cases you'll also face time management demands while you are on the job. Here are some tips to help you keep everything in balance:

If you have slack time on the job, get some studying done. Try to keep at least some of your textbooks, class notes, or notecards always with you so you can refer to them. Of course, you should never do schoolwork without your employer's prior agreement. If you don't get permission, you may jeopardize your job.

Use your lunch hour effectively. Although it's important to eat a nutritious lunch and not to wolf your food down, you may be able to use some of the time allotted to you for lunch to fit in some studying.

Ask your employer about flextime. If your job allows it, you may be able to set your own hours, within reason, as long as the work gets done. If this is an option for you, use it. Although it may create more time management challenges for you than would a job with set hours, it also provides you with more flexibility.

Accept new responsibilities carefully. If you've barely been keeping up with the demands of work and school, don't automatically accept new job responsibilities without carefully evaluating how they fit with your long-term priorities. If your job is temporary and you're not planning to stay, you might want to respectfully decline substantial new duties or an increase in the number of hours you work. On the other hand, if you plan to continue in the job once you're done with school, then accepting new responsibilities may be more reasonable.

"I had a friend who was taking classes to become a paralegal. He always complained about how he didn't have enough time between taking classes and holding down his job. But he was always inviting me and his other friends out to movies, insisting we stay at the bar for one more round. It wasn't a surprise when he eventually dropped out of school. It wasn't that he didn't have enough time. It was that he spent it on all the wrong things."

Bell Hansom, restaurant manager

On-the-Job Time Management

In the business world, schedules are unpredictable. Crises occur, perhaps due to manufacturing problems or client demands, which require sudden flurries of work. For employees with a demanding boss who may, without warning, give them an urgent assignment due the next morning, time is always at a premium. In some jobs, you may be forced to drop everything you normally work on and pitch in on a sudden new task. As a result, your plans to complete your everyday work may be disrupted completely.

Simply put, time management is an essential survival skill when developing your career. Learning the basic principles of time management now will help you well beyond your years in college, and throughout your later career. You'll also want to learn new time-management strategies specific to the working world. For instance, if you supervise other employees, it may be possible to delegate some work to them, allowing them to help you complete assignments on time. Or sometimes it may be possible to deflect assignments brought to you by a boss to some other unit or department. Always keep in mind what it is possible for you to do alone—and what is impossible without the aid of coworkers. Don't be afraid to ask for help. In the working world, the end result is what counts above all.

E Evaluate Checking Your Time

Evaluating how you use your time is pretty straightforward: You either accomplished what you intended to do in a given period, or you didn't. Did you check off all the items on your daily to-do list? If you go over your list at the end of every day, not only will you know how successful your time management efforts have been, but you will be able to incorporate any activities you missed into the next day's to-do list.

The checkoff is important because it provides an objective record of what you have accomplished on a given day. Just as important, it provides you with concrete reinforcement for completing the task. As we have noted, there are few things more satisfying than gazing at a to-do list with a significant number of check marks.

Of course, you won't always accomplish every item on your to-do list. That's not surprising, nor even particularly bad, especially if you've included some second- and third-level priorities that you don't absolutely have to accomplish and that you may not really have expected you'd have time for anyway.

Give yourself a virtual pat on the back for completing the things that you've accomplished. Successful time management is not easy, and if you've improved at all, you deserve to feel some personal satisfaction.

R Rethink Reflecting on Your Personal Style of Time Management

At the end of the day, after you've evaluated how well you've followed your time management plan and how much you've accomplished, it's time to rethink where you are. Maybe you've accomplished everything you set out to do, and every task for the day is completed, and every item on your to-do list has a check mark next to it.

Or maybe you have the opposite result. Your day has been a mess, and you feel as if nothing has been accomplished. Because of a constant series of interruptions and chance events, you've been unable to make headway on your list.

Or—most likely—you find yourself somewhere in between these two extremes. Some tasks got done, while others are still hanging over you. Now is the time to rethink in a broad sense how you manage your time by doing the following:

- **Reassess your priorities.** Are your long- and short-term goals appropriate? Are you expecting too much of yourself, given the constraints in your life? Reassess your priorities in order to be sure you're attempting to do what is most important to you.

- **Reconsider your personal style of time management.** We've outlined one method of time management. Although it works well for most people, it isn't for everyone. Some people just can't bring themselves to be so structured and scheduled. They feel hemmed in by to-do lists.

  If you're one of those people, fine. You don't need to follow the suggestions presented in this chapter exactly. In fact, if you go to your college bookstore or any office supply store, you'll find lots of other aids to manage your time. Publishing companies produce elaborate planners, such as DayTimers. In addition, software companies produce computerized time management software, such as Microsoft's Outlook or Novell's GroupWise, that reside on a computer and wireless handheld devices such as a BlackBerry or iPhone. Many cell phones contain a calendar system and alarm, and they can be set to provide periodic reminders.

  However you choose to manage your time, the important thing is to do so consistently. And remember that whatever approach to time management you take, it will work best if it is compatible with your own personal values and strengths. Keep experimenting until you find an approach that works for you.

- **Consider doing less.** If you keep falling behind, do less. There are only 24 hours in the day, and we need to sleep for about a third of the time. In the remaining hours, it may be nearly impossible to carry a full load of classes and work full-time and care for a child and still have some time left to have a normal life.

  Consequently, if you consistently fall behind in your work, it may be that you are just doing too much. Reassess your goals and your priorities, and make choices. Determine what is most important to you. It's better to accomplish less, if it is accomplished well, than to accomplish more, but poorly.

- **Do more.** Although it is a problem that many of us would envy, some people have too much time on their hands. Their classes may not be too demanding, or work demands may suddenly slacken off. If this happens to you, take advantage of your time. For example, you might use the extra time to simply relax and enjoy your more unhurried existence. There is a good bit to be said for having time to let your thoughts wander. We need to take time out to enjoy our friends, admire the flowers in the park, exercise, consider the spiritual side of our lives, and the like.

  > "Our costliest expenditure is time."
  > **Theophrastus, quoted in Diogenes Laertius's** *Lives and Opinions of Eminent Philosophers,* tr. R. D. Hicks

  On the other hand, if you consistently have more time than you know what to do with, reflect on what you want to accomplish and add some activities that help you reach your goals. For example, consider becoming involved in a service-learning activity. Volunteer your time to the community. Consider taking an extra course during the next term.

  But whatever you decide to do, make a real decision. Don't let the time slip away. Once it's gone, it's gone forever.

speaking of success

NAME: **Edmund Fixico**

SCHOOL: **Fort Berthold Community College, New Town, North Dakota**

Although he always had thoughts about going to college, until recently circumstances and opportunities were not right for Edmund Fixico.

"I had always planned to go to college, but I dropped out of high school in the eleventh grade," said Fixico. Two years later, he completed high school work, but higher education remained a distant dream.

Fixico started work as a bricklayer at age 19 and continued for more than two decades before finally enrolling in college. His job and starting a family took much of his time and energy.

"I had to work, but also I knew I had to go back to school someday," he said. "My wife encouraged me, and finally—at the age of 42—I enrolled at Fort Berthold Community College."

Fixico, who is pursuing a degree in Human Services, had apprehensions about his return to school.

"I was concerned that everyone would be younger than me. But the average age at Fort Berthold is about 31, which made me feel more comfortable. I also wasn't sure I could still do many basic things, like math and writing. I felt I would have to learn everything over again in a short span of time," he added.

Fixico puts in long hours of studying, staying up late after the rest of his family has gone to bed. He also learned to ask for assistance from faculty and advisors.

"I'm pretty much a shy person, so it was hard for me to ask for help," he noted. "But the classes are small, and you have more time with the instructor. You can get to know them well, and they offered a lot of support."

One of the courses that proved to be a tremendous help was a class in study strategies. "One of my first classes had a writing assignment that asked us to describe what is going on in our lives, and so I wrote about starting college," said Fixico. "I also learned how to schedule my time because I work full time."

Fixico is determined to succeed, and he is making good progress toward his degree. A member of the Cheyenne-Arapo tribe of Oklahoma, he is motivated by a desire to show future generations of American Indians the value of a college education.

Looking Back

How can I manage my time most effectively?

▸ Decide to take control of your time.

▸ Become aware of the way you use your time now.

▸ Set clear priorities.

▸ Use such time management tools as a master calendar, weekly timetable, and a daily to-do list.

How can I deal better with surprises and distractions?

▸ Deal with surprises by saying no, getting away from it all, working in silence, taking control of communications, and leaving slack in your schedule to accommodate the unexpected.

▸ Avoid procrastination by breaking large tasks into smaller ones, starting with the easiest parts of a task first; working with other people; and calculating the true costs of procrastination.

How can I balance competing priorities?

▸ Consider how your competing priorities relate to one another.

▸ Manage work time carefully, use slack time on the job to perform school assignments, use flextime, accept new responsibilities thoughtfully, and assign the proper priority to work.

[KEY TERMS AND CONCEPTS]

Time log (p. 32)

Priorities (p. 33)

Master calendar (p. 38)

Weekly timetable (p. 38)

Daily to-do list (p. 38)

Procrastination (p. 44)

[RESOURCES]

ON CAMPUS

The college official who determines when classes meet is known as the registrar. If you are having difficulty in scheduling your classes, the registrar's office may be helpful. In addition, your academic adviser can help you work out problems in enrolling in the classes you want.

For help with such issues as planning a study schedule for the upcoming term, dealing with multiple assignments and obligations on the same date, or tips on dealing with competing academic and work demands, consult with your campus learning center. The staff can help you sort out the various options you may have.

IN PRINT

Stephen Covey's *The Seven Habits of Highly Successful People* (Fireside, 2004) and Alan Axelrod and Brian Tracy's *Eat That Frog! 21 Great Ways to Stop Procrastinating and Get More Done in Less Time* (Berrett-Kohler, 2007) offer practical, hands-on guides to time management.

How to Do Everything with Microsoft Outlook (Osborne-McGraw-Hill, 2007), by Bill Mann, provides a quick, hands-on introduction to Microsoft's Outlook software, a popular time management program that is part of the Microsoft Office Suite.

Finally, Veronique Vienne and Erica Lennard's *The Art of the Moment: Simple Ways to Get the Most Out of Life* (Clarkson Potter, 2002) is an antidote to the impulse to schedule every minute of our days. The book celebrates taking time out and devoting it to oneself, providing a practical guide to rest and relaxation.

ON THE WEB

The *P.O.W.E.R. Learning* Web site at **www.mhhe.com/power** provides online versions of all the time management forms presented in this chapter. You can complete the forms online or download them and print out as many copies as you need. Although the Web addresses were accurate at the time the book was printed, check the *P.O.W.E.R. Learning* Web site for any changes that may have occurred.

> The University of Victoria's Office of Counseling Services provides two useful sites:

- Effective hints on how to plan study time, ideas about when to study, as well as tips on how to study (**www.coun.uvic.ca/learning/time-management/**).

- A handy self-management checklist that allows visitors to better achieve their goals with the time that they have (**www.coun.uvic.ca/learning/motivation/self-management.html**). It also provides effective techniques for avoiding procrastination and distractions, two major obstacles to effective time management.

> From Penn State University, try this nifty online interactive time management exercise (**www.ulc.psu.edu/studyskills/time_management.html#time_management_exercisetime_wasters**). This site also includes comprehensive links to a number of ways on how to manage your time while in college.

TAKING IT TO THE NET

1 Complete a weekly organizer online. Find a site on the Web that offers shareware or freeware featuring a weekly planner (for example, **www.studygs.net/schedule/Weekly.html** or **www.printablecalendar.ca/**). Create a weekly schedule sheet for yourself based on this design. Be sure to write in all of your classes, job obligations, and any other regular responsibilities that you have. Be sure to set specific times in your daily schedule to study. (If you already use Outlook or another kind of communications software, use its calendar function to do the same thing.)

2 Make a master calendar for the term, using the same software you used for the exercise above. If your calendar does not provide this information automatically, you can go to Yahoo! (**dir.yahoo.com**), click on "Reference," then again on "Calendars." Here you'll find many links to different calendar-related information such as when holidays occur. Be sure to indicate dates when important assignments are due and when exams occur.

The Case of . . .

Time Crunched

Ed Goddard couldn't believe it. He was working overtime at his delivery job because one of his coworkers was taking vacation. During a break from his shift, he got a text message from a college classmate asking if he wanted to study the next day for the exam they had to take the following Monday. Ed had forgotten all about the exam.

Even worse, Ed couldn't study with his classmate the next day because he'd promised his wife he would join her on her weekly visit to her mother. Although he wasn't looking forward to the two-hour drive, he knew his wife would be furious if he broke his promise. And on top of all that, he also had to find time in the next few days to work on a term paper due in one of his other classes.

As he was driving home thinking about all this, his car started to sputter and then stalled. He was unable to get it started. That was it. He sat there on the side of the road, feeling like his life had completely fallen apart and wondering how he'd ever get it back together again.

1. What might you tell Ed that could help solve his predicament?

2. Is there anything Ed could have done to prevent the situation he now faces from occurring in the first place?

3. What specific time management techniques might Ed have employed in the past to avoid these problems?

4. What strategies might Ed use now to take control over his limited time during the coming days?

5. What advice could you give Ed to try to prevent problems in time management for his next term?

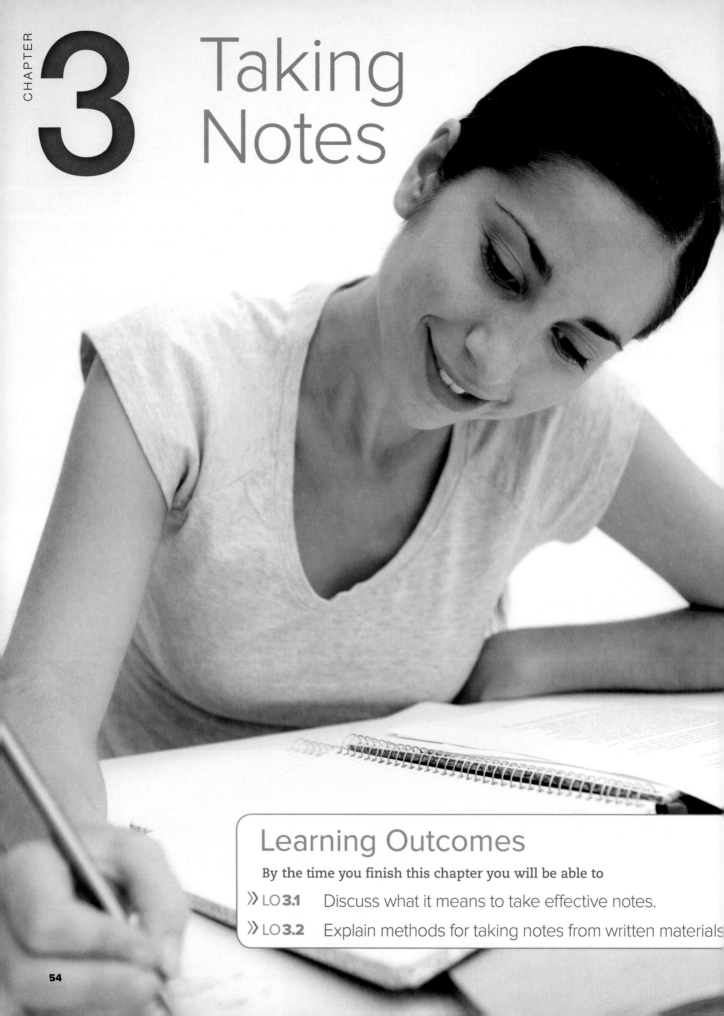

3 Taking Notes

Learning Outcomes

By the time you finish this chapter you will be able to

» **LO3.1** Discuss what it means to take effective notes.

» **LO3.2** Explain methods for taking notes from written materials

As he took his seat in the front row of his marketing class in his second term of college, Matt Ortiz realized that something fundamental had changed.

For the whole first term, Matt had sat in the back of the room during classes, just like he'd done in high school. He figured that just showing up to class was all that mattered. What difference did it make where he sat? Or if he occasionally sent text messages on his cell phone?

But then he received mostly C's in his first-term courses.

In a notetaking workshop Matt enrolled in afterward, he learned the importance of active listening and taking good notes in class. He also learned that one way to become more engaged in class is to sit close to the instructor.

Trying out the strategies he was taught in the workshop, Matt found—a bit to his surprise—that they helped. By the end of the term, he'd pulled his grades way up.

Looking Ahead

Matt Ortiz's move from the back to the front of the classroom was both a source and a symbol of his academic success. Matt's ability to take good notes is also likely to pay future dividends, because notetaking skills not only help produce academic success in college but also contribute to career success.

In this chapter we discuss effective strategies for taking notes during class lectures, during other kinds of oral presentations, and from written sources such as textbooks. There's a lot more to good notetaking than you probably think—and a lot less if you view notetaking as essentially "getting everything down on paper." As we explore the ins and outs of notetaking, we'll pause along the way to discuss the tools of the notetaking trade, how to be an active learner, how to think your way to good notes, and how to deal with disorganized instructors.

≫ LO 3.1 Taking Notes in Class

You know the type: the student who desperately tries to write down everything the instructor says—no spoken word goes unwritten. And you know what you think to yourself: "If only I took such thorough notes—I'd do much better in my classes."

Contrary to what many students think, good notetaking does not mean writing down every word that an instructor utters. With notetaking, less is often more. We'll see why as we consider the basic steps in P.O.W.E.R. notetaking.

P Prepare Considering Your Goals

As with other academic activities, preparation is a critical component of notetaking. The following steps will prepare you for action:

> **Identify the instructor's—and your—goals for the course.** On the first day of class, most instructors talk about their objectives, what they hope you'll get out of the class, and what you'll know when it's over. Most restate the information on the class syllabus, the written document that explains the assignments for the term. For example, they may say that they want you to "develop an appreciation for the ways that statistics are used in everyday life."
>
> The information you get during that first session and through the syllabus is critical. If the instructor's goals aren't stated explicitly, you should attempt to figure them out. In addition to those "external" goals, you should have your own goals. What is it you want to learn from the course? How will the information

P Prepare
Consider your goals

O Organize
Get the tools of notetaking together

W Work
Process–don't copy–information

E Evaluate
Think critically about your notes

R Rethink
Review your notes shortly after class to activate your memory

P.O.W.E.R. Plan

from the course help you to enhance your knowledge, improve your career prospects, achieve your dreams?

▶ **Complete assignments before coming to class.** Always go to class prepared. Complete all of your reading and other assignments beforehand. Instructors assume that their students have done what they've assigned, and their lectures are based upon that assumption. It's virtually impossible to catch on to the gist of a lecture if you haven't completed the assignments.

▶ **Accept the instructor, despite his or her limitations.** Not every instructor is a brilliant teacher. Accept the fact that, just as there are differences in skills among students, some instructors are more adept at teaching than others. Ultimately, it's your responsibility to overcome a lecturer's flaws. A bad lecturer is not an excuse to do poorly or to give up. Don't let a miserable lecture style—or the fact that the instructor has a bad haircut or a mouth that droops to one side or wrinkled clothing—get in the way of your education. You're going to notice these things, but don't let them interfere with your goals. Good notetaking requires being prepared to listen to the material.

> "The highest result of education is tolerance."
>
> Helen Keller, author

▶ **Perform a preclass warm-up.** No, this doesn't mean doing stretches just before each class. As you head to class or settle into your seat, skim your notes from the previous lecture, looking over what the instructor said and where that lecture left off. You should also briefly review the main headings or summary section of any reading you've been assigned.

The warm-up doesn't have to be long. The goal is simply to refresh yourself, to get yourself into the right frame of mind for the class.

Sometimes distracting seats have less to do with location and more to do with the person sitting next to you. Don't be afraid to put some physical distance between yourself and a distracting neighbor.

▶ **Choose a seat that will promote good notetaking.** You should certainly choose a seat that permits you to see and hear clearly, but there's more to your choice than that. Picking the right seat in a classroom can make a big difference.

Where is the best place to sit? Usually it's front and center. Instructors make more eye contact with the people near them, and they sometimes believe that the best, most-engaged students sit closest.

Furthermore, sitting in the back of the class may make you feel disengaged and out of touch with what is happening at the front of the room. In turn, this may make it easier for your mind to wander.

 Organize Getting the Tools of Notetaking Together

Do you have a favorite pen? A preferred type of notebook?

Most of us have distinct tastes in the type of tools we use for various tasks: a favorite screwdriver, a preferred style of mouse, a brand of running shoes we

Journal Reflections

How Do I Take Notes?

1. Describe your typical notetaking techniques in a few sentences. Do you try to write down as much of what the instructor says as possible? Do you tend to take only a few notes? Do you often find you need more time to get things down?

2. Overall, how effective would you say your notetaking techniques are?

3. In which classes do your techniques work best? Worst? Why?

4. Do your notes ever have "holes" in them—due to lapses of attention or times when you couldn't get down everything you wanted to? When do you usually discover them? What do you do about them?

find most comfortable. You should determine your preferred classroom "tools," too. Taking your favorite kind of notebook and pen to class can give you the confidence and focus you need to take effective notes.

There are several things to consider as you prepare for class:

▸ **Choose the appropriate writing utensil.** Generally, using a pen is better than using a pencil. Ink is less likely to smudge, and what you produce with ink is usually brighter and clearer—and therefore easier to use when studying. On the other hand, for math and accounting classes, where you may be copying down or even working through formulas in class, a pencil might be better, because it's easier to erase if you make a mistake when copying detailed, complex information.

Sometimes you may want to use a combination of pen and pencil. And in some cases you might use several different colors. One color—such as red—might signify important information that the instructor mentions will be on the test. Another color might be reserved for definitions or material that is copied from the board. And a third might be used for general notes on the lecture.

▸ **Choose a notebook that assists in notetaking.** Loose-leaf notebooks are particularly good for taking notes because they permit you to go back later and change the order of the pages or add additional material in the appropriate spot. But whatever kind of notebook you use, *use only one side of the page for writing: keep one side free of notes.* There may be times when you're studying when you'll want to spread your notes in front of you, and it's much easier if no material is written on the back of pages.

▸ **Consider the benefits of taking your textbook to class.** It's generally a good idea to take your textbook to class, unless your instructor advises you otherwise. Sometimes instructors will refer to information contained in it, and sometimes it's useful to have it handy to clarify information that is being discussed. You can also use it to look up key terms that may momentarily escape you. But don't, under any circumstances, use class time as an opportunity to read the textbook!

> **Consider the pros and cons of using a laptop computer to take notes in class.** There are several advantages: Legibility problems are avoided, and it's easy to go back and revise or add material after you've taken the notes.

There are also potential pitfalls. You may end up keyboarding more and thinking less. Or you may succumb to the temptation to check your e-mail or instant message your friends, rather than listening to your instructor.

Because of their drawbacks, some instructors have strong feelings against the use of laptops in their class. Consequently, be sure to ask for permission before using your laptop to take notes.

From the perspective of . . .

A STUDENT Using a laptop is advantageous for students who type faster than they write. What are some of the advantages of taking handwritten notes?

Processing—Not Copying—Information

W Work

With pen poised, you're ready to begin the work of notetaking. The instructor begins to speak, and you start to write as quickly as you can, taking down as many of the instructor's words as possible.

Stop! You've made your first mistake. The central act in taking notes is not writing; listening and thinking are far more important. The key to effective notetaking is to write down the right amount of information—not too much and not too little.

Successful notetaking involves not just *hearing* what is said, but *listening actively*. **Hearing** is the involuntary act of sensing sounds. The annoying drip of a faucet or the grating sound of a coworker's voice speaking on the phone in the next cubicle are two examples of how hearing is both involuntary and often meaningless. In contrast, **active listening** is the voluntary act of focusing on what is being said, making sense of it, and thinking about it in a way that permits it to be recalled accurately. Listening involves concentration. And it requires shutting out competing thoughts, such as what we need to pick up at the grocery store or why our date last night was so terrific. (To get a sense of your own listening skills, complete **Try It 1.**)

Keeping the importance of active listening in mind, consider the following recommendations for taking notes in class:

Hearing
The involuntary act of sensing sounds

Active listening
The voluntary act of focusing on what is being said, making sense of it, and thinking about it in a way that permits it to be recalled accurately

> **Listen for the key ideas.** Not every sentence in a lecture is equally important, and one of the most useful skills you can develop is separating the key ideas from supporting information. Good lecturers strive to make just a few main points. The rest of what they say consists of explanation, examples, and other supportive material that expands upon the key ideas.

Try It! POWER

Determine Your Listening Style

1

Consider the following pairs of statements. Place a check next to the statement in each pair that more closely describes your classroom listening style.

- [ ] 1a. When I'm listening in class, I lean back and get as comfortable as possible.
- [ ] 1b. When I'm listening in class, I sit upright and even lean forward a little.
- [ ] 2a. I let the instructor's words wash over me, generally going with the flow of the lecture.
- [ ] 2b. I try to guess in advance what the instructor is going to say and what direction the lecture is taking.
- [ ] 3a. I regard each lecture as a separate event, not necessarily related to what the instructor has said before or will say the next time.
- [ ] 3b. As I listen, I regularly ask myself how this relates to what was said in previous classes.
- [ ] 4a. When I take notes, I try to reproduce the instructor's words as closely as possible.
- [ ] 4b. When I take notes, I try to interpret and summarize the ideas behind the instructor's words.
- [ ] 5a. I don't usually question the importance of what the instructor is saying or why it's the topic of a lecture or discussion.
- [ ] 5b. I often ask why the content of the lecture is important enough for the instructor to be speaking about it.
- [ ] 6a. I rarely question the accuracy or logic of a presentation, assuming that the instructor knows the topic better than I do.
- [ ] 6b. I often ask myself how the instructor knows something and find myself wondering how it could be proved.
- [ ] 7a. I just about never make eye contact with the instructor.
- [ ] 7b. I often make eye contact with the instructor.

If you tended to prefer the "a" statements in most pairs, you have a more passive listening style. If you preferred the "b" statements, you have a more active listening style. Based on your responses, consider ways that you can become a more active listener.

To Try It online, go to www.mhhe.com/power.

Your job, then, is to distinguish the key ideas from their support. To do this, you need to be alert and always searching for your instructor's **meta-message**—that is, the underlying main ideas that a speaker is seeking to convey, or the meaning behind the overt message you hear.

How can you discern the meta-message? One way is to *listen for keywords*. Instructors know what's important in their lecture; your job is to figure it out, not just from what they say but from how they say it.

For instance, listen for clues about the importance of material. Phrases like "don't forget . . .," "be sure to remember that . . .," "you need to know . . .," "the most important thing that must be considered . . .," "there are four problems with this approach . . .," and—a big one—"this will be on the test . . ." should cause you to sit up and take notice. Another good sign of importance is repetition. If an instructor says the same thing in several ways, it's a clear sign that the material being discussed is important.

Be on the lookout for nonverbal signals too. Does an instructor get excited about a particular topic? Does he or she seem unenthusiastic when talking about something? Use nonverbal cues to gauge the importance of a particular part of a message relative to other things being said.

Meta-message
The underlying main ideas that a speaker is seeking to convey; the meaning behind the overt message

> "I had tons of notes—I copied *every word* the professor said. Actually, I was so busy writing that I didn't understand a thing."
> **Student, Saint Joseph's University[1]**

Finally, listen for what is not being said. Sometimes silence is not just golden, but informative as well. By noting what topics are not being covered in class, or are presented only minimally, you can gauge the relative importance of ideas in comparison with one another.

This is where preliminary preparation and organization come in. The only way to know what's left out of a lecture is to have done the assigned readings in advance. Also, don't be fooled into thinking that if a topic is not covered in class, it's unimportant: Most instructors believe students are responsible for all material that is assigned, whether or not it's explicitly covered in class.

> **Use short, abbreviated phrases—not full sentences—when taking notes.** Forget everything you've ever heard about always writing in full sentences. If you try to write notes in complete sentences, you'll soon become bogged down, paying more attention to your notes than to your instructor. In fact, if you use full sentences, you'll be tempted to try transcribing every word the instructor utters, which, as you now know, is not a good idea at all.

Instead, write in phrases, using only key words or terms. Save full sentences for definitions or quotes that your instructor clearly wants you to know word for word. For example, consider the following excerpt from a lecture:

There are two kinds of job analyses used by human resource experts: First, there are job- or task-oriented analyses, and second, there are worker- or employee-oriented analyses. Job analyses just describe the tasks that need to be accomplished by a worker. For example, heart surgeons need to be able to operate on patients in order to carry out their jobs. In contrast, employee-oriented job descriptions need to describe knowledge, skills, and abilities the employee must have to get the job done. For example, surgeons need to understand the different types of blood vessels in the heart in order to be successful. Most job analyses include elements of both job-oriented and employee-oriented types.

If you were taking notes, you might produce the following:

2 kinds job analyses:
    1. Job-oriented (=task-oriented): tasks needed to get job done. Ex: heart surgeon operates
    2. Worker-oriented (=employee-oriented): knowledge, skills, abilities, etc. necessary to do job. Ex: surgeon knows blood vessels
Most j.a. a combination

Note how the lecturer used almost 120 words, while the notes used only around 35 words—less than a third of the lecture.

> **Use abbreviations.** One way to speed up the notetaking process is through the use of abbreviations. Among the most common:

and	δ or +	with	w/	without	w/o
care of	c/o	leads to; resulting in	$\longrightarrow$	as a result of	$\longleftarrow$
percent	%	change	Δ	number	#
that is	i.e.	for example	e.g.	and so forth	etc.
no good	n.g.	question	?	compared with	c/w
page	p.	important!	!!	less than	<
more than	>	equals, same as	=	versus	vs.

> **Take notes in outline form.** It's often useful to take notes in the form of an outline. An outline summarizes ideas in short phrases and indicates the relationship among concepts through the use of indentations.

When outlining, it's best to be formal about it, using roman numerals, regular numbers, and capital and small letters (see the example in **Figure 3.1**). Or, if you prefer, you can also simply use outlining indentations without assigning numbers and letters.

From the perspective of . . .

Outlining serves a number of functions. It forces you to try to determine the structure of the lecture. Organizing the key points and noting the connections among them helps you remember the material better because you have processed it more. The effort involved in outlining also keeps your mind from drifting away from the lecture.

Use **Try It 2** on pages 62 and 63, "Outline a Lecture," to practice your outlining skills.

I. Difficulties faced by college students seeking affordable housing
   A. Students subjected to high rents close to campus
      1. Forced to share apartments
      2. Sometimes must live far from campus
   B. Made to sign harsh leases
II. Possible solutions
   A. College offers subsidized housing
      1. Advantage: Housing costs can be lowered
      2. Potential problems
         a. College becomes students' landlord
         b. College uses funds for housing instead of investing in education
   B. Rent control
      1. Advantage: Can provide fixed, reasonably priced rents
      2. Disadvantages
         a. Creates permanent expensive rent-control bureaucracy
         b. Landlords may neglect rent-control property
         c. Little incentive for owners to increase the number of rental units
         d. Strong competition for rent-fixed units
III. Summary
   A. Advantages and disadvantages to both solutions
   B. May need new, creative solutions

figure 3.1
A Sample Outline

2

Outline a Lecture

Working with others in a group, take turns slowly reading sections of the following lecture to each other.[2] As the paragraph is being read, outline the main arguments in the space on page 63.

In 1985 Joseph Farman, a British earth scientist working in Antarctica, made an alarming discovery. Scanning the Antarctic sky, he found less ozone than should be there—not a slight depletion but a 30% drop from a reading recorded 5 years earlier in the Antarctic!

At first the scientist thought that this "ozone hole" was an as-yet-unexplained weather phenomenon. Evidence soon mounted, however, pointing to synthetic chemicals as the culprit. Detailed analysis of chemicals in the Antarctic atmosphere revealed a surprisingly high concentration of chlorine, a chemical known to destroy ozone. The source of the chlorine was a class of chemicals called chlorofluorocarbons (CFCs). CFCs have been manufactured in large amounts since they were invented in the 1920s, largely for use as coolants in air conditioners, propellants in aerosols, and foaming agents in making Styrofoam. CFCs were widely regarded as harmless because they were chemically unreactive under normal conditions. But in the thin atmosphere over Antarctica, CFCs condense on to tiny ice crystals; warmed by the sun in the spring, they attack and destroy ozone without being used up.

The thinning of the ozone layer in the upper atmosphere 25 to 40 kilometers above the surface of the earth is a serious matter. The ozone layer protects life from the harmful ultraviolet (UV) rays from the sun that bombard the earth continuously. Like invisible sunglasses, the ozone layer filters out these dangerous rays. When UV rays damage the DNA in skin cells, it can lead to skin cancer. Every 1% drop in the atmospheric ozone concentration is estimated to lead to a 6% increase in skin cancers. The drop of approximately 3% that has already occurred worldwide, therefore, is estimated to have led to as much as a 20% increase in skin cancers.

The world currently produces about 1 million tons of CFCs annually, three-fourths of it in the United States and Europe. As scientific observations have become widely known, governments have rushed to correct the situation. By 1990, worldwide agreements to phase out production of CFCs by the end of the century had been signed. Nonetheless, most of the CFCs manufactured since they were invented are still in use in air conditioners and aerosols and have not yet reached the atmosphere. As these CFCs, as well as CFCs still being manufactured, move slowly upward through the atmosphere, the problem can be expected to grow worse. Ozone depletion has now been reported over the North Pole as well, and there is serious concern that the Arctic ozone hole will soon extend over densely populated Europe and the northeastern United States.

> ➤ **Copy key information written on the board or projected from overheads or PowerPoint slides.** If your instructor provides a definition, quotation, or formula, you probably should copy it. In fact, such prominently displayed material has "test item" written all over it. You might want to highlight such material in some way in your notes.

> ➤ **Take advantage of PowerPoint slides provided by your instructor.** Some instructors will post online their PowerPoint slides before class. If they do, print them and bring them to class. You can use them as the basis for your notes, filling in the details provided during the lecture on the printout. Even if your instructor doesn't post the slides until after class, it's still a good idea to print them out and keep them with the notes you create in class. The combination of your notes and the PowerPoints will be invaluable when reviewing and studying the material.

> ➤ **Pay particular attention to the points raised by instructors at the end of classes.** Instructors often provide a summary of the discussion, which is worthy of inclusion in your notes.

> ➤ **Ask questions.** One of the most important things you can do during a class is to ask questions. Raising questions will help you evaluate, clarify, and ultimately

2

After you have outlined the passage, compare your outline with that of others who took notes on the same passage.

- Did you all agree on the main ideas of each passage?
- How do your notes differ from others', and what are the similarities?
- How might you improve your notes to better capture the main points?
- Would a different topic produce greater or fewer difficulties?

Collectively, produce what you believe is the ideal outline, and compare it with that produced by other groups.

To Try It online, go to www.mhhe.com/power.

better understand what your instructor is saying. Even beyond these critical goals, questions serve several other purposes.

For one thing, raising questions will help you to personalize the material being covered, permitting you to draw it more closely into your own framework and perspective. Furthermore, when you ask a question and it is answered, you become personally engaged in what the instructor is saying. In very large classes, asking questions may be the only way that an instructor can get a sense of you as an individual.

Questioning also increases your involvement in the class as a whole. If you sit back and never raise questions in class, you are much less likely to feel a real part of the class. Becoming an active questioner will rightly make you feel like you have contributed something to the class. Remember, if you are unclear about some point, it is likely that others share your lack of clarity.

Finally, by asking questions in class, you serve as a role model for other students. Your questions may help break the ice in a class, making it easier for others to raise issues that they have about the material. And ultimately the answers that the instructor provides to others' questions may help you to better understand and/or evaluate your understanding of the material.

Use Special Techniques for "Problem Instructors"

He talks too fast . . . she mumbles . . . he puts down people when they ask a question . . . she rambles and goes off on boring tangents . . . she explains things in a way that doesn't make much sense.

Not every instructor comes to class with a clear, compelling lecture and then presents it beautifully. All of us have suffered through lectures that are deficient in one or more ways. What should you do when you find yourself in such a situation?

1. *Remember that this too shall pass.* First, keep in mind that this is a temporary condition; your experience usually won't last more than one term. Most instructors are conscientious and well prepared, and unless you have enormously bad luck, the unpleasant experience you're having now will not be routine.

2. *Ask questions about the material.* Even if you have no idea what is going on in class—or especially if you have no idea—ask questions. You are not the only one struggling with the instructor's shortcomings. You will be doing everyone in the class a favor if you admit you're not following what an instructor is saying and ask for clarification.

If you've ever been totally lost following a lecture, you may have discovered that speaking with your instructor immediately after class was helpful. Most instructors are very happy to go over and clarify key points that they've covered during class. They also appreciate your initiative and interest.

3. *Ask—privately and politely—for the instructor to alter the way material is presented.* It is not bad classroom etiquette to ask an instructor to speak a little slower. Instructors sometimes get carried away with enthusiasm and begin speaking faster and faster without even being aware of it. Very often a reality check from a student will be welcome. But don't couch your comment in a way that makes the instructor feel inept ("Could you slow down; you're going too fast and losing me"). Instead, keep the comment neutral, without placing blame. For instance, you might simply say, "I'm having trouble keeping up with you; would it be possible for you to speak a little more slowly?"

4. *Pool your resources.* Get together with other students in the class and work out a strategy for dealing with the situation. If an instructor speaks too fast and you just can't keep up with the flow of information, meet with your fellow students and compare what you've gleaned from the class. They may have understood or noted material that you missed, and vice versa. Together, you may be able to put the pieces of the puzzle together and get a fuller understanding of the material.

5. *Talk with the instructor after class.* If you feel totally lost after a lecture, or even if you've missed only a few points, speak with the instructor after class. Ask for clarification and get him or her to re-explain points that you missed. Such a dialogue will help you to understand the material better.

Keep a Balance between Too Many Notes and Too Few Notes

The key to effective notetaking is to keep a balance between too many and too few notes.

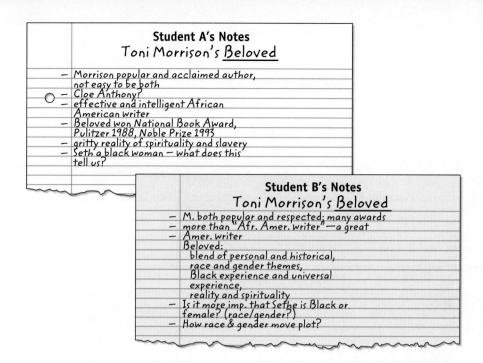

figure 3.2
Notes on a Lecture

Student A's Notes
Toni Morrison's <u>Beloved</u>

- Morrison popular and acclaimed author, not easy to be both
- Cloe Anthony?
- effective and intelligent African American writer
- Beloved won National Book Award, Pulitzer 1988, Noble Prize 1993
- gritty reality of spirituality and slavery
- Seth a black woman — what does this tell us?

Student B's Notes
Toni Morrison's Beloved

- M. both popular and respected; many awards
- more than "Afr. Amer. writer"—a great
- Amer. writer
  Beloved:
    blend of personal and historical,
    race and gender themes,
    Black experience and universal experience,
    reality and spirituality
- Is it more imp. that Sethe is Black or female? (race/gender?)
- How race & gender move plot?

The best way to achieve this balance is by paying close attention in class. By being alert, engaged, and involved in class, you'll be able to make the most of the techniques we've discussed. The result: notes that capture the most important points raised in class and that will optimize your recall and mastery of the course subject matter (see a sample of two students' notes in **Figure 3.2**).

Thinking Critically about Your Notes

Toward the end of class, take a moment to look over your notes. Now's the time—before the class has ended—to evaluate what you've written.

After being sure you can answer yes to the most basic question—can I read what I've written?—ask yourself these questions:

> Do my notes do a good job of representing what was covered in class?

> Do they reflect the emphases of the instructor?

> Are there any key points that are not entirely clear?

> Do I need help clarifying any of the points my instructor made?

Evaluating your notes is a critical part of the notetaking process. You can get a sense of how effective your notetaking has been while you still have a chance to ask your instructor to clarify anything that is still not clear.

Perhaps, for example, you've left out a keyword in a definition. Maybe you don't understand a concept fully, even though you've written about it in your notes. Possibly you've left out the third step in a list of six steps necessary to accomplish something.

If you look over your notes while you're still in class, you have time to ask your instructor for clarification. Or you can wait until the end of class and raise your question privately. Most instructors will be happy to answer questions from students who have obviously been actively listening. Just make sure that you add what they tell you to your notes so you'll be able to refer to them later. (To practice evaluating your notes, complete **Try It 3** on page 66.)

Try It!

Evaluate Your Class Notes

3

Take a set of notes you made recently during one of your classes and evaluate it on the following criteria.

Statement	Not Even Slightly	Slightly	Moderately	Pretty Well	Very Well
1. I can read my notes (i.e., they are legible).					
2. Someone else can read my notes.					
3. My notes are complete; I missed nothing important.					
4. My notes represent the key points that were covered in class.					
5. My notes reflect the instructor's emphases.					
6. The instructor's key points are clear and understandable.					
7. The notes contain only important points, with no extraneous material.					
8. I understand not only the notes but also the class content they reflect.					
9. Using only the notes, I will be able to reconstruct the essential content of the class in 3 months.					

 WORKING IN A GROUP

What do your answers tell you about the effectiveness of your notetaking skills? What might you do differently the next time you take notes?

Evaluate and compare the notes you took during the previous 20 minutes of the class you are in now. How do your notes compare with those of the other members of your group?

To Try It online, go to www.mhhe.com/power.

 Rethink Activating Your Memory

The lecture has ended and class is over. You put the top on your pen, close your notebook, stash everything in your bag, and head out for a cup of coffee before your next class.

Wait! Before you close up your notebook, finish the P.O.W.E.R. process. Rethink what you've heard. Spending 5 or 10 minutes reconsidering what you've written right now can save you *hours* of work later. The reason: Rethinking promotes the transfer of information into long-term memory (something discussed more in Chapter 5). As you link the new information you've taken down to what you already know and then integrate it, you essentially plug this information into your memory in a much more meaningful way, which means you can remember it better and more easily.

If you looked over your notes to clarify and evaluate the information in them in class, you've already begun the process. But once class is over, you need to review the material more formally. Here's how to do it:

> **Rethink as soon as possible.** Time is of the essence! The rethinking phase of notetaking doesn't have to take long; 5 to 10 minutes are usually sufficient. The more critical issue is *when* you do it. The longer you wait before reviewing your notes, the less effective the process will be.

There's no doubt that the best approach is to review the material just after the class has ended. As everyone else is leaving, just stay seated and go over your notes. This works fine for classes late in the day, when no other class is scheduled in the room. But what if you must vacate the room immediately after class? The next best thing is to find a quiet space somewhere nearby and do your rethinking there.

In any case, don't let the day end without examining your notes. In fact, reconsidering material just before you go to sleep can be particularly effective.

> **Make rethinking an active process.** Some people feel the notes they take in class are akin to historical documents in a museum, with Do Not Touch! signs hanging on them. On the contrary, think of your notes as a construction project and yourself as the person in charge of the project.

When you review your notes, do so with an eye to improving them. If any information is not entirely clear, change the wording in your notes, adding to or amending what's there. If certain words are hard to read, fix them; it won't be any easier to read them the night before a test—in fact, chances are you'll have even more trouble.

If, on rethinking the material, you don't understand something, ask your instructor or a friend to clarify it. And when you receive an explanation, add it to your notes so you won't forget it. (You might want to use a different-colored pen for additions to your notes, so you'll know they came later.)

> **Think critically about the material in your notes.** As you review the information, think about the material from a critical point of view. Go beyond the facts and pieces of information, integrating and evaluating the material.

In addition, as you rethink your notes, don't think of them only in terms of a single lecture or a single class. Instead, take a longer view. Ask yourself how they fit into the broader themes of the class and the goals that you and the instructor have for the term. How will the information be useful to you? Why did the instructor emphasize a particular point?

> **Create concept maps. Concept mapping** (sometimes called "mind mapping") is a method of structuring written material by graphically grouping and connecting key ideas and themes. In contrast to an outline, a concept map visually illustrates how related ideas fit together. The pictorial summary gives you another handle to store the information in memory, and it focuses your thinking on the key ideas from the lecture.

In a concept map, each key idea is placed in a different part of the map, and related ideas are placed near it—above, below, or beside it. What emerges does not have the rigid structure of an outline. Instead, a "finished" concept map looks something like a map of the solar system, with the largest and most central idea in the center (the "sun" position), and related ideas surrounding it at various distances. It has also been compared to a large tree, with numerous

Concept mapping
A method of structuring written material by graphically grouping and connecting key ideas and themes

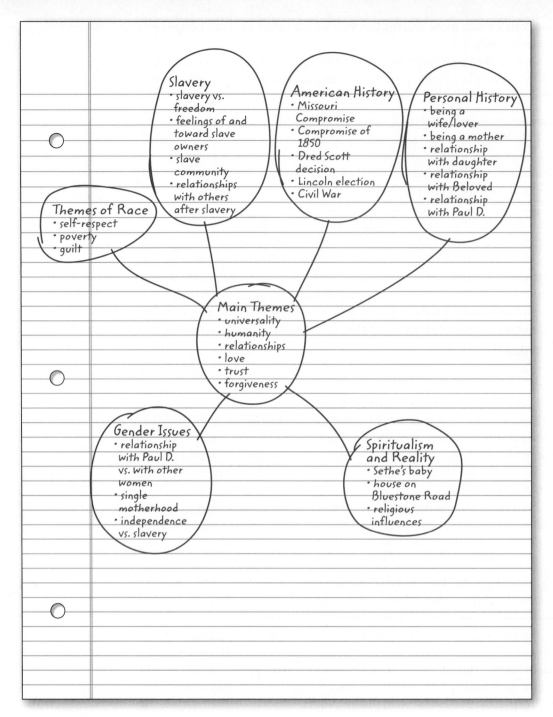

figure 3.3
A Concept Map of Toni Morrison's *Beloved*

branches and subbranches radiating out from a central trunk. (**Figure 3.3** presents a sample concept map.)

Building a concept map has several advantages. It forces you to rethink the material in your notes in a new style—particularly important if you used traditional outlining while taking the notes. In addition, it helps you to tie together the material for a given class session. Finally, it will help you to build a master concept map later, when you're studying the material for a final exam. (To practice the techniques we've been discussing, see **Try It 4** on page 69, "Practice Your Notetaking Skills.")

Practice Your Notetaking Skills

Practice your notetaking skills, using any techniques you find helpful, in one of the classes in which you are enrolled this term. Use these notes to answer these questions:

1. Which specific techniques did I use in taking notes?

2. Which of the notetaking techniques detailed in this chapter was I unable to use, and why?

3. Could I take the notes I made in class and redo them, using one of the techniques in this chapter, such as creating a concept map?

After you have taken notes, use the techniques discussed in this chapter to evaluate and rethink them. Creating a concept map on a separate sheet of paper may be particularly helpful.

To Try It online, go to www.mhhe.com/power.

»LO 3.2 Taking Notes as You Study

Weighing as much as five pounds, bulky and awkward, and filled with more information than you think anyone could ever need to know, it's the meat and potatoes of college work: your course textbook. You might feel intimidated by its size; you might be annoyed at its cost; you might think you'll never be able to read it, let alone understand, learn, and recall the material in it. How will you manage?

The answer involves taking **study notes,** notes taken for the purpose of reviewing material. They are the kind of notes that you take now to study from later. (We'll consider research notes, notes that you take to write a paper or prepare a report, in Chapter 4 when we discuss writing papers.)

Several strategies are useful for taking study notes from written material such as magazines, books, journals, and Web sites. Which approach works best depends on whether you're able to write on the material you wish to take notes on.

Study notes
Notes taken for the purpose of reviewing material

Taking Notes on Material You Can Write On

Here are some suggestions for creating study notes for material you own, on which you're free to write on the material by underlining, highlighting, or writing in the margins:

> **Integrate your text notes into your study notes.** Start by annotating the pages, using the techniques that work best for you: highlighting, underlining, circling, making marginal notes. (These techniques are discussed in detail in

Chapter 4; you may want to look ahead to that discussion.) Keep in mind that writing on the text, by itself, is not sufficient to promote learning—it's what you do next that counts.

Specifically, after you've finished reading and annotating the material, create study notes. The study notes should provide a summary of the key points, in outline form or in the form of concept maps. Either form of summary should supplement the annotations you've made on the printed page.

Furthermore, any notes you take should stand on their own. For instance, they should include enough information to be useful whether or not you have the book or article on hand.

> **Use flash cards.** If you feel confident that the annotations you've written in the book are sufficiently comprehensive, you might consider taking notes on flash cards. **Flash cards** are simply index cards that contain key pieces of information that you need to remember.
>
> Flash cards are particularly useful in subjects that present many small bits of information to remember, such as technical vocabulary words or scientific formulas. When you need to learn a new term, for instance, you can write the term on one side of a card and its definition on the other side.
>
> One of the greatest virtues of flash cards is their portability. Because they are small, they can fit into your pocket or handbag, and you can look at them at odd times when you have a spare moment.

Taking Notes on Material You Are Unable to Write On

Taking notes on material that can't be written on is a different story. Library books, magazines, journal articles, and materials on library reserve that are shared with others require a different approach.

> **Approach the written material as you would a class lecture.** The techniques we discussed earlier for taking notes in class can all be adapted for taking notes from written material. In fact, the task is often easier, because, as is not the case with the spoken word, you'll be able to refer back to what was said earlier—it's in black and white in front of you.
>
> **Laptops can be especially helpful in creating study notes.** If you're a good keyboarder, it's often easier and quicker to take notes using a word-processing program. On the other hand, don't be lured into typing too much. You need to be just as selective in what you input into your computer as you would be in taking notes during a class lecture.
>
> **Use the tricks of the trade we discussed earlier for taking notes from a class lecture.** Look for key ideas, definitions, quotations, and formulas, and include them in your notes. Use the headings that are included in the text, such as chapter and section titles. Bold or italic type is also a clue that an important point is being made. Graphs and charts often provide critical information.
>
> **Use the same form of notetaking that you use in class lectures.** If you write your notes in outline form, create an outline based on the written material. If you often create graphics such as concept maps, create them now. The point is to produce notes that are consistent with those you take during class lectures.

Taking Notes on the Job: Meetings of the Minds

The principles of good notetaking discussed in this chapter are useful not only in the classroom. They can also help you as you make your way in your career. For instance, you may need to take notes on lengthy memos or reports that detail company procedures you will need to master to do your job.

Further, one of the most important settings in which you'll want to take effective notes is in meetings. For many people, meetings take up a good part of their professional workdays and being able to take effective notes can provide a significant career advantage.

Meetings are similar to class discussions. During a meeting you will want to look for key topics and make note of the ideas that receive the most emphasis or enthusiastic response. Note these areas and keep them in mind as likely priorities.

During meetings, tasks are often assigned. Not only do you want to clearly note what you are to do and when you are supposed to do it, but keeping track of what others are doing will also be helpful, because you may need to get information from them or otherwise coordinate efforts. For instance, if you are assigned the task of managing the development of your company's Web site, you'll want to clarify in your notes who has agreed to do what portion of the task.

Taking notes when others are speaking also shows that you are paying attention to what the speaker is saying. It's a kind of compliment that suggests you find what the speaker is saying to be so important that you will want to refer to it later.

Finally, notetaking plays another role: It can make seemingly interminable meetings appear to proceed faster by providing something for you to do that's more active than simply listening. In short, not only can notetaking provide you with a clear record of what occurred in a meeting, but it can also keep you engaged in what is going on.

speaking of success

Thomas Nelson™
COMMUNITY COLLEGE
Explore. Excel. Succeed.

NAME: **Geraldine F. Mathey**

SCHOOL: **Thomas Nelson Community College, Hampton, Virginia**

Geraldine Mathey started—and stopped—her college education several times. But now, though, Mathey is on track to obtain a degree, and she's doing it while holding down a full-time job.

To meet this challenge, Mathey has styled her studying to meet the demands of her schedule.

"If I have a lot of reading to do, what works best for me is to do it during my lunch hour," she explained. "If I have a class later in the day, I'll use the few hours at the end of my work day to prepare for the class and review my notes."

The social science major is also a big proponent of asking questions, visiting the campus tutoring center, and meeting with faculty.

"I have no qualms about going to the instructor and asking questions," said Mathey. "I've found that instructors can offer helpful hints on studying, and some offer test review sheets," she added. "I tell other students that you can remember the information if you actually write out responses to the review topics. I believe if you write them out, there is more of a connection between hand and brain than just eye and page."

Mathey also is a proponent of TRIO, a federally funded student support program designed to motivate and support students from disadvantaged backgrounds in which she participates. Since her school adopted the program, they have found there was an 86% retention rate for students who participated in the program and a 55% retention rate for those who did not, she noted.

"You have to find out what your strengths and weaknesses are," she said. "If you need help, go to your instructor, or the library, or a tutoring center. Don't hesitate to ask for help."

Looking Back

What is effective notetaking?

▶ The central feature of good notetaking is listening and distilling important information—not writing down everything that is said.

How can I take good notes in class?

▶ Prepare for taking notes by identifying the instructor's and your own goals for the course, completing all assignments before arriving in class, and "warming up" for class by reviewing the notes and assignments from the previous class.

▶ Before writing notes, listen and think, processing the information that the instructor is attempting to deliver.

▶ Notes should be brief phrases rather than full sentences and, if possible, in outline form to reveal the structure of the lecture. Material written on the board should usually be copied word for word.

▶ Before leaving class, evaluate your notes, verifying that they are complete and understandable while there is still time to correct them. As soon as possible after class, actively rethink your notes.

What techniques apply to taking notes from written materials?

▶ Taking good study notes from written materials involves many of the principles that apply to taking good notes from oral presentations, although the source material can be consulted repeatedly, making it easier to get the information down accurately.

▶ Concept maps and flash cards can be helpful tools for notetaking from textbooks.

[KEY TERMS AND CONCEPTS]

Hearing (p. 58)

Active listening (p. 58)

Meta-message (p. 59)

Concept mapping (p. 67)

Study notes (p. 69)

Flash cards (p. 70)

[RESOURCES]

ON CAMPUS

If you are having difficulty taking class notes effectively, talk with your course instructor. Bring your notes with you soon after a class has ended, and let the instructor assess what you are doing correctly and what could stand improvement.

If your problems persist, and you have great difficulty translating the spoken word into notes, then there's a small possibility that you suffer from an auditory learning disability. Be tested by your college learning disabilities office or counseling office to rule this out.

IN PRINT

Judy Kesselman-Turkel and Franklynn Peterson's *Note-Taking Made Easy* (University of Wisconsin Press, 2003) provides a broad overview of how to take good notes in class, as does Bobbi DePorter and Mike Hernacki's *Quantum Notes* (Learning Forum, 2000).

In addition, Ron Fry's *Taking Notes* (Career Press, 1994) and *Noteworthy: Listening and Notetaking Skills* (2nd ed.), by Phyllis Lim and William Smalzer (William S. Hein & Co.,

1996) provide a fine overview of strategies for increasing your listening and notetaking expertise.

ON THE WEB

The following sites on the World Wide Web provide the opportunity to extend your learning about the material in this chapter. (Although the Web addresses were accurate at the time the book was printed, check the *P.O.W.E.R. Learning* Web site [**mhhe.com/power**] for any changes that may have occurred.)

> Dartmouth College has an online Academic Skills Center, with specific advice on taking good notes (**www.dartmouth.edu/~acskills/success/notes.html**). The site offers downloadable materials on effective listening, lecture notes, and more. The site also features plenty of other useful information on other important academic skills.

> Brigham Young University's Career and Counseling Center offers this page (**http://ccc.byu.edu/learning/note-tak.php**) on the Cornell Notetaking System. This notetaking system can help you improve the organization of your notes, while allowing you to make use of your existing strengths as a notetaker.

TAKING IT TO THE NET

1 The best way to improve notetaking skills is to practice. Locate a current news story of interest on the Internet and take notes while reading it. One possible strategy is to go to the "News" section of the Yahoo! home page (**http://dir.yahoo.com**). Click on one of the news categories (e.g., Sports, Politics, Business, etc.) and look for a story that sounds interesting.

2 Taking notes during lectures is an important part of classroom learning, but keeping up with a speaker for an entire hour can be difficult. You can improve your notetaking skills for lectures by taking notes while listening to recorded speeches on the Internet. For example, go to an Internet site containing recordings of speeches (you can find many at **www.youtube.com/**) and take notes while listening to a speech. Afterward, go back and indicate the key points and terms. You can check your comprehension by comparing the speech to news articles reporting on it. (You can also check the articles for bias!)

The Case of . . .
Not Missing a Thing

Some people write down a few things in class. Others write down most things. Jennifer Beck wrote down *everything*.

The woman was virtually a human dictation machine. She spent her time in class in a whirlwind of notetaking, writing down in a clear, meticulous script seemingly every word her instructor uttered. By the end of a term, her notebooks were so lengthy that they approached the size of telephone books from a small city.

Yet despite her thorough notes, Jennifer was only a mediocre student. She was a hard worker and studied her many notes thoroughly before tests. But she never managed to get grades higher than a C+. It seemed unbelievable to her. She worked incredibly hard in class taking good notes. Why wasn't it paying off?

1. How do you think Jennifer defines "good notetaking"?

2. Why does Jennifer's method of notetaking produce such poor results? What is she missing?

3. If you asked Jennifer to summarize the instructor's main ideas after a class lecture, how successful do you think she would be? Why?

4. Do you think it would be easy or hard to study for a final exam using Jennifer's notes? Why?

5. Do you think Jennifer evaluates her notes during or after class? Do you think she ever rethinks them? What questions would you ask to help her perform these steps?

6. In general, what advice would you give Jennifer on notetaking?

4

Taking Tests

Learning Outcomes

By the time you finish this chapter you will be able to

» LO **4.1**   Identify what kinds of tests you will take in college.

» LO **4.2**   Explain the best ways to prepare for and take various kinds of tests.

» LO **4.3**   Discuss the strategies for answering specific kinds of test questions.

onths of study and classes and reading and commuting to and from his college . . . and now it all came down to a test.

That was the thought that ran through Eddie Penn's head as he sat down to take the final exam in his computer programming course. Eddie knew the test would end up counting for 65 percent of his final grade. If he passed, he would have enough credits to get the graphic design degree he'd been working toward for years. If he failed . . . Eddie tried not to think about that.

He'd taken tests before, but the stakes had never seemed so high for a single exam. Although he was fairly confident—he had studied hard—he couldn't relax altogether. He told himself that he had always done well on tests in the past; he wasn't going to fail now. But still— Eddie couldn't help but feel like his entire career, maybe his entire future, was on the line.

Looking Ahead

Although many tests are not as critical as Eddie Penn's computer programming final, tests do play a significant role in everyone's academic life. Students typically experience more anxiety over tests than over anything else in their college careers. If you're returning to college after a long break, or perhaps struggled with tests earlier in your academic career, you may find the prospect of taking a test especially intimidating.

But tests don't have to be so anxiety-producing. There are strategies and techniques you can learn to reduce your fear of test-taking. In fact, learning how to take tests is in some ways as important as learning the content that they cover. Taking tests effectively does not just involve mastering information; it also requires mastering specific test-taking skills.

One of the most important goals of this chapter is to take the mystery out of the whole process of taking tests. To do that, you'll learn about the different types of tests and strategies you can start using even before you take a test. You'll gain insight into how different kinds of tests work and how best to approach them, and you'll also learn about the various types of test questions and strategies for responding most effectively to each type.

This chapter also explores two aspects of test-taking that may affect your performance: test anxiety and cramming. You will learn ways to deal with your anxiety and keep cramming to a minimum—but you will also learn how to make the most of cramming, if you do have to resort to it.

The chapter ends with suggestions for evaluating your performance toward the end of a test and for using what you learn to improve your performance the next time around.

» LO 4.1 Getting Ready

Tests may be the most unpopular part of college life. Students hate them because they produce fear, anxiety, apprehension about being evaluated, and a focus on grades instead of learning for learning's sake. Instructors often don't like them very much either, because they produce fear, anxiety, apprehension about being evaluated, and a focus on grades instead of learning for learning's sake. That's right: Students and instructors dislike tests for the very same reasons.

But tests are also valuable. A well-constructed test identifies what you know and what you still need to learn. Tests help you see how your performance compares with that of others. And knowing that you'll be tested on a body of material is certainly likely to motivate you to learn material more thoroughly.

However, there's another reason you might dislike tests: You may assume that tests have the power to define your worth as a person. If you do badly on a test, you may be tempted to believe that you've received some fundamental information about yourself from the instructor and the college, information that says you're a failure in some significant way.

Journal Reflections

How I Feel about Tests

1. How do you feel about tests in general?

2. What are your first memories of being in a testing situation? What were your feelings, and why?

3. What makes a test "good" and "bad" from your perspective?

4. What factors contribute to your success or failure on a particular exam? Which of these factors are under your control?

5. What strategies do you use when taking tests to maximize your performance? Which have been particularly effective, and why?

P Prepare
Ready test-taking strategies

O Organize
Bring the right tools to the test

W Work
Tackle the test

E Evaluate
Check your work

R Rethink
Reflect on what you've learned when you get a test back

P.O.W.E.R. Plan

This is a dangerous—and wrongheaded—assumption. If you do badly on a test, it doesn't mean you're a bad person. Or stupid. Or that you don't belong in college. If you don't do well on a test, you're the same person you were before you took the test—no better, no worse. You just did badly on a test. Period.

In short, tests are not a measure of your value as an individual. They are only a measure of how well (and how much) you studied, and your test-taking skills. Tests are tools; they are indirect and imperfect measures of what we know. Someone with a great deal of knowledge can do poorly on a test; tension or going at too slow a pace can lead to unwelcome results in some cases. Another person may know considerably less and still do better on the test simply because he or she may have learned some test-taking skills along the way.

How we do on a test depends on a number of considerations: the kind of test it is, the subject matter involved, our understanding of test-taking strategies, and, above all, how well we prepare for it. Let's turn, then, to the first step in test-taking: preparation. (The five steps are summarized in the P.O.W.E.R. Plan on the left.)

≫ LO 4.2 **P Prepare** ## Readying Your Test-Taking Strategies

Preparation for tests requires a number of strategies. Among the most important are the following.

Remember: Everything You Do in a Course Is Preparation for a Test

All the things you do during a course help to prepare you for a test. There is no surer way to get good grades on tests than to attend class faithfully and to complete all class assignments seriously and on time.

Preparing for tests is a long-term proposition. It's not a matter of "giving your all" the night before the test. Instead, it's a matter of giving your all to every aspect of the course.

Know What You Are Preparing For

Determine as much as you can about the test before you begin to study for it. The more you know about a test beforehand, the more efficient your studying will be.

To find out about an upcoming test, ask these questions:

> Is the test called a "test," "exam," "quiz," or something else? As you can see in **Table 4.1,** the names imply different things. For simplicity's sake, we'll use the term test throughout this chapter, but know that these distinctions exist, and they should affect the way you prepare.

> What material will the test cover?

> How many questions will be on it?

> How much time is it expected to take? A full class period? Only part of a period?

> What kinds of questions will be on the test?

> How will it be graded?

> Will sample questions be provided?

> Are tests from previous terms available?

> How much does the test contribute to my final course grade?

table 4.1 Quizzes, Tests, Exams . . . What's in a Name?
Although they may vary from one instructor to another, the following definitions are most commonly used:
Quizzes. A *quiz* is a brief assessment, usually covering a relatively small amount of material. Some quizzes cover as little as one class's worth of reading. Although a single quiz usually doesn't count very much, instructors often add quiz scores together, and collectively they can become a significant part of your final course grade.
Tests. A *test* is a more extensive, more heavily weighted assessment than a quiz, covering more material. A test may come every few weeks of the term, often after each third or quarter of the term has passed, but this varies with the instructor and the course.
Exams. An *exam* is the most substantial kind of assessment. In many classes, just one exam is given—a final exam at the end of the term. Sometimes there are two exams, one at the midpoint of the term (called, of course, a midterm) and the second at the end. Exams are usually weighted quite heavily because they are meant to assess your knowledge of all the course material covered up to that point.

Match Test Preparation to Question Types

Test questions come in different types (see **Table 4.2**), and each requires a somewhat different style of preparation.

> **Essay questions.** Essay tests focus on the big picture—ways in which the various pieces of information being tested fit together. You'll need to know not just a series of facts, but also the connections between them, and you will have to be able to discuss these ideas in an organized and logical way. A good study tactic is to play instructor: After carefully reviewing your notes and other course materials, think of likely exam questions. Then, without looking at your notes or your readings, answer each potential essay question, either aloud or by writing out the major points an answer should include. After you've answered the questions, check yourself by looking at the notes and readings once again.

> **Short-answer and fill-in questions.** Short-answer and fill-in questions are similar to essays in that they require you to recall key pieces of information rather than finding it on the page in front of you. However, short-answer and fill-in questions—unlike essay questions—typically don't demand that you integrate or compare different types of information. Consequently, the focus of your study should be on the recall of specific, detailed information.

> **Multiple-choice, true–false, and matching questions.** While the focus of review for essay questions should be on major issues and controversies, studying for multiple-choice, true–false, and matching questions requires more attention to the details.
>
> Almost anything is fair game for multiple-choice, true–false, and matching questions, so you can't afford to overlook anything when studying. True, these kinds of questions put the material right there on the page for you to

table 4.2	Types of Test Questions
Essay	Requires a fairly extended, on-the-spot composition about some topic. Examples include questions that call on you to describe a person, process, or event, or those that ask you to compare or contrast two separate sets of material.
Multiple-choice	Usually contains a question or statement, followed by a number of possible answers (usually 4 or 5 of them). You are supposed to choose the best response from the choices offered.
True–false	Presents statements about a topic that are either accurate or inaccurate. You are to indicate whether each statement is accurate (true) or inaccurate (false).
Matching	Presents two lists of related information, arranged in column form. Typically, you are asked to pair up the items that go together (e.g., a scientific term and its definition).
Short-answer	Requires brief responses (usually a few sentences at most) in a kind of mini-essay.
Fill-in	Requires you to add one or more missing words to a sentence or series of sentences.

react to—Did Columbus land in 1492, or not?—rather than asking you to provide the names and dates yourself (as in the case of the essay question). Nevertheless, to do well on these tests you must put your memory into high gear and master a great many facts.

It's a particularly good idea to write down important facts on index cards. Remember the advantages of these cards: They're portable and available all the time, and the act of creating them helps drive the material into your memory. Furthermore, you can shuffle them and test yourself repeatedly until you've mastered the material.

It also can be helpful to write the name of a particular concept or theory on one side of a note card, and then to generate and write an example of it on the other side. Studying the cards will ensure that you fully understand the concepts and theories and can generalize them to different situations.

Test Yourself

Once you feel you've mastered the material, test yourself on it. There are several ways to do this. Often textbooks are accompanied by Web sites that offer automatically scored practice tests and quizzes. (*P.O.W.E.R. Learning* does: Go to **www.mhhe.com/power** to try one!)

From the perspective of . . .

A STUDENT You will take many types of courses during your academic career. Can you think of how test-taking strategies will work in an English course versus a science course?

You can also create a test for yourself, in writing, making its form as close as possible to what you expect the actual test to be. For instance, if your instructor has told you the classroom test will be primarily made up of short-answer questions, your test should reflect that.

You might also construct a test and administer it to a classmate or a member of your study group. In turn, you could take a test that someone else has constructed. Constructing and taking practice tests are excellent ways of studying the material and cementing it into memory. (To be sure you're fully prepared for your next test, complete **Try It 1** on page 82.)

Deal with Test Anxiety

What does the anticipation of a test do to you? Do you feel shaky? Frantic, like there's not enough time to get it all done? Do you feel as if there's a knot in your stomach? Do you grit your teeth?

Test anxiety is a temporary condition characterized by fears and concerns about test-taking. Almost everyone experiences it to some degree, although for some people it's more of a problem than for others. The real danger with test anxiety is that it can become so overwhelming that it can hurt test performance. (To assess your own test-taking style and the degree of anxiety around tests that you experience, see **Try It 2** on page 83.)

Test anxiety
A temporary condition characterized by fears and concerns about test-taking

Try It!

Complete a Test Preparation Checklist

It takes more than simply learning the material to prepare for a test. You also need a strategy that will help you understand what it is you are studying for. To do that, learn as much as you can about what the test will be like. The more you understand about the kind of test and what it will cover, the better you'll be able to target your studying.

To focus your studying, complete the following test preparation checklist before your next test.

TEST PREPARATION CHECKLIST

- ☐ I know whether it's a quiz, test, or exam.
- ☐ I know what kinds of questions will be on the test.
- ☐ I understand what material will be covered.
- ☐ I know how many questions will be on the test.
- ☐ I know how long I will have to complete the test.
- ☐ I know how the test will be graded, and how the grade contributes to my final course grade.
- ☐ I obtained sample questions and/or previous tests, if available.
- ☐ I formed or participated in a study group.
- ☐ I used different and appropriate preparation strategies for different types of questions.
- ☐ I read and studied my class notes.
- ☐ I composed some questions of the kind that will be on the exam.
- ☐ I answered essay questions aloud.
- ☐ I actively memorized facts and details.
- ☐ I made and used index cards.
- ☐ I created and used a test like the real test.

After completing the checklist, ask yourself these questions: How can I use this checklist to study more effectively for tests? How might completing the checklist change the way I study for tests? What new strategies might I follow in order to prepare for tests more effectively in the future?

To Try It online, go to www.mhhe.com/power.

You'll never eliminate test anxiety completely, nor do you want to. A little bit of nervousness can energize us, making us more attentive and vigilant. Like any competitive event, testing can motivate us to do our best. You might think of moderate test anxiety as a desire to perform at your peak—a useful quality at test time.

On the other hand, for some, anxiety can spiral into the kind of paralyzing fear that makes their minds go blank. There are several ways to keep this from happening to you:

1. *Prepare thoroughly.* The more you prepare, the less test anxiety you'll feel. Good preparation can give you a sense of control and mastery, and it will prevent test anxiety from overwhelming you.

2. *Take a realistic view of the test.* Remember that your future success does not hinge on your performance on any single exam. Think of the big picture: Put the task ahead in context, and remind yourself of all the hurdles you've passed so far.

3. *Eat right and get enough sleep.* Good mental preparation can't occur without your body being well prepared.

4. *Learn relaxation techniques.* You can learn to reduce or even eliminate the jittery physical symptoms of test anxiety by using relaxation techniques. The basic process is straightforward: Breathe evenly, gently inhaling and exhaling. Focus

Try It!

2

Measure Your Test-Taking Style

Do you feel anxious at the very thought of a test, or are you cool and calm in the face of testing situations? Get a sense of your test-taking style by checking off every statement below that applies to you.

- [ ] **1.** The closer a test date approaches, the more nervous I get.
- [ ] **2.** I am sometimes unable to sleep on the night before a test.
- [ ] **3.** I have "frozen up" during a test, finding myself unable to think or respond.
- [ ] **4.** I can feel my hands shaking as I pick up my pencil to begin a test.
- [ ] **5.** The minute I read a tough test question, all the facts I ever knew about the subject abandon me and I can't get them back no matter how hard I try.
- [ ] **6.** I have become physically ill before or during a test.
- [ ] **7.** Nervousness prevents me from studying immediately before a test.
- [ ] **8.** I often dream about an upcoming test.
- [ ] **9.** Even if I successfully answer a number of questions, my anxiety stays with me throughout the test.
- [ ] **10.** I'm reluctant to turn in my test paper for fear that I can do better if I continue to work on it.

If you checked off more than four statements, you have experienced fairly serious test anxiety. If you checked off more than six statements, your anxiety is probably interfering with your test performance. In particular, statements 3, 5, 6, 7, and 10 may indicate serious test anxiety.

If, based on your responses to this questionnaire and your previous experience, your level of test anxiety is high, what are some of the steps described in this chapter that might be helpful to you?

To Try It online, go to www.mhhe.com/power.

your mind on a pleasant, relaxing scene such as a beautiful forest or a peaceful farm, or on a restful sound such as that of ocean waves breaking on the beach.

5. *Visualize success.* Think of an image of your instructor handing back your test marked with a big fat "A." Or imagine your instructor congratulating you on your fine performance the day after the test. Positive visualizations that highlight your potential success can help replace images of failure that may fuel test anxiety.

What if these strategies don't work? If your test anxiety is so great that it's getting in the way of your success, make use of your college's resources. Most provide a learning resource center or a counseling center that can provide you with personalized help. (For more on dealing with test anxiety, see the **Course Connections** feature.)

Form a Study Group

Study groups are small, informal groups of students who work together to learn course material and study for a test. Forming such a group can be an excellent way to prepare for any kind of test. Some study groups are formed for particular tests, whereas others meet consistently throughout the term.

Study groups can be extremely powerful tools because they help accomplish several things:

> They help members organize and structure the material to approach their studying in a systematic and logical way.

Study groups

Small, informal groups of students whose purpose is to help members work together and study for a test

Special Techniques for Dealing with Math Anxiety

For many students, the greatest test anxiety comes when they're taking a test involving math. Math seems to bring out the worst fears in some people, perhaps because it's seen as a discipline in which answers are either totally right or totally wrong, or because they've felt they've "hit the wall" and they'll never be able to understand a new concept, no matter how hard they try.

Such feelings about math can be devastating, because they can prevent you from doing well even if you know the material. If you suffer from math anxiety, keep these things in mind:

- Math is like any other subject: the greatest component of success is the effort you put in, not whether you have a "math gene" that makes you naturally good at math. It's not true that you either are born "good at math" or not and that there's some "secret" about math that some people know and others don't.

- It's also not true that there's only one way to solve a math problem. Sometimes there are a variety of routes to coming up with a solution. And keep in mind that the solution to math problems often calls for creativity, not just sheer logic.

- It's a false stereotype that women are not as good at math as men, but it's a stereotype that many women buy into. Research has shown that when men do badly on a math test, they're most likely to think that they haven't put in enough effort. But when women don't do well on a math test, they're three times more likely than men to feel that they don't have enough ability to be successful.[1] That's an erroneous view of the world. Don't become a prisoner of stereotypes.

Use these special strategies to deal with math problems on exams:

BEFORE TESTS:

1. Math is cumulative, building on prior concepts and knowledge. Make sure you review math fundamentals before moving on to more advanced topics.
2. Ask questions in class. Don't be afraid that you'll ask the wrong question in the wrong way. Instructors want you to understand their subject.
3. Make use of review sessions and other study resources.
4. Practice, practice, practice. The more experience you have completing math problems under pressure, the better you'll do. Practice math problems using a timer in order to simulate an actual test.

DURING TESTS:

1. Analyze math problems carefully. What are the known quantities or constants, and what pieces of information are missing? What formula(s) or theorem(s) apply?
2. Consider drawing a diagram, graph, or probability tree.
3. Break down calculations into their component parts.
4. Check your math carefully.
5. Be neat and logical in your presentation, and show every step as you solve problems. Your instructor may give you partial credit if you lay out every step you're going through. In addition, some instructors may require you to show your work.

> They allow students to share different perspectives on the material.
> They make it more likely that students will not overlook any potentially important information.
> They force members to rethink the course material, explaining it in words that other group members will understand.

Study groups, made up of a few students who study together for a test, can help organize material, provide new perspectives, and motivate members to do their best. Do you think you would function well in a study group? Why or why not?

There are some potential drawbacks to keep in mind. Study groups don't always work well for students with learning styles that favor working independently. In addition, "problem" members—those who don't pull their weight—may cause difficulties for the group. In general, though, the advantages of study groups far outweigh their disadvantages. (To set up your own study group, see **Try It 3** on page 86.)

Use Your Campus Learning or Tutorial Center Resources

Many colleges have a learning center, tutorial center, or other office that can help you study for a test. Don't wait until after you do badly on a test to visit your campus learning or tutorial centers. A visit prior to your first test is a good use of your time, even if you feel it's not essential. Just knowing what resources are available can boost your confidence.

Cramming: You Shouldn't, But . . .

You know, of course, that **cramming,** hurried, last-minute studying, is not the way to go. You know that you're likely to forget the material the moment the test is over because long-term retention is nearly impossible without thoughtful study. But . . .

> . . . it's been one of those weeks where everything went wrong
>
> . . . the instructor sprang the test on you at the last minute
>
> . . . you forgot about the test until the night before it was scheduled.

Whatever the reason, there may be times when you can't study properly. What do you do if you have to cram for an exam?

Don't spend a lot of time on what you're unable to do. Beating yourself up about your failings as a student will only hinder your efforts. Instead, admit you're human and imperfect like everyone else. Then spend a few minutes developing a plan about what you can accomplish in the limited time you've got.

Cramming
Hurried, last-minute studying

Try It!

WORKING IN A GROUP

3

Form a Study Group

The next time you have to prepare for a test, form a study group with three to five classmates. They may have a variety of study habits and skills, but all must be willing to take the group seriously.

The first time you meet, compare notes about what is likely to be on the test and brainstorm to come up with possible test questions. If the instructor hasn't given you detailed information about the test (i.e., number and types of questions, weighting, etc.), one of you should be delegated to ask for it. Plan to meet once more closer to the test date to discuss answers to the questions you've come up with, share any new insights, and quiz each other on the material.

After you've taken the test and gotten your results, meet again. Find out if members felt the group was effective. Did the members feel more confident about the test? Do they think they did better than they would have without the group? What worked? What didn't? What could you do differently next time?

To Try It online, go to **www.mhhe.com/power.**

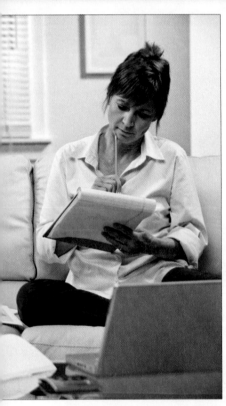

Cramming can be exhausting, but it is on occasion necessary. With the many family and personal responsibilities many students face, sometimes it can't be avoided. There are, however, strategies you can use to help you make the best use of limited time.

The first thing to do is choose what you really need to study. You won't be able to learn everything, so you have to make choices. Figure out the main focus of the course, and concentrate on it.

Once you have a strategy, prepare a one-page summary sheet with hard-to-remember information. Just writing the material down will help you remember it, and you can refer to the summary sheet frequently over the limited time you do have to study.

Next, read through your class notes, concentrating on the material you've underlined and the key concepts and ideas that you've already noted. Forget about reading all the material in the books and articles you're being tested on. Instead, only read the passages that you've underlined and the notes you've taken on the readings. Finally, maximize your study time. Using your notes, index cards, and concept maps, go over the information. Read it. Say it aloud. Think about it and the way it relates to other information. In short, use all the techniques we've talked about for learning and recalling information.

Just remember: When the exam is over, material that you have crammed into your head is destined to leave your mind as quickly as it entered. If you've crammed for a midterm, don't assume that the information will still be there when you study for the final. In the end, cramming often ends up taking more time for worse results than does studying with appropriate techniques.

Organize Facing the Day of the Test

You've studied a lot, and you're happy with your level of mastery. Or perhaps you have the nagging feeling that there's something you haven't quite gotten to. Or maybe you know you haven't had enough time to study as much as you'd like, and you're expecting a disaster.

Whatever your frame of mind, it will help to organize your plan of attack on the day of the test. What's included on the test is out of your hands, but you can control what you bring to it.

For starters, bring the right tools to the test. Have at least two pens and two pencils with you. It's usually best to write in pen because, in general, writing tends to be easier to read in pen than pencil. But you also might want to have pencils on hand. Sometimes instructors will use machine-scored tests, which require the use of pencil. Or there may be test questions that involve computations, and solving them may entail frequent reworking of calculations.

You should also bring a watch to the test, even if there will be a clock on the wall of the classroom. You will want to be able to pace yourself properly during the test. Also, if you usually use a cell phone to determine the time, remember that some instructors may not allow you to look at them during the test.

Sometimes instructors permit you to use notes and books during the test. If you haven't brought them with you, they're not going to be much help. So make sure you bring them if they're permitted. (Even for closed-book tests, having such material available when you arrive in the classroom allows you a few minutes of review before the test actually starts.) And don't be lulled into thinking an open-book test is going to be easy. Instructors who allow you to use your notes and books during a test may not give you much time to look things up, so you still need to study.

On the day of a test, avoid the temptation to compare notes with your friends about how much they've studied. Yes, you might end up feeling good because many of your fellow classmates studied less than you did. But chances are you'll find others who seem to have spent significantly more time studying than you, and this will do little to encourage you.

In addition, you might want to plan on panicking. Although it sounds like the worst possible approach, permitting yourself the option of spending a minute feeling panicky will help you to recover from your initial fears.

Finally, listen carefully to what an instructor says before the test is handed out. The instructor may tell you about a question that is optional or worth more points or inform you of a typographical error on the test. Whatever the instructor says just before the test, you can be sure it's information that you don't want to ignore.

» LO 4.3 Taking the Test

 W Work Tackling the Test

Take a deep breath—literally.

There's no better way to start work on a test than by taking a deep breath, followed by several others. The deep breaths will help you to overcome any initial panic and anxiety you may be experiencing. It's OK to give yourself over for a moment to panic and anxiety, but, to work at your best, use the relaxation techniques that we spoke about earlier to displace those initial feelings. Tell yourself, "It's OK. I am going to do my best."

Read test instructions carefully. Even if instructors talk about what a test will be like beforehand, at the last minute they may make changes. Consequently, it's critical to read the instructions for the test carefully. In fact, you should skim through the entire exam before you begin. Look at the kinds of questions and pay attention to the way they will be scored. If the point weighting of the various parts of the exam is not clear, ask your instructor to clarify it.

Knowing the point weighting is critical, because it will help you to allocate your time. You don't want to spend 90 percent of your time on an essay that's worth only 10 percent of the points, and you want to be sure to leave time at the end of the test to check your answers.

An initial read-through will also help you verify that you have every page of the exam and that each one is readable. It may also provide you with "intratest knowledge," in which terms defined or mentioned in one part of a test trigger memories that can help answer questions in another part of the test.

If there are any lists, formulas, or other key facts that you're concerned you may forget, jot them down now on the back of a test page or on a piece of scrap paper. You may want to refer to this material later during the test.

Once this background work is out of the way, you'll be ready to proceed to actually answering the questions. These principles will help you to do your best on the test:

> **Answer the easiest questions first.** By initially getting the questions out of the way that are easiest for you, you accomplish several important things. First, you'll be leaving yourself more time to think about the tougher questions. In addition, moving through a series of questions without a struggle will build your confidence. Finally, working through a number of questions will build up a base of points that may be enough to earn you at least a minimally acceptable grade.

> **Write legibly and only on one side of the paper.** If an instructor can't read what you've written, you're not going to get credit for it, no matter how brilliant your answer. So be sure to keep your handwriting legible.

> It's also a good idea to write your answers to essay questions on only one side of a page. This will allow you to go back later and add or revise information.

> **Master machine-scored tests.** Tests will sometimes be scored, in part, by computer. In such cases, you'll usually have to indicate your answers by filling in—with a pencil—circles or squares on a computer answer sheet.

> Be careful! A stray mark or smudge can cause the computer scanner to misread your answer sheet, producing errors in grading. Be sure to bring a good eraser in addition to a pencil; the biggest source of mistakes in machine grading is incomplete erasing.

> It's best to write your answers not only on the answer sheet, but also on the test itself (if the test is not intended for future reuse). That way you can go back and check your answers easily—a step you should take frequently. It's also a good idea to match up your answers on the test with the spaces on the answer sheet every five or so items. This will help you make sure you haven't skipped a space or gotten off track in some other way. If you catch such problems early, they're easy to fix.

"Computerized test-scoring isn't perfect. Smudges can kill you. If your grade seems incorrect, ask to see the answer sheet."
Graduate, Physiology, Michigan State University[2]

A variant of machine-scored testing is online testing. In such cases, you'll be taking an exam on a computer outside of class. Although we'll talk more about such tests in Chapter 7, for now keep in mind that you shouldn't wait until the final deadline to start your test. Technical difficulties may prevent you from logging in or not allow you enough time to finish. In addition, be sure to have paper and pencil available. Even though you use the computer to record your answers, you'll want to be able to jot down ideas, notes, and do calculations the traditional way: by hand.

Use Strategies Targeted to Answering Specific Types of Test Questions

Every type of question requires a particular approach. Use these strategies below:

> **Essay questions.** Essay questions, with their emphasis on description and analysis, often present challenges because they are relatively unstructured.

Unless you're careful, it's easy to wander off and begin to answer questions that were never asked. To prevent that problem, the first thing to do is read the question carefully, noting what specifically is being asked. If your essay will be lengthy, you might even want to write a short outline.

Pay attention to keywords that indicate what, specifically, the instructor is looking for in an answer. Certain action words are commonly used in essays, and you should understand them fully. For instance, knowing the distinction between "compare" and "contrast" can spell the difference between success and failure. **Table 4.3** defines common action words.

table 4.3   Action Words for Essays
These words are commonly used in essay questions. Learning the distinctions among them will help you answer essay questions effectively.
Analyze: Examine and break into component parts.
Clarify: Explain with significant detail.
Compare: Describe and explain similarities.
Compare and contrast: Describe and explain similarities and differences.
Contrast: Describe and explain differences.
Critique: Judge and analyze, explaining what is wrong—and right—about a concept.
Define: Provide the meaning.
Discuss: Explain, review, and consider.
Enumerate: Provide a listing of ideas, concepts, reasons, items, etc.
Evaluate: Provide pros and cons of something; provide an opinion and justify it.
Explain: Give reasons why or how; clarify, justify, and illustrate.
Illustrate: Provide examples; show instances.
Interpret: Explain the meaning of something.
Justify: Explain why a concept can be supported, typically by using examples and other types of support.
Outline: Provide an overarching framework or explanation—usually in narrative form—of a concept, idea, event, or phenomenon.
Prove: Using evidence and arguments, convince the reader of a particular point.
Relate: Show how things fit together; provide analogies.
Review: Describe or summarize, often with an evaluation.
State: Assert or explain.
Summarize: Provide a condensed, precise list or narrative.
Trace: Track or sketch out how events or circumstances have evolved; provide a history or timeline.

Use the right language in essays. Be brief and to the point in your essay. Avoid flowery introductory language. Compare the two sentences that follow:

"Management techniques have evolved to a point never before seen in the history of our country, or perhaps even our world."

"Many new management techniques have been developed in recent years ."

The second sentence says the same thing much more effectively and economically.

Essays are improved when they include examples and point out differences. Your response should follow a logical sequence, moving from major points to minor ones, or following a time sequence. Above all, your answer should address every aspect of the question posed on the test. Because essays often contain several different, embedded questions, you have to be certain that you have answered every part to receive full credit. (After reviewing Table 4.3, complete **Try It 4** on page 91.)

> **Short-answer and fill-in questions.** Short-answer and fill-in questions basically require you to generate and supply specific information. Unlike essays, which are more free-form and may have several possible answers, short-answer and fill-in questions are usually quite specific, requiring only one answer.

Use both the instructions for the questions and the questions themselves to determine the level of specificity that is needed in an answer. Try not to provide too much or too little information. Usually, brevity is best.

> **Multiple-choice questions.** If you've ever looked at a multiple-choice question and said to yourself, "But every choice seems right," you understand what can be tricky about this type of question. However, there are some simple strategies that can help you deal with multiple-choice questions.

First, read the question carefully. Note any specific instructions. In most cases, only one answer will be correct, but some questions will you ask you to select multiple items.

Then, *before you look at the possible answers, try to answer the question in your head.* This can help you avoid confusion over inappropriate choices.

Next, *carefully read through every possible answer.* Even if you come to one that you think is right, read them all—there may be a subsequent answer that is better.

Look for absolutes like "every," "always," "only," "none," and "never." Choices that contain such absolute words are rarely correct. For example, an answer choice that says, "A U.S. president has never been elected without having received

Understand Action Verbs in Essay Questions

4

Answer the following questions about the Second Amendment to the United States Constitution by outlining your responses to them, paying attention to the different action verbs that introduce questions.

The Second Amendment states:

A well-regulated militia, being necessary to the security of a free State, the right of the people to keep and bear arms, shall not be infringed.

1. Summarize the Second Amendment to the Constitution.

2. Analyze the Second Amendment to the Constitution.

3. Discuss the Second Amendment to the Constitution.

How do your answers differ for the each of the questions? Which of the questions provoked the lengthiest response? Which of the questions could you answer best?

To Try It online, go to www.mhhe.com/power.

---

the majority of the popular vote" is incorrect due to the presence of the word "never." On the other hand, less-absolute words, such as "generally," "usually," "often," "rarely," "seldom," and "typically" may indicate a correct response.

Be especially on guard for the word "not," which negates the sentence ("The one key concept that is not embodied in the U.S. Constitution is . . ."). It's easy to gloss over "not," and if you have the misfortune of doing so, it will be nearly impossible to answer the item correctly.

If you're having trouble understanding a question, underline key words or phrases, or try to break the question into different short sections. Sometimes it is helpful to work backwards, *Jeopardy!* style, and look at the possible answers first to see if you can find one that is clearly accurate or clearly inaccurate.

*Use an **educated guessing** strategy*—which is very different from wild or random guessing. Unless you are penalized for wrong answers (a scoring rule by which wrong answers are deducted from the points you have earned on other questions, rather than merely not counting at all toward your score), it always pays to guess.

The first step in educated guessing is to eliminate any obviously false answers. The next step is to examine the remaining choices closely. Does one response choice include an absolute or qualifying adjective that makes it

Educated guessing

The practice of eliminating obviously false multiple-choice answers and selecting the most likely answer from the remaining choices unlikely ("the probability of war *always* increases when a U.S. president is facing political difficulties")? Does one choice include a subtle factual error? For example, the answer to a multiple-choice question asking why Columbus took his journey to the new world that says "the French monarchy was interested in expanding its colonial holdings" is wrong because it was not the French, but the Spanish monarchy, that funded his journey.

> **True–false questions.** Although most of the principles we've already discussed apply equally well to true–false questions, a few additional tricks of the trade may help you with this type of question.
>
> Begin a set of true–false questions by answering the ones you're sure you know. But don't rush; it's important to read every part of a true–false question, because key words such as "never," "always," and "sometimes" often determine the appropriate response.
>
> If you don't have a clue about whether a statement is true or false, here's a last-resort principle: Choose "true." In general, more statements on a true–false test are likely to be true than false.

> **Matching questions.** Matching questions typically present you with two columns of related information, which you must link, item by item. For example, a list of terms or concepts may be presented in one column, along with a list of corresponding definitions or explanations in the second column. The best strategy is to reduce the size of both columns by matching the items you're most confident about first; this will leave a short list in each column, and the final matching may become apparent.

About Academic Honesty

Academic honesty

Completing and turning in only one's own work under one's own name

Plagiarism

Taking credit for someone else's words, thoughts, or ideas

It's tempting: A glance at a classmate's test may provide the one piece of information that you just can't remember. But you owe it to yourself not to do it. Copying from a classmate's paper is no different from reaching over and stealing that classmate's calculator or cell phone. It is a violation of **academic honesty,** one of the foundations of civility in the classroom, as well as in society. Unless the work you turn in under your own name is your work, you are guilty of academic dishonesty.

Violations of academic honesty can take many forms. It may involve **plagiarism,** taking credit for another's words, thoughts, or ideas. Academic dishonesty may also include using a calculator when it's not allowed, discussing the answer to a question, copying a computer file when it's unauthorized, taking an exam for another person, or stealing an exam. It can take the form of ripping a page out of a book in the library, or lying to an instructor about the reason for a late paper. It includes using your textbook or conferring with a friend when taking a closed-book exam in an online, distance-learning course.

You may feel that "everyone does it," so cheating is not so bad. Wrong. Everyone doesn't do it, just as most people don't embezzle from their companies or steal from others. Although you may know of a few cases of exceptionally dishonest classmates, most of your classmates try to be honest—you just don't notice their honesty.

Whatever form it takes, academic dishonesty is just plain wrong. It lowers the level of civility in the classroom, it makes the grading system unfair, and it ultimately reduces the meaning of your grade. It certainly hinders academic and personal growth. It can't help but reduce one's self-esteem, and it robs the cheater of self-respect.

Tests for a Lifetime

If you think the last tests you'll ever have to take are the final exams just before you graduate from college, you're probably wrong.

Increasing numbers of professions require initial licensing exams, and some even require periodic exams to remain in good standing within the profession. For example, in some states, people who wish to become teachers must pass an exam. And even experienced teachers are required to take periodic tests throughout their careers to remain in the teaching field.

In short, good test-taking skills won't just bring you success in college. They're something that may benefit you for a lifetime as you pursue your career.

Finally, academic dishonesty violates the regulations of every college (rules that you should familiarize yourself with), and instructors feel it is their obligation to uphold standards of academic honesty. Violations of honesty policies will lead to any number of potentially devastating scenarios: failing the exam on which the cheating has taken place, failing the entire course, being brought before a disciplinary board, having a description of the incident permanently placed on your grade transcript, being placed on academic probation, or even being thrown out of school. A single instance of cheating can permanently prevent you from embarking on the career of your choice. Cheating is simply not worth it.

 E Evaluate

Taking Your Own Final Examination

The last few minutes of a test may feel like the final moments of a marathon. You need to focus your energy and push yourself even harder. It can be make-or-break time.

Save some time at the end of a test so you can check your work. You should have been keeping track of your time all along, so plan on stopping a few minutes before the end of the test period to review what you've done. It's a critical step, and it can make the difference between a terrific grade and a mediocre one. It's a rare person who can work for an uninterrupted period of time on a test and commit absolutely no errors—even if he or she knows the material backwards and forwards. Consequently, checking what you've done is crucial.

Start evaluating your test by looking for obvious mistakes. Make sure you've answered every question and haven't skipped any parts of questions. If there is a separate answer sheet, check to see that all your answers have been recorded on the answer sheet and in the right spot.

If the test has included essay and short-answer questions, proofread your responses. Check for obvious errors—misspellings, missing words, and repetitions.

Make sure you've responded to every part of each question and that each essay, as a whole, makes sense.

Check over your responses to multiple-choice, true–false, and matching questions. If there are some items that you haven't yet answered because you couldn't remember the necessary information, now is the time to take a stab at them. As we discussed earlier, it usually pays to guess, even randomly if you must. On most tests, no answer and a wrong answer are worth the same amount—nothing!

What about items that you initially guessed at? Unless you have a good reason to change your original answer—such as a new insight or a sudden recollection of some key information—your first guess is likely your best guess.

Know When to Stop

After evaluating and checking your answers, you may reach a point when there is still some time left. What to do? If you're satisfied with your responses, it's simply time to tell yourself, "Let it go."

Permit yourself the luxury of knowing that you've done your best, and hand the test in to your instructor. You don't have to review your work over and over just because there is time remaining and some of your classmates are still working on their tests. In fact, such behavior is often counterproductive, because you might start overinterpreting and reading things into questions that really aren't there.

Disaster! I've run out of time! It's a nightmarish feeling: The clock is ticking relentlessly, and it's clear that you don't have enough time to finish the test. What should you do?

Stop working! Although this advice may sound foolish, in fact the most important thing you can do is to take a minute to calm yourself. Take some deep breaths to replace the feelings of panic that are likely welling up inside you. Collect your thoughts, and plan a strategy for the last moments of the test.

If there are essays that remain undone, consider how you'd answer them if you had more time. Then write an

From the perspective of . . .

A LEGAL ASSISTANT Even though tests are uncommon in professional careers, deadlines are frequent occurences. How might test-taking strategies help you when you are faced with a tight schedule?

outline of each answer. If you don't have time even for that, write a few keywords. Writing anything is better than handing in a blank page, and you may get at least some credit for your response. The key principle here: Something is better than nothing, and even one point is worth more than zero points.

The same principle holds for other types of questions. Even wild guesses are almost always better than not responding at all to an item. So rather than telling yourself you've certainly failed and giving up, do as much as you can in the remaining moments of the exam.

The Real Test of Learning

Your instructor is about to hand the graded exams back. All sorts of thoughts run through your head: How did I do? Did I do as well as my classmates? Will I be happy with my results? Will the results show how much I studied? Will I be embarrassed by my grade?

Most of us focus on the evaluative aspects of tests. We look at the grade we've received on a test as an end in itself. It's a natural reaction.

But there's another way to look at test results: They can help guide us toward future success. By looking at what we've learned (and haven't learned) about a given subject, we'll be in a better position to know what to focus on when we take future exams. Furthermore, by examining the kinds of mistakes we make, we can learn to do better in the future.

When you get your test back, you have the opportunity to reflect on what you've learned and to consider your performance. Begin by actively listening to what your instructor says as he or she hands back the test. You may learn about things that were generally misunderstood by the class, and you'll get a sense of how your performance compares with that of your classmates. You also may pick up some important clues about what questions will be on future exams.

> "The test of any man lies in action."
>
> Pindar, author, *Odes*

Then examine your own mistakes. Chances are they'll jump out at you since they will be marked incorrect. Did you misunderstand or misapply some principle? Was there a certain aspect of the material covered on the test that you missed? Were there particular kinds of information that you didn't realize you needed to know? Or did you lose some points because of your test-taking skills? Did you make careless errors, such as forgetting to fill in a question or misreading the directions? Was your handwriting so sloppy that your instructor had trouble reading it?

Once you have a good idea of what material you didn't fully understand or remember, get the correct answers to the items you missed—from your instructor, fellow classmates, or your book. If it's a math exam, rework problems you've missed. Finally, summarize—in writing—the material you had trouble with. This will help you study for future exams that cover the same material.

Finally, if you're dissatisfied with your performance, talk to your instructor—not to complain, but to seek help. Instructors don't like to give bad grades, and they may be able to point out problems in your test that you can address readily so you can do better in the future. Demonstrate to your instructor that you want to do better and are willing to put in the work to get there. The worst thing to do is crumple up the test and quickly leave the class in embarrassment. Remember, you're not the first person to get a bad grade, and the power to improve your test-taking performance lies within you. (Now, take a deep breath and complete **Try It 5** on page 96.)

Try It!

Take a Test-Taking Test

Take the following test on test-taking skills, which illustrates every question type discussed in this chapter. Answers to all questions except short-answer and essay questions are provided on page 101.

Before taking the test, think of the test-taking strategies we've discussed in the chapter and try to employ as many of them as possible.

MULTIPLE-CHOICE SECTION

Choose one of the possible responses following each question.

1. Tests are useful tools for which of the following purposes?
   a. Determining people's likely level of future career success.
   b. Indicating strengths and gaps in people's knowledge.
   c. Defining people's fundamental abilities and potentials.
   d. Evaluating people's individual worth and contributions.

2. One of the main advantages of study groups is that
   a. Every individual must contribute equally to the group.
   b. Group members can help each other during the test.
   c. Each member has to memorize only a fraction of the material.
   d. They allow each member to share different perspectives on the material.

3. Which of the following is a good way to deal with test anxiety?
   a. Visualizing success on the test.
   b. Drinking coffee or other stimulants.
   c. Telling yourself to stop worrying.
   d. Focusing on the importance of the test.

MATCHING SECTION

_____ 1. Essay question

_____ 2. Multiple-choice question

_____ 3. Matching question

_____ 4. Fill-in question

_____ 5. Guessing penalty

_____ 6. Cramming

_____ 7. Academic dishonesty

A. A question in which the student supplies brief missing information to complete a statement.

B. Hurried, last-minute studying.

C. A question in which the student must link information in two columns.

D. A question requiring a lengthy response in the student's own words.

E. Deduction of points for incorrect responses.

F. Representing another's work as one's own.

G. A question that requires selection from several response options.

FILL-IN SECTION

1. Fear of testing that can interfere with test performance is called _____.

2. The primary source of error on machine-scored tests is incomplete _____.

TRUE–FALSE SECTION

1. The best way to prepare for an essay test is to review detailed factual information about the topic. T _____ F _____

2. True–false questions require students to determine whether given statements are accurate or inaccurate. T _____ F _____

3. You should never permit yourself to feel panicky during a test. T _____ F _____

4. A good evaluation strategy toward the end of a test is to redo as many questions as time permits. T _____ F _____

5. In a multiple-choice question, the words "always" and "never" usually signal the correct response. T _____ F _____

6. If you run out of time at the end of a test, it is best to write brief notes and ideas down in response to essay questions rather than to leave them completely blank. T _____ F _____

SHORT-ANSWER SECTION

1. What are five things you should find out about a test before you take it?

2. What is academic honesty?

ESSAY SECTION

1. Discuss the advantages of using a study group to prepare for an examination.

2. Why is academic honesty important?

(Answers can be found on page 101 at the end of the chapter.)

After you have completed the test, consider these questions: Did you learn anything from taking the test that you might not have learned if you hadn't been tested? How effective were the test-taking strategies you employed? Were any types of strategies easier for you to employ than others? Were any types of questions easier for you to answer than others?

 WORKING IN A GROUP

Exchange your essay responses with a classmate, and critique the essay. How do the responses of your partner compare with your own?

To Try It online, go to www.mhhe.com/power.

speaking of success

NAME: Sonia Sotomayor

SCHOOL: Princeton University, B.A., 1976 (Summa Cum Laude); Yale Law School, J.D, 1979

U.S. Supreme Court Justice Sonia Sotomayor's educational journey was not an easy one, but hard work, determination, and a supportive family helped her become the first Latina and the third woman to serve in the Supreme Court's 220 year history.

Sotomayor's parents moved from Puerto Rico to New York City in the 1950s, and she grew up in a working-class Bronx neighborhood where both of her parents worked. At the age of 9 her father's death was an emotional blow, but she immersed herself in books—particularly the Nancy Drew series, which started her thinking about crime solving. That, and doing her homework in front of the TV while watching lawyer Perry Mason, ignited her goal of pursuing law.

She went on to graduate from Cardinal Spellman High School in New York City and was able to earn a scholarship to college. Although her undergraduate years were challenging, she was ultimately successful, graduating with honors. After graduation, she went on to law school.

"Although I grew up in very modest and challenging circumstances, I consider my life to be immeasurably rich," Sotomayor said.

"My mother taught us that the key to success in America is a good education," Sotomayor said at her Senate confirmation hearing. "And she set the example, studying alongside my brother and me at our kitchen table so that she could become a registered nurse."

Close to her family, the Supreme Court Justice notes that her mother, who worked six days a week as a nurse to support her and her brother, is her greatest inspiration. And while her achievements have been attained through hard work, she points to an appreciation for the opportunities she has had.

"It is our nation's faith in a more perfect union that allows a Puerto Rican girl from the Bronx to stand here now," she said during her swearing-in ceremony. "I am struck again by the wonder of my own life and the life we in America are so privileged to lead."

Looking Back

What kinds of tests will I encounter in college?

▸ Although tests are an unpopular fact of college life, they can provide useful information about one's level of knowledge and understanding about a subject.

▸ There are several types of tests, including brief, informal quizzes; more substantial tests; and even more weighty exams, which tend to be administered at the midpoint and end of a course.

What are the best ways to prepare for and take various kinds of tests?

▸ Good test preparation begins with doing the course assignments, attending class regularly, and paying attention in class. It also helps to find out as much as possible about a test beforehand and to form a study group to review material.

▸ If cramming becomes necessary, focus on summarizing factual information broadly, identifying key concepts and ideas, and rehearsing information orally.

▸ When you first receive the test, skim it to see what kinds of questions are asked, figure out how the different questions and sections will be weighted, and jot down complex factual information that is likely to be needed for the test.

▸ Answer the easiest questions first, write legibly, use only one side of each sheet of paper, mark answer sheets carefully, and record answers in the test book as well as the answer sheet.

What are the best strategies for answering specific kinds of test questions?

▸ For essay questions, be sure to understand each question and each of its parts, interpret action words correctly, write concisely, organize the essay logically, and include examples.

▸ The best strategy for short-answer and fill-in questions is to be very sure what is being asked. Keep answers complete but brief.

▸ For multiple-choice questions, read the question very carefully and then read all response choices. Educated guessing based on eliminating incorrect response choices is usually a reasonable strategy.

▸ For true–false and matching questions, answer all the items that you are sure of quickly and then go back to the remaining items.

[KEY TERMS AND CONCEPTS]

Test anxiety (p. 81)   Cramming (p. 85)   Academic honesty (p. 92)
Study groups (p. 83)   Educated guessing (p. 91)   Plagiarism (p. 92)

[RESOURCES]

ON CAMPUS

Colleges provide a variety of resources for students having difficulties with test-taking. Some offer general workshops for students, reviewing test-taking strategies. Furthermore, if you are planning to take a specific standardized test, you may be able to sign up for a course offered through your college (or through such commercial organizations as Princeton Review or Kaplan).

If you are experiencing difficulties in a specific course, you may be able to find a tutor to help you out. Some colleges have tutoring centers or campus learning centers that can provide one-to-one assistance. It's also important to speak to your instructor, who more than likely has encountered many students with similar problems and may have some useful test-taking strategies.

If you find that you are experiencing significant test anxiety when taking a test or in the days leading up to it, talk to someone at your campus counseling center or health center. They can help you learn relaxation techniques and can provide counseling to help make your anxiety manageable.

IN PRINT

In *How to Ace Any Test* (Wiley, 2004), Beverley Chin provides a variety of techniques designed to improve your performance on any kind of test.

Eileen Tracy's *The Student's Guide to Exam Success* (Open University Press, 2006) gives an overview of strategies for test-taking success.

Finally, *Test Anxiety and What You Can Do About It* (National Professional Resources, 2005), by Joseph Casbarro, is a professional guide to dealing with test anxiety, providing a variety of concrete suggestions.

ON THE WEB

The following sites on the World Wide Web provide opportunities to extend your learning about the material in this chapter. (Although the Web addresses were accurate at the time the book was printed, check the *P.O.W.E.R. Learning* Web site [**www.mhhe.com/power**] for any changes that may have occurred.)

>   "The Multiple Choice Exam," an online handout from the University of Victoria's Learning Skills Program (**www.coun.uvic.ca/learning/exams/multiple-choice.html**) offers some valuable suggestions on how to approach multiple-choice exams. Several types of multiple-choice questions are described and strategies for answering them are explained. There are also helpful hints about what to look for in the wording of both the questions and the answer choices.

>   "Simplified Plans of Action for Common Types of Question Words," another online handout from the University of Victoria's Learning Skills Program (**www.coun.uvic.ca/learning/essays/simple-answers.html**), gives examples of question words that are often found in essay assignments or in essay questions on exams. Possible "plans of action" for each of the question types are outlined. These outlines can be useful as a starting point for understanding how to approach essay questions.

>   "Tactics for Managing Stress and Anxiety" (**www.coun.uvic.ca/personal/stressanxiety.html**) offers several suggestions that you might find helpful in managing and reducing your level of stress and anxiety. The techniques may help you deal with test-related anxiety as well as academic anxiety in general. Not all of the techniques work for everyone. Try them and use the ones that work best for you.

1   Seeing exams from other classes can help you get an idea of the kinds of questions that are often asked on exams. Use an Internet search engine to locate examples of exams from other colleges and universities. (One strategy would be to use the Google search engine—**www.google.com**—and type "examples of exams" [including the quotes] at the search prompt.) Look at several exams. How many of the questions on these exams were true–false? How many were multiple-choice? How many were essays?

2   Practice answering essay questions by comparing and contrasting the information different Web pages offer about the same topic. For example, go to Yahoo! (**www.yahoo.com/**) and enter the phrase "essay exams" (using quotes). Read the strategies for essay exams offered in the two different Web sites. Then write a paragraph describing the information both sites had in common, and another paragraph describing the information that was unique to each site.

[ANSWERS TO THE ITEMS IN TRY IT 5]

Multiple-choice: 1b, 2d, 3a

Matching: 1D, 2G, 3C, 4A, 5E, 6B, 7F

Fill-in: test anxiety, erasing

True–False: 1F, 2T, 3F, 4F, 5F, 6T

Short answer:

1. Possible answers include what the test is called, what it will cover, how many questions will be on it, how much time it will take, what kinds of questions will be on it, how it will be graded, whether sample questions will be provided, and whether tests from prior terms are available.

2. Academic honesty is completing and turning in only one's own work under one's own name.

Essay:

1. Strong essays would include a brief definition of a study group, followed by a discussion of the advantages of using study groups (including such things as helping to organize and structure material, providing different perspectives, and rethinking material). A mention of the disadvantages of study groups would also be reasonable.

2. After starting with a brief definition of academic honesty, the bulk of the answer should concentrate on the reasons why academic honesty is important and what are the consequences of academic dishonesty.

The Case of . . .
That Sinking Feeling

This was going to be easy, Debbie Mallery said to herself as she sat down to take her test, a midterm exam covering the basics of restaurant management. She had spent a few hours the previous night and an hour right before class studying key terms and concepts. She felt she knew the material. She felt ready.

Debbie was surprised to see, though, that the exam had two parts: a multiple-choice section and an essay section. Debbie hadn't really thought about what she might say in an essay. But she figured working on the multiple-choice questions might help give her some ideas.

The first two multiple-choice questions Debbie answered easily, but she got stuck on the third one. She went back and forth over two possible answers

and finally decided just to leave that question blank. The pattern was the same for the rest of the multiple choice questions. A few questions Debbie would answer easily, then she'd get stuck on a hard one.

Finally, Debbie finished the multiple-choice questions and came to the essay. Only then did she notice the instructions that indicated the essay was worth 50 points, and the multiple-choice questions 25 points. Then Debbie got another shock: She realized she had only 10 minutes left to write her essay! Her mind froze—and Debbie had the horrible feeling that she didn't have enough time to complete the test. Even though she had studied, Debbie now felt certain she would fail.

1. What mistakes did Debbie make in her test preparation that probably harmed her performance?

2. What mistakes did Debbie make during the test that hurt her?

3. What was right about Debbie's initial approach to the test?

4. What should Debbie have done differently in calculating the amount of time to devote to each portion of the test? Why?

5. What specific strategies would have helped Debbie with the multiple-choice questions? What strategies could she have used on the essay?

6. If you were in Debbie's shoes, what would you do with only 10 minutes left in the test?

Learning Outcomes

By the time you finish this chapter you will be able to

» **LO5.1**   Identify the essential elements of successful reading.

» **LO5.2**   Explain how to improve concentration and read more effectively.

» **LO5.3**   Discuss techniques for memorizing large amounts of information.

» **LO5.4**   Analyze how best to retain what you have read.

Reading and Remembering

"Read the next chapter in the textbook by Tuesday." "Read the first two articles in the course pack by next class." "The test will cover the first hundred pages in your book, so be sure you've read it."

One day, three different reading assignments, Jeff Knowles thought as the instructor of his last class of the day delivered this last instruction to read. It would be hard enough for Jeff to complete all this reading during an ordinary week. But this week he had to finish painting his garage and had volunteered to help his brother move. On top of that, there was his part-time landscaping job—and, Jeff suddenly remembered, he'd agreed to work overtime on Friday.

Still, Jeff figured that even with all his work, family, and household obligations, he could still find time to do all his reading—except Jeff believed he was an unusually slow reader. When he pushed himself to read quicker and absorb more, he actually read and retained less. For Jeff, the problem wasn't just completing the reading—it was remembering it when test time rolled around.

Looking Ahead

For people like Jeff, reading assignments are the biggest challenge in college. The amount of required reading is often enormous. Even skilled readers may find themselves wishing they could read more quickly and effectively. On the job, too, many people struggle with all the memos, e-mails, manuals, and so forth that they need to read.

Fortunately, there are ways to improve your reading skills. In this chapter, we'll go over a number of strategies to make reading more effective.

We'll also discuss ways to improve memory skills, not just as they relate to reading, but in general, too. Most of us have experienced the challenge of memorizing a seemingly impossible amount of information, and we tend to focus on our failures far more than on our successes. But the truth is that our memory capabilities are truly astounding. For instance, if you are like the average college student, your vocabulary contains some 50,000 words, you know hundreds of mathematical facts, and you can recall detailed images from events you witnessed years ago. In this chapter, you'll learn how to harness your memory's power.

≫LO 5.1 Sharpen Your Reading and Memory Skills

One of the reasons many people struggle with reading, especially in college, is they feel they *shouldn't* have to struggle with it. Reading, after all, is something almost all of us master as children . . . right?

In fact, it is not so simple. Reading, as we will see in this chapter, involves more than just recognizing words. The task of reading large amounts of information and remembering the essential points takes time to master.

To begin, consider the way you read now. In other words, what kind of reader are you? Ask yourself first of all about your reading *preferences:* What do you *like* to read, and why? What makes you pick up a book and start reading—and what makes you put one down?

Before going any further, think about your own reading preferences by completing the **Journal Reflections.**

Journal Reflections

My Reading Preferences

Think about what you like and don't like to read by answering these questions.

1. Do you read for pleasure? If so, what do you read (e.g., magazines, newspapers, novels, humor, short stories, nonfiction, illustrated books)?

2. What makes a book enjoyable? Have you ever read a book that you "couldn't put down"? If so, what made it so good?

3. What is the most difficult book you are reading this semester? Why is it difficult? Are you enjoying it?

4. Think about when you read for pleasure compared with when you read material for a class. How does the way you read differ between the two types of material?

5. How well do you remember the last book or magazine you read for pleasure? Do you remember it better than your last college reading assignment? Why do you think this might be?

» LO 5.2   Read for Retention, Not Speed

You may have come across advertisements on the Web promoting reading "systems" that promise to teach you to read so quickly that you'll be reading entire books in an hour and whizzing through assigned readings in a few minutes.

Unfortunately it's not going to happen. Research has shown that claims of speed-reading are simply groundless. But even if it were physically possible to read a book in an hour, ultimately it probably doesn't matter very much. If we read too fast, comprehension and ultimately retention plunge. Reading is not a race, and the fastest readers are not necessarily the best readers.

The act of reading is designed to increase our knowledge and open up new ways of thinking. It can help us achieve new levels of understanding and get us to think more broadly about the world and its inhabitants. Speed matters far less than what we take away from what we've read. That's not to say we shouldn't try to become more efficient readers who comprehend and recall more effectively. Ultimately, though, the key to good reading is understanding—not speed.

In describing how you can use the principles of *P.O.W.E.R. Learning* to become a better reader with a more complete memory of what you read, we'll focus on

P Prepare
Approach the
written word

O Organize
Gather the tools
of the trade

W Work
Get the most out
of your reading

E Evaluate
Consider what it means
and what you know

R Rethink
Get it the second time

P.O.W.E.R. Plan

Advance organizers

Broad, general ideas related to material that is to be read or heard, which pave the way for subsequent learning

the type of reading that is typically called for in academic pursuits—textbook chapters, articles, handouts, and the like. However, the same principles will help you get more benefit and enjoyment out of your recreational reading as well. Crucially also, the reading skills you learn and employ in the classroom will also help you read more efficiently and effectively on the job.

P Prepare   Approaching the Written Word

Preparation to begin reading isn't hard, and it won't take very long, but it's a crucial first step in applying P.O.W.E.R. Learning (summarized in the P.O.W.E.R. Plan here). Your aim in preparation is to become familiar with **advance organizers**—outlines, overviews, section objectives, or other clues to the meaning and organization of new material—provided in the material you are reading. Most textbooks have them built in; for an example, look at the start of every chapter in this book, which includes a "Learning Outcomes" list and a "Looking Ahead" section. You can also create your own advance organizers by skimming material to be read and sketching out the general outline of the material you'll be reading.

Advance organizers pave the way for subsequent learning. They help you tie information that you already know to new material you're about to encounter. This connection between old and new material is crucial in helping build memories of what you read. If you approach each new reading task as something entirely new and unrelated to your previous knowledge, you'll have enormous difficulty recalling it. On the other hand, if you connect it to what you already know, you'll be able to recall it far better.

In short, the more we're able to make use of advance organizers and our own prior knowledge and experiences, the better we can understand and retain new material. (To prove the value of advance organizers, complete **Try It 1,** "Discover How Advance Organizers Help.")

What's the Point of the Reading Assignment?

Before you begin an assignment, think about what your goal is. Will you be reading a textbook on which you'll be thoroughly tested? Is your reading supposed to provide background information that will serve as a context for future learning but that won't itself be tested? Is the material going to be useful to you personally? Realistically, how much time can you devote to the reading assignment?

Your goal for reading will help you determine which reading strategy to adopt. You aren't expected to read everything with the same degree of intensity. Some material you may feel comfortable skimming; for other material you'll want to put in the maximum effort.

Understand the Point of View of the Material Itself

What are you reading—a textbook, an essay, an article? If it is an essay or article, why was it written? To prove a point? To give information? To express the author's personal feelings? Knowing the author's purpose (even if his or her specific point and message aren't yet clear) can help you a great deal as you read.

Discover How Advance Organizers Help

Read this passage. What do you think it means?

The procedure is actually quite simple. First you arrange items into different groups. Of course, one pile may be sufficient, depending on how much there is to do. If you have to go somewhere else due to lack of facilities, that is the next step; otherwise, you are pretty well set. It is important not to overdo things. That is, it is better to do too few things at once than too many. In the short run this may not seem important but complications can easily arise. A mistake can be expensive as well. At first, the whole procedure will seem complicated. Soon, however, it will become just another facet of life. It is difficult to foresee any end to the necessity for this task in the immediate future, but then one can never tell. After the procedure is completed, one arranges the materials into different groups again. Then they can be put into their appropriate places. Eventually, they will be used once more and the whole cycle will then have to be repeated. However, this is a part of life.[1]

If you're like most people, you don't have a clue about what this all means and won't be able to remember anything about it in five minutes. But suppose you had been given some context in advance, and you knew before reading it that the description had to do with washing laundry. Now does it all fall into place? Do you think it will be easier to remember? Read the passage once more, and see how having an advance organizer (in this case, *washing laundry*) helps out.

To Try It online, go to www.mhhe.com/power.

Start with the Frontmatter

If you'll be using a text or other book extensively throughout the term, start by reading the preface and/or introduction and scanning the table of contents—what publishers call the **frontmatter.** Instructors often don't formally assign the front-matter, but reading it can be a big help because it is there that the author has a chance to step forward and explain, often more personally than elsewhere in an academic book, what he or she considers important. Knowing this will give you a sense of what to expect as you read.

> **Frontmatter**
> The preface, introduction, and table of contents of a book

Create Advance Organizers

To provide a context for your reading, create your own advance organizers by skimming through the table of contents, which provides the main headings of what you will be reading. Textbooks often have chapter outlines, listing the key topics to be covered, which also provide a way of previewing the chapter content. As you read over the outline, you can begin to consider how the new material in the book may relate both to what you know and to what you expect to learn—from the reading assignment itself and from the course.

Textbooks also often have end-of-chapter summaries, and many articles include a final section in which the author states his or her conclusions. Take a look at these ending sections as well. Even though you haven't read the material yet and the summary probably won't make complete sense to you, by reading the summary, you'll get an idea of what the author covers and what is important.

Your instructor may also provide an advance organizer for readings. Sometimes instructors will mention things to pay particular attention to or to look for, such as "When you read Thomas Paine's *Common Sense,* notice how he lays out his argument and what his key points are." Sometimes they will say why they assigned a reading. Such information provides clues that can help you develop a mental list of the reading's key ideas.

However you construct advance organizers, be sure they provide a framework and context for what you'll be reading; this framework and context can spell the difference between fully comprehending what you read and misunderstanding it.

Now it's time to put all this practice to good use. Create an advance organizer for a textbook chapter in **Try It 2.**

Identify What You Need to Remember

No matter how important a reading assignment is to a course, you will not be expected to remember every word of it—nor should you try! The average textbook chapter has something like 20,000 words. If you had to recall every word of the chapter, it would be nearly impossible. Furthermore, it would be a waste of time. Being able to spew out paragraphs of material is quite different from the more important ability to recall and deeply understand material in meaningful ways.

Within those 20,000 words, there may be only 20 different concepts that you need to learn. And perhaps there are only 10 keywords. *Those* are the pieces of information that should be the focus of your efforts to memorize.

How do you know what's so important that you need to recall it? One way is to use the guides built into most textbooks. Key concepts and terms are often highlighted or in boldface type. Chapters often have summaries that recap the most important information. Use such guideposts to understand what's most critical in a chapter.

Write down what you determine is important. Putting critical information in writing not only helps you manage what you need to remember, but the very act of writing it down makes it easier to memorize the information later.

In short, the first step in building a better memory of your reading is to determine just what it is that you wish to recall. By extracting what is important from what is less crucial, you'll be able to limit the amount and extent of the material that you need to recall. You'll be able to focus, laserlike, on what you need to remember.

Gathering the Tools of the Trade

It's obvious that the primary item you'll need to complete a reading assignment is the material that you're reading. But there are other essential tools you should gather, potentially including the following:

- Pencils or pens to write notes in the margin.
- Highlighters to indicate key passages in the text.
- A copy of the assignment, so you'll be sure to read the right material.
- A pad of paper and/or index cards for notetaking if the material is particularly complex. If you routinely use a word processor to take notes, get it ready.
- A dictionary. You never know what new words you'll encounter while you're reading. If a dictionary is not handy, you'll be tempted to skip over unfamiliar words—a decision that may come back to haunt you. Note that some word-processing software includes a dictionary; there are also many good dictionaries available online (e.g., Merriam-Webster's at **www.m-w.com,** where you will also find an online thesaurus). The point is to use what's available—but use something!

Create an Advance Organizer

Use any information you have available to create an advance organizer for a chapter in a text that you are using this term. Skim the section headings in the chapter, read the chapter summary, consult the book's frontmatter, and recall anything your instructor may have said about the chapter.

Complete the following statements to prepare your organizer:

The general topics that are covered in the chapter are . . .

The most critical topics and concepts in the chapter are . . .

The most difficult material in the chapter includes . . .

Words, phrases, and ideas that are unfamiliar to me include . . .

Ways that the material in this chapter relates to other material that I've previously read in the text include . . .

Use this Try It as a starting point for advance organizers for future chapters in the book.

To Try It online, go to www.mhhe.com/power.

Give Yourself Time

There's one more thing you need to prepare successfully for a reading assignment: enough time to complete it. The length of reading assignments is almost never ambiguous. You will typically be given a specific page range, so you will know just how much material you will need to cover.

Now get a watch and time yourself as you read the first three pages of your assignment, being sure to pay attention to the material, not the time! Timing how long it takes to read a representative chunk of material provides you with a rough measure of your reading speed for the material—although it will vary even within a single reading assignment, depending on the complexity of the material.

Attention span
The length of time that attention
is typically sustained

You'll also need to consider an aspect of your personal learning style: your reading attention span. **Attention span** is the length of time that a person usually is able to sustain attention. People with long attention spans can read for relatively lengthy periods without getting jumpy, while those with shorter ones can only maintain attention for a short while. You can get a general sense of this by using **Try It 3,** "Discover Your Attention Span."

Use the three pieces of information you now have—the length of the assignment, your per-page reading speed at full attention, and your typical attention span—to estimate roughly how long it will take you to complete the reading assignment. For example, if you are asked to read 12 pages, you have found that you need approximately 4 minutes to read a page, and your reading attention span is, on average, 25 minutes long, you can expect your reading to take at least 60 minutes, assuming you'll take a short break when your attention begins to fade after 25 minutes.

In addition, you may need to interrupt your reading to look up words in the dictionary, get a drink, stretch, or answer the phone. You may also decide to break your reading into several short sessions, in which case your total reading time may be greater since you will have to get reacquainted with the reading assignment each time you sit down again.

Remember that you can use this strategy for estimating the amount of time reading will take you for reading tasks outside the classroom, too. If your employer asks you to read a set of customer feedback forms, for example, you can figure out how much time in your day you'll need to block off to complete the work by factoring in the total length of all the forms, your per-page reading speed, and your attention span. Remember, though, that reading on the job is different from reading in a college library or at your desk at home. You can expect many more distractions as you try to read—coworkers asking questions, e-mails coming in, the phone ringing. Take into account these inevitable workplace distractions when making your reading time estimate.

Getting the Most Out of Your Reading and Using Proven Strategies to Memorize New Material

Once you've familiarized yourself with the material as a whole and gathered the necessary tools, it's time to get down to work and start reading. Here are several things that will help you get the most out of the reading process.

Stay Focused

The TV show you watched last night . . . your husband forgetting to meet you at the bus stop . . . the new toothbrush you need to buy for your daughter . . . your grumbling stomach. There are a million and one possible distractions that can invade your thoughts as you read. Your job is to keep distracting thoughts at bay and focus on the material you are supposed to be reading. It's not easy, but the following are things you can do to help yourself stay focused:

> **Read in small bites.** If you think it is going to take you 4 hours to read an entire chapter, break up the 4 hours into more manageable time periods. Promise

Try It! 3

Discover Your Attention Span

You should be aware of your attention span, the length of time you usually are able to sustain attention to a task, as you prepare for reading assignments. To get an idea of the length of your current attention span for reading, perform this exercise over the next few days.

1. Choose one of the textbooks that you've been assigned to read this semester.
2. Start reading a chapter, without any preparation, noting in the chart below the time that you start reading.
3. As soon as your mind begins to wander and think about other subjects, stop reading and note the time on the chart below.
4. Using the same textbook, repeat this process four more times over the course of a few days, entering the data on the chart below.
5. To find your reading attention span, calculate the average number of minutes across the five trials.

Trial #1   Starting time: _____   Ending time: _____

Number of minutes between start and end times: _____

Trial #2   Starting time: _____   Ending time: _____

Number of minutes between start and end times: _____

Trial #3   Starting time: _____   Ending time: _____

Number of minutes between start and end times: _____

Trial #4   Starting time: _____   Ending time: _____

Number of minutes between start and end times: _____

Trial #5   Starting time: _____   Ending time: _____

Number of minutes between start and end times: _____

Reading attention span (the average of the number of minutes in the last column, found by adding up the five numbers and dividing by 5) = _____ minutes

---

Ask yourself these questions about your reading attention span:

1. Are you surprised by the length of your reading attention span? In what way?
2. Does any number in the set of trials stand out from the other numbers? For instance, is any number much higher or lower than the average? If so, can you account for this? For example, what time of day was it?
3. Do the numbers in your trials show any trend? For instance, did your attention span tend to increase slightly over the course of the trials, did it decrease, or did it stay about the same? Can you explain any trend you may have noted?
4. Do you think your attention span times would be very different if you had chosen a different textbook? Why or why not?
5. What things might you do to improve your attention span?

To Try It online, go to www.mhhe.com/power.

If you are reading a long assignment, taking a break can be a reward and reinvigorate you.

yourself that you'll read for 1 hour in the afternoon, another hour in the evening, and the next 2 hours spaced out during the following day. One hour of reading is far more manageable than a 4-hour block.

> **Take a break.** Actually, plan to take several short breaks to reward yourself while you're reading. During your break, do something enjoyable—eat a snack, watch a bit of a ball game on television, text message a friend, or the like. Just try not to get drawn into your break activity to the point that it takes over your reading time.

> **Deal with mental distractions.** Sometimes problems have a way of popping into our minds and repeatedly distracting us. If a particular problem keeps interrupting your concentration—such as a difficulty you're having on the job—try to think of an action-oriented strategy to deal with it. You might even write your proposed solution down on a piece of paper. Putting it down in words can get the problem off your mind, potentially making it less intrusive.

> **Manage interruptions.** You can't prevent your children from getting into a fight and needing immediate attention. But there are some things you can do to reduce interruptions and their consequences. For instance, you can schedule reading to coincide with periods when you know you'll be alone. You can also plan to read less critical parts of assignments (such as the summaries or book frontmatter) when distractions are more likely, saving the heavier reading for later. Or, if you are a parent with small children, you can get them involved in an activity that they can perform independently so you'll be free to concentrate.

Write While You Read

Writing is one of the most important aspects of reading. If you haven't underlined, jotted notes to yourself, placed check marks on the page, drawn arrows, constructed diagrams, and otherwise defaced and disfigured your book while you're reading, you're not doing your job as a P.O.W.E.R. reader.

The idea of writing on a book page may go against everything you've been taught in the past. (And of course you should never write on a library book or one that you've borrowed.)

However, once you've bought your book, *you own it and you should make it your own.* Don't keep your textbooks spotless so they will fetch a higher price if you sell them later. Instead, think of textbooks as documents recording your active learning and engagement in a field of study. In addition, you should look at your

Textbook Tips: Starting Off on the Right Page

You've just come back from the bookstore, weighted down with a bookbag filled with the textbooks and other materials for the upcoming term. Now is the time to take some preliminary steps to make the most of your investment.

- Make sure you've bought the correct textbooks. Look at each syllabus from your classes to ensure you've bought the appropriate text. Sometimes there are multiple sections of a course, and each section uses a different text and the right edition. Be sure the book you've bought matches the description in the syllabus.

- Make the book your own. Write your name, e-mail address, and/or telephone number in the front of the book. If you misplace your book during the term, you want the person who finds it to be able to return it to you.

- Orient yourself to each of your textbooks. Take a quick look at each of the books, examining the table of contents, introduction, and/or preface (as we discussed earlier). Get a sense of the content and the general reading level of the book.

- Get yourself online. Many textbooks contain a card or insert with a password that gives you access to online material. Follow the directions and enter the book's Web site, making sure the password allows you to register. If you have trouble making the site work, call the tech support number that should be included with the password.

textbooks as the foundation of your personal library, which will grow throughout your lifetime. In short, writing extensively in your book while you're reading is an important tactic for achieving success. (For more on using textbooks, see the **Course Connections** feature.)

From the perspective of . . .

A STUDENT To truly retain what you are reading, you must give your reading your undivided attention. Make a list of your biggest distractions and consider strategies for avoiding those distractions when you read.

The ability to add your own personal notes, underlining, and other annotations to a clean text while you're reading is one of the reasons it usually pays to buy new, rather than used, textbooks. Why would you want a stranger's comments on something you own? Can you really trust that person's judgment over your own regarding what's important to underline? New books allow you to mark them up in your own personal style, without the distraction of competing voices.

What should you be writing while you are reading? There are several things you should write down:

▸ **Rephrase key points.** Make notes to yourself, in your own words, about what the author is trying to get across. Don't just copy what's been said. Think about the material, and rewrite it in words that are your own.

Writing notes to yourself in your own words has several consequences, all good. First, you make the material yours; it becomes something you now understand and part of your own knowledge base. This is an essential aid to memorization. When you try to recollect your reading, you won't be trying to summon the thoughts of someone else—you'll be trying to remember *your own* thinking.

Second, trying to summarize a key point in your own words will make it very clear whether you truly understand it. It's easy to be fooled into thinking we understand something as we're reading along. But the true test is whether we can explain it to ourselves (or someone else) on our own, without referring to the book or article.

Third, the very act of writing engages an additional type of perception—involving the physical sense of moving a pen or pressing a keyboard. This will help you learn the material in a more active way.

Finally, writing notes and phrases will help you study the material later. Not only will the key points be highlighted, but your notes will also quickly bring you up to speed regarding your initial thoughts and impressions.

> **Highlight or underline key points.** Very often the first or last sentence in a paragraph, or the first or last paragraph in a section, will present a key point. Before you highlight anything, though, read the whole paragraph through. Then you'll be sure that what you highlight is, in fact, the key information. Topic sentences do not always fall at the beginning of a paragraph.
>
> Be selective in your highlighting and underlining. A page covered in yellow highlighter may be artistically appealing, but it won't help you understand the material any better. Highlight only the key information. You might find yourself highlighting only one or two sentences or phrases per page. That's fine. *In highlighting and underlining, less is more.* One guideline: No more than 10 percent of the material should be highlighted or underlined.
>
> Keep in mind, too, as you highlight and underline that the key material you are marking is the material you will likely need to remember for exams or class discussions. To aid in your recall of such material, read it over a time or two after you've marked it, and consider also reading it aloud. This will reinforce the memories you are building of the essential points in the assignment.

> **Use arrows, diagrams, outlines, tables, timelines, charts, and other visuals to help you understand and later recall what you are reading.** If there are three examples given for a particular point, number them. If a paragraph discusses a situation in which an earlier point does not hold, link the original point to the exception by an arrow. If a sequence of steps is presented, number each step.
>
> For example, after you have annotated *this* page of *P.O.W.E.R. Learning,* it might look something like what is shown in **Figure 5.1**.
>
> Particularly if your learning style is a visual one, representing the material graphically will get you thinking about it—and the connections and points in it—in new and different ways. Rather than considering the material solely in verbal terms, you now add visual images. The act of creating visual annotations will not only help you to understand the material better but it will also ease its later recall. Practice this technique on the sample textbook page in **Try It 4** on page 116.

> **Look up unfamiliar words in a dictionary.** Even though you may be able to figure out the meaning of an unfamiliar word from its context, use a dictionary anyway. This way you can be sure that what you think it means is correct. A dictionary will also tell you what the word sounds like, which may be important if your instructor uses the word in class.

understand and part of your own knowledge base. This is an essential aid to memorization. When you try to recollect your reading, you won't be trying to summon the thoughts of someone else—you'll be trying to remember *your own* thinking.

Second, trying to summarize a key point in your own words will make it very clear whether you truly understand it. It's easy to be fooled into thinking we understand something as we're reading along. But the true test is whether we can explain it to ourselves (or someone else) on our own, without referring to the book or article.

Third, the very act of writing engages an additional type of perception—involving the physical sense of moving a pen or pressing a keyboard. This will help you learn the material in a more active way.

Finally, writing notes and phrases will help you study the material later. Not only will the key points be highlighted, but your notes will also quickly bring you up to speed regarding your initial thoughts and impressions.

Topic sentence

Read whole paragraph before highlighting

Highlight or underline key points. Very often the first or last sentence in a paragraph, or the first or last paragraph in a section, will present a key point. Before you highlight anything, though, read the whole paragraph through. Then you'll be sure that what you highlight is, in fact, the key information. Topic sentences do not always fall at the beginning of a paragraph.

Be selective in your highlighting and underlining. A page covered in yellow highlighter may be artistically appealing, but it won't help you understand the material any better. Highlight only the key information. You might find yourself highlighting only one or two sentences or phrases per page. That's fine. *In highlighting and underlining, less is more.* One guideline: No more than 10 percent of the material should be highlighted or underlined.

Reread key points to help memory

Keep in mind, too, as you highlight and underline that the key material you are marking is the material you will likely need to remember for exams or class discussions. To aid in your recall of such material, read it over a time or two after you've marked it, and consider also reading it aloud. This will reinforce the memories you are building of the essential points in the assignment.

Use visuals →

Use arrows, diagrams, outlines, tables, timelines, charts, and other visuals to help you understand and later recall what you are reading. If there are three examples given for a particular point, number them. If a paragraph discusses a situation in which an earlier point does not hold, link the original point to the exception by an arrow. If a sequence of steps is presented, number each step.

For example, after you have annotated *this* page of *P.O.W.E.R. Learning*, it might look something like what is shown in **Figure 5.1**.

Particularly if your learning style is a visual one, representing the material graphically will get you thinking about it—and the connections and points in it—in new and different ways. Rather than considering the material solely in verbal terms, you now add visual images. The act of creating visual annotations will not only help you to understand the material better but it will also ease its later recall. Practice this technique on the sample textbook page in **Try It 4** on page 116.

Look up words in dictionary

Look up unfamiliar words in a dictionary. Even though you may be able to figure out the meaning of an unfamiliar word from its context, use a dictionary anyway. This way you can be sure that what you think it means is correct. A dictionary will also tell you what the word sounds like, which may be important if your instructor uses the word in class.

figure 5.1
Sample of Annotated Page

Memorize Key Material

Many of the reading strategies discussed above will help fix key material in your mind. Rephrasing key points, highlighting or underlining essential material and then rereading it, and creating visuals will all help you recall the information you've read.

Sometimes, though, these strategies are not enough. You may need to memorize a great deal of information, more than you'll be able to recall just through the

Mark Up a Book Page

First, working alone, read the excerpt in **Figure 5.2** on the opposite page. Then use the techniques we've discussed for marking up a page to highlight its key points.

Next, working in a group, compare and contrast your annotations with those of some classmates, and answer the following questions:

1. How do others' annotations differ from yours?

2. Why did they use the annotations they did?

3. Which annotation techniques worked best for you? Which did others prefer? Why?

4. How might these annotations help you to remember what is important?

5. If there were different sorts of material presented on the page, such as mathematical formulas, would you use different kinds of annotations?

To Try It online, go to **www.mhhe.com/power.**

The more parents speak to their children, the better their children's language skills.

Understanding Language Acquisition: Identifying the Roots of Language

Anyone who spends even a little time with children will notice the enormous strides that they make in language development throughout childhood. However, the reasons for this rapid growth are far from obvious. Two major explanations have been offered: one based on learning theory and the other on innate processes.

The **learning-theory approach** suggests that language acquisition follows the principles of reinforcement and conditioning discussed in Chapter 6. For example, a child who utters the word "mama" is hugged and praised by her mother, which reinforces the behavior and makes its repetition more likely. This view suggests that children first learn to speak by being rewarded for making sounds that approximate speech. Ultimately, through a process of shaping, language becomes more and more like adult speech (Skinner, 1957).

learning-theory approach: The theory suggesting that language acquisition follows the principles of reinforcement and conditioning

The learning theory approach is supported by research that shows that the more parents speak to their young children, the more proficient the children become in language usage (see Figure 8-11). In addition, higher levels of linguistic sophistication in parents' speech to their young children are related to a greater rate of vocabulary growth, vocabulary usage, and even general intellectual achievement by the time the children are 3 years of age (Hart & Risley, 1997).

On the other hand, the learning theory approach is less successful when it comes to explaining the acquisition of language rules. Children are reinforced not only when they use proper language, but also when they respond incorrectly. For example, parents answer the child's "Why the dog won't eat?" as readily as they do the correctly phrased question "Why won't the dog eat?" Both sentences are understood equally well. Learning theory, then, has difficulty in providing the full explanation for language acquisition.

Pointing to such problems with learning theory approaches to language acquisition, Noam Chomsky (1968, 1978, 1991), a linguist, provided a ground-breaking alternative. Chomsky argued that humans are born with an innate linguistic capability that emerges primarily as a function of maturation. According to his analysis, all the world's languages share a similar underlying structure called a **universal grammar.** Chomsky suggests that the human brain has a neural system, the **language-acquisition device,** that both permits the understanding of the structure of language and provides strategies and techniques for learning the unique characteristics of a given native language.

universal grammar: Noam Chomsky's theory that all the world's languages share a similar underlying structure

language-acquisition device: A neural system of the brain hypothesized to permit understanding of language

figure 5.2
Sample Page to Annotate

process of reading, underlining, and so forth. Many people find extensive memorization daunting. But one of the good things about the work of memorization is that you have your choice of literally dozens of techniques. Depending on the kind of material you need to recall and how much you already know about the subject, you can turn to any number of methods.

As we sort through the various options, keep in mind that no one strategy works by itself. (And some strategies don't seem to work: For example, forget about supplements like gingko biloba—there's no clear scientific evidence that they are effective.[2]) Instead, try the following proven strategies and find those that work best for you. Feel free to devise your own strategies or add those that have worked for you in the past.

> ▸ **Rehearsal.** Think it again: rehearsal. Say it aloud: rehearsal. Think of it in terms of the three syllables that make up the word: re—hear—sal. OK, one more time—say the word "rehearsal."
>
> If you're scratching your head over the last paragraph, it's to illustrate the point of **rehearsal:** to transfer material that you encounter into memory. If you don't rehearse information in some way, it will end up like most of the information to which we're exposed: on the garbage heap of lost memory.
>
> To test if you've succeeded in transferring the word "rehearsal" into your memory, put down this book and go off for a few minutes. Do something entirely unrelated to reading this book. Have a snack, catch up on the latest sports scores on ESPN, or read the front page of the newspaper.
>
> Are you back? If the word "rehearsal" popped into your head when you picked up this book again, you've passed your first memory test. You can be assured that the word "rehearsal" has been transferred into your memory.
>
> Rehearsal is the key strategy in remembering information. If you don't rehearse material, it will never make it into memory. Repeating the information, summarizing it, associating it with other memories, and above all thinking about it when you first come across it will ensure that rehearsal will be effective in pushing the material into memory.

> ▸ **Mnemonics.** This odd word (pronounced in an equally odd fashion, with the "m" silent—"neh MON ix") describes formal techniques used to make material more readily remembered. **Mnemonics** are the tricks of the trade that professional memory experts use, and you too can use them to nail down the sort of information you will often need to recall for tests.
>
> Among the most common mnemonics are acronyms. You're already well acquainted with **acronyms,** words or phrases formed by the first letters of a series of terms. For instance, although you may not have known it, the word "laser" is actually an acronym for "light amplification by stimulated emissions of radiation," and "radar" is an acronym for "radio detection and ranging." If you took music lessons, you may know that FACE spells out the names of the notes that appear in the spaces on the treble clef music staff ("F," "A," "C," and "E," starting at the bottom of the staff).
>
> The benefit of acronyms is that they help us to recall a complete list of steps or items. P.O.W.E.R. stands for—well, by this point in the book, you probably remember.
>
> After learning to use the acronym "FACE" to remember the notes on the spaces of the music staff, many beginning musicians learn that the names of the lines on the staff form the acrostic, "Every Good Boy Deserves Fudge." An **acrostic** is a sentence in which the first letters spell out something that needs to be recalled. The benefits—as well as the drawbacks—of acrostics are similar to those of acronyms. (You can explore acronyms and acrostics in **Try It 5.)**

Rehearsal
The process of practicing and learning material to transfer it into memory

Mnemonics
Formal techniques used to make material more readily remembered

Acronyms
A word or phrase formed by the first letters of a series of terms

Acrostic
A sentence in which the first letters of the words correspond to material that is to be remembered

Try It!

POWER

5

Do-It-Yourself Acronyms and Acrostics

In the first part of this Try It, work individually to create an acronym and an acrostic.

1. Figure out an acronym to remind you of the names of the five Great Lakes, using the first letters of their names (which are Erie, Huron, Michigan, Ontario, Superior).

2. Devise an acrostic for the nine planets in order of their average distance from the sun. Their names, in order, are Mercury, Venus, Earth, Mars, Jupiter, Saturn, Uranus, Neptune, Pluto. (Bonus question: Because many astronomers no longer believe Pluto is a planet, devise an acrostic that omits Pluto and just contains the first eight planets.)

After you've tried to create the acronym and acrostic, meet in a group and discuss these questions: How successful were you in devising effective acronyms and acrostics? Do some of the group members' creations seem more effective than others? Why? Is the act of creating them an important component of helping to remember what they represent, or would having them created by someone else be as helpful in recalling them? For your information, a common acronym for the Great Lakes is HOMES (**H**uron, **O**ntario, **M**ichigan, **E**rie, **S**uperior), and a traditional acrostic for the order of the planets is **M**y **V**ery **E**ducated **M**other **J**ust **S**erved **U**s **N**ine **P**izzas. (As for the bonus question that omits Pluto, future generations may use the acrostic **M**y **V**ery **E**ducated **M**other **J**ust **S**erved **U**s **N**oodles.)

To Try It online, go to **www.mhhe.com/power**.

Although mnemonics are helpful, keep in mind that they have a number of significant shortcomings. First, they don't focus on the meaning of the items being remembered. Because information that is learned in terms of its surface characteristics—such as first letters that form a word—is less likely to be retained than information that is learned in terms of its meaning, mnemonic devices are an imperfect route to memorization.

There's another problem with mnemonics: Sometimes it takes as much effort to create a mnemonic device as it would to memorize the material in the first place. And because the mnemonic itself has no meaning, it can be forgotten.

Despite their drawbacks, mnemonics can be useful. They are particularly helpful when the material being memorized includes a list of items or a series of steps.

▸ **Involve multiple senses.** The more senses you can involve when you're trying to learn new material, the better you'll be able to remember. Here's why: Every time we encounter new information, all of our senses are potentially at work. For instance, if we witness a car crash, we receive sensory input from the sight of the two cars hitting each other, the sound of the impact, and perhaps the smell of burning rubber. Each piece of sensory information is stored in a separate location in the brain, and yet all the pieces are linked together in extraordinarily intricate ways.

What this means is that when we seek to remember the details of the crash, recalling a memory of one of the sensory experiences—such as what we heard—can trigger recall of the other types of memories. For example, thinking about the *sound* the two cars made when they hit can bring back memories of the way the scene looked.

When you learn something, use your body. Don't sit passively at your desk. Instead, move around. Stand up; sit down. Touch the page. Trace figures with your fingers. Talk to yourself. Think out loud. It may seem strange, but doing this increases the number of ways in which the information is stored.

> **Visualize. Visualization** is a technique by which images are formed to ensure that material is recalled. For instance, memory requires three basic steps: the initial recording of information, the storage of that information, and, ultimately, the retrieval of the stored information. As you read the three steps, you probably see them as logical and straightforward processes. But how do you remember them?

You might visualize a computer, with its keyboard, disks, and monitor (see **Figure 5.3**). The keyboard represents the initial recording of information. The disk represents the storage of information, and the monitor represents the display of information that has been retrieved from memory. If you can put these images in your mind, it will help you to remember the three basic memory steps later.

> **Overlearning.** Think back to when you were learning your basic multiplication facts ($1 \times 1 = 1$; $2 \times 2 = 4$; and so forth). Let's suppose you had put each multiplication problem on a flash card, and you decided to go through your entire set of cards, trying to get every problem right.

The first time you went through the set of cards and answered all the problems correctly, would you feel as if you'd memorized them perfectly and that you'd never again make an error? You shouldn't. You would need several instances of perfect performance to be sure you had learned the multiplication facts completely.

Visualization

A memory technique by which images are formed to help recall material

Overlearning

Studying and rehearsing material past the point of initial mastery to the point at which recall becomes automatic

Lasting learning doesn't come until you have overlearned the material. **Overlearning** consists of studying and rehearsing material past the point of initial mastery. Through overlearning, recall becomes automatic. Rather than searching for a fact, going through mental contortions until perhaps the information surfaces, overlearning permits us to recall the information without even thinking about it.

To put the principle of overlearning to work, don't stop studying at the point when you can say to yourself, "Well,

figure 5.3
Visualizing Memory

Recording of information

Storage of information in memory

Display of information retrieved from memory

I'll probably pass this test." You may be right, but that's all you'll do—pass. Instead, spend extra time learning the material until it becomes as familiar as an old pair of jeans.

Dealing with Learning Disabilities

If you, like millions of people in the United States, have a learning disability of one sort or another, reading and remembering may prove to be particularly challenging. **Learning disabilities** are defined as difficulties in processing information when listening, speaking, reading, or writing; in most cases, learning disabilities are diagnosed when there is a discrepancy between learning potential and actual academic achievement.

One of the most common kinds of learning disabilities is *dyslexia,* a reading disability that produces the misperception of letters during reading and writing, unusual difficulty in sounding out letters, spelling difficulties, and confusion between right and left. Although its causes are not yet completely understood, one likely explanation is a problem in the part of the brain responsible for breaking words into the sound elements that make up language.

Another common disability is *attention deficit hyperactivity disorder* (or *ADHD*), which is marked by an inability to concentrate, inattention, and a low tolerance for frustration. For the 1 to 3 percent of adults who have ADHD, planning, staying on task, and maintaining interest present unusual challenges. These challenges are present not only in college, but they also affect job performance.

People with learning disabilities are sometimes viewed as unintelligent. Nothing could be further from the truth: There is no relationship between learning disabilities and IQ. For instance, dozens of well-known and highly accomplished individuals suffered from dyslexia, including physicist Albert Einstein, U.S. General George Patton, poet William Butler Yeats, and writer John Irving.

By the time they reach college, most people with learning disabilities have already been diagnosed. If you do have a diagnosed learning disability and you need special services, it is important to disclose your situation to your instructors and other college officials.

In some cases, students with learning disabilities have not been appropriately evaluated prior to college. If you have difficulties such as mixing up and reversing letters frequently and suspect that you have a learning disability, there usually is an office on campus that can provide you with guidance. One place to start is your college counseling or health center.

Many sorts of treatments, ranging from learning specific study strategies to the use of medication, can be effective in dealing with learning disabilities. In addition, colleges that accept support from the federal government have a legal obligation to provide people with diagnosed learning disabilities with appropriate support. This obligation is spelled out in the Americans with Disabilities Act, and it provides important legal protections.

However, just because you are having trouble with reading assignments doesn't automatically mean that you have a learning disability. Not only is the kind of reading you do in college more difficult than in other contexts, but there's also more of it. It's only when reading represents a persistent, long-term problem—one

Learning disabilities
Difficulties in processing information when listening, speaking, reading, or writing, characterized by a discrepancy between learning potential and actual academic achievement

A disability in no way dictates what sort of accomplishments you are capable of.

that won't go away no matter how much work you do—that a learning disability becomes a possible explanation.

>> LO 5.4   **E Evaluate**   # What Does It Mean? What Do I Know?

Evaluation is a crucial step in reading. You need to be able to answer the seemingly simple question: "What does all this mean?"

But there's another aspect to evaluation. You need to evaluate, truthfully and honestly, your own level of understanding. What do you know as a result of your reading? Evaluation, then, consists of the following steps:

> **Identify the main ideas and themes and their value *to you personally.*** Try to determine the take-home message of the material you've read. For example, the take-home message of a chapter on accounting ethics might be, "In the long run, honest accounting practices benefit the long-term health of any business."

From the perspective of . . .

AN EDITORIAL ASSISTANT The ability to discern what is important within what you read is a key job function for editors. How might you apply your reading evaluation skills to an author's first draft?

Sometimes the main ideas and themes are spelled out, and at other times you will have to deduce them for yourself. Evaluating the main ideas and themes in terms of how they relate to you personally will help you understand and remember them more easily.

> **Prioritize the ideas.** Of all the information that is presented, which is the most crucial to the main message and which is the least crucial? Make a list of the main topics covered and try to rank them in order of importance.

> **Think critically about the arguments presented in the reading.** Do they seem to make sense? Are the author's assertions reasonable? Are there any flaws in the arguments? Would authors with a different point of view dispute what is being said? How would they build their own arguments?

> **Pretend you are explaining the material (talking—out loud!—about the material) to a fellow classmate who missed the assignment.** This is one time when talking out loud when no one is around is not only normal, but beneficial. Summarize the material aloud, as if you were talking to another person.

Talking out loud does two things. First, it helps you identify weak spots in your understanding and recall. Talking to yourself will help you nail down concepts that are still not clear in your own mind. Second, and equally important, because you are transforming the written word into the spoken word, you are thinking about the information in another way, which will help you remember it better.

The Job of Reading

Memos. Annual reports. Instructions. Continuing education assignments. Professional journals.

Each of these items illustrates the importance of developing critical reading skills for on-the-job success. Virtually every job requires good reading expertise, and for some professions, reading is a central component. Polishing your reading skills now will pay big dividends when you enter the world of work. The better you are at absorbing and remembering written information, the better you'll be at carrying out your job.

For instance, in many corporations, vital information is transmitted through the written word, via e-mails, hard-copy memos, technical reports, or Web-based material. The job of repairing broken appliances or automobiles requires reading of numerous service manuals to master the complex computer diagnostic systems that are now standard equipment. Nurses and others in the health-care field must read journals and reports to keep up with the newest medical technologies.

Furthermore, because not all supervisors are effective writers, you'll sometimes need to read between the lines and draw inferences and conclusions about what you need to do. You should also keep in mind that there are significant cultural differences in the way in which people write and the type of language they use. Being sensitive to the cultural background of colleagues will permit you to more accurately interpret and understand what you are reading.

In short, reading is a skill that's required in virtually every profession. Developing the habit of reading critically while you are in college will pave the road for future career success.

> **Use in-text review questions and tests.** Many textbook chapters end with a quiz or a set of review questions about the material. Some have questions scattered throughout the chapter. Don't ignore them! Not only do such questions indicate what the writer of the book thought was important for you to learn, but they can also provide an excellent opportunity for evaluating your memory.

> **Team up with a friend or use a study group.** When it comes to evaluating your understanding of a reading, two heads (or more!) are often better than one. Working with a classmate or study group—especially others who may have a different preferred learning style from your own—can help you test the limits of your understanding and memory of material and assess areas in which you need work.

> **Be honest with yourself.** Most of us are able to read with our minds on cruise control. But the net result is not much different from not reading the passage at all. If you have drifted off while you've been reading, go back and reread the passage.

℞ Rethink   Getting It the Second Time

You're human, so—like the rest of us—when you finish a reading assignment you'd probably like nothing more than to heave a sigh of relief and put the book away.

By now you know that there's a crucial step you should take that will assist you in cementing what you've learned into memory: rethinking what you've read. If you do it within 24 hours of first reading the assignment, it can save you hours of work later.

The best way to rethink an assignment is to reread it, along with any notes you've taken. "Yeah, right," you're probably

> "Reading furnishes the mind only with materials of knowledge; it is thinking that makes what we read ours."
>
> **John Locke, author, *Of the Conduct of the Understanding*, 1706**

thinking. "Like I have time for that." The goal, though, is not a literal rereading. In fact, it isn't necessary to reread word for word. You already know what's important and what's not important, so you can skim some of the less important material. But it is wise to reread the more difficult and important material carefully, making sure that you fully understand what is being discussed and that you'll remember the key details.

What's most critical, though, is that you think deeply about the material, considering the take-home message of what you've read. You need to be sure that your understanding is complete and that you're able to answer any questions that you had earlier about the material. Rethinking should be the central activity as you reread the passage and your notes.

The benefits of rethinking the material can't be overstated. Rethinking transfers material from your short-term memory to your long-term memory. It solidifies information so that it will be remembered far better over the long haul.

Speaking of **Success**

NAME: **James S. Cook**

SCHOOL: **Art Institute of Houston, Houston, Texas**

James Cook readily admits he wasn't a very diligent student when in high school, skipping classes and not working very hard. He felt he would never make it to college.

His outlook would have almost become a reality if it were not for his love of art.

"I've always been an artistic person and had an eye for design," Cook said. "I started out doing graffiti on buildings, but I knew that I had to put my skills into an actual profession where I could succeed and not be the starving artist."

To further his education, he enrolled in the Art Institute of Houston, pursing a degree in graphic design. But he was not able to focus on his studies.

"I still had fuzzy goals, and I was stuck in trying to be social, instead of academic," he noted. "I wanted to succeed, but I wasn't fully engaged. If a class met three days a week, I'd be there for two and a half days."

He fell further and further behind, and became involved in activities that eventually led to a run-in with the law, causing Cook to drop out of college temporarily. However, it led Cook to turn his life around.

"I grew up and put away my childish ways," Cook said. "I hoped to return to the Art Institute, but I wasn't sure if they would let me back in."

Through the efforts of two administrators who saw his promise, Cook did return, with a new major in multimedia and Web design and, more important, with a new set of goals.

"The major thing I did was set a goal," he explained. "I said to myself that I'm going to graduate, and I'm going to do it on time. I also set little goals for myself along the way, helping me to know that I was on the right path.

"One of my main goals is to bring up my grade point average, which is now 3.1, to where I will qualify for the National Vocational Technical Honor Society, and I expect to do that the next quarter," he added. "Another goal is to use my hardheadedness within the system instead of against it."

Cook has kept busy. To support himself financially he has waited tables and has started a business designing Web sites and producing multimedia presentations. For spiritual support, he has become a youth leader in his church's youth ministry—in addition to carrying close to a full load of courses.

"Once I got back into school, my goals and focus were clear," Cook said. "I saw I could reach those goals. I knew I had to study and work hard in class."

Looking Back

What are the essential elements of successful reading?

› The most important aspect of reading is understanding, not speed. Finishing a reading assignment quickly is far less important than understanding it fully.

› One problem people have with reading is a limited attention span. However, attention span can be increased with self-awareness and practice.

How can I improve my concentration and read more effectively?

› Reading should be approached with a clear sense of purpose and goals, which will vary from assignment to assignment. Examining the frontmatter of a book and creating advance organizers is also useful.

› As your read, identify and focus on the key material you will need to remember later. Don't try to memorize everything you read.

› Maintain focus by breaking down the reading into small chunks, taking breaks as needed, dealing with distractions, and writing while reading.

What are some techniques I can use for memorizing large amounts of information?

› Many memory techniques are available to improve memorization. Rehearsal is a primary one, as is the use of mnemonics such as acronyms and acrostics.

› Other memory techniques are visualization and the use of multiple senses while learning new material.

› Overlearning is a basic principle of memorization.

How can I best retain what I have read?

› Understanding of reading assignments can be cemented in memory by identifying the main ideas, prioritizing them, thinking critically about the arguments, using in-text questions and tests, and explaining the writer's ideas to someone else.

› Quickly rereading assignments and notes taken on them can greatly help in solidifying memories of what has been read.

[KEY TERMS AND CONCEPTS]

[RESOURCES]

ON CAMPUS

If you are experiencing unusual difficulties in reading or remembering material, you may have a learning disability. If you suspect this is the case, take action. Many colleges have an office that deals specifically with learning disabilities. You can also talk to someone at your college's counseling center; he or she will arrange for you to be tested, which can determine whether you have a problem.

IN PRINT

The fourth edition of Joe Cortina and Janet Elder's book, *Opening Doors: Understanding College Reading* (McGraw-Hill, 2008), provides a complete set of guidelines for reading textbooks and other kinds of writing that you will encounter during college. Another useful volume is the seventh edition of *Breaking Through: College Reading* (Longman, 2009) by Brenda Smith.

In *Improving Your Memory* (Johns Hopkins, 2005), Janet Fogler and Lynn Stern provide an overview of practical tips on maximizing your memory. Barry Gordon and Lisa Berger provide insight into the functioning of memory and how to improve it in *Intelligent Memory* (Penguin, 2004).

Finally, *The Memory Doctor* by Douglas Mason and Spencer Smith (New Harbinger Publications, 2005) offers simple techniques for improving memory.

ON THE WEB

The following sites on the World Wide Web provide the opportunity to extend your learning about the material in this chapter. (Although the Web addresses were accurate at the time the book was printed, check the *P.O.W.E.R. Learning* Web site [**www.mhhe.com/power**] for any changes that may have occurred.)

> Increasing Textbook Reading Comprehension by Using SQ3R is the title of this site offered by Virginia Tech University (**www.ucc.vt.edu/lynch/TextbookReading.htm**). Offered here is a clear and detailed outline on how to use the SQ3R reading method, as well as links to other reading comprehension aids such as critical reading, proofreading, and selective reading.

> Need a mnemonic? Have one you'd like to share? Then just go to (**www.mnemonic-device.com/**) a new site devoted entirely to mnemonics. This fun and educational site covers a variety of subjects from astronomy to weather.

> Mind Tools, a bookstore specializing in works on memory, offers a number of free online articles (**www.mindtools.com/memory.html**) detailing methods for improving memory. It includes examples of how each technique can be applied to such topics as remembering lists and foreign languages.

TAKING IT TO THE NET

1 Go to a newspaper's Web site, such as that of *The New York Times* (**www.nyt.com**) or the *Atlanta Constitution* (**www.ajc.com**), and read one of the current editorials. Take notes on the editorial, concentrating on evaluating the strength of the argument(s). How persuasive was the editorial, and why?

2 Practice the rehearsal technique for storing information in memory. Go to Yahoo! (**dir.yahoo.com**) and click on "Regional" and again on "U.S. States." Click on your state, then on "Government," and finally on "Elected and Appointed Officials" to find the names of your state's U.S. senators. Repeat the names several times. Now explore another, unrelated site on the Web. After a few minutes, write down the names of your state's U.S. senators from memory. How did you do?

The Case of . . .
The Five-Hundred-Pound Reading Packet

The instructor dropped the thick packet of course readings on Delila Meade's desk. It landed with a loud *thunk*.

"We'll be reading this packet over the next four weeks," the instructor announced.

But staring at the packet, all Delila could think was, *I don't think I could even lift that, let alone read it in just a month!*

Sure, Delila thought, she was interested in the topics of the readings. They all dealt with the history of computer programming, and Delila was in college to get her degree in that same field. She told herself a lot of the information in the readings would probably be very useful, both in college and throughout her programming career.

But still—all Delila could focus on as she stared at the packet were nagging questions. How could she possibly read all of it in four weeks? How would she remember all that material for tests or on the job? And perhaps most urgently of all, how would she even get the massive packet home?

1. How would you advise Delila to prepare for her course reading?

2. How would you suggest Delila organize her time so she could finish the readings in the allotted four weeks?

3. How might Delila stay focused on her reading? How might she most effectively use writing as a way to accomplish her task?

4. What techniques might Delila use to memorize long lists or other key material from her reading?

5. In what ways can Delila use rethinking techniques to improve her understanding of the readings in the packet?

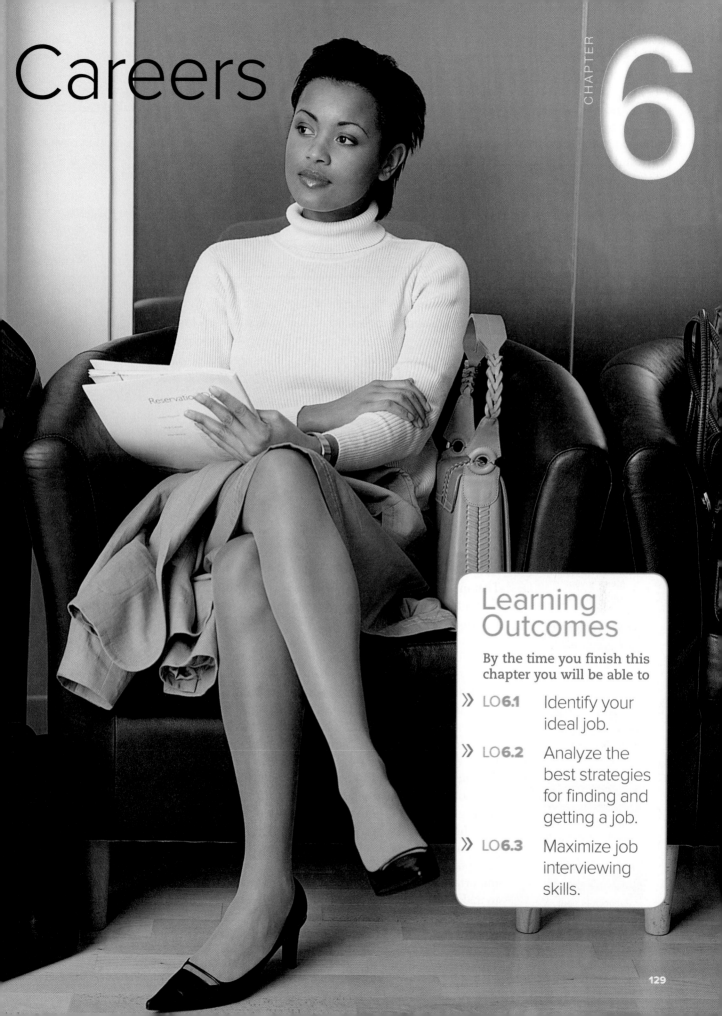

Careers

Learning Outcomes

By the time you finish this chapter you will be able to

» LO**6.1**   Identify your ideal job.

» LO**6.2**   Analyze the best strategies for finding and getting a job.

» LO**6.3**   Maximize job interviewing skills.

Michelle Edmunds felt ready for her first job interview. In fact, she felt more than ready.

The interview, for a position as a broker in a local real estate firm, had been scheduled the week before. And ever since then Michelle had been mentally preparing answer after answer about her background and about the position. She'd researched the real estate company online, reviewed her own job experience, and even scanned some real estate ads in the local newspaper to try to get a sense of the area real estate market.

But when the interviewer, seemingly out of the blue, asked her, "How many piano tuners are there in your home state?" she was clueless. How should she know? And, more to the point, what did that question have to do with being a real estate broker?

Looking Ahead

Luckily for Michelle, what she later called the "piano crisis" was a turning point. Once she got beyond her initial shock, she realized that the aim of the question was to test not her knowledge of piano tuners but her problem-solving skills. After first considering the population of her home state, and then guessing at how many of those people might own pianos, she was able to come up with a rough estimate of how many piano tuners there might be. The interviewer, clearly satisfied, moved on to other, more predictable questions.

Job interviews can be anxiety-producing events. But they are just one of a series of challenging activities that are part of the process of finding a job. In the last few chapters of *P.O.W.E.R. Learning,* we've been looking at skills that are usually applied in a classroom setting: notetaking, test-taking, and so forth. In this chapter, we explore strategies that will help you in the world of work. We address ways to identify your career goals and the best methods to achieve them. To put it simply, we consider the things you need to know to get the job you want.

≫LO 6.1 Career Planning

P Prepare
Identify your career goals

O Organize
Find career opportunities

W Work
Create a career portfolio

E Evaluate
Get feedback on your résumé and cover letter

R Rethink
Reconsider your career choices

P.O.W.E.R. Plan

At this point, you're in college to learn the skills to start down a specific career path. That means you've made up your mind about your career . . . right?

In fact, the answer is no. Even those on their way to acquiring training to work within a particular field need to think and plan carefully with regard to their professional ambitions.

For instance, imagine you are on your way to earning a degree in accounting. Clearly, you've made an important decision about your career. But consider these questions: Do you want to work independently or as an employee of a business? If you want to work for a business, would you rather it be a small company or a large corporation? Do you want a job that will pay less initially but at which you can advance, or would you rather trade the possibility of moving up the ladder for a better starting salary?

Further, do you want to work locally, or would you be willing to relocate for the right job? What kind of hours are you willing to work? What kind of hours *can* you work, given demands of family and other obligations?

These are just some of the questions people need to answer as they approach their careers. Keep in mind that you don't need to have all the answers right now. Few people know *exactly* how they'd like their professional lives to unfold. What's important to realize is that even if you've chosen a field, you still have lots of decisions to make and options to choose from as you pursue your career. Remember: Career planning is not a decision you make once. Rather, it is an ongoing process. (To explore your thinking about work and careers, complete the **Journal Reflections**.)

Journal Reflections

Thinking about Work

At some point in your life, you've almost surely had a job. Maybe you have one right now. And whether you realize it or not, there's no doubt you have developed some strong ideas about what it's like to work. Take some time now to consider your thoughts about work more fully.

1. What was most rewarding about the best job you ever had: the ability to earn money, social aspects involving your fellow employees, enjoyment of the work itself, or something else?

2. What would you see as the positive and negative aspects of supervising other people? Would you like to supervise others at some point in your career?

3. How important is the amount of money that you're paid for the work you do?

4. Do you see work as something you must do in order to earn a living, or something that is a central and important aspect of life in and of itself?

5. How important is variety in what you do? How important is stability in what you do?

 Prepare Identifying Your Career Goals

Some people take a job for the money. Some people take a job for the health benefits. Some people show up at work because they love to crunch numbers or treat patients or make filet mignon. Other people go to the office because they believe that hard work is the key to happiness.

These are all valid reasons for doing a job. As you think about the kind of job you want to find, it's essential to consider your own goals. Apart from what you might do during the day, do you want a job that helps others? A job that pays very well? One with flexible hours? Is having an impact on future generations important to you? Use **Try It 1** on page 132 to identify your long-term career goals.

 » LO 6.2 **Organize** Finding Career Opportunities

Research, research, research. That's the name of the game when it comes to charting your career. Even if you know the general direction you want your career to

Try It!

1 Identifying Your Long-Term Career Goals

Consider each of these areas as you determine your long-term goals:

- Achievement
- Advancement opportunities
- Challenge
- Contribution to society
- Control, power
- Creativity

- Financial
- Friendships with coworkers
- Helping others
- Independence
- Leadership
- Learning new things

- Loyalty
- Prestige
- Recognition from others
- Security
- Variety
- Working with others

Using this list, create a set of your three most important occupational goals. For example, three primary goals might be to (1) be challenged to reach my potential, (2) work with others in a cooperative environment, and (3) make a lasting contribution to society. However, don't be influenced by these examples—choose goals that are your own.

My Primary Career Goals Are to:

1.

2.

3.

Stating your career goals up front, even before you consider the range of jobs that you have to choose from, is important. Identifying your goals helps you know what it is that *you* want out of work. Future employers are more interested in what you bring to your job, rather than how well a job fulfills your important goals. It's crucial that you consider what has significance to you before making career decisions. If a career opportunity doesn't fulfill your major goals, it will not be a good choice for you.

take, you'll want to get a feel for the specific opportunities within your chosen field, as well as how your field is developing and changing.

Be sure to keep notes about what you find. Your notes don't have to be elaborately written or suitable for handing in to an instructor. Just keep them simple, legible, and organized, and make sure that they include the source of the information you're describing.

Books and Web Sites

A good first step in obtaining career information is the U.S. Department of Labor's *Occupational Outlook Handbook (OOH)*. The *OOH,* published every two years, categorizes occupations into 11 broad groupings. It provides information on kinds of work, working conditions, job outlook, earnings, education and training requirements, and expected job prospects.

You can also visit the Department of Labor Web site at **www.bls.gov/oco/,** which provides a wealth of additional information. Among the most interesting features of the Web site is a compilation of the most up-to-date information on the hottest professions, in terms of projected future growth. (This information, summarized in **Table 6.1** on page 134, must be used with care: The mere fact that a job is expanding rapidly doesn't necessarily mean that there are huge numbers of openings. A quickly growing profession may have only a few openings, and even with rapid growth, the absolute number of jobs may still be relatively small in coming years.)

From the perspective of . . .

A STUDENT Part of your growth as a student involves an honest assessment of career possibilities. What careers appeal to you most?

You are likely to find the *OOH,* and a wealth of other information, either in the career center of your college or in its library. In addition, almost every public library has a reference section on careers, and state employment centers often have extensive materials to help identify careers.

In addition to books, you may find CD-ROMs, pamphlets, and other helpful material at career centers, libraries, and employment centers. These resources also may offer on-site computers with software that can help you gather job-related information. For example, the *Discover Career Guidance and Information System* and *SIGI PLUS (System of Interactive Guidance and Information)* are widely used computer programs that have proven helpful to those engaged in career searches.

Home health-care aides, forensic science technicians, and dental hygienists are all career areas on the rise. Have you considered any of the careers on this list?

table 6.1 Fastest-Growing Occupations, 2006–2016

2006–2016 Predicted Typical Educational Occupation	Percentage Increase	Training Required
Network systems and data communications	53.4	Bachelor's degree
Personal and home care aides	50.6	Short-term on-the-job training
Home health aides	48.7	Short-term on-the-job training
Computer software engineers, applications	44.6	Bachelor's degree
Veterinary technologists and technicians	41.0	Associate degree
Personal financial advisors	41.0	Bachelor's degree
Makeup artists, theatrical and performance	39.8	Postsecondary vocational award
Medical assistants	35.4	Moderate-term on-the-job training
Veterinarians	35.0	First professional degree
Substance abuse and behavioral disorder counselors	34.3	Bachelor's degree
Skin care specialists	34.3	Postsecondary vocational award
Financial analysts	33.8	Bachelor's degree
Social and human service assistants	33.6	Moderate-term on-the-job training
Gaming surveillance officers and gaming investigators	33.6	Moderate-term on-the-job training
Physical therapist assistants	32.4	Associate degree
Pharmacy technicians	32.0	Moderate-term on-the-job training
Forensic science technicians	30.7	Bachelor's degree
Dental hygienists	30.1	Associate degree
Mental health counselors	30.0	Master's degree
Mental health and substance abuse social workers	29.9	Master's degree
Marriage and family therapists	29.8	Master's degree
Dental assistants	29.2	Moderate-term on-the-job training
Computer systems analysts	29.0	Bachelor's degree
Database administrators	28.6	Bachelor's degree
Computer software engineers, systems software	28.2	Bachelor's degree
Gaming and sports book writers and runners	28.0	Short-term on-the-job training
Environmental science and protection technicians, including health	28.0	Associate degree
Manicurists and pedicurists	27.6	Postsecondary vocational award
Physical therapists	27.1	Master's degree
Physician assistants	27.0	Master's degree

Source: U.S. Bureau of Labor Statistics, *Occupational Outlook Handbook,* 2008–09 edition.

Personal Interviews

To get an up-close-and-personal look at a profession, another strategy is to talk with people who are already in it. People love to talk about their jobs, whether they love them or hate them, so don't be afraid to ask for an interview. You don't need a lot of their time—just enough to get an inside view of what it's like to work in their profession. Some questions you might want to ask:

> What's your typical day like?
> How did you find your job?
> What are the best and worst aspects of being in your profession?
> What do you look for in someone who wants to enter your field?

Keep in mind, of course, that the answers you get will be the opinions of one individual, reflecting his or her unique, personal experience. That's why it is a good idea to talk to several practitioners of a particular occupation, and to consider what they say in the context of other research that you have conducted.

Be sure to write a thank-you note following an interview. Not only is it a common courtesy, but it also serves the additional purpose of reinforcing who you are and your interest in their profession. You never know: One day, they might have a job opening, and you might want to ask them for a job!

 ## Creating a Career Portfolio

The research you've done on career options forms the foundation for creating a Career Development Portfolio. A **Career Portfolio** is a dynamic record that documents your skills, capabilities, achievements, and goals, as well as provides a place to keep notes, ideas, and research findings related to careers. Such a portfolio will provide an easy-to-access history of your job-related activities, and it will include material that will be helpful for you and, later, for potential employers. You'll want to keep and update your Career Portfolio as long as you are pursuing a career.

Your Career Portfolio will consist of two main parts. The first part, background information, will hold information to help you keep track of your accomplishments and notes on your research; the second part, which includes your résumé and cover letter, will be material that you share with potential employers.

Your Career Portfolio can either be in the form of a traditional, hard-copy version, or you can create an e-Portfolio online. Some colleges provide online templates or "wizards" that guide you through the process of creating a Career Portfolio. E-Portfolios have the advantage of being easily modified, and—since they reside on the Web—they are accessible anywhere you have access to the Web.

Career Portfolio

A dynamic record that documents your skills, capabilities, achievements, and goals, as well as provides a place to keep notes, ideas, and research findings related to careers

Career Portfolio Part I: Background Information

The information in this section of your Portfolio is meant to help you make career-related decisions and record your thinking about your career. This part is for your eyes only. Although you will draw on the material for the "public" part of your Portfolio that potential employers will see, think of it as your own, private repository of information.

> **Basic personal data.** Keep a record of data and identification numbers that you think you'll never forget—but, even with the best intentions, you probably

Instructors as Career Guides

Each of your instructors has a job—that of college instructor. But despite the similarity in job title, each got that job in a different way, using different tactics and strategies. Each followed his or her own particular career path and has a distinct educational background. Furthermore, your instructors may have had a variety of positions, and possibly a number of previous careers, prior to becoming a college instructor.

You can learn a great deal about career opportunities and the process of getting a job by talking to your course instructors about their own careers. Set up an appointment with each of your course instructors, and ask questions such as these:

- What is your educational and professional background?
- How did you get your current job?
- What students have you had that have been particularly successful careerwise? What qualities did they have that set them apart from other students of yours?
- What general advice do you have for someone looking for a job?
- Knowing me from your course, what skills would you encourage me to work on and develop in order to increase my chances of successfully getting a job?

You can gain valuable insights into navigating a career from your course instructors. Furthermore, talking with your course instructors can help you get to know them better, and it may eventually pave the way for your course instructors to provide letters of recommendation. Instructors also sometimes get leads on jobs, and if they know your career goals, they may pass the leads on to you. Finally, if you build a relationship with your instructor, it may help you do better academically in your course—no small benefit!

---

will not remember at the least opportune moment. For example, include your social security number, addresses (home and college), college ID number, and telephone numbers. If you're a renter, keep a record of your landlord's name and address; you might need a credit reference one day.

▸ **Career research notes.** Whether you have notes collected from books, Web-based research, or interviews with people in a particular occupation, they belong in your Career Portfolio. They will provide a record of your career-related activities.

▸ **Syllabus and outline from courses you have taken.** Include a copy of the syllabus and course outline of every course you take, along with the grade you received in the course. The information contained in a course syllabus and outline will serve to jog your memory about the material the course covered. Without these materials, you're at the mercy of your memory when you're trying to recall the content of a course you may have taken several years earlier and that has direct relevance to your career.

For further documentation relating to your courses, you could include a copy of the course description from the college catalog and, if the class had a list of competencies that students were to attain, a copy of these as well.

▸ **Transcripts.** Include the most recent version of your transcript, listing the courses that you took, credits earned, and grades you received in your classes.

▸ **Your personal history.** If someone were to write your biography, what are the key events that you'd want him or her to know about?

The events that would be included in your biography can form the core of a list that you should make of every significant experience you've had. Although the list should include every employment-related experience you've had, even part-time jobs or summer jobs when you were in high school, don't limit yourself only to job experiences. Also include other accomplishments, such as the community service you perform. Personal events that have had a major impact on who you are should also earn a place in your personal history, such as the car accident you had or notable athletic achievements. Use **Try It 2** on page 138 to help make this list, which you'll use later to create a résumé.

- ▶ **Long-term career goals.** Your Career Portfolio should have the statement of your long-term career goals that you developed in Try It 1.

- ▶ **Writing samples.** Add examples of your best writing. These can be papers that you've handed in for classes or other writing you have done on your own or on the job. The idea is to have a sample of your writing easily available should a potential employer ask for one.

- ▶ **Credentials.** Include copies of any credentials you have earned. For example, place in the portfolio a copy of diplomas you have earned, certificates of workshop or training participation you have received, proof of noncredit continuing education courses you have taken, and the like. You never know when an employer might want to see documentation of your accomplishments.

Career Portfolio Part II: Résumé and Cover Letter

This section of your Career Portfolio encompasses information that you will share with potential employers. Whereas the material in the first part of your portfolio provides the background for your career planning, this is the public face of your portfolio.

Think of the components of the first part as the equivalent of the backstage of a play, with a director and crew working behind the scenes to pull things together. In contrast, this second part of the portfolio is the play the audience sees, the part that should proceed flawlessly. You want the critics to offer nothing less than raves for your production.

The two primary elements that belong in the second part of your Career Portfolio are your résumé and your cover letter.

Résumé

A résumé (pronounced res-oo-may) is a brief summary of your qualifications for a job. It is the first thing that potential employers see and should serve to arouse their interest. Actually, a human may not even initially see it: An increasing number of employers use computers to screen résumés. The computers look for key skills, and if they are lacking, they send an automatic rejection.

Consequently, the résumé must be crafted with great precision and care. If you've created a personal history statement earlier for Part I of your Career Portfolio, use it to get started.

The key elements of a résumé include the following and are illustrated in a sample résumé in **Figure 6.1** on page 139.

- ▶ **Contact information.** Include your name, address (current and permanent if they're different), phone number(s), and e-mail address. *Don't* include your sex, age, race, or marital status. Not only are they irrelevant, but employers who take them into consideration are breaking antidiscrimination laws.

- ▶ **Job objective.** If you are targeting a specific job, include a specific objective (such as, "to obtain a position as a buyer for a major retail department store").

Try It!

2

Cataloging Your Personal History

	Activity or Event	When Activity or Event Took Place	Where Event Occurred (e.g., company, hospital, social agency)	Responsibilities or Actions Performed	Skills or Talents Used	Achievements, Results, or Insights
Did you work during or before high school?						
Were you a member of any clubs or other organizations in high school?						
How many paid jobs have you held since high school?						
Have you performed any community service?						
Have you provided any services to a religious institution?						
Are you working, while at college?						
Are you in any clubs or organizations at college?						
Have you had any personally significant life experiences?						
Have you ever been called upon to exercise skills or talents you didn't know you had?						
Have you ever solved a tough problem and felt great satisfaction?						
Have you ever worked in a group to solve a problem?						
Have you ever organized a complex task on your own?						
Have you ever led a group in the performance of a large task?						
What is the best thing you have ever done?						

 WORKING IN A GROUP

Compare your responses to those of other students in the group. What are the unique capabilities that you have, the things that set you apart from others in the group? How could you take advantage of those unique capabilities when you are seeking a job?

figure 6.1
Sample Résumé

However, if you're willing to be flexible, provide a more general job objective (for example, "to obtain an entry-level position in retail sales").

> **Education.** Include the colleges you've attended or are currently attending, with the actual or anticipated year of graduation and degree earned.

> **Awards and honors.** If you've won any awards or honors (such as membership in an honors program or inclusion on the Dean's List) mention them. If you have none that you want to include, leave this category off your résumé.

> **Campus and community activities.** Include activities in which you've participated, and indicate any in which you've had a leadership role. You want to demonstrate that you are an involved, contributing member of your community.

> **Professional memberships.** Do you belong to any professional organizations that are relevant to the job you'll be seeking? If so, include them.

> **Work experience.** List your experience, starting with your most recent job and working backward. Include the job title, dates, and your major on-the-job responsibilities.

> *Don't* feel you need to include every job you're ever held (for example, leave out the occasional pet sitting). Instead, focus on the key positions that illustrate your ability to hold a job and to carry out responsibilities. Furthermore, as you present your work experience, always remember that the focus should be on how your past work can get you a job in the profession you want in the future.

> **Particular skills.** Do you know how to program in Linux? Can you speak Spanish fluently? Are you a certified lifeguard? Can you use an Excel spreadsheet or PowerPoint?

> Include a brief list of the special skills you have. Once again, make sure that the skills you list are related to the job you're seeking. For example, if you're seeking a job in information technology, Linux programming is relevant, but it may not be if you're looking for a job in medical services.

> **References.** A "reference" category is optional, but if you include it simply say "References available upon request." Don't list specific names, but have them available should you be asked for them. (We'll discuss whom to ask and how to obtain references later in the chapter.)

As you create a résumé, keep in mind some general rules. First, keep it short. In a résumé, less is more. Generally, résumés should be no longer than one page.

Second, make it look good. Your résumé should appear professional. Use plenty of white space, with one-inch margins on every side. Use strong action words, such as those in **Table 6.2.** Avoid articles (such as "the," "a," and "an") and pronouns (such as "I" or "we"); don't write in full sentences.

Finally, proofread, proofread, proofread. You want to be sure that no typographical errors or misspellings find their way into your résumé.

The same rules hold for the second element of Part II of your Career Portfolio, your cover letter, which we discuss next. Before moving on, though, get a start on creating a résumé by completing **Try It 3** on page 142.

Cover Letter

Although your résumé is the centerpiece of your presentation to potential employers, your cover letter is no less important. It shows that you can string words together into well-crafted sentences, and it gives you the opportunity to bring life to the list of qualifications on your résumé. It also gives you the opportunity to say how enthusiastic you are about the job for which you're applying and to illustrate how well your qualifications match the job requirements.

In writing a cover letter, keep in mind the perspective of the person who is reading it. Potential employers have a problem that they need to solve: identifying someone to do work that they need done so much that they're willing to pay someone to do it. The better you can provide them with a solution to this problem, the more attractive you will be.

What this means is that your cover letter should be oriented toward helping employers solve *their* problem, not toward how the job will solve *your* problems. Consequently, don't talk about how you think the job will fulfill you as

table 6.2　Action Words

Using strong action words and making sentences short will help you prepare a professional and eye-catching résumé. Here is a list of action words to get you started. Use words that best describe what you do and who you are.

Achieved	Directed	Investigated
Administered	Discovered	Launched
Advised	Drafted	Led
Aided	Edited	Managed
Approved	Educated	Moderated
Arranged	Enabled	Monitored
Archived	Established	Negotiated
Assigned	Evaluated	Operated
Assisted	Examined	Organized
Authored	Expanded	Oversaw
Budgeted	Expedited	Performed
Built	Extracted	Recommended
Calculated	Facilitated	Recruited
Cataloged	Fashioned	Regulated
Chaired	Granted	Remodeled
Classified	Forecasted	Reported
Coached	Formulated	Restored
Collected	Founded	Reversed
Compiled	Generated	Reviewed
Computed	Guided	Saved
Conducted	Identified	Scheduled
Contracted	Illustrated	Solved
Controlled	Improved	Strengthened
Coordinated	Increased	Summarized
Counseled	Influenced	Supervised
Created	Informed	Trained
Critiqued	Initiated	Translated
Delegated	Inspected	Trimmed
Demonstrated	Installed	Tutored
Designated	Instituted	Upgraded
Designed	Instructed	Validated
Developed	Integrated	Worked
Devised	Interviewed	Wrote
Diagnosed	Invented	

a person or how much you need it to pay your bills. Instead, orient your letter toward describing how well your own unique qualifications match the specific job requirements.

POWER Try It!

3

Creating a Résumé

It's time to use some of the pieces you have been thinking about and working on to create a résumé. You have explored your ideas about your occupational goals **(Try It 1)**, and you have gathered important elements of your personal history **(Try It 2)**. Now put the pieces together by filling in the worksheet below. Then use the worksheet to create a clean, one-page résumé that you can have reviewed and proofread.

Contact Information:

Your name, address, phone number(s), and e-mail address.

Job Objective:

Use your ideas about your occupational goals. Write one statement, beginning with the word "To," that sums up your goals. Be specific ONLY if you are applying for a job you understand and want to focus on; otherwise, state your goals broadly and generally.

Education:

List any colleges attended, including your current college, starting with the most recent. If you have taken college courses without being formally enrolled, list those too.

Awards and Honors (Optional):

List any honors you have received. Academic honors are of primary importance, but honors and awards from social, religious, and community groups (e.g., 4-H, Red Cross, Rotary Club) may be worth including if they testify to personal characteristics that may help you gain employment, such as leadership, perseverance, or a sense of civic duty.

Campus and Community Activities (Optional):

List any clubs, teams, or activities in which you participated since high school. Include high school activities only if they were significant and are related to your career goals. Also list community activities in which you have participated, especially those in which you had a leadership role.

Professional Memberships (Optional):

List any professional organizations related to your career goals of which you are or have been a member. Professional organizations are groups such as the Modern Language Association; any of a number of national honor societies; the National Student Speech, Language, and Hearing Association; National Art Education Association; Student Sports Medicine Association; and the like.

Work Experience (If You've Had Any):

List all jobs you have had, including paid jobs (on campus and off), apprenticeships, internships, and similar "real" jobs. List your most recent work experience first and work backward through time. Include the title of the job, organization for which you worked, dates of work, and major responsibilities. Understand that you may be asked about any of the jobs you list, including your reasons for moving to the next job.

Particular Skills (Optional):

List anything you are particularly good at that might transfer to a work setting; for example, the ability to speak a foreign language, to fix computer hardware problems, to write and debug software programs, to repair engines, to create Web sites, and so forth. You can draw this list from your academic, work, and even personal/recreational life.

References:

Available on request.

July 29, 2010

Mr. Reginald Pelly
Assistant Vice President
WorldWide Publishing Corp
New York, NY 10011

Dear Mr. Pelly:

Jennifer Windsor, Director of Editorial Development at WorldWide Publishing, advised me of an opening in your company for an entry-level trade book editor. From my enclosed résumé, you will find that both my experience and my education fully meet the requirements you have outlined for the position.

My current position as a copy editor at a medium-sized daily newspaper has given me experience in dealing with deadlines and working closely with others. Having served as a reporter for six years, I can relate to the needs of writers as well. My colleagues consider me both outgoing and diplomatic, traits that have served me well in my work as an editor.

I will contact you Monday to learn when we can meet for an interview.

Sincerely,

Martina L. Veschova

Enclosure: Résumé

figure 6.2
Two Sample Cover Letters

Although every cover letter should be tailor-written to a specific position (see the two sample letters in **Figure 6.2,** they typically contain the following elements:

> **Introduction: Catching the reader.** Describe why you are writing, how you learned about the job, and why you are interested in it. Emphasize the connection between the position requirements and your qualifications.

> **Letter body: Drawing in the reader.** Here's where you describe, in very brief terms, who you are and what makes you unique. Highlight major accomplishments and qualifications from your personal history, making the argument that your skills are a close match to the job. Show enthusiasm!

Martin L. Chen

14A Orchard Street
Boise, Idaho 83702   email: marlchen@mrnr.com   Phone: 207 889-3763

July 29, 2010

Ms. Arlene Washington
Director, Human Services
Mercy General Hospital
18 Medical Plaza
Chicago, IL 60604

Dear Ms. Washington:

I am writing in response to the position advertised July 22, 2007, in the *Chicago Tribune* seeking a Lead Cost Analyst Accountant. My professional experience and education match well with the position requirements listed. Enclosed is my résumé.

In addition to being self-motivated, I work well under pressure and welcome new challenges and opportunities. Among some of my accomplishments are the following:

- Analyzed, defined, and produced appropriate budgets for wages and salary costs, materials, expenses, and workload.
- Provided extensive, timely, and appropriate reporting for all aspects of the various budgets.
- Investigated variations from budget.
- Performed cost benefit analyses and assisted with capital expenditure proposals.

My experience in supervising a team of four co-workers has taught me patience and has strengthened my organizational skills. My greatest satisfaction in a job comes from selecting, training, and motivating personnel. I believe I have the qualities that can help a department become more efficient and productive.

I am familiar with Mercy General Hospital from news stories on breakthrough cancer research conducted there, and I have further researched your hospital and its contributions to medicine. I feel there is a good fit between my career goals and your needs. I welcome the opportunity to discuss the position further, and look forward to hearing from you soon. Thank you for your consideration.

Yours truly,

Martin L. Chen

Enclosure

figure 6.2
Two Sample Cover Letters (*concluded*)

You can also include information that does not appear on your résumé; for instance, if you paid for your education entirely on your own, mention that fact. In addition, you can write about what you hope to accomplish on the job.

Finally, show that you know something about the organization to which you are applying. Do some homework to learn about the employer, and state specifically what you find attractive about them.

▸ **Conclusion: A call for action.** End the letter by restating your interest in the position and suggesting that you would like to discuss the position further.

State that you are available to meet for an interview. Thank the employer for considering your application.

Like your résumé, the cover letter should read well and look good. Before you send it, be sure to proofread it carefully.

The point of including a sample cover letter in your Career Portfolio is to be ready at a moment's notice to revise the sample and send it off. Job opportunities sometimes appear unexpectedly, and it will be much easier for you to respond quickly, and respond well, if you already have a sample letter on file.

Unless you are certain of the job you'll be seeking in the future, you might want to prepare several cover letters, targeted at the different job possibilities you are considering. In addition, the act of writing cover letters for a variety of professions may actually help you come to a decision regarding the path you ultimately choose to follow.

One final note about your Career Portfolio: Keep in mind that it is a work in progress, a living document that is meant to be revised as your interests and aspirations change. That's why it may be a good idea to keep your Career Portfolio in virtual form, rather than as a hard copy. By creating an e-Portfolio, you will be able to make revisions easily. An e-Portfolio also simplifies the process of producing your résumé and cover letter for an actual job opening.

 ## Getting Feedback on Your Résumé and Cover Letter

After you have created the key elements of your Career Portfolio—your résumé and cover letter—it's time to evaluate their effectiveness. Start by asking a trusted person, such as one of your course instructors or someone on the staff of your college's career center, to review what you've created. Ask them to provide honest and concrete suggestions, because the more feedback you receive, the better the finished product will be.

Once you've received an initial review, one of the best strategies is to ask individuals working in the field in which you're interested to review your résumé and cover letter. Requesting feedback from one or two people who are already working in your desired profession, particularly if they have hired people in the past, serves several purposes. First, your reviewers will be in the best position to know what employers are looking for, and they can tell you how to present yourself most effectively. Not only can they help you say the right things, but they can also help you avoid saying the wrong thing.

But there's an extra bonus from seeking advice from someone currently working in the field: You become a known quantity to them, and at some point in the future they may have a job opening and you may spring to mind. Or if you contact them in the future, they may be able to steer you to a job opening.

 ## Reconsidering Your Career Choices

Going through the process of identifying your goals, researching careers, and building a Career Portfolio may lead you to solidify your ideas about which occupation you'd like to pursue. That's great—that's the point of career exploration.

But even if you are sure about what you intend to do professionally, it's important to take some time to reconsider your choices. The most important thing is to avoid what psychologists call "foreclosure." Foreclosure is making a premature decision and sticking with it so persistently that you ignore other possibilities, even ones that hold considerable promise. Keeping an open mind by reconsidering your choices will help you be sure that you've made the best decisions.

From the perspective of . . .

A SECOND-CAREER EMPLOYEE It is possible to work for years in one field before deciding on a new career path. What are some things to consider if you are contemplating a second career?

What if you haven't been able to narrow things down? What if you're still completely up in the air about what path you'd like to pursue? First, realize that it's natural to be undecided. It's almost inevitable that you'll have some uncertainty with regard to decisions as important as where you work.

Also, keep in mind that even if you are certain about the general shape you want your career to take, there will inevitably be moments of backtracking and reconsideration. Very few people take one job at one organization and work there until they retire. The point is that you will have many opportunities to rethink your decisions. Don't feel that any one decision will forever shape the rest of your career, or your life.

If you're close to the point where you need to start work, and you still don't have a clue about what you want to do, then maybe you need to rethink your approach. Assuming you've considered various possibilities, you may want to reconsider the career-planning strategies you've been using. Ask yourself these questions:

> ➤ Have you been too restrictive or too selective in considering possibilities?
> ➤ Have you done sufficient research?
> ➤ Have you rejected job opportunities that seem somewhat interesting without carefully considering what they have to offer?
> ➤ Have you underestimated (or overestimated) your skills?
> ➤ Have you taken full advantage of all the resources your college offers in terms of career planning?

"Your true pilot cares nothing about anything on earth but the river, and his pride in his occupation surpasses the pride of kings."
Mark Twain, author, *Life on the Mississippi*, 1883

Your References:
Who Says What About You

Getting the job you want sometimes can hinge less on what you say about yourself and more on what others say about you. A good reference can make the difference between getting a job and getting passed over. A bad reference can destroy your chances of being offered a position.

That's why finding just the right people to supply potential employers with a reference can be the key to obtaining the job you want. That's why it's critical to identify people who are willing to speak on your behalf well before you face a deadline.

Identifying People to Provide References

Several categories of individuals can provide you references, including:

> Former job supervisors

> Colleagues in previous positions

> Class instructors

> Community service supervisors

> Coaches, club advisers, or heads of professional groups to which you belong

> People who can provide character references (e.g., clergy)

The most effective references come from people who know you well—very well—and can speak to your skills, abilities, accomplishments, motivation, and character. In addition, people who can speak to the specific requirements of the job you're seeking (especially those who have worked with you in environments similar to that of the potential job) are highly effective.

The least effective references are those from family members or friends or, even worse, friends of friends. For instance, a reference from someone famous who happens to play tennis occasionally with your uncle will rarely be helpful, unless that person knows you well. Remember a key rule of references: The ability of a reference provider to describe in detail *your* strengths and *your* accomplishments is considerably more important than the identity of the reference provider, whatever *his or her* strengths and accomplishments.

The necessity of having people to act as references points out the importance of networking. Even while you're in college, it's critical to build up a network of people who can vouch for you. To network effectively, be sure to keep in touch with people who know and like you. And try to expand your network of contacts. For example, whenever you're at a social event, talk to people you don't know and don't just hang out with people you're familiar with.

Asking for a Reference

When choosing someone to be a reference, **always ask permission.** Never give out the names of people who you think will provide references without asking them beforehand. Not only is seeking permission common courtesy, but asking first avoids violating another rule of references: *No reference is better than a bad reference.* You need to check that the reference someone provides will be an explicitly positive one.

Although you can't directly ask someone if they can provide a positive reference (it's very hard for someone to tell you straight out that they can't), you can approach the issue indirectly. When asking someone to serve as a reference, ask them if they have any reservations. If they do, no matter how minor, turn to someone else to provide the recommendation.

You should also offer some guidelines for those providing recommendations. Let them know why you're asking them in particular, and remind them of the context in which they've known you. If there is something you'd like them to specifically address in providing you with a reference—such as, for example, the unusual creativity you showed in a previous position or the fact that you wrote exceptionally good papers in a class—let them know. The more explicit information you can provide them, the better.

Starting Over: Once You Have a Job You Want

What's the best time to start looking for a job? When you already have one and don't need to find a new position.

Even if you feel happy and secure in your job, it makes sense to be prepared for the unexpected. Perhaps you'll get a new boss whom you can't work with, or your current job's activities and requirements change for the worse. Or maybe the company will downsize or be merged with another corporation, causing widespread layoffs.

For a variety of reasons, then, you'll want to keep your résumé and Career Portfolio updated, even if you've just started a new job. You will want to stay in contact with the people who have provided you with references in the past.

Above all, take every opportunity to learn new skills. As the economy and technology change, you'll want to have cutting-edge skills that will allow you to compete effectively.

In short: Be prepared!

Using the Web in Your Job Hunt

The Web has changed some of the rules for conducting a job search. It permits you to post your résumé and have the potential for thousands of possible employers to screen it. It also permits employers to post their job needs and have the potential for thousands of possible employees to see them. You can even apply for jobs online. Internet services can help you to conduct automated searches, exposing you to job listings in your chosen field and receiving e-mails containing job postings that fit your skills.

The advantages of electronic job searches—such as the potentially wide exposure of your résumé—come at some potential costs. First, your résumé quite likely will be "read" by a computer. That means you must be extremely precise and follow some specific stylistic rules to avoid its being misread or ignored. Second, there are security issues, since you never know who may be reading your résumé.

In using the Web for a job search, you need to cast your net widely. Although general interest job sites such as **monster.com** and **careerbuilder.com** post millions of jobs each year, there are more focused boards that can help you identify possible jobs in specific industries (see **Table 6.3** on page 150). In addition, most large companies post job openings on their own Web sites.

There are several general guidelines to follow when posting your résumé on an online employment site:

> Be very precise in the words you employ. For example, use action verbs and other words that are standard within an industry.

> Use simple type styles, such as Arial or Times New Roman.

> Avoid elaborate formatting, such as tabs or italics.

> Use a standard 80 characters per line.

> As always, proofread, proofread, proofread. A typographical error is more than embarrassing: Computers screening your résumé may reject your application before a human ever sees it because they do not recognize a misspelled word.

table 6.3 Finding the Right Site on the Web[1]

Specific Sites	
www.HigherEdJobs.com	Teaching
www.EngineerJobs.com	Engineering
www.ShowBizJobs.com	Acting
www.Medzilla.com	Doctors, nurses
www.RXCareerCenter.com	Pharmaceuticals
www.HR.com	Human resources
www.dice.com	Information technology
www.LegalStaff.com	Legal
www.AgCareers.com	Agriculture

»LO6.3 Job Interviews:
Putting Your Best Foot Forward

For a potential employer who has never met you, a job interview puts a face to what has previously been an impression based on mere words written on a page. The interview is your chance to show who you are, to demonstrate your enthusiasm for a potential position, and to exhibit what you can bring to a position.

The fact that interviews are so important may make them seem intimidating and overwhelming. However, remember that the mere fact that you've been invited to an interview means you've overcome some of the highest hurdles already. Furthermore, you can follow a variety of concrete strategies to ensure that you maximize the opportunity an interview presents. Among the most important are the following.

Before the Interview

▸ **Learn about the potential employer.** It's important to learn as much as you can about the position and the company that is offering it. Go to the potential employer's Web site and find out as much as you can about the organization's management style and company culture. Then try to find magazine and newspaper articles to gain a sense of the success and effectiveness of the organization. The bottom line: If an interviewer asks, "What do you know about our organization?" be prepared to answer, "Quite a bit, because I've researched it thoroughly."

▸ **Prepare with questions.** Come to the interview prepared with questions. Think up a set of questions and write them down so you can remember them—it's perfectly fine to refer to them during the interview. Having targeted questions shows that you've spent time thinking about the position. (Don't ask about salary during the interview; salary issues are usually addressed if you get an actual job offer.)

▸ **Prepare answers.** Finally, come prepared with answers to likely questions. For instance, it shouldn't be a surprise if an interviewer asks you to "tell me about yourself." So have an answer ready, a two- or three-minute response that touches on your career goals, your skills, your experiences, and your personality. Obviously, this is a lot to cover in just a few minutes, so practice it until you can do it comfortably within that short time frame. Going longer than three minutes runs the risk of boring your interviewer. Furthermore, don't just practice it by yourself. Have someone else listen to it and give you feedback.

Other favorite interview questions include "What are your major strengths and weaknesses?" "Why do you want to leave your current position?" "What are your major qualifications?" "What are your short-term and long-range goals?" and "Why should I hire you?" Although you can't prepare for every possible question in advance, thinking through some of the most likely possibilities will help you feel more confident and ready to deliver polished responses.

During the Interview

> **Be punctual.** Allow yourself enough time to arrive well ahead of the scheduled interview. That will help you find a parking space, locate the building and room, and generally get composed.

> **Dress appropriately.** Wear the right clothes for the interview. Stop by beforehand to see how people dress. If you're unsure of how formal to be, keep in mind that it's almost always better to be overdressed than to be underdressed. This is not the time to make a fashion statement. You want to look professional.

> **Use your social skills effectively.** Shake hands firmly, and look the interviewer in the eye. Show that you're interested in the interviewer as a fellow human being, not just as someone who might give you a job. Listen attentively to what he or she has to say, and be responsive. Above all, try to think confidently. Thinking positive, confident thoughts will help you appear positive and confident.

> **Ask questions.** If you have prepared for the interview, you've got some questions to ask about the organization with which you're looking for a job. Be sure to ask them. Interviewers almost always ask if you have any questions, but if they don't, try to work them in when you sense that the interview is almost over. It's also a good idea to ask about the hiring process the employer is using. Ask how long it will be before they will be making a decision and when you will be hearing from them again.

> **Above all, be yourself and be honest.** You do yourself no favor by pretending to be someone other than who you are. Getting a job under false pretenses virtually guarantees that neither you nor your employer ultimately will be satisfied with your job performance. You may end up doing things you don't like to do and may not be very good at, and neither you nor your employer will find that acceptable for very long. (To get experience interviewing, complete **Try It 4** on page 152.)

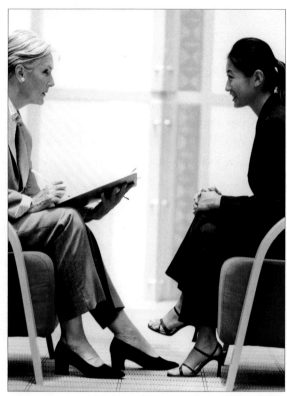

Interviews can be a nervous experience, but preparation and a coolheaded approach can make all the difference. Don't forget that you are interviewing a potential employer, as well as being interviewed as a potential employee!

"Rule No. 1: Just be yourself. Unless, of course, you're sloppy, lazy, or otherwise undesirable, in which case, be someone else. Be ready to humbly sell yourself, and if someone asks about your weak points, say, 'Occasionally I just work too hard.' "

Rainbow Rowell, the *Daily Nebraskan*[2]

Try It!

4

Interviewing

Nothing will prepare you better for an upcoming interview than a number of prior interviews. To get practice interviewing, ask an instructor, a person who has had experience in hiring, or even a fellow student to role-play an interview with you in which they will interview you, the potential job applicant. Tell them that you will prepare for your role carefully and that you will treat the practice interview seriously.

Follow these steps:

- Choose a company or organization that you would like to work for, and provide the person who will interview you with some details about it, such as information from the company Web site.

- You should also research your chosen company as a potential interviewee would, to gain enough knowledge to answer potential interview questions well.

- Hold the interview. You should be serious and try to play your role well. If you like, you can "dress the part" to help you set the right tone. You may also want to tape-record the session.

- After you've concluded the interview, ask your interviewer for a critique of your performance. Ask the interviewer to make as candid a judgment as he or she can as to which category you would fit into based solely on the interview: (A) Offer a job; (B) Don't offer a job; or (C) Call back for another interview to follow up with additional questions.

After you've completed the steps outlined above, answer the following questions:

1. What did you learn from the interview?

2. Critically assess your performance as an interviewee. What was your greatest strength as an interviewee? Your greatest weakness?

3. What would you do differently during an actual interview?

4. How can you better prepare for an actual interview in the future?

After the Interview

> **Evaluate your interview performance.** Are you pleased with how you presented yourself in the interview? What did you do particularly well? What things could you have done better?

Jot down your impressions of the interview while they're still fresh in your mind and place them in your Career Portfolio. These notes will be valuable when you prepare for future interviews.

> **Consider if you still want the position.** Suppose, for a moment, you were actually offered the job. Do you really want it?

It's important to ask yourself whether, given what you learned about the position, you would accept it if it were actually offered to you. You probably found out things about the position that interested you, and others that may be worrisome. Evaluate the job, and if there are too many negatives, rethink whether you'd actually want it.

However, unless there are so many negatives that you're certain that under no circumstances would you take the job, don't withdraw your application. It may be that if you are offered the job, you could negotiate with your potential employer to eliminate the factors that you find undesirable.

> **Write a thank-you note.** It's common courtesy to thank someone for giving you his or her time during an interview.

It's also strategically important. It shows that you are polite and can be counted on to do the right thing. It demonstrates your interest in the job. And it gives you one more opportunity to show you have the "right stuff."

Although you shouldn't turn your thank-you note into a sales pitch, do indicate your continued interest in the position. Write about the aspects of the job that were of particular interest to you and explain how you can see yourself fitting in well with the company.

> **Follow up.** If you haven't heard from the employer in a few weeks, and it's past the point where you were told you'd be contacted, it's perfectly reasonable to e-mail or call. The purpose is not to badger the employer into hiring you—that's not going to work—but to simply check up on where the process stands. Of course, it also serves another purpose: to remind a potential employer of your continued interest in the position. You can also use the opportunity to provide additional information or to inform the employer of another job offer.

NAME: **Dr. Ben Carson**

SCHOOL: **Yale University, B.A.; University of Michigan Medical School, M.D.**

Few who knew Ben Carson as a fifth grader would have guessed that he would become a surgeon whose skills would save the lives of hundreds of patients.

Dr. Carson grew up in a poor, single-parent household in Detroit. His mother, who had only a third-grade education, worked two jobs cleaning bathrooms.

To his classmates—and even to his teachers—he was thought of as "the dumbest kid in the class," according to his own not-so-fond memories. He had a terrible temper and once tried to stab another child.

Dr. Carson was headed down a path of self-destruction until a critical moment in his youth: His mother, convinced that she had to do something dramatic to prevent him from leading a life of failure, laid down some rules. He could not watch television except for two programs a week, could not play with his friends after school until he finished his homework, and had to read two books a week and write book reports about them.

His mother's strategy worked. As he wrote his weekly book reports for his mother, worlds opened to him.

"Of course, we didn't know she couldn't read, so there we were submitting these reports," he said. "She would put check marks on them like she had been reading them. As I began to read about scientists, economists, and philosophers, I started imagining myself in their shoes."[3]

As he got in the habit of hard work, his grades began to soar. Ultimately, he received a scholarship to attend Yale University, and later he was admitted to the University of Michigan Medical School. He is now head of pediatric neurosurgery at Johns Hopkins University, one of the most prestigious medical schools in the world; he is also the author of three books.

Dr. Carson tries to pass on to others the lessons he learned as a child. He has established a fund for students in grades 4 through 12 who maintain a 3.75 grade point average. Each month, 800 children come to his hospital, where he underscores the importance of education. As he says, "There is absolutely nothing in this world that you can't become simply through the acquisition of knowledge, because knowledge creates power and you make yourself into a more valuable person."[4]

Looking Back

How do I identify my ideal job?

> Careful and systematic research is the key to identifying possible career options.

> Books, Web sites, and informational interviews provide useful information about careers.

> A Career Portfolio can document a person's skills, capabilities, achievements, and goals, as well as provide a place to keep notes and research findings relating to jobs. It also includes one's résumé and cover letter.

What are the best strategies for finding and getting a job?

> It is important to find appropriate references.

> The Internet not only provides substantial information about potential jobs and companies, but also can play an important role in getting a job.

How can I maximize my job interviewing skills?

> Job interviews require a significant amount of preparation.

> Useful interview strategies include being punctual, dressing appropriately, using social skills effectively, asking questions, being oneself, and being honest.

> After an interview, follow up with the interviewer.

[KEY TERMS AND CONCEPTS]

Career Portfolio (p. 135)

[RESOURCES]

ON CAMPUS

Your campus almost certainly has an office devoted to career planning. In addition, your college library, as well as any public library, will surely have books that can help you research careers and find a job.

IN PRINT

There are thousands of books that can help you with career planning. One classic is Richard Bolles's *What Color Is Your Parachute?* (Ten Speed Press, 2008), which comes out in a new edition almost every year.

Another useful guide is Frank Satterthwaite and Gary D'Orsi's *The Career Portfolio Workbook* (McGraw-Hill, 2003).

Finally, *Acing the Interview: How to Ask and Answer Questions That Will Get You the Job* (AMACOM, 2008) offers a great variety of pointers that will help you prepare for interviews more effectively.

ON THE WEB

The following sites on the Web provide opportunities to extend your learning about the material in this chapter. (Although the Web addresses were accurate at the time the book was printed, check the *P.O.W.E.R. Learning* Web site [**www.mhhe.com/power**] for any changes that may have occurred.)

> The Planning a Career section of Mapping Your Future's Web site (**www. mappingyour-future.org/planning/**) discusses everything from developing a career plan to writing a résumé. It offers an abundance of other information related to students and schooling as well.

> Welcome to Resumania (**www.resumania.com/**)—a fun but practical look at those things you shouldn't put into a résumé. The term "Resumania" was coined by Robert Half, founder of the specialized staffing firm Robert Half International Inc. (RHI), to describe errors made by job seekers on résumés, applications, and cover letters.

> From the University of Texas at Austin (**www.gslis.utexas.edu/careers/resume_assistance.php**), this site provides dozens of tips on various topics, including how-to articles on résumé writing, interview behavior, and how to dress for an interview.

TAKING IT TO THE NET

1   Use the Internet to identify two companies that you would be interested in working for (e.g., using the HotJobs section of **www. yahoo.com**). Find out what you can about the companies, trying to go beyond the public relations statements that you will find on their Web sites. Write down your impressions about such features as their location, current financial situation, history, work setting and atmosphere, dress code, and benefits, as well as your need for prior experience in the field, your chances for advancement, and anything else of interest to you. Note similarities and differences between the two companies. Can you tell enough about the two companies to prefer one over the other? Would your preparation for an interview with each company be different?

2   Explore at least two Web sites that offer advice about interviewing. See if you can find sample questions that are often asked at interviews (including both traditional questions and brainteasers), tips on what to do and not do at an interview, hints for making a good impression and improving your chances of success, and other advice. Write down the names of the Web sites you found helpful and take notes on the advice they offer.

The Case of . . .
Interviewophobia

Dale had found his dream job.

A few weeks before finishing college to get his degree in fitness training, Dale found an online job posting for an entry-level training job with the professional basketball team that played in his area. Dale had long been a fan of the team. The salary and benefits were excellent. The facility where the team trained was only ten minutes from Dale's house. In short, the job was perfect, and Dale was thrilled when, a week after submitting his résumé, he received a call about scheduling an interview.

But then Dale started to get nervous. He had failed miserably at the only job interview he had ever had,

for a sales position at a retail company after he finished high school. He'd actually gotten into an argument with his interviewer. What if the interview for the fitness trainer position went just as poorly?

Other worries started creeping into Dale's mind. What if the interviewer asked questions about Dale's limited training experience? What if Dale forgot to mention the key experiences on his résumé? What if he wore the wrong clothes?

As the interview approached, Dale went from excited to terrified. He was certain he would blow the interview. So much for my dream job, he thought.

1. What advice would you give Dale? How is this interview different from the one he experienced just after finishing high school?

2. What steps could Dale take to ready himself for the interview? How could he build his confidence?

3. What could Dale do to prepare for questions about his work experience?

4. What tactics could Dale employ to make sure the interview remains cordial, and to get him on his interviewer's good side?

Learning Outcomes

By the time you finish this chapter you will be able to

» LO**7.1** Explain the educational uses of technology.

» LO**7.2** Identify what is available on the Web.

» LO**7.3** Define distance learning.

» LO**7.4** Discuss how to develop information competency.

» LO**7.5** Explain what to keep in mind when using the Web to gather information.

Technology and Information Competency

Tara Mallory had never been comfortable with technology. Raised in a small rural community, she'd never had a computer—much less the Internet—in her home growing up. Now, unlike most of her friends, she rarely used e-mail. She wasn't even sure she knew what an "Instant Message" was.

So when Tara's psychology instructor announced on the first day of class that her course required extensive use of the Web, Tara was not very enthusiastic. And when the instructor went on to say that the course would involve mandatory participation in online discussion groups, Tara became downright nervous.

Tara struggled with the computer-based assignments for the first few weeks. But then something happened that Tara didn't expect. Not only did she get the hang of surfing the Web and communicating with classmates online—she actually started to enjoy it. She saw that it was easier to keep up with friends and family via e-mail than through phone calls. And the fact that there were computers in her office at work and in her apartment made it easy for her to do schoolwork when she found she had a spare twenty minutes.

In short, Tara realized technology was not something that should intimidate her. In fact, she found that in many ways, it was a powerful ally.

Looking Ahead

The technology that Tara utilized in her psychology course didn't even exist 15 years ago. Education is changing, just like every other aspect of society, as "virtual" resources—e-mail, the Web, texting, and so forth—become more and more a part of how we live our lives. Today, businesspeople hold meetings and instructors teach courses without even being in the same room with their coworkers or students.

Technology is making a profound difference in how we are taught, the ways we study and carry out our work, and how we communicate with our loved ones. It is changing the way you can access the vast quantities of information published each year—tens of thousands of books, journals, and other print materials, and literally billions of Web pages. But successfully wading through all that information requires significant new skills in information competence that weren't necessary in the past.

In this chapter we discuss how technological advances increase your opportunities to achieve success in college and on the job. We'll first consider the basic educational uses of technology. We'll also talk about distance learning, an approach to education that involves studying with an instructor who may be thousands of miles away. Finally, we'll consider how you can use technology to develop information competency—locating and using both the information traditionally held in print *and* information created for, and in, the virtual world of cyberspace. Information competency is an essential skill in our increasingly technology-driven classrooms and offices.

» LO 7.1 You and Technology

It's a great tool that can help you achieve success in your classes. It can save you hours of time on your job, whether you work in a cubicle or a garage. At the same time, it can be extremely frustrating, annoying, and maddening. And sometimes instead of saving time, it can eat up hours of your time.

"It," of course, is technology. Today, it's as much a necessity to use technology as it was for you to learn to write using pen and paper earlier in your schooling. No one facing the job market in the 21st century will want to leave college without a strong working knowledge of a variety of technologies and what they can do for you. (To explore your feelings about technology and computers, complete the **Journal Reflections** on page 160.)

Journal Reflections

Could I Live without Technology?

1. What do you use technology for most? Texting? E-mail? Surfing the Web? Tasks at work? Classwork?

2. How much time do you spend using technology? How does it affect your social relationships?

3. What technological device could you live without? What devices could you *not* live without?

4. How much and what kinds of technology would you like to have in your courses? Why?

If you are not yet at ease with technology, relax. No one is born with technology expertise. With practice, however, using a broad range of technologies can become second nature. (If you need to brush up on the fundamentals of computer use, there's a section on the *P.O.W.E.R. Learning* Web site that will get you up to speed. Go to **www.mhhe.com/power**.)

Technology and Your Academic Life

Even if you don't feel particularly proficient with technology in general, it already plays a big role in your life. Computers run your car's engine, make your digital camera work, allow you to record iPod tunes, and make sure the bus you're waiting for runs on time.

Technology has revolutionized academic life as well. Here are some of the ways you may encounter technology in your classes:

> **Course Web sites.** Many college courses have a Web site associated with them. The Web site may reside in a nationally developed course management software system (such as Blackboard, desire2learn, or eCollege) with which your college has a licensing agreement. In other cases, colleges develop their own course management systems.
>
> Whatever course management system is used, the Web site will probably contain basic information about the course, such as a copy of the syllabus. Or it may provide important emergency updates, such as class cancellations or changes in a paper's due date.
>
> In other classes, the Web site may be much more elaborate and play a central role in the class. For instance, class Web sites that require a username

and password for access may contain exercises and quizzes to be completed (and scored) online. They may be the home for online discussion groups and forums. All your grades for the class may be stored on the Web site, accessible to you at any time of the day or night.

In some classes, you may electronically deposit papers and essays onto the class Web site. Later, your instructor can read them online, post comments on your submissions, and return them to you on the Web site. You may carry out group projects on the Web site, or hold virtual discussions on the site. You may even be required to take your major tests and final exams on the Web site.

▸ **CD-ROMs.** Textbooks frequently come with a CD that contains exercises, demonstrations, and other interactive media. For example, a psychology textbook might come with a CD that includes interactivities that allow you to participate in simulations of famous experiments, such as training Pavlov's dogs.

▸ **Textbook Online Learning Centers and Companion Web Sites.** Most textbooks have a Web site that is tied to the book. The Web site typically includes chapter summaries, interactive reviews, flash cards, and practice tests. These resources, which are usually described in the preface to most textbooks, can be extremely valuable study tools. (The Online Learning Center for *P.O.W.E.R. Learning* can be found at **www.mhhe.com/power.**)

▸ **Podcasts.** In some classes, instructors sometimes produce an audio or a video recording, called a **podcast,** of lectures or other instructional material relevant to the class. You can either access podcasts on the Web or download them to a mobile device (such as an iPod) that permits you to listen to and view them outside of class whenever you want.

▸ **Blogs.** Some instructors maintain blogs of their own. A **blog** is a kind of Web-based public diary in which a writer offers ideas, thoughts, short essays, and commentary. If your instructor has a blog and tells you to read it, get in the habit of checking it routinely. It not only will contain information relevant to the course that you'll need to know, but also may reveal personal insights that can help you know your instructor better.

> ▸ **Classroom presentation programs.** Many instructors use technology during class itself. For example, rather than using transparencies and overhead projectors, an increasing number of instructors present material electronically using PowerPoint slides or some other presentation program. Presentation programs help instructors to create professional-

Podcast
An audio or video recording that can be accessed on the Internet and viewed on a computer or downloaded to a mobile device

Blog
A Web-based public diary in which a writer provides commentary, ideas, thoughts, and short essays on topics

From the perspective of . . .

A STUDENT What technology do you find intimidating in the classroom? What steps can you take to overcome your anxiety?

looking slides that contain not only text, but often graphics such as photos, charts, maps, and animations.

If you are lucky, your instructor might later place the slides projected in class onto the class Web site, where they can be reviewed after class. Sometimes instructors even put the slides on Web sites before class. That gives you the chance to print them out and bring them to class, writing class notes on them. (For tips on making best use of instructors' presentation programs in class, see the **Course Connections** box on page 162.)

Getting the Most Out of Instructors' PowerPoint Presentations

Traditional "chalk-and-talk" lectures are a thing of the past in many classes. Instead, increasing numbers of instructors are using presentation programs such as PowerPoint to project material in their classes.

This newer technology calls for fresh strategies for taking notes and absorbing the information. Here are some tips:

- **Listening is more important than seeing.** The information that your instructor projects on screen, while important, ultimately is less critical than what he or she is saying. Pay primary attention to the spoken word and secondary attention to the screen.

- **Don't copy everything that is on every slide.** Instructors can present far more information on their slides than they would if they were writing on a blackboard. Oftentimes there is so much information that it's impossible to copy it all down. Don't even try. Instead, concentrate on taking down the key points.

- **Remember that key points on slides are . . . key points.** The key points (typically indicated by bullets) often relate to central concepts. Use these points to help organize your studying for tests, and don't be surprised if test questions directly assess the bulleted items on slides.

- **Check to see if the presentation slides are available online.** Some instructors make their class presentations available on the Web to their students, either before or after class time. If they do this before class, print them out and bring them to class. Then you can make notes on your copy, clarifying important points. If they are not available until after a class is over, you can still make good use of them when it comes time to study the material for tests.

- **Remember that presentation slides are not the same as good notes for a class.** If you miss a class, don't assume that getting a copy of the slides is sufficient. Studying the notes of a classmate who is a good notetaker will be far more beneficial than studying only the slides.

≫7.2 Using the Internet and the Web

Internet
A vast network of interconnected computers that share information around the world

Web
A highly graphical interface between users and the Internet that permits users to transmit and receive not only text but also graphical, video, and audio information

E-mail
Electronic mail, a system of communication that permits users to send and receive messages via the Internet

The Internet and the Web have revolutionized communication. And we haven't seen anything yet: Visionaries say it won't be too long before it will allow our refrigerators to order milk when supplies are running low or permit our physicians to constantly monitor our vital organs.

Although many people use the two terms interchangeably, the Internet and the Web are actually different, although related, concepts. The **Internet** is the electronic network that connects millions of computers together. Hooking up to this network permits a user to share information with virtually anyone else who has a computer. The **Web** (or, as it was originally called, the *World Wide Web*), provides a graphical means of locating and accessing information on the Internet. Using the Web has become the standard way to find and use such information. The Web provides a way to transmit typewritten text, visual material, and auditory information—graphics, photos, music, sound bites, video clips, and much more.

The Internet provides the backbone of virtual communication. Among its most common uses are the following:

- ▸ **E-mail. E-mail,** short for "electronic mail," offers a way for people to send and receive messages with incredible speed. On most college campuses, e-mail is the most common form of communication among students and faculty.

- **Text messaging (or texting).** Text messaging (or **texting**) permits you to send short messages from mobile phones to other phones or e-mail accounts. They are typically limited to 160 characters or less. Using text messaging, you can communicate with others in real time. You can also sign up to receive automatic text messages, such as receiving information whenever there are breaking news events.

- **Instant messaging (IM).** If you want to communicate in real time with friends, coworkers, and instructors, use instant messaging. With **instant messaging,** you create a list of other users with whom you wish to keep in touch. If others on your list are online at the same time you are, you'll know instantly, and you'll be able to send messages back and forth. Instructors sometimes hold virtual office hours using instant messaging, and businesses increasingly use instant messaging to facilitate employee communication.

- **Listservs.** A **listserv** is a subscription service that automatically e-mails messages on general topics of shared interest to people who have added their names to its mailing list. Members can respond to messages by replying to the listserv, and their responses will be distributed automatically to everyone on the mailing list. (In most cases it's also possible to respond directly to an individual who posts a message of interest, without sending that response to all members of the listserv.) Among the thousands of listservs online are those relating to jazz, tourism, privacy issues, and libertarianism.

- **RSS feeds.** RSS, which stands for both "Really Simple Syndication" or "Rich Site Summary," permits you to subscribe to your favorite Web site, which feeds you new information without you having to visit the site. RSS feeds provide news, listings of events, and scientific discoveries. To use RSS feeds, you need a news reader, software that checks feeds and allows you to read new material.

Using E-Mail Effectively

Although e-mail (illustrated in **Figure 7.1** on page 164) has become the preferred means of written communication for many of us, you may be unaware of some of the basics of how it works. For example, every e-mail address contains three basic elements:

- **Mailbox name.** The mailbox name—the name assigned to your account on an e-mail system—is often some variant of your own name (e.g., conan_obrien), though it may also be totally fictitious (e.g., hepcat9).

- **@.** The "at" sign.

- **Domain name.** The domain name is the name of the organization that hosts the e-mail "post office" to which the user subscribes—often an institution (e.g., umass.edu or mcgraw-hill.com), an Internet service provider (e.g., aol.com or earthlink.net), or a multifaceted system such as yahoo.com or hotmail.com. *Host computers* are connected directly to the Internet. You can usually tell what kind of an organization hosts an e-mail account by the last part of the address (the *extension*): for example, *.edu* is an educational organization, *.com* is a commercial organization, *.org* is a nonprofit or charitable organization, *.mil* is the military, and *.gov* is a governmental organization (see **Table 10.1** on page 164).

Text messaging (texting)

This communication method permits you to send short messages from mobile phones to other phones or e-mail accounts

Instant messaging

A system that allows one to use a computer to communicate in real time with friends and instructors

Listserv

A subscription service through which members can post and receive messages via e-mail on general topics of shared interest.

figure 7.1
E-Mail

E-mail sent via Google's Gmail.

table 10.1	Domain Extensions	
E-Mail Address	**Extension**	**Type of Organization**
jasper.johns@asu.edu	.EDU	Arizona State University—Educational
dowd@nytimes.com	.COM	*The New York Times*—Commercial
send.help@redcross.org	.ORG	American Red Cross—Charitable or nonprofit
general@army.mil	.MIL	United States Army—Military
head.counter@census.gov	.GOV	U.S. Census Bureau—Government

Many e-mail providers (e.g., Gmail or Yahoo! Mail) have their own, unique e-mail systems on which e-mail can be retrieved anywhere you have access to the Web. Others use particular software programs such as Microsoft's Outlook or Outlook Express to send and receive mail; you must have that software installed on your computer to retrieve your e-mail. Sometimes colleges have their own unique e-mail system that you can access through your college Web site.

Writing Effective E-Mail Messages

Even if you are an experienced e-mail user, you can do several things to improve the effectiveness of the messages you send. Among the most important to keep in mind when writing formal e-mail messages:

- **Use an informative subject line.** Don't say "IMPORTANT" or "meeting" or "question." None of those help recipients sort out your message from the dozens of others that may be clogging their in-boxes. Instead, something like "Reminder: supervisor applications due 5:00pm 10/11" is considerably more useful. In addition, *always* use a subject line: some recipients routinely delete messages without a subject line, fearing they contain viruses.

- **Make sure the recipient knows who you are.** If you are writing someone you know only casually, jog their memory with a bit of information about yourself. If you don't know them at all, identify yourself early in the message ("I am a college student who is interested in an internship . . .").

- **Keep messages short and focused.** E-mail messages are most effective when they are short and direct. If at all possible, keep your message short enough that it fits on one screen without scrolling down to see the rest. The reason is simple: Recipients sometimes don't read beyond the beginning of a message. If you do need to include a good deal of material, number each point or set them off by bullets so recipients will know to read down.

- **Try to include only one major topic per e-mail.** It's often better to write separate e-mails rather than including a hodgepodge of unrelated points in an e-mail. This is especially true if you want a response to each of the different points.

- **Put requests near the beginning of the e-mail.** If you want the recipient to do something in response to your message, respectfully put the request at the very beginning of your message. Be explicit, while being polite.

- **Keep attachments to a minimum.** If possible, include all relevant information in the body of your e-mail. Large attachments clog people's e-mail accounts and may be slow to download. In addition, recipients who don't know you personally may fear your attachment contains a virus and will not open it.

- **Avoid abbreviations and emoticons in formal e-mails.** When writing informal e-mails to friends, abbreviations such as AFAIK ("as far as I know"), BTW ("by the way"), CYA ("see ya"), OIC ("oh, I see"), and WTG ("way to go") are fine. So are **emoticons (or smileys),** which signal the emotion that you are trying to convey. However, they should be avoided in formal e-mails. Recipients may not be familiar with them, and they may make your e-mail seem overly casual.

- **Above all, always be respectful and courteous.** It always pays to be polite. In fact, as we discuss next, there are certain guiding principles that govern civility on the Web and which you should always keep in mind when writing e-mail.

Emoticons (or smileys)
Symbols used in e-mail messages that provide information on the emotion that the writer is trying to convey. Emoticons usually look like faces on their side, with facial expressions related to the intended emotion or tone.

Netiquette: Showing Civility on the Web

Although e-mail and text communication is usually less formal than a letter, it is essential to maintain civility and demonstrate good etiquette, which in the technology world is known as *netiquette*. Here are some rules:

- **Don't write anything in an e-mail or text message that you'll regret seeing on the front page of the newspaper.** Yes, e-mail and texts are usually private; but the private message you write can easily be forwarded by the recipient to another person or even scores of other people. Worse yet, it's fairly easy to hit "reply all" when you mean simply to "reply": in this case, you might think that you are responding to an individual, when in fact the e-mail will go to everyone who received the message, along with you.

- **Be careful of the tone you convey.** It is harder in e-mail and texts to express the same kind of personality, and often the same degree of subtlety, that our voice, our handwriting, or even our stationery can add to other forms of communication. This means that attempts at humor and especially sarcasm can backfire. If you're using humor, consider adding an emoticon to clarify the intent of your message.

- **Never write anything in an e-mail or text that you wouldn't say in person.** If you wouldn't say something in a face-to-face conversation, don't say it electronically.

- **Don't use all capital letters.** Using all caps MAKES IT LOOK AS IF YOU'RE SHOUTING.

- **Never send an e-mail or text when you are angry.** No matter how annoyed you are about something someone has written in a message, don't respond in kind—or at least wait until you've cooled down. Take a deep breath, and wait for your anger to pass.

- **Be especially polite and professional when writing to instructors and on-the-job supervisors.** In many cases, instructors get scores, and sometimes hundreds, of e-mails and texts from their students every week. In many offices, supervisors receive just as many messages. To make sure your message gets maximum attention, use a clear subject line (if you're writing your instructor, be sure to include the name of the relevant course), address the recipient of the e-mail politely, and always end with a thank you and your full name.

To consider e-mail and text message netiquette more closely, complete **Try It 1.**

In-Person Netiquette: Using Technology Appropriately

In many situations, there are standards for appropriate use of technology. An instructor does not want you to answer a cell phone call while he or she is speaking; neither does your boss.

Follow these guidelines to ensure you don't offend anyone with how you use technology:

- **Turn off your cell phone in formal settings.** If you're in a meeting or a class, keep your cell phone off (or set in "vibrate" mode). Cell phones ringing at random times are distracting and annoying.

- **Don't send text messages or make calls while someone else is speaking.** It's obvious that you should be paying attention to what coworkers, classmates, or instructors are saying, rather than what's going on in the rest of the world.

- **If you use your laptop to take notes, stay on task.** No matter how tempting it is to check your e-mail messages, IM with a friend, or surf the Web, avoid the temptation. Use your laptop to take notes, and nothing else.

- **Never use your cell phone to text answers to problems in class.** Cheating is cheating, whether done using high-tech or low-tech methods. Don't do it.

Protecting Yourself: Spam Management and Safety

The downside of e-mail is *spam,* the virtual equivalent of junk mail. Spam may range from get-rich-quick schemes to advertisements for body enhancements or pornography. Spam is more than a nuisance; it takes up valuable transmission resources ("bandwidth"), disk space, and computer time.

Using E-Mail Netiquette

Read the e-mail below, written by a student to his instructor, and respond to the questions that follow.

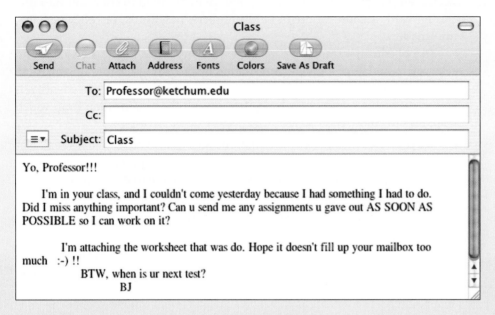

1. What rules of "netiquette" does the e-mail violate?

2. If you were the instructor to whom the e-mail message was sent, how do you think you would react to receiving it? What questions would you have about the message?

3. Based on the e-mail, what opinion might you have of the student who wrote it?

4. Rewrite the e-mail so that it is consistent with good netiquette.

To Try It online, got to **www.mhhe.com/power**.

Some e-mail systems apply a filter that uses a few simple rules to separate the wheat (e-mail you actually want to read) from the chaff (spam). Unfortunately, these systems are not perfect: They sometimes let junk through and can even at times dispose of messages you want. The only absolutely reliable way to deal with spam is to delete it yourself as quickly as possible.

Here are a few tips for dealing with spam:

▸ Consider using two e-mail addresses—one for personal messages and one you use when you visit newsgroups and chat rooms.

- Don't use anything similar to your actual name as your username or screen name.

- *Never* give anyone your password, and change your password frequently.

- *Never* respond to an e-mail that asks for personal or financial information, even if it appears to be legitimate. Such requests may originate in *crimeware,* programs that steal personal financial information. For instance, in a practice called *phishing,* spam or pop-up messages are used to trick you into disclosing bank account or credit card numbers, passwords, or other personal information.

    In a phishing scam, the e-mail appears to be from a legitimate source and asks you to update or validate information by providing account information. In reality, such messages are from con artists seeking to steal your identity. If you think such a request may be legitimate, call the organization from which it appears to come.

- *Do not click* on any links in the e-mail message until you're sure it's real. Not only can such links lead to the disclosure of personal information about you, but they may lead to the secret installation of software that can spy on you.

- *Never* open an attachment from someone you don't know. Computer viruses, which can ruin everything on your hard drive, are often spread through e-mail attachments.

- Finally, if your e-mail program has a spam filter, periodically check your spam folder to make sure no legitimate e-mails may have been directed there by mistake.

Keeping Safe

There's an even darker side to the Web than financial criminals looking to steal from you. Specifically, you need to be wary of sexual predators who use the Web to identify potential victims. To help protect yourself, use these guidelines:

1. Don't give out personal information to strangers such as your name, phone number, address, hometown, or your future schedule—anything that can be used to identify you.

2. Never send photos of yourself or friends or family to someone you don't know.

3. Don't reply to e-mails that are offensive, weird, or distressing in any way.

4. Don't arrange to meet anyone whom you've only met on the Web.

5. If you do have problems with someone over e-mail, immediately contact your college or local police.

Social Networking Web Sites

Many people today use social networking Web sites such as Facebook.com or MySpace.com to stay in touch with their friends and to make new acquaintances. In fact, Facebook has more than 150 million active users.

Although social networking Web sites offer many possibilities for interacting with friends and making new acquaintances, they need to be used appropriately. Don't post information about yourself or photos that you wouldn't want your instructors, children, or employer seeing. In fact, employers increasingly are using information they find on Facebook and MySpace in hiring decisions. In short, be thoughtful of what you post about yourself.

≫ LO 7.3 Distance Learning: Classes without Walls

Do you find that your schedule changes so much from one day to the next that it's hard to fit in a course that meets at a regularly scheduled time? Interested in an unusual course topic that your own college doesn't offer? Want to take a class during the summer, but your college doesn't have a summer program?

The solution to your problem may be to enroll in a **distance learning** course. Distance learning is a form of education in which students participate via the Web or other kinds of technology. Although most distance learning courses are taught via the Web, some use teleconferencing, fax, and/or express mail.

The key feature of distance learning courses is the nature of interaction between instructor and students. Rather than meeting in a traditional classroom, where the instructor, you, and the other students are physically present, distance learning classes are most often virtual. Although some schools use "Webcasts" of lectures with virtual discussion rooms or employ lectures on videotape or CDs, most students in distance learning courses will never sit through a lecture or even participate in a real-time conversation with students in the class. They may never even know what their instructor or classmates look like or hear their voices.

If you take a distance learning course, you may read lecture notes posted on the Web, search and browse Web sites, write papers, post replies to discussion topics on a *message board,* and take online quizzes and exams. You will see your instructor's and classmates' responses through comments they post on the Web. You may be expected to read a textbook entirely on your own.

You may already be familiar with the kinds of technologies used in distance learning courses, because many traditional, face-to-face courses already contain elements of distance learning. In **blended (or hybrid) courses,** instruction is a combination of the traditional face-to-face classroom interaction and a significant amount of online learning. Students in blended courses generally spend more time working alone or in collaboration with others online.

In contrast to blended courses, all instruction takes place online in distance learning classes. However, distance learning is not for everyone. Whether you're a good candidate for it or not depends on your preferred style of course-taking. Complete **Try It 2** on page 170 to see whether you are suited to learn at a distance.

Distance learning classes have both advantages and disadvantages. On the plus side, distance learning courses offer the following:

- **You can take a Web-based distance learning course anywhere that you have access to the Web.** You can be at home, at the office, or on vacation on the beach and still participate.

- **Distance learning classes are more flexible than traditional classes.** You can participate in a course any time of the day or night. You set your own schedule. This is particularly helpful for those with time-consuming family obligations such as child care.

- **Distance learning classes are self-paced.** You may be able to spread out your work over the course of a week, or you may do the work in a concentrated manner on one day.

- **You may have more contact with your instructor than you do with a traditional class.** Even though you may not have face-to-face contact, you may have greater access to your instructor, via e-mail and the Web, than in traditional classes. You can leave messages for your instructor any time of

Distance learning
The teaching of courses at another institution, with student participation via video technology or the Web

Blended (or hybrid) courses
Instruction is a combination of the traditional face-to-face classroom interaction and a significant amount of online learning

2 Assess Your Course-Taking Style

Your preferred course-taking style—how you participate in classes, work with your classmates, interact with your teachers, and complete your assignments—may make you more or less suitable for distance learning. Read the following statements and indicate whether you agree or disagree with them to see if you have what it takes to be a distance learner.

	Agree	Disagree
1. I need the stimulation of other students to learn well.		
2. I need to see my teacher's face, expressions, and body language to interpret what is being said.		
3. I participate a lot in class discussions.		
4. I prefer to hear information presented orally rather than reading it in a book or article.		
5. I'm not very good at keeping up with reading assignments.		
6. I'm basically pretty easily distracted.		
7. I'm not very well organized.		
8. Keeping track of time and holding to schedules is NOT a strength of mine.		
9. I need a lot of "hand-holding" while I work on long assignments.		
10. I need a close social network to share my feelings, ideas, and complaints with.		
11. I'm not very good at writing.		
12. Basically, I'm not very patient.		

The more you disagree with these statements, the more your course-taking style is suited to distance learning. Interpret your style according to this informal scale:

Disagreed with 10–12 statements = Excellent candidate for distance learning

Disagreed with 7–9 statements = Good candidate for distance learning

Agreed with 6–9 statements = Probably better taking classes on campus

Agreed with 10–12 statements = Avoid distance learning

To Try It online, go to www.mhhe.com/power.

the night or day; most instructors of distance learning classes respond in a timely way.

> **Shy students may find it easier to "speak up" in a distance learning class.** You can think through your responses to make sure you are communicating just what you wish to say. You don't have to worry about speaking in front of other people. For many people, distance learning is liberating.

> **You can become a better writer.** Because distance learning usually involves more writing than traditional courses, you receive more practice writing—and more feedback for it—than in traditional classes.

On the other hand, distance learning has disadvantages that you should keep in mind:

> **You are a prisoner of technology.** If you lose access to a computer and the Web, you won't be able to participate in the class until the problem is fixed.

> **You won't have direct, face-to-face contact with your instructor or other students.** Distance learning can be isolating, and students sometimes feel alone and lost in cyberspace.

> **You won't get immediate feedback.** In a distance learning class, it may be hours, or sometimes days, before you receive feedback on what you have posted to a message board, depending on how well the pace of other students matches your own.

> **Distance learning classes require significant discipline, personal responsibility, and time management skills.** You won't have a set time to attend class as you do in traditional courses. Instead, you must carve out the time yourself. Although instructors provide a schedule of when things are due, you have to work out the timing of getting them done.

Consequently, many students believe that distance learning courses are more difficult than traditional classes. You must be focused and committed to keeping up with the course. You need to be prepared to work hard on your own for a substantial number of hours each week.

Despite these potential challenges to distance learning courses, they are becoming increasingly popular. More and more colleges are offering them. Many companies encourage employees with crowded schedules to take distance learning as a way of providing continuing education.

If you are considering taking a distance learning course, follow these steps, which are summarized in the P.O.W.E.R. Plan here.

P **Prepare**
Identify distance learning course possibilities

O **Organize**
Obtain access to technology

W **Work**
Participate in a distance learning plan

E **Evaluate**
Consider your "classroom" performance

R **Rethink**
Reflect on what and how you have learned

P.O.W.E.R. Plan

 Prepare ## Identifying Distance Learning Course Possibilities

How do you find a distance learning course? In some cases, your own college may offer courses on the Web and list them in your course catalog. In other cases, you'll have to find courses on your own.

The best place to look is on the Web itself. By searching the Web, you can find distance learning courses ranging from agronomy to zoology. Don't be deterred by the physical location of the institution that offers the course. It doesn't matter where the college is located, because for most distance learning classes, you'll never have to go to the campus itself.

But before you sign up for a potential course that you would like to count toward your degree, *make sure that your own college will give you credit for it.* Check with your adviser and registrar's office to be certain.

You should also find out what the requirements of a course are before you actually sign up for it. Check the syllabus carefully and see how it meshes with your schedule. If it is a summer course and you are going to be away from your computer for a week, you may not be able to make up the work you miss.

Finally, try to talk with someone who has taken the course before. Was the instructor responsive, providing feedback rapidly? If necessary, could you speak with the instructor by phone? Was the course load reasonable? (**Try It 3** on page 172 will help you to work through the process.)

Try It!

WORKING IN A GROUP

3 Get Some Distance on the Problem

Working by yourself initially, see if you can find distance learning courses of interest to you. Start by checking your school's course catalog to see what might be offered there. If you're already comfortable online, you might also try the following:

- *The Chronicle of Higher Education's* Distance Education: Daily Updates (**chronicle.com**).
- The World Lecture Hall (**www.utexas.edu/world/lecture/index.html**), hosted by the University of Texas, which provides a list of distance learning courses offered worldwide.

Try to find five courses you would be interested in and list them below. After you have completed your list, share your list with others in a group.

1. How diverse were the courses you were able to find?

2. Were particular subject areas better represented than others?

3. Why do you think this might be?

To Try It online, go to **www.mhhe.com/power**.

 Organize Obtaining Access to Technology

Although you don't need to be a computer expert, you will need some minimal e-mail and Web skills to take a distance learning course. If you don't have sufficient technological expertise, beef up your computer skills by taking a computer course or workshop *before* you actually sign up for the distance learning course.

You'll also need access to a computer connected to the Internet. It doesn't have to be your own computer, but you will certainly need regular and convenient access to one. Make sure that the computer you plan to use has sufficient internal resources to quickly connect to the Internet; a very slow connection is frustrating.

Be sure to make all your arrangements for computer access prior to the start of a course. It can take several weeks to set up Internet service on a home computer if you don't have it already.

Participating in a Distance Learning Class

Successfully participating in a distance learning course involves several skills that are distinct from those needed for traditional classes. To get the most out of a distance learning course, you'll need to do the following:

> **Manage your time carefully.** You won't have the luxury of a regular schedule of class lectures, so you'll have to manage your time carefully. No one is going to remind you that you need to sit down at a computer and work. You will need every bit of self-discipline to be successful in a distance learning course.

> **Check in frequently.** Instructors may make crucial changes in the course requirements. Make sure to check for any changes in due dates or class expectations.

> **Find a cyberbuddy.** At the start of the semester, try to make personal contact with at least one other student in the class. You can do this by e-mailing, phoning, or actually meeting the student if he or she is geographically nearby. You can share study strategies, form a study group, and share notes. Connecting with another student can help you avoid feelings of isolation that may interfere with your success.

> **Make copies of everything.** Don't assume everything will go well in cyberspace. Make a printed copy of everything you submit, or alternatively have a backup stored on another computer.

> **Have a technology backup plan.** Computers crash, your connection to the Internet may go down, or an e-mailed assignment may be mysteriously delayed or sent back to you. Don't wait until the last minute to work on and submit assignments, and have a plan in place if your primary computer is unavailable.

Considering Your "Classroom" Performance

As with any class, you'll be receiving feedback from your instructor. But unlike many courses, in which almost all the feedback comes from the instructor, much of the feedback in a distance learning course may come from your fellow students. Consider what you can learn from their comments, while keeping in mind that they are, like you, students themselves.

At the same time you'll be receiving feedback, you will likely be providing feedback to your classmates. Consider the nature of feedback you provide, and be sure that you use the basic principles of classroom civility.

Reflecting on What and How You Have Learned

Distance learning is not for everyone. If your preferred learning style involves extensive, face-to-face interaction with others, you may find that your experience is less than satisfying. On the other hand, if you are at ease with computers and enjoy working on your own, you may find distance learning highly effective.

As you reflect on your distance learning experience, go beyond the technology and think about the learning outcomes. Ask yourself whether you learned as much as you would have in a traditional class. You should also consider ways that the experience could have been more effective for you. And think about whether you were so absorbed by the technology that you lost sight of the real goal of the course: learning new material.

Most educational experts believe that distance learning will play an increasingly important role in higher education. Furthermore, because it offers an efficient way of educating people in far-flung locales, it is a natural means of promoting lifelong learning experiences. In short, the first distance learning class you take is likely not to be your last.

»LO 7.4 Fact Finding: Developing Information Competency

One of the greatest advances brought about by technology involves the area of research. More than ever, people require **information competency,** the ability to determine what information is necessary, and then to locate, evaluate, and effectively use that information. The sheer abundance of material available today makes information competency a critical skill.

We'll consider the ways in which you can use the two primary storehouses of information available today to boost your own level of information competency. One you can walk or drive to—the library. The other—the Web—doesn't have a physical location. Both are indispensable in anyone's quest for information.

Libraries

No matter how imposing or humble their physical appearance, whether they contain only a few hundred volumes or hundreds of thousands of them, libraries are a good place to focus your efforts as you seek out and gather information. Although every library is different, all share two key elements: the material they hold—their basic collections—and tools to help you locate the material you need.

What Can Be Found in a Library's Basic Collection?

Libraries obviously contain books, but they typically have a lot more than that, including some or all of the following:

> **Periodicals.** *Periodicals* include magazines published for general audiences, specialized journals for professionals in a field, and newspapers. Magazines and journals are often bound and stored by year; newspapers are usually kept in *microform,* in which documents have been photographed and stored on either microfilm (reels of film) or microfiche (plastic sheets).

> **Indexes and Online Databases.** An index provides a listing of periodical articles by title, author, and subject. Some indexes also provide a short summary, or *abstract,* of the contents of each article.

"Knowledge is of two kinds: we know a subject ourselves, or we know where we can find information upon it."

Samuel Johnson

Most indexes come in both print and electronic form. In their electronic form, they are known as an **online database,** an organized body of information on a related topic. For example, the National Center for Biotechnology

Information (NCBI) maintains *Medline,* an online public database that provides information on medical research. The advantage of online databases over traditional, print-based indexes is that the database sometimes provides the full text of material they identify in a search.

> **Encyclopedias.** Some encyclopedias, such as the *Encyclopaedia Britannica* or *World Book Encyclopedia,* attempt to cover the entire range of knowledge, and they may take up many volumes. Others are more specialized, covering only a particular field, such as the *Encyclopedia of Human Behavior* or the *Encyclopedia of Religion.* Most are printed as multivolume sets of books, although an increasing number are available electronically, on CD-ROM or online. Encyclopedias provide a good general view of a topic, but they lack depth: Use them at the earliest stage of your hunt for information for an overview of key issues, and move from there to more specific and current sources.

> **Government documents.** Census records, laws, and tax codes are some of the millions of government documents that are stored in libraries.

> **Musical scores.** The music to *Rent,* the Brahms *Alto Rhapsody,* and The Beatles' greatest hits are among the musical scores you can find in libraries.

> **Reserve collections.** Reserve collections hold heavily used items that instructors assign for a class. Sometimes reserve material can be checked out for only an hour or two and used in the same room; in other cases the material can be used overnight or for a few days.

Locating Information in a Library

The place to begin searching for information in a library is the library catalog. Catalogs list all materials that are held in the library and provide their location. Most library catalogs are computerized, though a few still use name cards filed in drawers or microform (microfiche or microfilm). You are usually able to access computerized catalogs from home or residence hall rooms as well as from computers housed in the library itself.

Library catalogs traditionally allow searches by title, author name, and subject; electronic catalogs also typically allow searching by keyword. Individual catalog entries generally include additional information about the material, such as the publisher, date of publication, number of pages, and similar information.

Say, for example, you're writing a paper on Ernest Hemingway. To find books he *wrote* in an electronic catalog, you would enter his name in the "author" field. You may be presented with the listing shown in **Figure 7.2** on page 176.

Of course, you could also search on "Hemingway" as the subject, which would yield a list of books *about* him and his work; if you entered his name in a "keyword" search, the catalog would return a more comprehensive list of books both by *and* about him.

The key piece of information in a catalog entry is the book's **call number,** a code that tells you exactly where to find it. Most college libraries use the Library of Congress classification system, which assigns to each book a unique combination of letters and numbers.

Because the record illustrated in Figure 7.2 is from an electronic search, it contains further helpful information. The word "Available" under "Due Date" tells you that one copy of the book has not been checked out by another patron and should be sitting on the shelf. You'll need to familiarize yourself with your library's particular system to know precisely how you can make most efficient use of the catalog. Chances are there's a handout or a posted set of instructions nearby.

Call number

A unique classification number assigned to every book (or other resource) in a library. Call numbers are used for ease of location.

figure 7.2
Online Catalog Entry

Online catalog entry for a book called *The Old Man and the Sea*. Note especially the call number and due date: These will tell you where the book is to be found and whether it is on the shelves or is checked out.

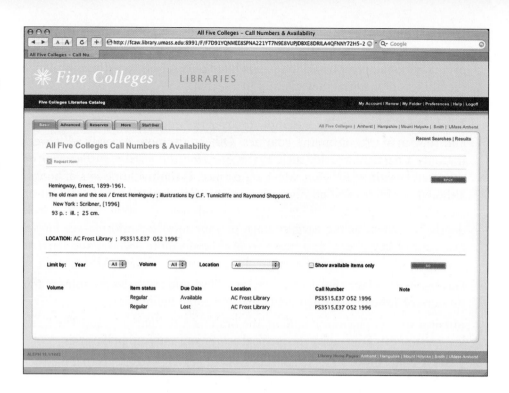

Stacks

The shelves on which books and other materials are stored in a library

Recall

A way to request library materials from another person who has them

Interlibrary loan

A system by which libraries share resources, making them available to patrons of different libraries

Once you have identified the material you need and where it is located, you'll need to go find it. In all but the biggest libraries, you can simply go into the **stacks,** the place containing shelves where the books and other materials are kept, and—using the call number—hunt for it. In libraries with closed stacks, you must fill out a form with the call numbers of the books you want. A library aide will find and deliver the material to a central location.

What if you go to the location in the stacks where the material is supposed to be and you can't find it? The material may be checked out, in use by someone else at that time, incorrectly shelved, or simply lost. Whatever the reason, *don't give up.* If the material is checked out to another user, ask a librarian if you can **recall** the material, a process by which the library contacts the person who has the book and asks him or her to return it.

If the librarian informs you that the material is not checked out, wait a few days and see if it appears on the shelf. Someone may have been using it while you were looking for it. If it was misshelved, the librarian may be able to find it. If the material is truly lost, you may be able to get it from another library through **interlibrary loan,** a system by which libraries share resources.

Finally, even if you do find exactly what you were looking for, take a moment to scan the shelves. Because books and other materials are generally grouped by topic, you may find other

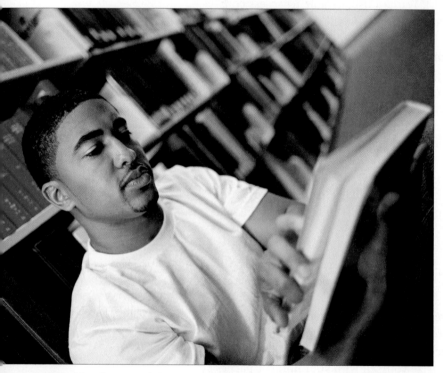

Searching for materials in the library stacks can be frustrating if they are not on the shelves. However, you may unexpectedly find relevant and interesting material while browsing.

useful titles in the same place. One of the pleasures of libraries is the possibility of finding an unexpected treasure—material that your catalog search did not initially identify but that may provide you with exactly what you need.

» LO 7.5 Finding Information on the Web

The Web is vast—sometimes frustratingly so. In fact, no one knows how much material exists on the Web. Not only is more information added to the Web every day, but the information also resides on thousands of individual computers. Anyone with minimal Web savvy and access to a *server* (a computer with a permanent Internet connection) can set up a personal Web site.

The fact that anyone can put information on the Web is both the biggest asset and greatest disadvantage of using the Web as an information source. Because minimal computer skill is the only expertise a person needs to set up a Web page, there may be as much misinformation on the Web as there is information. Consequently, keep the usual consumer rule in mind: Buyer beware. Unless the Web site has been established and is maintained by a reliable organization, the information it contains may not be accurate.

A number of key factors are involved in each Web search. They include a browser, Web pages, links, and search engines.

> **Browsers.** To use the Web, your computer has to have a browser. A **browser,** as its name implies, is a program that provides a way of looking at the information on the Web. Among the major browsers are Microsoft's Internet Explorer and Firefox's Mozilla (see **Figure 7.3** on page 178).

Using a browser is a bit like taking a taxi: once you get in, you get to where you want to go by providing an address. The address, also known as a URL (Uniform Resource Locator), identifies a unique location on the Web, a *Web site* or a *Web page* (one of the parts of a site).

Browser
A program that provides a way of navigating around the information on the Web

From the perspective of . . .

A LAW ENFORCEMENT PROFESSIONAL Technology is changing the approach to many long-established career fields. What technology changes could potentially impact your chosen profession?

Web addresses are combinations of letters and symbols. They typically start off with "**www.[domain_name].[xxx]**"—the address of the hosting Web site (e.g., **www.iastate.edu,** the home page for Iowa State University). If you're looking for a subsite or a particular page on the site, the address becomes increasingly specific: **www.iastate.edu/visitors/** will take you to a "visitors" site—a collection of pages—hosted by **iastate.edu.** A *page* on that site—for example, **www.iastate.edu/visitors/directions.shtml,** which offers directions to campus—ends with a specific name, usually followed by ".htm," ".html," or ".shtml." Because most addresses begin with "http://," this part of the address is often dropped in references to a site.

You can often get a decent idea of what kind of site you're going to by taking a careful look at the Web address: you can tell that **www.mhhe.com/power,** for example, is a site that has something to do with "power" and is hosted by a

figure 7.3

Internet Browser

Home page for Microsoft's
Internet Explorer browser.

Web page

A location (or site) on the Web
housing information from a
single source and (typically)
links to other pages

Link

A means of "jumping"
automatically from one Web
page to another

Search engine

A computerized index to
information on the Web

commercial entity (which you might or might not recognize as McGraw-Hill Higher Education). (Hmm, might be worth checking out . . .)

> **Web pages.** Web pages are the heart of the Web. A **Web page** is a document that presents you with information. The information may appear as text on the screen, to be read like a book (or more accurately, like an ancient scroll). It might include a video clip, an audio clip, a photo, a portrait, a graph, or a figure. It might offer a news service photo of the president of the United States or a backyard snapshot of someone's family reunion.

> **Links.** Web sites typically provide you with **links**—embedded addresses to other sites or documents that, at a click, cause your browser automatically to "jump" there. Just as an encyclopedia article on forests might say at the end, "See also Trees," Web pages often refer to other sites on the Web—only it's easier than with a book. You just have to click on the link with your mouse and—*poof!*—you're there.

> **Search engines.** A **search engine** is simply a computerized index to information on the Web. When you know what information you want to find but don't have an address for it, a search engine can often steer you toward relevant sites.

The various parts of the Web are similar to the components of traditional libraries, as illustrated in **Figure 7.4**. A Web browser is equivalent to a library card; it gives you access to vast quantities of material. Web sites are like the books of a library; Web pages are the book pages, where the content resides. Links are analogous to "see also" portions of books that suggest related information. And search engines are like a library's card catalog, directing you to specific locations.

"Go ask your search engine."

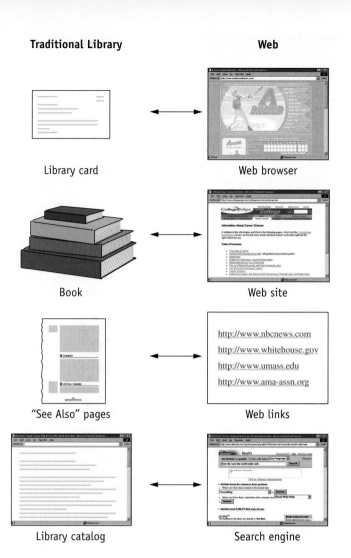

figure 7.4
Comparison of Library and Web
The various parts of the Web are similar to the components of a traditional library.

Traditional Library

Library card

Book

"See Also" pages

Library catalog

Web

Web browser

Web site

http://www.nbcnews.com
http://www.whitehouse.gov
http://www.umass.edu
http://www.ama-assn.org

Web links

Search engine

Locating Information on the Web

There is no central catalog of the contents of the Web; instead, there are a number of different search engines. Furthermore, depending on the search engine you use and the type of search you do, you'll identify different information.

Search engines themselves are located on the Web, so you have to know their addresses. After you reach the "home" address of a search engine, you enter your search terms. The search engine then provides a list of Web sites that may contain information relevant to your search.

Some search engines, such as Yahoo!, specialize in organizing information by subject, making it easy to search for information on, say, different dog breeds, the Islamic religion, or car repair. Using Yahoo! for its subject directories is like searching for information using the subject entries in a library catalog (see **Figure 7.5** on page 180).

Other search engines, such as Google or AltaVista, catalog many more pages than Yahoo! but don't group them by subject. Due to the breadth of their coverage, they might be more useful when you are looking for obscure pieces of information or for numerous sources for different perspectives on a topic. Using Google or AltaVista is like performing a keyword search in a library catalog.

Finally, a third type of search engine is exemplified by Ask.com and AlltheWeb.com. Known as metasearch tools, these sites send your search commands to other search engines, compiling the results into a single, unified list.

figure 7.5
Using a Search Engine
Yahoo! search page on
animal rights.

"First, they do an online search."

> "Don't let that little glowing screen
> become an adversary. If you
> plan correctly, the computer can
> become your most useful tool at
> college—next to your brain."
>
> Greg Gottesman, author

There's no single search engine that works best. Most people develop their own preferences based on their experience. The best advice: Try out several of them and see which works best for you. To get started, work through **Try It 4,** "Work the Web: Information, Please!" on page 181.

Becoming a Savvy Surfer

The process you use to search the Web couldn't be easier—or more difficult. The vast amounts of material online and the relative ease of navigation afforded by the Web make finding information quite simple: What is hard is finding appropriate information.

Consider the search illustrated in **Figure 7.6** on page 181. It is the result of entering How do I use the Web? into the home page of Google. The search identified over 2.8 *billion* Web sites related to the topic.

Using the list of sites generated by the search is simple. With the mouse, click on the site address of the relevant document, and the home page of the site will (eventually) appear on your computer screen. You can then take notes on the material, in the same way you'd take notes on material in a book.

Many of the million sites Google returned, however, may well be of little use. It's easy in such a search to end up in a virtual dead end, in which the information you have found is only minimally related to the topic you're researching. If you do find yourself at a site that's of no use to you, simply hit the "back" button on your browser until you return to where you started.

How can you limit your search in the first place, so that you find sites more directly relevant? The following tips can help you to get the most from a search[1]:

1. **Before you type anything into your computer, phrase your search as a question.**

2. **Identify the important words in that question.** Then think of words that are related to the important words. Write all the words down.

3. **Go to your favorite search engine.** Google is the most popular today, but preferences vary.

Work the Web: Information, Please!

4

Try to find the answer to the first question below on Yahoo! (**www.yahoo.com**), Google (**www.google.com**), *and* Dogpile (**www.dogpile.com**). Then use whichever search engine you prefer to find answers to the remaining questions.

1. What was the French Revolution and when did it occur?

2. Who is Keyser Soze?

3. What are the words of Dr. Martin Luther King Jr.'s "I have a dream" speech?

4. Is the birthrate in the United States higher or lower than that in Brazil?

5. What is the ecu?

How easy was it for you to find the answers to the questions? Which search engine(s) did you prefer, and why?

To Try It online, go to **www.mhhe.com/power.**

4. **Type in two or three words from your list,** making sure they are spelled correctly, then search. Note: You can do a few things here to limit the number of results returned, thus making your search more efficient. Most search engines allow you to use the following:

figure 7.6
Starting a Search
This search on Google on How do I use the Web? identified more than 2.8 billion sites.

- *Quotation marks,* to denote a phrase—words that should appear together, in a specific order (e.g., "animal rights").
- *Plus signs,* used before terms that must appear in all results returned (+ "animal rights" + experimentation).
- *Minus signs,* before terms you do not want to appear in results (+ "animal rights" + experimentation − fur).
- *Boolean operators*—words like AND, OR, AND NOT, and NEAR (e.g., "animal rights" AND experimentation NOT fur).

Check the "Help" section of your preferred search engine for more precise information on limiting your searches.

5. **Open a new window,** type in a different arrangement of your terms, and search again.

6. **Identify the common links between the two searches.** Read the very brief summaries provided.

7. **When you choose a Web site, open the page in a new window** so that you can go back to your list of hits.

8. **Open a text editor window.** Copy and paste the site's address into that window and follow it with an annotation of your own. Do that for five sites.

9. **See if you have found the answer you were looking for.** If not, reformulate your question to come up with new key words.

10. **Resist the temptation to simply cut and paste the material into a new document,** once you've found the information you're looking for. It's too easy to succumb to plagiarism if you simply copy material. Instead, take notes on the material using the critical thinking and notetaking skills you've developed for use with other, more traditional information sources.

Then save your notes. You can save your notes on a computer's hard drive, a flash drive, or a network drive (if you have space on one). You can also print out hard copies of what you create virtually.

However you do it, *make sure you save material frequently and make backup copies.* Nothing is more frustrating than laboring over a document for hours and having it disappear into cyberspace.

Evaluating the Information You Find on the Web

In most instances, you'll find more information than you need, and you'll have to evaluate the information you have found. Some of the important questions you must address before you can feel confident about what you've found include the following:

> **How authoritative is the information?** It is absolutely essential to consider the source of the material. Approach every piece of information with a critical eye, trying to determine what the author's biases might be. The best approach is to use multiple sources of information. If one source diverges radically from the others, you may reasonably question the reliability of that source.

"On the Internet, nobody knows you're a dog."

Using the Web at Work

The skills you learn at finding and sorting information on the Web will have many uses in your working life. Nearly every modern office is equipped with Internet-ready computers. Your employer will probably expect you to be able to find specific pieces of information—addresses, dates, phone numbers, and so forth—using the Web, regardless of your specific profession. Further, in many industries, Web skills are crucial. Real estate agents, for example, need to be able to use the Web to assess markets and post offerings; accountants need to be able to research costs; salespeople need to be able to get background on present and potential clients.

Even if you don't work in an office setting, you will find great use for the Web. Whatever professional problem you are facing—from an engine you can't fix to a patient who won't cooperate—there are others who have faced it before, and probably more than one of these people has shared his or her experiences online. Your evaluation skills will be crucial in applying what you find on the Web to your job, but it's likely that there is helpful, reliable information online to be found.

Another approach is to consider the publisher of the material or sponsoring institution. For instance, sites established by well-known publishers and organizations are more likely to contain accurate information than those created by unknown (and sometimes anonymous) authors. Remember, the Web is completely unregulated: *Anyone* can put *anything* on the Web.

> **How current is the information?** No matter what the subject, information is changing at a rapid rate. Consider whether what you've found is the most recent and up-to-date material. Compare older sources to newer ones to identify changes in the ways in which the topic is considered.

> **How well are claims documented?** Are there references and citations to support the information? Are specific studies identified?

A Final Word

The Information Age presents us with great promise and opportunity. Through the use of media such as e-mail and the Internet, we have at our fingertips the ability to communicate with others around the world. We can break the bounds of our physical location and reach across geography to learn about others. The computer keyboard truly can be said to contain keys to the entire earth and its peoples.

NAME: **Jordan M. Miller**

SCHOOL: **Surry Community College, Dobson, North Carolina**

For Jordan Miller, there were three keys to academic success that permitted him to make a successful transition to college: developing good organizational skills, learning new reading strategies, and learning to speak up in class and ask the right questions. Until he mastered those skills, academic success was elusive.

"I was struggling in my junior year at high school," he recalled, "and noticed that my peers were preparing to go on to college and realized that I wasn't where I wanted to be at the time."

One immediate solution was to find a personal place to study, which helped him organize his studying.

"Everyone has different study habits," he noted, "but for me, I had to find a place where I could always go to study. Before that, I was studying all over the house. But after I got more organized, I found a specific place to study and saw I could concentrate better, and things would go faster."

Miller's pursuit of new study habits and approaches were further expanded when he enrolled in Surry Community College and took a reading class.

"I noticed that when I would read something, by the time I reached the end of the page I forgot what I had read," he said. "Through a reading class at Surry, I began to slow my reading. I started to highlight sections and annotate important bits of information such as names and dates in the margins. This helped a lot."

"As a result I didn't have to go back and re-read the book. Instead, I could just review my notes and annotations," Miller added. "In addition, I noticed that I, as well as other students, would often skip over graphs and figures. But I came to the conclusion that they were very important."

Miller, who plans to continue his education at the University of North Carolina at Wilmington, also overcame his fear of speaking up in class and asking questions, which proved to be a key skill.

"I always sat in the back of the class, but I found there were too many distractions. Just about anything would sidetrack me," he said. "As soon as I moved to the front, things changed.

"But I was scared to ask questions, fearing the other students would think I wasn't smart enough," Miller added. "It was only after I started asking questions that I realized that all my classmates had the same questions."

"I would urge all students to ask questions and seek out the teacher for explanations. And remember, if you have a question about the material, others probably have the same question, too," he said.

Looking Back

What are the educational uses of technology?

▸ Course Web sites, CD-ROMs, textbook Web sites, podcasts, blogs, and classroom presentation programs are among the major educational uses of technology.

What is available on the Web?

▸ The Internet is a vast network that connects millions of computers. It has numerous useful features, including e-mail, text messaging, instant messaging, listservs, and the Web.

▸ E-mail and the Web are the most frequently used features of the Internet.

▸ E-mail permits instant communication across the world. Users can reply to messages, forward them, and include attachments.

What is distance learning?

▸ Distance learning is a form of education that does not require the physical presence of a student in a classroom. It is usually conducted over the Web.

▸ Distance learning requires some adjustments for students, but it is likely to increase in popularity in future years.

How can I develop information competency?

▸ There are two main sources of information today: libraries and the Web.

▸ Information in libraries is available in print form, electronic form, and microform.

▸ Library resources can be found through the use of the library catalog, which may be print based but is increasingly likely to be digital.

▸ The Web is another major source of information. Web users access Web pages (or sites) by using a browser, locate information by using search engines, and move from site to site by following links on each Web page.

What do I need to keep in mind as I use the Web to gather information?

▸ Using the Web effectively to find information can be tricky. It has many dead ends, false trails, and distractions, and the accuracy of the information presented as fact can be difficult to assess.

▸ Information on the Web must be carefully evaluated by considering how reliable the source is, how current the information is, and how well the source's claims are documented.

[KEY TERMS AND CONCEPTS]

Podcast (p. 161)
Blog (p. 161)
Internet (p. 162)
Web (p. 162)
E-mail (p. 162)
Text messaging (texting) (p. 163)
Instant messaging (p. 163)

Listserv (p. 163)
Emoticons (or smileys) (p. 165)
Distance learning (p. 169)
Blended (or hybrid) courses (p. 169)
Information competency (p. 174)
Online database (p. 174)
Call number (p. 175)

Stacks (p. 176)
Recall (p. 176)
Interlibrary loan (p. 176)
Browser (p. 177)
Web page (p. 178)
Link (p. 178)
Search engine (p. 178)

[RESOURCES]

ON CAMPUS

If you are having difficulty connecting to or surfing the Web, the first place to turn is your college's computer center. Most campuses have consultants who can help you with the technical aspects of computer usage.

If you need access to computers, most colleges have computer labs. Typically, these labs provide computers with Web access, as well as printers. It's important to check their hours, as they usually are not open 24/7. In addition, you may have to wait in line for a computer, so it is a good idea to bring some other work to the lab so you have something to do while waiting. You may also need to provide printer paper if you want to print something out.

The librarians at your college library are the people to whom you should turn first if you need help in locating information. In recent years, librarians—most of whom hold advanced degrees—have undergone a significant change in what they do, and most are equally at home using traditional print material and searching electronic information storehouses.

IN PRINT

A good introductory guide to computers is Michael Miller's *Absolute Beginner's Guide to Computer Basics* (Que, 2007). *Web Search Savvy: Strategies and Shortcuts for Online Research* by Barbara Friedman (Lawrence Erlbaum, 2004) provides a step-by-step guide to locating information of all sorts. Finally, *Peterson's Guide to Online Learning* (Peterson's, 2005) offers clear instruction on becoming an effective online learner.

ON THE WEB

Many sites on the Web provide the opportunity to extend your learning about the material in this chapter. (Although the Web addresses were accurate at the time the book was printed, check the *P.O.W.E.R. Learning* Web site [**www.mhhe.com/power**] for any changes that may have occurred.)

> ➤ Imperial College (London)'s Department of Computing offers FOLDOC (Free Online Dictionary of Computing) at **foldoc.org.** If you're having a hard time trying to figure out some computer jargon, this site—a dictionary of computer terminology—might help. Topics are listed alphabetically and a search engine helps locate specific information.

> ➤ The WWW Virtual Library (**www.vlib.org/**) is one of the oldest catalogs of the Web, providing useful links to thousands of subjects.

> ➤ Yahoo! (**www.yahoo.com**) is a very popular Internet search engine and subject directory. Unlike Google and Alta Vista, as a subject directory, Yahoo! allows browsing through prearranged categories (e.g., education, health, social science, and more). It also offers easy access to news, weather, maps, the Yellow Pages, and much more.

1   Using the search engine of your choice, find the address for the Web site of the libraries of the University of California at Berkeley. Once there, try to find "Finding Information on the Internet: A Tutorial." Try the tutorial, which will help you understand many of the basic skills needed to use the Internet effectively. (Would taking the tutorial *first* have helped you to find it?)

2   To see for yourself how the Web can be a great resource for locating information on important issues, try to find the answer to this question: "What are the effects of media violence on children?" Go to a search engine (try **www.google.com**) and type in the phrase: "media violence and children" (being sure to include the quotation marks). Look over the first page of documents that the search engine turns up. Are they in fact about the effects of media violence on children? Do they answer the question you are asking? What is the answer to the question?

The Case of . . .

The Empty Page

It had already been a long day for Joelle.

She'd worked two hours of overtime at her job supervising a call center. She'd driven home and immediately sat down at her computer to start work on her paper for her marketing class the next day. It was already 11:00 PM by the time she finished her research on the Web. Then she began writing, opening a new file in her word processing program.

Joelle worked hard, drinking coffee to help her concentrate on the paper—and to keep her eyes open.

When she was about three-quarters of the way done, her computer screen suddenly froze. Joelle pushed every button she could think of, but finally had to switch her computer off and then switch it back on. She opened the file for her paper . . . and saw an empty page.

To her horror, Joelle realized that her paper had been lost. She looked at the clock—it was almost 3:00 AM. Did she really need to start her paper *all over again?*

1. How well did Joelle use her time to work on her paper? What advice would you give her about the preparation stage of working on a paper?

2. Clearly, Joelle should have saved her work frequently while she was working. What else should she have done while working on her paper to help her recover from such a catastrophe?

3. Do you think Joelle's instructor would be sensitive to her problem? Do you think he or she would be willing to give her an extension? What could Joelle do to make her case that she had nearly finished the paper?

4. What should Joelle do next to begin reconstructing her paper and recovering as much of her work as possible?

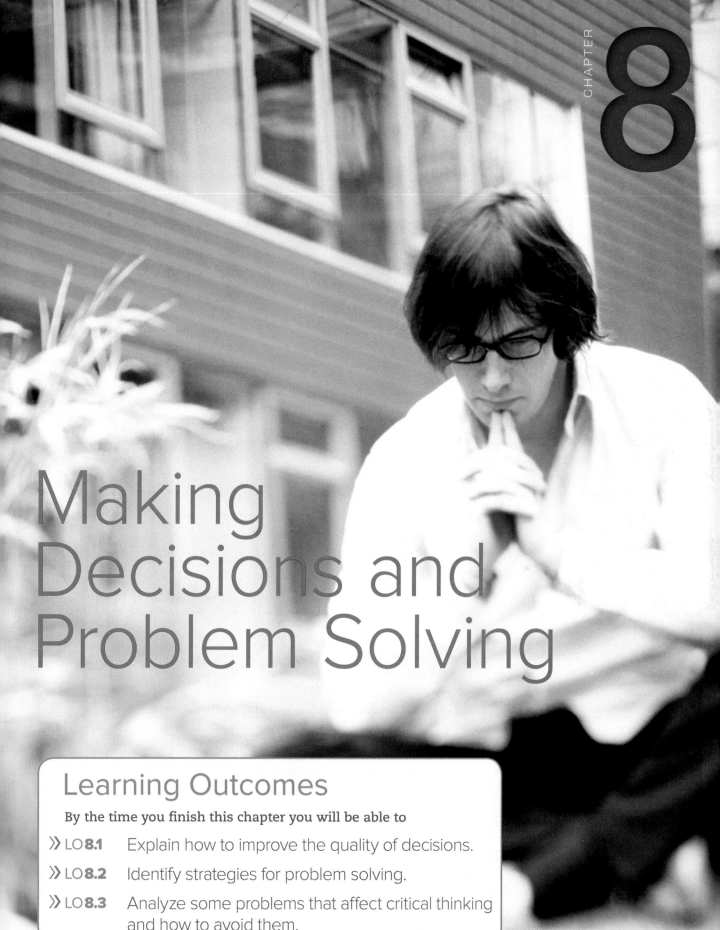

Making Decisions and Problem Solving

Learning Outcomes

By the time you finish this chapter you will be able to

» **LO 8.1** Explain how to improve the quality of decisions.

» **LO 8.2** Identify strategies for problem solving.

» **LO 8.3** Analyze some problems that affect critical thinking and how to avoid them.

Ron Taubman had a tough decision coming up.

In three weeks, he would earn his electrician's degree. It had taken a great deal of effort and the sacrifice of a lot of free time, but he was almost there. It was what to do next, though, that was giving Ron problems.

All through college he had worked for a local contractor, picking up construction jobs when the contractor needed an extra pair of hands. Now that Ron was graduating with his electrician's degree, the contractor had offered to make him a permanent member of his construction crew. In short, he was being offered more work at a better salary.

Ron knew it was a great offer—but it was not Ron's only option. A friend he had met in college wanted to start his own electrician business, and he wanted Ron to be his partner. Working together, Ron's friend said, they could build the business quickly, and they would earn more and have more flexibility than if they worked for someone else.

As graduation approached, Ron knew he had to make up his mind. But he kept going around in circles. Was security more important than flexibility? How much was running his own business worth to him?

Ron knew he had to make up his mind. But how?

Looking Ahead

Like Ron, all of us face important decisions in our lives at one time or another. How can we make the right decisions? The best way is to employ some basic techniques that can help improve the quality of our decision making.

This chapter will give you a sense of what decision making is and is not, and it discusses a structured process that can help make your decisions the right ones. We'll also consider the related issue of problem solving. You'll confront a variety of problems as you proceed through college and your career. We'll look at a number of proven techniques that will help you solve them.

Neither making decisions nor solving problems is easy. Sometimes the best decision or solution to a problem is one that we don't see at first; we all have mental blind spots. The best problem solvers and decision makers have learned how to use critical thinking to see around these blind spots. To help you improve your critical thinking skills, we'll examine some common problems that can affect our thinking and discuss several biases that can make us jump too quickly to conclusions.

» LO 8.1 Making Good Decisions: A Framework

Decision making

The process of deciding among various alternatives

Decision making is the process of deciding among various alternatives. Whether you are trying to decide between a Ford and a Honda; between an apartment that is close to your job and one that is close to family; or simply between a hamburger and a pizza—every one of these choices requires a decision. Some decisions are easily made and have few consequences, but others, such as whether to take one job or another, can involve the deepest examination of our beliefs and values.

Whatever you're deciding, you need to think critically in order to make a reasoned decision. You need to actively apply your past knowledge, synthesize and evaluate alternatives, and reason and reflect on a course of action. The greater your depth of thinking about the components of the decision, the more likely it is that you'll come up with the best choice.

To make a good decision, map out a strategy for making the choice that is best for you. Every decision can benefit from your systematically thinking through the options involved, based on the P.O.W.E.R. Plan illustrated here.

P.O.W.E.R. Plan

 # Identifying Your Goals

Every decision starts with the end you have in mind: the goals you wish to accomplish by making the decision.

For example, suppose you are trying to decide how to spend a little extra money: on a gym membership or on a distance learning course in computer programming. To decide, you need to consider both your short- and long-term goals. For instance, the gym membership may raise your level of fitness and help you lose weight, something you promised yourself you'd do. The programming class will be interesting, but the skills you'll learn aren't really applicable to your current job. In terms of short-term goals, then, the gym membership may be the better choice. On the other hand, while the programming class may not provide as clear-cut an immediate payoff, it may help you meet your longer-term goal of entering the technology industry.

In short, every decision should start with a consideration of what our short- and long-term goals are. Identifying the goals that underlie decisions ensures that we make decisions in the context of our entire lives and not just to provide short-term answers to immediate problems.

 # Considering and Assessing the Alternatives

Every decision is based on weighing various alternatives. Determining what those alternatives are, and their possible consequences, is often the most difficult part of decision making.

> "Nothing is more difficult, and therefore more precious, than to be able to decide."
>
> Napoleon I, *Maxims*, 1804–15

Develop a List of Alternatives

It's important not only to think thoroughly about the obvious alternatives, but also to consider those that are less obvious. For many decisions, there are choices beyond the "this or that" alternatives that can dominate our thinking. How can you be sure that you've considered all the possible alternatives? Using the technique of freewriting can help.

In **freewriting,** one writes continuously for a fixed period of time, perhaps 5 or 10 minutes. During this period, the idea is to write as many different ideas as possible, without stopping. It makes no difference whether the alternatives are good or bad or even whether they make sense. All that matters is that you let yourself brainstorm about the topic for a while and get it down on paper.

With freewriting, evaluating the worth of the ideas you've generated comes later. After you have produced as many possibilities as you can, then you go back and sift out the reasonable ones from those that are truly unlikely or just plain wacky. It's OK if you have to delete quite a few alternatives from your list; the process is likely to have liberated some truly reasonable alternatives that you might not otherwise have come up with. (Try the technique in the "Use Freewriting" exercise—see **Try It 1** on page 193.)

Freewriting
A technique involving continuous, nonstop writing, without self-criticism, for a fixed period of time

We've all been there: facing a mind-boggling array of similar choices. However, by systematically assessing the alternatives, we can make informed decisions that will satisfy us.

Assess Alternatives

Once you have generated as extensive a list of alternatives as possible, assess them. You need to follow three key steps when assessing each alternative:

1. *Determine the possible outcomes for each alternative.* Some outcomes are positive, some negative. Consider as many as you can think of. For example, if you are considering ways of solving transportation problems, one alternative might be to purchase a car. That alternative produces several potential outcomes. For example, you know that it will be easier to get wherever you want to go, and you might even have a better social life—clearly positive outcomes. But it is also true that buying and owning a car will be expensive, or it may be difficult to find convenient parking—both significant negative outcomes.

2. *Determine the probability that those outcomes will take place.* Some outcomes are far more likely than others. To take this into account, make a rough estimate of the likelihood that an outcome will come to pass, ranging from 100 percent (it is certain that it will occur) to 0 percent (it is certain that it will never occur). Obviously, the probabilities are just guesses, but going through the exercise of estimating them will make the outcomes more real and will permit you to compare the various alternatives against one another more easily.

3. *Compare the alternatives, taking into account the potential outcomes of each.* Systematically compare each of the alternatives. Then ask yourself the key question: Which alternative, on balance, provides the most positive (and most likely) outcomes?

Obviously, not every decision requires such an elaborate process. In fact, most won't. But when it comes to major decisions, those that could have a large impact upon you and your life, it's worthwhile to follow a systematic process.

Take a look at **Career Connections** on page 194 for another process that you can follow to help you make a career decision.

Making and Carrying Out the Decision

Working through the previous steps will lead you to the point of decision: choosing one of the alternatives you've identified. Having carried out the steps will make the actual decision easier, but not necessarily easy.

Choosing among Alternatives

The reason that important decisions are difficult is that the alternatives you have to choose from carry both benefits and costs. Choosing one alternative means that you have to accept the costs of that choice and give up the benefits of the other alternatives.

Use Freewriting

Use freewriting to think of as many answers as you can to each of the following questions. The ground rules are that you should spend three minutes on each question, generating as many ideas as possible—regardless of whether they are feasible. To give yourself maximum freedom, write each answer on a separate page.

1. How can you make room in your schedule to take one more course next term than you're taking this term?

2. How can someone get from the 3rd floor to the 20th floor of a building?
   - elevator
   - stairs

3. What should you do if you suspect that one of your coworkers is a space alien?

4. What would happen if the average life span were extended to 125 years?

After generating ideas, go back and evaluate them. How many were actually feasible or realistic? Do you think freewriting led to the production of more or fewer ideas than you would have come up with if you hadn't used the process? Did the quality of ideas change?

 WORKING IN A GROUP

After you have answered the questions above, form a group of classmates and compare your answers with those of others. As a group, try to identify the best answers to each question.

To Try It online, go to **www.mhhe.com/power.**

What if, after going through the steps of the process laid out here, you still can't make up your mind? Try these strategies:

> **Give the decision time.** Sometimes waiting helps. Time can give you a chance to think of additional alternatives. Sometimes the situation will change, or you'll have a change in viewpoint.

From the perspective of . . .

A STUDENT Balancing education and life can be fraught with many alternatives and choices. How do you prioritize options when making a decision?

> **Make a mental movie, acting out the various alternatives.** Many of us have difficulty seeing ourselves in the future and envisioning how various options would play out. One way to get around this difficulty is to cast yourself into a series of "mental movies" that have different endings depending on the decision you make. Working

Weighing Job Possibilities

One of the most difficult decisions you'll ever make is choosing between job offers. Although it's a tough position to be in, keep in mind that it is a *good* position, too—you are lucky to have multiple options.

Here's one method that can help you decide on the right job:

- Generate a selection of choices to consider. Include not only the job options you have, but also alternative ideas such as pursuing other jobs, earning a degree, starting your own business, and so forth. Even if you doubt you'll select one of these other options, considering them will help you assess what you truly want to do.

- Determine life-satisfaction considerations that are important to you. Generate a list of criteria to use in weighing the possibilities. For instance, you might want to consider the following:

    Benefits (vacation, health insurance, etc.)
    Income
    Spouse's opinions
    Friends' opinions
    Interest in the activity
    Prestige
    Job security
    Time off
    Benefit to society
    Practicality/attainability
    Everyday working conditions

- Determine how well a particular option fulfills each of the life-satisfaction factors you consider important. By systematically considering how a potential path fulfills each of the criteria you use, you'll be able to compare different options. One easy way to do this is to create a chart like the one in **Table 8.1** (which shows an example of how two job options for a massage therapist might fulfill the various criteria).

- Compare different choices. Using the chart, evaluate your possibilities. Keep in mind that this is just a rough guide and that it's only as accurate as (a) the effort you put into completing it and (b) your understanding of a given choice. Use the results in conjunction with other things you find out about the jobs—and yourself.

table 8.1 Making Career Decisions

Life-Satisfaction Considerations	Possible Choice #1 Massage therapist at Vida Spa	Possible Choice #2 Sports massage therapist at State University	Possible Choice #3	Possible Choice #4
Benefits		√		
Income	√	√		
Spouse's opinion		√		
Friends' opinions		√		
Interest in the activity	√	√		
Prestige				
Job security/job openings		√		
Time off	√			
Benefit to society	√	√		
Practicality/attainability	√	√		
Everyday working conditions	√			
Other				
Other				
Other				
Other				
Other				

through the different scripts in your head makes potential outcomes far more real and less abstract than they would be if you simply left them as items on a list of various options.

> **Toss a coin.** This isn't as crazy as it sounds. If each alternative seems equally positive or negative to you, pull out a coin—make option A "heads" and B "tails." Then flip it.

The real power of the coin-toss strategy is that it might help you discover your true feelings. It may happen while the coin is in the air, or it may be that when you see the result of the coin toss, you won't like the outcome and will say to yourself, "No way." In such a case, you've just found out how you really feel.

> **Ask for advice.** Although Western society teaches the virtues of rugged individualism, asking others for their advice is often an excellent strategy. A friend, an instructor, a parent, or a counselor can provide helpful recommendations—sometimes because they've had to make similar decisions themselves. You don't have to take their advice, but it can help to listen to what they have to say.

> **Go with your gut feeling.** Call it what you like—gut feeling, intuition, hunch, superstition—but sometimes we need to go with our hearts and not our minds. If you've thought rationally about a decision and have been unable to determine the best course of action but have a gut feeling that one choice is better than another, follow your feelings.

Following a gut feeling does not mean that you don't need to consider the pros and cons of a decision rationally and carefully. In fact, generally our "intuitions" are best when informed by the thoughtfulness of a more rational process.

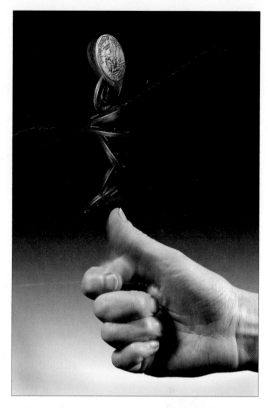

If all else fails, toss a coin to decide what alternative to follow. Tossing a coin at least brings you to a decision. Then, if you find you're unhappy with the result, you'll have gained important information about how you really feel regarding a particular choice.

Carrying Out the Decision

Ultimately, decisions must move from thought to action—they have to be carried out. Consequently, the final stage in making a decision is to act upon it. You need to turn your decision into behavior.

 E Evaluate   Considering the Outcomes

> "In any moment of decision, the best thing you can do is the right thing, the next best thing is the wrong thing, and the worst thing you can do is nothing."
>
> **President Theodore Roosevelt**

Did you make the right decision?

Even if you've spent time and mental effort in thinking through a decision, you still need to consider the results. Even well-considered decisions can end up being wrong, either because you neglected to consider something or because something has changed: either you or the situation.

Remember, it's never too late to change your mind. In fact, even major life decisions are often reversible. That's why it's so important to evaluate your choices. If you chose the wrong alternative, reverse course and reconsider your options.

It's not a bad thing to change your mind. In fact, admitting that a decision was a mistake is often the wisest and most courageous course of action. You don't want to

Journal Reflections

My Decision Crossroads

Have you ever made a decision that proved to be of great importance in terms of the direction your life would take? For example, perhaps you broke off a romantic relationship, or decided to quit a job to go back to school, or took a stand on a controversial political issue. Reflect on that decision by answering these questions.

1. What was an important decision that you made that had significant effects on your life?

2. What have been the main benefits and disadvantages that you derived from the decision?

3. Every decision to do something is also a decision not to do other things. What did your decision keep you from doing?

4. Considering both the benefits and disadvantages of the decision, would you say that you made a good decision?

5. Thinking critically about the approach you used to make the decision, what alternative approaches might you have used to make it? Could these alternatives have produced a different decision? How?

be so rigidly committed to a decision that you're unable to evaluate the consequences objectively. Give yourself permission to be wrong.

 ## Reconsidering Your Goals and Options

We can get to most places by multiple routes. There's the fastest and most direct route, which will get us to our destination in the least amount of time. Then there's the longer, more scenic route, where the trip itself provides pleasure. You can "take the long way home," as the song goes. Is one route better than the other? Often not. Both take us to our destination. However, the experience of reaching our goal will have been very different.

Decisions about how to achieve a goal are similar to traveling down different routes. There's often no single decision that is best, just as there's often no single road to a particular place. Consequently, it's important to periodically reconsider the major decisions that we've made about our lives.

Ask yourself these questions:

> Are my decisions still producing the desired consequences?

> Are my decisions still appropriate, given my circumstances and changes in my life?

> Are my decisions consistent with what I want to get out of life?

Periodically taking stock like this is the best way to make sure that your decisions are taking you where you want to go. Taking stock also helps you to be more effective in making future decisions.

» LO 8.2 Problem Solving: Applying Critical Thinking to Find Solutions

Two trains are approaching one another, each moving at 60 miles an hour. If the trains continue moving at the same speed, how long will it be before . . .

If this is what comes to mind when you think of problem solving, think again. **Problem solving** encompasses more than the abstract, often unrealistic situations portrayed in math texts. It involves everyday, commonplace situations: How do we divide the restaurant bill so that each person pays a fair share? How do I keep my 1-year-old from tumbling down the stairs when there seems to be no way to fasten a gate at the top? How can I stop a faucet from dripping? How do I manage to study for a test and do the laundry the same evening?

Problem solving
The process of generating alternatives to work on

While decision making is most focused on choosing among various alternatives, the central issue in problem solving is *generating* alternatives. Since many problems require that decisions be made regarding alternatives, decision making and problem solving are often related.

What's the Problem?

The first step in solving any problem is to be as clear as you can about what the problem is. This may sound easy, but often it isn't. In fact, it may take some time to figure out just what is at stake. The reason is that some problems are big and hard to define, while others are quite precise, such as mathematical equations or the solution to a jigsaw puzzle. Determining how to stop terrorism or finding peace in the Middle East are big, ill-defined problems. Simply determining what information is required to solve such problems can be a major undertaking.

To determine what the problem is and set yourself on a course for finding a solution, ask yourself these questions:

> What is the initial set of facts?

> What is it that I need to solve?

> Which parts of the problem appear to be most critical to finding a solution?

> Is there some information that can be ignored?

The more systematically you approach a problem, the better. For instance, you can apply the five P.O.W.E.R. steps to problems, similar to how it can be used to make decisions. When you consider a problem systematically and think through your options, your choices will become clearer to you.

As you clarify what the problem is, you may find that you have encountered similar problems before. Your experience with them may suggest the means to the solution of the current problem. For example, consider the problem of the trains rushing toward each other. If you have worked on this kind of problem before, you might know a fairly simple equation you can write to determine how long it will take before they meet. If someone asks you about the problem she has in keeping her toddler from tumbling down the stairs, you might offer your experience in keeping your own children from visiting an off-limits area of your house.

On the other hand, to solve many of the problems we face in our daily lives, we have to do more than reach into our memories of prior situations. Instead, we need to devise novel approaches. How do you do this? There are several strategies you might use.

Strategies for Solving Life's Messier Problems

> **Break the problem down into smaller, more manageable pieces.** Divide a problem into a series of subgoals. As you reach each subgoal, you get closer to your overall goal of solving the problem. For example, if your goal is to find a job in Montreal, a subgoal might be to learn French. By reaching this subgoal, you move closer to reaching your ultimate goal—a job in a country that interests you.

> **Work backward.** Sometimes you know the answer to the problem, but not how to get there. Then it's best to work backward. A **working backward** strategy starts at the desired solution or goal and works backward, moving away from the goal. For example, if your in-laws show up unexpectedly and you are faced with the problem of preparing a quick dinner, you might imagine the end result—the meal on the table—and then work backward to consider how to prepare it.

Working backward
The strategy of starting at the desired solution or goal and working toward the starting point of the problem

> **Use a graph, chart, or drawing to redefine the problem.** Transforming words into pictures often can help us to devise solutions that otherwise would elude us. One good example is this problem:

A hiker climbs a mountain on Saturday, leaving at sunrise and arriving at the top near sunset. He spends the night at the top. The next day, Sunday, he leaves at daybreak and heads down the mountain, following the same path that he climbed the day before. The question is this: Will there be any time during the second day when the hiker will be at exactly the same point on the mountain as he was at exactly the same time on the first day?

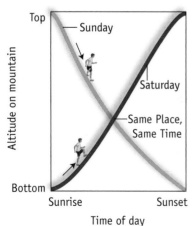

figure 8.1
Up and Down the Mountain: The Paths to a Solution

Trying to solve the problem through the use of math or words is quite difficult. However, there's a simpler way: drawing the two paths. As you can see from **Figure 8.1,** the drawing helps provide a solution.

- **Consider the opposite.** Problems can sometimes be solved by considering the opposite of the problem you're seeking to solve. For example, to define "good mental health" you might try to define "bad mental health."

- **Use analogies.** Some problems can be solved through the use of an **analogy,** which is a comparison between concepts or objects that are alike in some respects, but dissimilar in most others. For instance, if you liken a disastrous experience family vacation to a voyage on the *Titanic,* you're using an analogy.

    Analogies may help us gain additional insight into the problem at hand, and they may provide an alternative framework for interpreting the information that is provided. For instance, the manufacturers of Pringles potato chips found that they could cut packaging costs if they slightly moistened the chips before packaging them—an idea that came when researchers noticed that dry tree leaves, which normally crumble easily, could be packed together tightly when they were wet.

- **Take another's perspective.** By viewing a problem from another person's point of view, it is often possible to obtain a new perspective on the problem that will make the problem easier to solve.

- **Forget about it.** Just as with decision making, sometimes it's best simply to walk away from a problem for a while. Just a few hours or days away from a problem may give us enough of a break to jar some hidden solutions from the recesses of our minds. The idea of "sleeping on it" also sometimes works; we may wake up refreshed and filled with new ideas.

    Test these problem-solving strategies in **Try It 2** on page 200.

Analogy
A comparison between concepts or objects that are alike in some respects, but dissimilar in most others

Assessing Your Potential Solutions

If a problem clearly has only one answer, such as a math problem, this step in problem solving is relatively easy. You should be able to work the problem and figure out whether you've been successful. In contrast, messier problems have several possible

Exercise Your Problem-Solving Skills

Working in a group, try to solve these problems.[1] To help you devise solutions, a hint regarding the best strategy to use is included after each problem.

1. One cold, dark, and rainy night, a college student has a flat tire on a deserted stretch of country road. He pulls onto the shoulder to change it. After removing the four lug nuts and placing them into the hub cap, he removes the flat tire and takes his spare out of the trunk. As he is moving the spare tire into position, his hand slips and he upsets the hub cap with the lug nuts, which tumble off into the night where he can't find them. What should he do? (*Hint:* Instead of asking how he might find the lug nuts, reframe the problem and ask where else he might find lug nuts.)

2. Cheryl, who is a construction worker, is paving a walk, and she needs to add water quickly to the concrete she has just poured. She reaches for her pail to get water from a spigot in the front of the house, but suddenly realizes the pail has a large rust hole in it and cannot be used. As the concrete dries prematurely, she fumbles through her toolbox for tools and materials with which to repair the pail. She finds many tools, but nothing that would serve to patch the pail. The house is locked and no one is home. What should she do? (*Hint:* When is a pail not a pail?)

3. What day follows the day before yesterday if two days from now will be Sunday? (*Hint:* Break it up or draw a diagram.)

4. Carrie has four chains, each three links long. She wants to join the four chains into a single, closed chain. Having a link opened costs 2 cents and having a link closed costs 3 cents. How can Carrie have the chains joined for 15 cents? (*Hint:* Can only end links be opened?)

5. What is two-thirds of one-half? (*Hint:* Reverse course.)

6. Juan has three separate large boxes. Inside each large box are two separate medium-sized boxes, and inside each of the medium boxes are four small boxes. How many boxes does Juan have altogether? (*Hint:* Draw it.)

After working to solve these problems, consider these questions: Which problems were the easiest to solve, and which were more difficult? Why? Were the hints helpful? Do you think there was more than one solution to any of the problems? Did your initial assumptions about the problem help or hinder your efforts to solve it? (*Note:* Answers to the problems are found on page 210.)

To Try It online, go to www.mhhe.com/power.

solutions, some of which may be more involved and costly than others. In these cases, it's necessary to compare alternative solutions and choose the best one. For example, suppose you want to surprise your best friend on her birthday. She is working in Omaha, about 90 miles from you, and you need to find a way to get there. Perhaps you could rent a car, take a bus, or find some other way. Money is an issue. You will want to figure out how much each alternative costs before choosing one as your solution to the problem. Since every penny you spend getting there is a penny less that you will have to celebrate, you will want to weigh the options carefully.

Finally, spend a bit of time seeing whether there is a way to refine the solution. Is the solution you've devised adequate? Does it address all aspects of the problem? Are there alternative approaches that might be superior? Answering these questions, and refining your solution to address them, can give you confidence that the solution you've come up with is the best. For example, if you're trying to get to Omaha, you might decide to use the ride board at your school to try to find a ride with someone going to Omaha that day. Maybe your friend's family is going to be driving in and could pick you up or could even lend you a car for the trip.

Remember that not every problem has a clear-cut solution. Sometimes we need to be satisfied with a degree of uncertainty and ambiguity. For some of us, such a lack of clarity is difficult, making us uneasy, and it may push us to choose solutions—any solution—that seems to solve the problem. Others of us feel more comfortable with ambiguity, but this may lead us to let problems ride, without resolving the situation.

Either way, it's important to consider what your own problem-solving style is when you seek to identify solutions. And keep in mind that often there is no perfect solution to a problem—only some solutions that are better than others.

From the perspective of . . .

A PHARMACY TECHNICIAN The ability to ask questions is a trait that will continue to matter in your career. What are some of the potential consequences of not asking questions in a field that presents possible health risks?

Reflect on the Process of Problem Solving

It's natural to step back and bask in the satisfaction of solving a tough problem. That's fine—but take a moment to consider your success. Each time we solve a problem we end up a couple steps ahead, but only if we've thought about the process we went through to solve it.

Go back and consider what it took to solve the problem. Can the means you used to come up with your solution be applied to more complex kinds of problems? If you arrived at a solution by drawing a chart, would this work on similar problems in the future? Taking a moment to rethink your solution can provide you with an opportunity to become an expert problem solver and, more generally, to improve your critical thinking skills. Don't let the opportunity slip away.

≫ LO 8.3 Don't Fool Yourself: Avoiding Everyday Problems in Critical Thinking

Being able to think clearly and without bias is the basis for critical thinking. As you have probably noticed already, the quality of the thinking you do regarding problems and decisions plays a crucial role in determining how successful you are.

Unfortunately, it is sometimes the alternative you *didn't* think of that can end up being the most satisfactory decision or solution. So how can we learn to think critically and avoid blind spots that hinder us in our decision making and problem solving? We can start by considering the common obstacles to critical thinking.

Here are some of the decision-making and problem-solving pitfalls to look out for. Avoiding them will improve your critical thinking greatly.

Using Critical Thinking in Your Classes

Nowhere is critical thinking more important to use—and demonstrate to your instructors—than when you're in your classes. Here are some strategies to foster your skills as a critical thinker when you are in class:

- **Ask questions.** Most instructors welcome questions. Even if an instructor doesn't have time to provide a full response, the very act of formulating a question will help you think more critically about the course material.

- **Accept that some questions have no right or wrong answers.** Understanding that some questions have no simple answer is a sign of mental sophistication. Sometimes the best an instructor can do is present competing theories. Although you may want to know which theory is right, accept that sometimes no one knows the answer to that question—that's why they're theories, not facts!

- **Keep an open mind.** Your instructor and classmates have their own perspectives and opinions. Even if you disagree with them, try to figure out why they hold their views. It will help you to see the multiple sides of different issues.

- **Don't deny your emotional reactions—manage them.** There may be times that an instructor or classmate says something that is bothersome or even makes you angry. That's OK. But be sure to manage your emotions so that they don't overwhelm your rational self. And use your emotional reactions to gain self-understanding into what's important to you.

- **Don't be afraid of looking unintelligent.** No one wants to look foolish, especially in front of a roomful of classmates. But don't let self-defeating feelings prevent you from expressing your concerns. Take intellectual risks!

> **Don't assume that giving something a name explains it.** The mere fact that we can give an idea or problem a name doesn't mean we can explain it. Yet we often confuse the two.

For instance, consider the following sequences of questions and answers:

Q. *Why do I have so much trouble falling asleep?*
A. *Because you have insomnia.*

Q. *Why is he so unsociable?*
A. *Because he's an introvert.*

Q. *Why did the defendant shoot those people?*
A. *Because he's insane.*

Q. *How do you know he's insane?*
A. *Because only someone who was insane would shoot people in that way.*[2]

It's clear that none of these answers is satisfactory. All use circular reasoning, in which the alleged explanation for the behavior is simply the use of a label.

> **Don't accept vague generalities dressed up as definitive statements.** Read the following personality analysis and think about how well it applies to you:

You have a need for other people to like and admire you and a tendency to be critical of yourself. You also have a great deal of unused potential that you have not turned to your advantage, and although you have some personality weaknesses, you are generally able to compensate for them. Nonetheless, relating to members of the opposite sex has presented problems to you, and while you appear to be disciplined and self-controlled to others, you tend to be anxious and insecure inside.

If you believe that these statements provide an amazingly accurate description of your unique qualities, you're not alone: Most college students believe that the descriptions are tailored specifically to them.[3] But how is that possible? It isn't. The reality is that the statements are so vague that they are virtually meaningless. The acceptance of vague but seemingly useful and significant statements about oneself and others has been called the *Barnum effect,* after showman and circus master P. T. Barnum, who coined the phrase "there's a sucker born every minute."

> **Don't confuse opinion with fact.** Opinions are not fact. Although we may be aware of this simple formula, almost all of us can be fooled into thinking that someone's opinion is the same as a fact.

A fact is information that is proven to be true. In contrast, an opinion represents judgments, reasoning, beliefs, inferences, or conclusions. If we accept some bit of information as a fact, we can use it to build our opinions. But if we are presented with an opinion, we need to determine the facts on which it is built to judge its reliability.

The difference between fact and opinion can sometimes be subtle. For instance, compare these two statements:

1. Every college student needs to take a writing course during the first term of college.

2. Many college students need to take a writing course during the first term of college.

The first statement is most likely an opinion, because it is so absolute and unqualified. Words such as "every," "all," and "always" are often evidence of opinion. On the other hand, the second statement is more likely a fact, since it contains the qualifier "many." In general, statements that are qualified in some way are more likely to be facts.

Complete **Try It 3** on page 204 to see the difficulties sometimes involved in distinguishing between fact and opinion.

> **Avoid jumping to conclusions.** Read this riddle and try to answer it:

A father and his son were driving along the interstate highway when the father lost control of the car, swerved off the road, and crashed into a utility pole. The father died instantly, and his son was critically injured. An ambulance rushed the boy to a nearby hospital. A prominent surgeon was summoned to provide immediate treatment. When the surgeon arrived and entered the operating room to examine the boy, a loud gasp was heard.
"I can't operate on this boy," the surgeon said. "He is my son."

How can this be?

If you find this puzzling, you've based your reasoning on an assumption: that the surgeon is a male. But suppose you had assumed that the surgeon was a female. Suddenly, the riddle becomes a lot easier. It's far easier to guess that the surgeon is the son's *mother* if we don't leap to embrace a faulty assumption.

Why is it so easy to jump to conclusions? One reason is that we sometimes aren't aware of the assumptions that underlie our thinking. Another is our reliance on "common sense."

> **Be skeptical of "common sense."** Much of what we call common sense makes contradictory claims. For example, if you believe in the notion "Absence makes the heart grow fonder," you may assume that your girlfriend, now working at a

3

Distinguish Fact from Opinion

Read the following statements and try to determine which are facts (put "F" on the line that follows the item) and which are opinions (put "O" on the line that follows the item).

1. College students should get at least 7 hours of sleep every night. _____

2. The average college student sleeps less than 7 hours a night. _____

3. Nikes offer better styling and comfort than any other brand of shoe. _____

4. Two out of five sports figures surveyed preferred Nikes over Converse shoes. _____

5. The U.S. government spends too much money on guns and missiles and not enough money on education. _____

6. Government figures show spending is much higher for guns and missiles than for education. _____

7. In general, U.S. high school students receive less classroom instruction in foreign languages than their counterparts in Europe and Asia. _____

8. No student in the United States should graduate without having studied a language other than English for at least 4 years. _____

9. Michael Jordan is the most outstanding, most exciting, and certainly most successful basketball player who ever stepped onto a court. _____

Items 1, 3, 5, 8, and 9 are opinions; the rest are facts. What are the main differences between opinion and fact?

To Try It online, go to **www.mhhe.com/power.**

job in another city, will arrive home at Christmas even more in love with you than before. But what about "Out of sight, out of mind," which suggests a less positive outcome? Common sense often presents us with contradictory advice, making it a less than useful guide to decision making and problem solving.

> **Don't assume that just because two events occur together one causes the other.** Just because two events appear to be associated with one another, we cannot conclude that one event has caused the other to occur. For example, suppose you read that a study showed that 89 percent of juvenile delinquents use marijuana. Does this mean that smoking marijuana *causes* juvenile delinquency?

No, it doesn't. It is pretty safe to say that 100 percent of juvenile delinquents grew up drinking milk. Would you feel comfortable saying that milk causes delinquency? With the association between marijuana use and delinquent behavior, it is very likely that there's some third factor—such as influence of peers—that causes people both to (a) try drugs and (b) engage in delinquent behavior. The bottom line: We do not know the cause of the delinquency just because delinquents often smoke marijuana.

In short, we need to be careful in assuming causality. Even if two events or other kinds of variables occur together, it does not mean that one causes the other. To see this for yourself, take a look at the statements in **Try It 4** on pages 206 and 207, "What's the Real Explanation?"

Try It!

What's the Real Explanation?

Even though two events are related to each other, it doesn't mean that one causes the other. Instead, there is often some other factor that is the actual cause of the relationship.

To see this for yourself, consider each of the following (actual!) findings. What might be a plausible explanation for each one?

1. Ice cream sales and the timing of shark attacks are highly related. Why?

2. The number of cavities children have and the size of their vocabulary are closely related. Why?

3. Skirt hemlines tend to rise as stock prices rise. Why?

4. Women with breast implants have a higher rate of suicide than those without breast implants. Why?

5. People who own washing machines are more likely to die in car accidents than those who don't. Why?

6. Men who carry their cell phones in their front pants pockets have a lower sperm count than those who don't carry them in their front pants pockets. Why?

Once you've completed this **Try It,** look at the possible explanations listed below. Keep in mind that these are simply theories; we don't know for sure if they're correct:

1. The actual cause is probably the temperature, which causes both sales of ice cream and ocean swimming to increase.

2. Both the number of cavities children have and the size of their vocabularies are related to their age.

3. Skirt hemlines go up, as does the stock market, when people are feeling less conservative and more optimistic.

4. Having breast implants and committing suicide both may be a result of unhappiness or a poor self-image.

5. People who own washing machines are more likely to own cars, and therefore they stand a higher risk of dying in a car crash.

6. Men with high-stress jobs may be more likely to have cell phones, and it is the stress that produces the low sperm count—not the placement of a phone in their pocket.

To Try It online, go to **www.mhhe.com/power.**

speaking of success

NAME: **Francine Sanchez**

SCHOOL: **Lehman College, New York, NY, BA;**
University of Pennsylvania, MA in Social Work

In her senior year of high school, Francine Sanchez suddenly found herself as the oldest of four siblings in what had become a single-parent family. As a result, she was forced to take on a more significant role in her household, helping care for her three younger brothers and sisters.

With these unexpected demands thrust upon her, Sanchez realized that time management was crucial to meet the challenges she faced. Despite the circumstances, she committed herself to pursue a college education full time.

"I was determined not to go into debt for college, and I knew that my family could not afford to provide me with financial assistance," said Sanchez, who is now Education Program Development Coordinator for the New York City Administration for Children's Services. "At one point I juggled three part-time jobs," she added.

"I learned a lot about myself in college, and learned my own strengths that have helped me," said Sanchez, who went on to graduate with honors from Lehman College. She eventually completed a masters degree in Social Work at the University of Pennsylvania.

Through her years of undergraduate and graduate school, Sanchez was always involved in many activities outside of academics, requiring her to manage her time carefully.

"During my first year as an undergraduate, I learned a lot of things though academic experiences, and one was to be able to say 'no' when I felt I had a lot on my plate," said Sanchez. "There came a point where I realized my limitations." Sanchez also said that it was very important to make time for herself, especially when weighed down with work.

"If ever I got to the point where I felt overwhelmed or stressed out, I would just stop and take a short break," she added. "For me it was watching something light on TV. For someone else it could be taking a walk, working out, or talking to a friend. It's important to learn to do that and decompress."

Looking Back

How can I improve the quality of my decisions?

➤ A structured process of decision making can clarify the issues involved, expand our options, and improve the quality of our choices.

➤ Good decision making begins with understanding your short- and long-term goals.

➤ Decision making is improved if you have a large number of alternatives.

➤ For difficult decisions, strategies include giving the decision time, acting out alternatives, tossing a coin to test our feelings, seeking advice, and acting on gut feelings.

What strategies can I use for problem solving?

➤ Problem solving entails the generation of alternatives to consider.

➤ We need to first understand and define the problem and to determine the important elements in coming to a solution to a problem.

➤ Approaches to generating solutions include breaking problems into pieces, working backward, using pictures, considering the opposite, using analogies, taking another's perspective, and "forgetting" the problem.

➤ Problem solving ultimately requires the evaluation and refinement of the solutions that have been generated.

What are some problems that affect critical thinking, and how can I avoid them?

➤ Labeling, using vague generalities, accepting opinion as fact, jumping to conclusions, mistaking common sense, and assuming causation all pose threats to critical thinking.

[KEY TERMS AND CONCEPTS]

Decision making (p. 190)   Problem solving (p. 197)   Analogy (p. 199)

Freewriting (p. 191)   Working backward (p. 198)

[RESOURCES]

AT SCHOOL

Some colleges offer courses in critical thinking, and they are a good bet to help increase decision-making and problem-solving skills. In addition, courses in logic and philosophy will help improve critical thinking skills.

If you are having a personal problem that is difficult to solve, don't hesitate to turn to staff at the counseling center or mental health center. Trained counselors and therapists can help sort through the different options in an objective manner. They may identify possibilities for solutions that you didn't even know existed. Even if the person with whom you speak initially is not the right one, he or she can direct you to someone who can help.

IN PRINT

If you have trouble making good decisions, then check out *Learning to Think Things Through: A Guide to Critical Thinking Across the Curriculum,* by Gerald M. Nosich (Prentice Hall, 2008). It is an excellent, concise guide to increasing your decision-making skills.

In addition, *Asking the Right Questions: A Guide to Critical Thinking* (8th ed.) (Prentice Hall, 2006) teaches readers how to effectively consider alternative points of view while making personal choices.

ON THE WEB

The following sites on the Web provide the opportunity to extend your learning about the material in this chapter. (Although the Web addresses were accurate at the time the book was printed, check the *P.O.W.E.R. Learning* Web site [**www.mhhe.com/power**] for any changes that may have occurred.)

> "Basic Guidelines to Problem Solving and Decision Making" (**www.managementhelp. org/prsn_prd/prob_slv.htm**) by Carter McNamara, PhD, provides basic guidelines to problem solving and decision making in seven steps. This site is rich in links to comprehensive approaches to decision making, critical and creative thinking, time management, and organizing yourself.

> "Critical Thinking Core Concepts" (**http://mcckc.edu/longview/ctac/corenotes.htm**), by Lauren Miller and Michael Connelly of Longview Community College, presents principles of critical thinking with exercises and examples. The site contains a short history of logic and answers the question: "What is the point of studying critical thinking?"

[ANSWERS TO TRY IT 2 PROBLEMS]

1. Remove one lug nut from each of the other three tires on the car and use these three to attach the spare tire. This will hold until four more lug nuts can be purchased.
2. Dump the tools out of the toolbox and use it as a pail.
3. Thursday.
4. Open all three links on one chain (cost = 6 cents) and use them to fasten the other three chains together (cost = 9 cents; total cost = 15 cents).
5. It is the same as one-half of two-thirds, or one-third.
6. 33 boxes (3 large, 6 medium, 24 small).

[TAKING IT TO THE NET]

1 Making good decisions can depend on distinguishing legitimate appeals (good reasons) from fallacious appeals (bad reasons). Go to San Jose State University's "Mission: Critical," an interactive tutorial in critical thinking (**www.sjsu.edu/depts/ itl/graphics/adhom/appeal.html**). After reading the description of the different kinds of fallacious appeals, do the related exercises.

2 Locate three problem-solving strategies on the Internet. Possible strategy: Go to Yahoo! (**www.yahoo.com**) or AltaVista (**www.altavista.com**), and enter the key phrase "problem solving." Search the results until you find at least three different problem-solving strategies. Are these strategies similar to the ones described in the book? If not, how are they different?

The Case of . . .
The Missing Tenant

Chloe had a problem.

She and her husband owned their own house, and to help with the mortgage they rented out the extra room over their garage. For three years they'd been renting it to one of Chloe's cousins, but a few months earlier Chloe's cousin had gotten married and moved in with her new husband.

That wasn't the problem, though. Chloe had known for months that her cousin would be leaving, so she'd had time to find someone new to rent the garage room: a local nursing student. The nursing student had signed a six-month lease and scheduled a day to move in. The problem was that on the day she was meant to arrive . . . the nursing student didn't show up.

Concerned, Chloe called her—and the nursing student brusquely told her she'd found a better place and wouldn't be renting from Chloe. Then she hung up. Suddenly Chloe was left without a tenant, with an empty room—and without money she'd been counting on to pay the mortgage.

1. Of the problem-solving strategies outlined in this chapter, which would you use to approach this problem?

2. What alternatives does Chloe have for dealing with the situation?

3. How should Chloe go about evaluating the outcomes for each alternative?

4. Based on your analysis of the problem, what advice would you give Chloe for dealing with the situation?

5. Is there anything Chloe could have done to avoid this problem in the first place? (Hint: If you've signed a lease in the past, did you have to pay any money up front?)

Diversity and Relationships

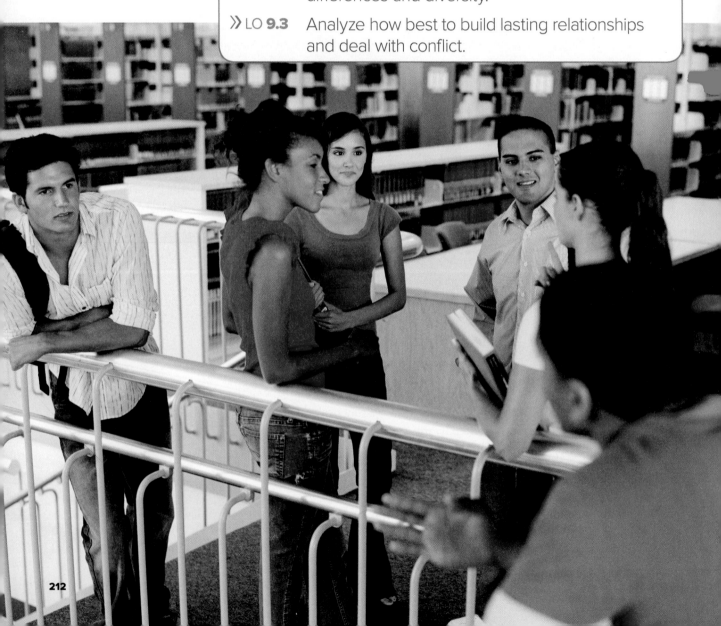

Learning Outcomes

By the time you finish this chapter you will be able to

» LO **9.1**   Explain why the increasing racial, ethnic, and cultural diversity of society are important.

» LO **9.2**   Identify strategies to become more at ease with differences and diversity.

» LO **9.3**   Analyze how best to build lasting relationships and deal with conflict.

He was born in the Kapi'olani Maternity and Gynecological Hospital in Honolulu, Hawaii. His mother was an American of primarily English descent from Wichita, Kansas. His father was born in Africa, in Nyang'oma Kogelo, Nyanza Province, Kenya. His parents met while taking a Russian language class. He spent most of his childhood in Hawaii, except for a few years in Indonesia.

In describing his childhood, he later said, "The opportunity that Hawaii offered—to experience a variety of cultures in a climate of mutual respect—became an integral part of my world view, and a basis for the values that I hold most dear."

He is Barack Obama, who grew up to be President of the United States.

Looking Ahead

Whether you have skin that is black or white or brown, are Jewish or Muslim or Greek Orthodox or Hindu, were born in Cuba or Vietnam or Boise, are able-bodied or physically challenged, college presents a world of new opportunities. College permits you to encounter people with very different backgrounds from your own. If you take the opportunity to form relationships with a variety of individuals, you will increase your understanding of the human experience and enrich your life. This will also benefit you greatly in your career, because whatever your field, you will inevitably find yourself in situations where success will depend on your ability to collaborate effectively with people different from yourself.

In this chapter, we consider how social diversity and relationships affect your life experience. We examine the increasing diversity of American society and consider the meanings and social effects of race, ethnicity, and culture. We look at practical strategies for acknowledging—and shedding—prejudice and stereotypes and being receptive to others on their own merits.

We next discuss relationships from a broader perspective, exploring ways that you can build lasting friendships with others. Finally, the chapter discusses the conflicts that can arise between people and what you can do to resolve them.

» LO 9.1 Living in a World of Diversity

No matter where we live, our contacts with others who are racially, ethnically, and physically different from us are increasing. The Web is bringing people from across the globe into our homes, as close to us as the computer sitting on our desk. Businesses now operate globally, so coworkers are likely to come from many different countries and cultures. Being comfortable with people whose backgrounds and beliefs may differ from our own is not only a social necessity, but it is virtually a requirement for career success.

By the mid-21st century, the percentage of people in the United States of African, Latin American, Asian, and Arabic ancestry will be greater than the percentage of those of Western European ancestry—a profound statistical, and social, shift.

Furthermore, it's not just racial and ethnic characteristics that compose diversity. As you can see in the Diversity Wheel in **Figure 9.1** on page 214, diversity encompasses characteristics such as gender, sexual orientation, age, and mental and physical characteristics. Layer on top of that factors such as education, religion, and

figure 9.1

Diversity Wheel

Diversity is composed of many different characteristics as exemplified by the Diversity Wheel.[1]

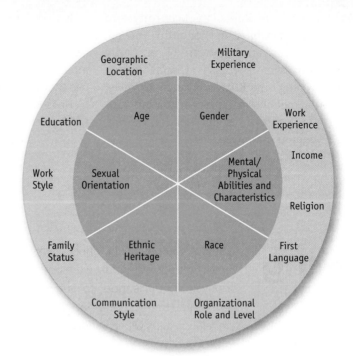

income level, and the complexity of others—and ourselves—becomes apparent. (You can examine the diversity of your own community by completing **Try It 1.**)

Race, Ethnicity, and Culture

Are you African American or Black? Caucasian or white or Euro-American? Hispanic or Latino? American Indian or Native American?

The language we use to describe our ethnic and racial group membership, and those of other people, is in constant flux. And what we call people matters. The subtleties of language affect how people think about members of particular groups, and how they think about themselves.

One of the difficulties in understanding diversity is that many of the terms we use are ill-defined and often overlapping. The term **race** is generally used to refer to obvious physical differences that set one group apart from others. According to such a definition, whites, Blacks, and Asian Americans are typically thought of as belonging to different races, determined largely by biological factors.

Ethnicity refers to shared national origins or cultural patterns. In the United States, for example, Puerto Ricans, Irish, and Italian Americans are categorized as ethnic groups. However, ethnicity—like race—is very much in the eye of the beholder. For instance, a Cuban American who is a third-generation citizen of the United States may feel few ties or associations to Cuba. Yet whites may view her as "Hispanic," and Blacks may view her as "white."

Finally, **culture** comprises the learned behaviors, beliefs, and attitudes that are characteristic of an individual society or population. But it's more than that: Culture also encompasses the products that people create, such as architecture, music, art, and literature. Culture is created and shaped by people, but at the same time it creates and shapes people's behavior.

Race, ethnicity, and culture shape each of us to an enormous degree. They profoundly influence our view of others, as well as who we are. They affect how others treat us, and how we treat them in turn. They determine whether we look people in the eye when we meet them, how early we arrive when we're invited to

Race

Traditionally, biologically determined physical characteristics that set one group apart from others

Ethnicity

Shared national origins or cultural patterns

Culture

The learned behaviors, beliefs, and attitudes that are characteristic of an individual society or population, and the products that people create

Determine the Diversity of Your Community

Try to assess the degree of diversity that exists in your community. *Community* can be a loosely defined term, but for this **Try It** think of it as the group of people you encounter and interact with on a regular basis. When thinking of diversity, remember to include the many different ways in which people can be different from one another, including race, ethnicity, culture, sexual orientation, physical challenges, and so on.

Overall, how diverse would you say your community is?

Are there organizations in your community that promote diversity? Are there organizations that work to raise the visibility and understanding of particular groups within your community?

What is the nature of your college's *student* diversity in terms of statistics regarding membership in different racial, ethnic, or cultural groups? (You may be able to find these statistics on your college's website.)

Is your college community more or less diverse than your community at large? Why do you think this might be?

How does the diversity on your community compare to the following statistics on diversity in the United States as of the 2006 census: white, 74 percent; Hispanic or Latino, 15 percent; Black or African American, 13 percent; Asian, 4 percent; two or more races, 2 percent; American Indian and Alaska Native, .7 percent; Native Hawaiian and other Pacific Islander, .1 percent; other race, 6 percent? (Note: Percentages add up to more than 100 percent because Hispanics may be of any race and are therefore counted under more than one category.)

To Try It online, go to **www.mhhe.com/power**.

dinner at a friend's house, and even, sometimes, how well we do in school or on the job.

Because many of us grow up in neighborhoods that are not ethnically diverse, we may have little or even no experience interacting with people who are different from us. Some college campuses don't have much diversity, either, and consequently even in college your exposure to people who have different backgrounds may be limited.

At some time, though, that will change. As the United States becomes increasingly diverse, it's not a matter of "if" but "when" you will be exposed to people who have profoundly different backgrounds from your own. Whether in the workplace or the neighborhood in which you reside, living in a diverse environment will be part of your life.

Workplace colleagues are increasingly diverse.

» LO9.2 Building Cultural Competence

We're not born knowing how to drive a car or cook. We have to learn how to do these things. The same is true of developing a basic understanding of other races, ethnic groups, and cultures. Called **cultural competence,** this knowledge of others'

Cultural competence
Knowledge and understanding about other races, ethnic groups, cultures, and minority groups

Prepare

Accept diversity as a valued part of your life

Organize

Explore your own prejudices and stereotypes

Work

Develop cultural competence

Evaluate

Check your progress in attaining cultural competence

Rethink

Understand how your own racial, ethnic, and cultural background affects others

P.O.W.E.R. Plan

customs, perspectives, background, and history can teach us a great deal about others, as well as ourselves. Cultural competence also provides a basis for civic engagement, permitting us to act with civility toward others and to make the most of our contributions to society.

Building cultural competence proceeds in several steps, outlined in the P.O.W.E.R. Plan.

Prepare

Accepting Diversity as a Valued Part of Your Life

In the title of her book on social diversity, psychologist Beverly Tatum asks, *"Why Are All the Black Kids Sitting Together in the Cafeteria?"*[2] She might just as well have asked a similar question about the white kids, the Asian American kids, and so forth. It often appears as if the world comes already divided into separate racial, ethnic, and cultural groups.

It's more than appearances: We form relationships more easily with others who are similar to us than with those who are different. It's easier to interact with others who look the same as we do, who come from similar backgrounds, and who share our race, ethnicity, and culture because we can take for granted certain shared cultural assumptions and views of the world.

But that doesn't mean that "easy" and "comfortable" translate into "good" or "right." We can learn a great deal more, and grow and be challenged, if we seek out people who are different from us. If you look beyond surface differences and find out what motivates other people, you can become aware of new ways of thinking about family, relationships, earning a living, and the value of education. It can be liberating to realize that others may hold very different perspectives from your own and that there are many ways to lead your life.

Letting diversity into your own life also has very practical implications: As we discuss in **Career Connections** on page 218, learning to accept and work with people who are different from you is a crucial skill that will help you in whatever job you hold.

From the perspective of . . .

A STUDENT Having a varied classroom can help you see the world in a broader way. Have you ever had a classmate relate an experience that impacted your thought process?

Organize

Exploring Your Own Prejudices and Stereotypes

Arab. Gay. African American. Hispanic. Female. Disabled. Overweight.

Quick: What comes into your mind when you think about each of these labels? If you're like most people, you don't draw a blank. Instead, a collection of images and feelings comes into your mind, based on what you know, have been told, or assume about the group.

Journal Reflections

Thinking about Race, Ethnicity, and Culture

1. Were race and ethnicity discussed in your family as you were growing up? In what ways?

2. Do you demonstrate—through your behavior, attitudes, and/or beliefs—your own ethnic background? How?

3. Are there cultural differences between you and members of other races or ethnicities? What are they?

4. Are you proud of your ethnicity? Why?

5. Think what it would be like to be a member of a racial group or ethnicity other than your own. In what ways would your childhood and adolescence have been different? How would you view the world differently?

The fact that we don't draw a blank when thinking about each of these terms means that we already have a set of attitudes and beliefs about them and the groups they represent. Acknowledging and then examining these preexisting assumptions is a first step toward developing cultural competence: We need to explore our own prejudices and stereotypes.

Prejudice refers to evaluations or judgments of members of a group that are based primarily on their membership in the group, rather than on their individual characteristics. For example, the auto mechanic who doesn't expect a woman to understand auto repair or a job supervisor who finds it unthinkable that a father might want to take a leave for child care are engaging in gender prejudice. *Gender prejudice* is evaluating individuals on the basis of their being a male or female and not on their own specific characteristics or abilities. Similarly, prejudice can be directed toward individuals because of their race, ethnic origin, sexual orientation, age, physical disability, or even physical attractiveness.

Prejudice

Evaluations or judgments of members of a group that are based primarily on membership in the group and not on the particular characteristics of individuals

Diversity in the Workplace

Diversity, and issues relating to it, are a part of today's workplace. For example, in one California computer assembly company with several thousand employees, 40 different languages and dialects are spoken among people representing 30 nationalities.[3] Furthermore, employers must deal with issues ranging from whether time off for religious holidays should count as vacation time to whether the partner of a gay or lesbian worker should be covered by the worker's medical insurance.

The gulf in the workplace between people with different cultural backgrounds may be wide. For instance, an immigrant from Japan might consider it the height of immodesty to outline his or her accomplishments in a job interview. The explanation? In Japan, the general cultural expectation is that people should stress their incompetence; to do otherwise would be considered highly immodest.

The increasing diversity of the workplace means that increasing your cultural competence will serve you well. It will help you perform on work teams that are composed of people of different races and ethnic backgrounds; it will help you supervise people whose native language and customs may be different from yours; and it will help you to work for a boss from another country and cultural background.

Equally important, gaining cultural competence will help you respond to the legal issues that surround diversity. It is illegal for employers to discriminate on the basis of race, ethnic background, age, gender, and physical disability. Cultural competence will help you not only to deal with the letter of the law, but also to understand why embracing diversity is so important to getting along with others in the workplace.

Stereotypes
Beliefs and expectations about members of a group that are held simply because of their membership in the group

Prejudice leads to discrimination. *Discrimination* is behavior directed toward individuals on the basis of their membership in a particular group. Discrimination can result in exclusion from jobs and educational opportunities. It also may result in members of particular groups receiving lower salaries and benefits.

Prejudice and discrimination are maintained by **stereotypes,** beliefs and expectations about members of a group. For example, do you think that women don't drive as well as men? Do you agree that "white men can't jump"? Do you believe that people raised in the jungles of South America are less intelligent than those raised in a Western society? Do you think that people on welfare are lazy? If you answered yes to any of these questions, you hold stereotypes about the group being referred to. It is the degree of generalization involved that makes stereotypes inaccurate. Some white men can't jump. But the fact is, many can—and do—and the stereotypes ignore this diversity.

To develop cultural competence, it's important to identify our prejudices and stereotypes and to fight them. Sometimes they are quite subtle and difficult to detect. For instance, a wealth of data taken from observation of elementary school classrooms shows that teachers are often more responsive to boys than to girls. The teachers don't know they're doing it; it's a subtle, but very real, bias.

Why does this happen? In part it's because we're exposed to stereotypes from a very young age. Parents and relatives teach them to us, sometimes unwittingly, sometimes deliberately. The media illustrate them constantly and often in very subtle ways. For instance, African Americans and Latinos are often portrayed as unemployed or as criminals, women are less likely than men to be shown as employed, and gay men are frequently depicted as effeminate.

But it's not only stereotypes that lead us to view members of other groups differently from those of our own. For many people, their own membership in a cultural or racial or ethnic group

"Prejudice is the child of ignorance."
William Hazlitt, essayist

is a source of pride and self-worth. There's nothing wrong with this. However, these feelings can lead to a less desirable outcome: the belief that their own group is superior to others. As a result, people inflate the positive aspects of their own group and belittle groups to which they do not belong. The bottom line is continuing prejudice.

To overcome stereotypes and to develop cultural competence, we must first explore and identify our prejudices. To begin that process, complete **Try It 2** on page 220, "Check Your Stereotype Quotient."

W Work Developing Cultural Competence

Although it's neither easy nor simple to increase your understanding of and sensitivity to other cultures, it can be done. Several strategies are effective:

> **Study other cultures and customs.** Take an anthropology course, study religion, or learn history. If you understand the purposes behind different cultural customs, attitudes, and beliefs, you will be able to understand the richness and meaning of other people's cultural heritage.

> **Travel.** There is no better way to learn about people from other cultures than to see those cultures firsthand. Vacations offer you the time to travel, and relatively inexpensive direct flights can take you to Europe, Asia, and other places around the globe. Sometimes, in fact, it's cheaper to take a trans-oceanic flight than to travel to closer locations in the United States.

Travel provides us with an opportunity to become immersed in very different cultures and to see the world—and ourselves—through different eyes.

If you can't afford airfare, take a car or bus ride to Mexico or Canada. In many parts of Canada, French is spoken and the culture is decidedly different from that in the United States (or the rest of Canada, for that matter).

Travel needn't be international, however. If you are from the northern states, head south. If you are from California, consider heading east. If you live in a large metropolitan area, travel to a different area from ones you're familiar with. No matter where you go, simply finding yourself in a new context can aid your efforts to learn about other cultures.

> **Participate in community service.** By becoming involved in community service, such as tutoring middle-school students, volunteering to work with the homeless, or working on an environmental cleanup, you get the opportunity to interact with people who may be very different from those you're accustomed to.

> **Don't ignore people's backgrounds.** None of us is color-blind. Or blind to ethnicity. Or to culture. It's impossible to be completely unaffected by people's racial, ethnic, and cultural backgrounds. So why pretend to be? Cultural

Try It!

2

Check Your Stereotype Quotient

Do you hold stereotypes about other people? How pervasive do you think they are? Respond to the following informal questionnaire to get a sense of your susceptibility to stereotyping.

1. When you see five African American students sitting together in a cafeteria, do you think that they are exhibiting racism? Do you think the same thing when you see five white students sitting together in a cafeteria?

2. When you are speaking with a person who has a speech-related disorder such as stuttering, are you likely to conclude that the person is less intelligent than a fluent speaker?

3. When an elderly woman can't remember something, do you assume her forgetfulness is because she is old or perhaps has Alzheimer's disease?

4. When an attractive blond female coworker states an opinion, are you surprised if the opinion is intelligent and well expressed?

5. If a person with a mobility disorder turns down your offer for assistance, would you be offended and resentful?

6. If you found out that a star professional football player is gay, would you be surprised?

What do you think your answers tell you about yourself and your views of others?

 WORKING IN A GROUP

Compare your answers with those of your classmates. What do you think causes the similarities and differences in responses?

To Try It online, go to www.mhhe.com/power.

heritage is an important part of other people's identity, and to pretend that their background doesn't exist and has no impact on them is unrealistic at best, and insulting at worst. It's important, though, to distinguish between accepting the fact that other people's backgrounds affect them and pigeonholing people and expecting them to behave in particular ways.

> **Don't make assumptions about who people are.** Don't assume that someone is heterosexual just because most people are heterosexual. Don't assume that someone with an Italian-sounding last name is Italian. Don't assume that a Black person has two Black parents.

> **Accept differences.** Different does not mean better. Different does not mean worse. Different just means not looking, acting, or believing exactly the same as you. We shouldn't attach any kind of value to being different; it's neither better nor worse than being similar.

In fact, even people who seem obviously different on the surface probably share many similarities with you. Like you, they have commitments to family or loved ones; they have fears and anxieties like yours; and they have aspirations and dreams, just as you do.

The important point about differences is that we need to accept and embrace them. Think about some differences you may have with people who are similar to you. Perhaps you really can't stand baseball, yet one of your childhood friends has followed the game since he was five and loves it. Chances are you both accept that you have different tastes and see this difference as part of who each of you is.

 ## Checking Your Progress in Attaining Cultural Competence

Because cultural groups are constantly changing, developing cultural competence is an ongoing process. To evaluate where you stand, ask yourself the following questions:

> Do I make judgments about others based on external features, such as skin color, ethnic background, cultural customs, gender, weight, or physical appearance?

> Who are my friends? Do they represent diversity or are they generally similar to me?

> Do I openly express positive values relating to diversity? Do I sit back passively when others express stereotypes and prejudices, or do I actively question their remarks?

> Am I educating myself about the history and varying experiences of different racial, ethnic, and cultural groups?

> Do I give special treatment to members of particular groups, or am I even-handed in my relationships?

> Do I recognize that, despite surface differences, all people have the same basic needs?

> Do I feel so much pride in my own racial, ethnic, and cultural heritage that it leads me to look less favorably upon members of other groups?

> Do I seek to understand events and situations through the perspectives of others and not just my own?

Course Connections

Diversity in the Classroom

The increasing diversity of classrooms presents both opportunity and challenge. The opportunity comes from the possibility of learning on a firsthand basis about others and their experiences. The challenge comes when people who may be very different from us call into question some of our most fundamental beliefs and convictions.

Here are some ways that you can be better equipped to deal with the classroom challenges involved in diversity:

- **Present your opinions in a respectful manner.** Don't get annoyed or angry when others disagree with your point of view. Be tolerant of others' perspectives and their thinking.
- **Don't assume you can understand what it's like to be a member of another race, ethnicity, cultural group, or gender.** Talk about your own experiences, and don't assume you know what others have experienced.
- **Don't treat people as representatives of the groups to which they belong.** Don't ask someone how members of his or her racial, ethnic, or cultural group think, feel, or behave with respect to a particular issue. No single individual can speak for an entire group. Furthermore, group members are likely to display little uniformity on most issues and in most behaviors. Consequently, this type of question is ultimately impossible to answer.
- **Seek out students who are different from you.** If you are assigned a group project, volunteer to work with others who are different from you. You may learn more working with others who are dissimilar than those who are like you.
- **Don't be afraid to offer your opinion out of concerns for "political correctness."** If you offer an opinion in a respectful, thoughtful, and tolerant manner, you should feel free to voice your opinion. Even if your views are minority opinions, they deserve to be considered.

 R Rethink

Understanding How Your Own Racial, Ethnic, and Cultural Background Affects Others

If you are a member of a group that traditionally has been the target of prejudice and discrimination, you probably don't need to be told that your race, ethnicity, and cultural background affect the way that others treat you. But even if you are a member of a traditionally dominant group in society, the way in which others respond to you is, in part, a result of others' assumptions about the group of which you are a part.

In short, both how we view others and how we ourselves are viewed are affected by the groups to which we—and others—belong. But keep this in mind: No matter how different other students, coworkers, or community members are from you in terms of their race, ethnicity, and cultural background, they undoubtedly share many of the same concerns you do. Like all of us, they question themselves, wonder whether they will be successful, and fret about making ends meet. Bridging the surface difference between you and others can result in the development of close, lasting social ties—a topic we consider next.

≫ LO 9.3 Building Lasting Relationships

Few of us lead our lives in isolation. There's a reason for this: Relationships with others are a critical aspect of our sense of well-being. The support of friends and relatives helps us feel good about ourselves. In fact, studies have found that our physical and psychological health may suffer without friendships. The social support of others acts as a guard against stress and illness. And if we do get sick, we recover more quickly if we have a supportive network of friends.

Our relationships with others also help us understand who we are. To understand our own abilities and achievements, we compare them with those of others who are similar to ourselves. Our attitudes, beliefs, and values are influenced—and shaped—by others. We are who we are largely because of the people with whom we come in contact.

> "I have met the most amazing individuals and made the most incredible friends in such a short amount of time."
>
> **Student, Wittenberg University**[4]

Making Friends

Although some of us naturally make friends with ease, for others making friends is more difficult. But building relationships is not a mystery. Here are several ways to go about it:

> ➤ **Invest time in others.** There's no better way to demonstrate that you are interested in being friends than investing time. Relationships need to be nourished by the commitment of time. You can't expect friendships to flourish unless you spend time with people.

> ➤ **Reveal yourself.** Good friends understand each other. The best way to make that happen is to let others get to know you. Be open and honest about the things you like and dislike. Talk about where you come from, what your family is like. By honestly communicating your beliefs and attitudes, you give others the chance to learn those things you have in common.

> ➤ **Show concern and caring.** This is really the substance of friendship and the basis for the trust that develops between friends. Don't be afraid to show your interest in the fortunes of others and to share the sadness when they suffer some setback or loss.

> ➤ **Be open to friendships with people who are very different from you.** Don't assume the only "appropriate" friends are your peers who are similar to you, such as other college students. Open yourself to friends who are older, who are younger, who work at your school, and who are different from you in fundamental ways.

> ➤ **Not everyone makes a good friend.** People who put you down, consistently make you feel bad, or behave in ways that violate your own personal standards are not friends. Choose your friends based on the good feelings you have when you are with them and the concern and care they show for you. Friendship is a two-way street.

The R-Word: Relationships

Relationships move beyond friendship. They occur when two people feel emotionally attached, fulfill each other's needs, and generally feel interdependent. When a true relationship exists, several components are present:

> ➤ **Trust.** Relationships must be built on a foundation of trust. We need to be able to count on others and feel that they will be open with us.

> ➤ **Honesty.** No relationship can survive if the partners are not honest with one another. Each partner must share a commitment to the truth. Your life does not have to be a completely open book—it's the rare individual who has no secrets whatsoever—but it is important to be honest about your fundamental

beliefs, values, and attitudes. Those in good relationships accept one another, blemishes and all. A relationship based on untruths or even half-truths lacks depth and meaning.

> **Mutual support.** Healthy relationships are characterized by mutual support. A partner's well-being should have an impact on you, and your well-being should affect your partner. In good relationships, the partners seek out what is best for both, and they act as advocates for and defend each other.

> **Loyalty.** The mark of a good relationship is loyalty. Loyalty implies that relationship partners are supportive of each other, even in times of adversity and difficulty.

> **Acceptance.** In good relationships small annoyances don't get in the way of the deeper connection between you and another person. We don't have to like everything others do to maintain relationships with them. We don't even have to appreciate or approve of every aspect of their personality. What is crucial is the willingness to accept others as they are, without constantly yearning for changes.

> **Willingness to embrace change.** Change is part of everyone's life. As people grow and develop, they change. So do relationships.

We need to accept change as a fundamental part of relationships and build upon that change. In fact, we need to welcome change. Although change brings challenges with it, it also helps us to understand ourselves and our own place in the world more accurately.

It is only natural that some relationships will fade over time. People do outgrow each other. That's inevitable. What's important is not to live in fear that your relationship is so fragile that you have to avoid or ignore changes in who you and a partner are. Instead, both partners in a relationship should do their best to accept transformations in the relationship as a part of life.

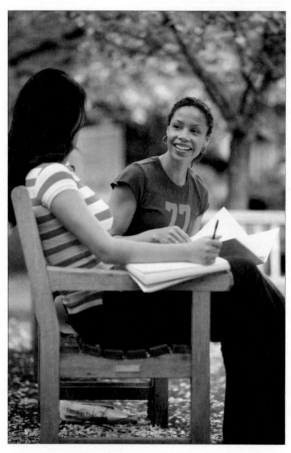

What you *don't* say matters. Close, lasting relationships are often built on good listening skills.

Communicating in Relationships

Communicating well in personal relationships is a blend of talking and listening. Not only does it help to do both well, but it is also important to know when it's time to listen and when it's time to speak up. Listening is an often overlooked skill in personal relationships. We may be so busy trying to communicate our feelings and interests that we overlook the need of the other person to be heard. As friendships develop into personal relationships, simply talking isn't enough. How you express yourself, especially in moments of difficulty, can be very important to getting your message across.

Being a Good Listener: The Power of Supportive Silence

When it comes to building relationships, how you listen is sometimes more important than what you say. The silence involved in listening is a powerful force, one that can bind us more closely to others.

We've already discussed the art and science of listening as it applies to academic success in Chapter 3. The same principles that promote learning about lecture topics also promote learning about our friends. You can't call yourself a good friend without knowing what others are like and what they are thinking. Good listening is one of the ways to enhance your understanding of others.

When we are heard, we appreciate it because we get the message that our listeners care about us, not just about themselves. Similarly, when we listen, we show that we have respect for those who are speaking, are interested in their ideas and beliefs, and are willing to take the time to pay attention to them.

There are several ways you can improve your ability to listen:

1. **Stop talking!** Are you the kind of person who revels in telling stories about what happened to you? Do you wait eagerly for others to finish what they are saying so that you can jump in with a response? Do you accidentally cut other people off or finish their sentences while they are speaking?

   No one likes to be interrupted, even in casual conversation. In more personal relationships, it is a sign of not respecting what the other person has to say and is hurtful.

2. **Demonstrate that you are listening.** Linguists call them "conversational markers"—those nonverbal indications that we're listening. They consist of head nods, uh-huhs, OKs, and other signs that we're keeping up with the conversation. Eye contact is important too. Listening this way shows that we're paying attention and are interested in what the other person is saying.

   In addition, don't multitask. If you're having a serious conversation, turn off your cell phone. If it does ring, don't look at caller ID. Even glancing at your phone for a moment shows you're not paying full attention.

> "The reason why we have two ears and only one mouth is that we may listen the more and talk the less."
>
> Zeno of Citium, philosopher

3. **Use reflective feedback.** Carl Rogers, a respected therapist, developed a very useful way to lend support to someone and draw him or her out. In **reflective feedback,** a listener rephrases what a speaker has said, trying to echo the speaker's meaning. For example, a listener might say, "as I understand what you're saying . . .," or "you seem to feel that . . .," or "in other words, you believe that . . ."

   In each case, the summary statement doesn't just "play back" the speaker's statements literally. Instead, it is a rephrasing that captures the essence of the message in different words.

   Reflective feedback has two big benefits. First, it provides speakers with a clear indication that you are listening and taking what they're saying seriously. Second, and equally important, it helps ensure that you have an accurate understanding of what the speaker is saying.

   Reflective feedback
   A technique of verbal listening in which a listener rephrases what a speaker has said, trying to echo the speaker's meaning

4. **Ask questions.** Asking questions shows that you are paying attention to a speaker's comments. Questions permit you to clarify what the speaker has said, and he or she can move the conversation forward. Further, people feel valued when others ask them about themselves.

5. **Admit when you're distracted.** We've all had those moments: Something is bothering you and you can't get it out of your mind, or you've simply got to finish something and don't really have time to chat. If at the same time someone wants to engage you in conversation, your distraction will undoubtedly show, making the other person feel you are not interested in her or him.

   The way to deal with this situation is to admit that you're distracted. Simply saying, "I'd love to talk, but I've got to finish reading a chapter," is enough to explain the situation to a classmate who wants to talk about his date.

Loneliness

Loneliness
A subjective state in which people do not experience the level of connection with others that they desire

Loneliness is a subjective state: We can be totally alone and not feel lonely, or we can be in the midst of a crowd and feel lonely. Loneliness occurs when we don't experience the level of connection with others that we desire. There are also different types of loneliness. Some of us feel lonely if we lack a deep emotional attachment to a single person, which can occur even if we have many friends. Others feel loneliness because they believe they don't have enough friends.

The reality is that there is no standard that indicates the "right" number of relationships. There's no standard against which to measure yourself and the number, and kind, of relationships that you have. It's something you need to decide,

Remember, also, that loneliness is not inevitable. There are several strategies you can use to deal with the feeling. You can become involved in a new activity, volunteering for a service organization or joining a recreational sports league. If you don't work, consider taking a job. Not only will you have some more income, you'll have the chance to socialize with coworkers and perhaps form bonds of friendship with them, as well. You should also take advantage of the social opportunities you do have. Even if you don't think of yourself as a "people person," accept invitations to parties and other gatherings. You never know when you might meet someone you truly connect with.

What if your feelings of loneliness are extreme and you experience a sense of complete isolation and alienation from your classmates? If the feeling persists, it's wise to talk to someone at your college counseling center, a health service provider, or a trusted family member. Although everyone feels isolated at times, such feelings shouldn't be extreme. Counselors can help you deal with them.

It's Not Just Talk: Avoiding and Handling Conflicts in Relationships

Listening communicates a great deal in personal relationships, but, as discussed previously, it is also important to put yourself forward. Generally, close relationships are built on good communication, so day to day there may be no problem in this regard. But when misunderstandings or conflicts occur—as they definitely will from time to time—communication can fall apart. In these situations your ability to communicate in words is tested, and more sensitive listening and more careful ways of saying what you think and feel are needed.

The Subject Is "I," and Not "You"

Suppose a close friend says something with which you disagree: "All you guys are the same—you expect to get everything your way!" You might respond by directing anger at the other person, directly or indirectly accusing the person of some imperfection. "You're always looking for something to complain about!" Such responses (and, as you will notice, the initial statement) typically include the word *you*. For instance, consider these possible responses to indicate disagreement: "*You* really don't understand"; "*You're* being stubborn"; and "How can *you* say that?"

These types of statements cast blame, make accusations, express criticism, and make assumptions about what's inside the other person's head. And they lead to defensive replies that will probably do little to move the conversation forward: "I am *not!*"; "I do so understand"; "I'm not being stubborn"; and "I can say that because that's the way I feel."

A far more reasonable tactic is to use "I" statements. **"I" statements** cast responses in terms of yourself and your individual interpretation. Instead of saying,

"I" statements
Statements that cast responses in terms of oneself and one's individual interpretation

for example, "You really don't understand," a more appropriate response would be, "I think we're misunderstanding each other." "You're being stubborn" could be rephrased as "I feel like you're not really listening." And "Why don't you call when you're going to be late?" becomes "I worry that something has happened to you when you don't call if you are going to be late." In each case, "I" statements permit you to state your reaction in terms of your perception or understanding, rather than as a critical judgment about the other person. (Practice using "I" statements in **Try It 3** on page 228.)

From the perspective of . . .

A HUMAN RESOURCES SPECIALIST Relationships are a key part of a successful professional environment. What might you need to know about fostering positive relationships in your professional life?

Resolving Conflict: A Win–Win Proposition

Even with careful attention to putting our own feelings forward instead of making accusations, whenever two people share their thoughts, concerns, fears, and honest reactions with each other, the chances are that sooner or later some sort of conflict will arise.

Conflict is not necessarily bad.

Often, people are upset simply by the fact that they are having a conflict. It is as though they believe conflicts don't occur in "good" relationships. In fact, however, conflict is helpful in some very important ways. It can force us to say what is really on our minds. It can allow us to clear up misconceptions and miscommunications before they begin to undermine the relationship. It can even give us practice at resolving conflicts with others with whom we might not share such good relations.

Outside the context of close relationships, conflict is not necessarily a bad thing, either. In the working world, conflict is often inevitable. Yet as in relationships, conflicts on the job can be beneficial. Inefficiencies can be removed, misconceptions cleared up, and new processes devised when coworkers engage in honest, passionate discussion.

Like anything else, though, there are good ways to resolve conflict, and there are bad ways. Good ways move people forward, defining the problem and promoting creative problem solving. Bad ways make the situation worse, driving people apart rather than bringing them together. The following are some fundamental principles of conflict resolution that you can use when conflict occurs in personal and professional relationships:

➤ **Stop, look, and listen.** In the heat of an argument, all sorts of things that otherwise would go unsaid get said. If you find yourself making rash or hurtful statements, stop, look at yourself, and listen to what you and the other person are saying.

   Stopping works like a circuit breaker that prevents a short circuit from causing a deadly fire. You've probably heard about counting to 10 to cool off when you're angry. Do it. Take a break and count to 10 . . . or 20 . . . or more. Whether you count to 10 or 100, stopping gives you time to think and not react rashly.

Try It!

3

Switch "You" to "I"

Working in a group or in pairs, turn the following "you" statements into less aggressive "I" statements. For example, a possible "I" statement alternative to "You just don't get it, do you?" would be "I don't feel I'm making my feelings clear."

1. You just don't get it, do you?

2. You never listen to what I say.

3. You don't see where I'm coming from.

4. You don't really believe that, do you?

5. You never try to see my point of view.

6. Please stop interrupting me and listen to what I'm saying for a change.

7. Stop changing the subject!

8. You're not making sense.

9. You keep distorting what I say until I don't even know what point I'm trying to make.

10. You use too many "you" statements. Use more "I" statements when you're talking to others.

To Try It online, go to www.mhhe.com/power.

- **Defuse the argument.** Anger is not an emotion that encourages rational discourse. When you're angry and annoyed with someone, you're not in the best position to evaluate logically the merits of various arguments others may offer. It may feel exhilarating to get our fury off our chests in the heat of an argument, but you can bet it isn't taking anyone any closer to resolving the problem.

  Don't assume that you are 100 percent right and the other person is 100 percent wrong. Make your goal *solving the problem* rather than winning an argument.

- **Get personal.** Perhaps you've heard others suggest that you shouldn't get personal in an argument. In one sense that's true: Accusing people you're arguing with of having character flaws does nothing to resolve real issues.

  At the same time, you should be willing to admit personal *responsibility* for at least part of the conflict. The conflict would not exist without you, so you need to accept that the argument has two sides and that you are not automatically blameless. This creates some solid ground from which you and the other person can begin to work on the problem.

- **Listen to the real message.** When people argue, what they say is often not the real message. There's typically an underlying communication—a subtext—that is the source of the conflict.

  It's important, then, to dig beneath what you're hearing. If someone accuses you of being selfish, the real meaning hidden in the accusation may be that you don't give anyone else a chance to make decisions. Remember, arguments are usually about behavior, not underlying character and personality. What people *do* is not necessarily synonymous with who they *are*.

  If you rephrase the person's statement in your own mind, it moves from an insult ("You're a bad person") to a request for a change of behavior ("Let me participate in decision making"). You're much more likely to respond reasonably when you don't feel that the essence of your being is under attack.

- **Show that you're listening.** It's not enough only to listen to the underlying message that someone is conveying. You also need to acknowledge the *explicit* message. For example, saying something like "OK. I can tell you are concerned about sharing the burden on our group project, and I think we should talk about it" acknowledges that you see the issue and admit that it is worthy of discussion. This is a far more successful strategy than firing back a countercharge each time your coworker makes a complaint.

- **If you are angry, acknowledge it.** Don't pretend that everything is fine if it isn't. Ultimately, relationships in which the partners bottle up their anger may suffer more than those in which the partners express their true feelings. If you're angry, say so.

- **Ask for clarification.** As you're listening to another person's arguments, check out your understanding of what is being said. Don't assume that you know what's intended. Saying something like "Are you saying . . ." or "Do you mean that . . ." is a way of verifying that what you *think* someone means is really what is meant.

- **Make your requests explicit.** If you're upset that your spouse leaves clothes lying around your apartment, remarking that he or she is a "pig" shows more than that you are angry. It also shows that your intent is to hurt rather than to solve the problem.

  It's far better to be explicit in your concerns. Say something like "It would make me feel better if you would pick up your clothes from the floor." Couching your concern in this way changes the focus of the message from your spouse's personality to a specific behavior that can be changed.

> **Always remember that life is not a zero-sum game.** Many of us act as if life were a **zero-sum game,** a situation in which when one person wins, the other person automatically loses. It's what happens when you make a bet: If one person wins the bet, the other person loses.

Life is not like that. If one person wins an argument, it doesn't mean that others automatically have to lose it. And if someone loses an argument, it doesn't mean that others have automatically won. In fact, all too often conflict escalates so much that the argument turns into a lose-lose situation, where everyone ends up a loser.

However, life can be a win-win situation. The best resolution of conflict occurs when both parties walk away with something they want. Each may not have achieved *every* goal but will at least have enough to feel satisfied.

> **Finally, if a relationship involves emotional or physical abuse, you must seek help or decide to end the relationship immediately.** If a partner is emotionally or physically abusive to you, seek assistance from trained counselors. Don't wait. It is virtually impossible to deal with abuse on your own. Your college counseling center, mental health center, or medical center can offer you help. If you are physically threatened or injured, call 911.

When Relationships Are Over: Dealing with Endings

Not all relationships last a lifetime. Sometimes they just wind down, as the two people involved slowly lose interest in maintaining their partnership. At other times, they break apart, as disagreements build and there is not a strong enough bond to hold the two parties together. Or there may be an abrupt rupture if some event occurs that destroys one partner's feeling of trust.

Caring for others is rewarding, but risky. When relationships don't work out, their endings can be painful, even devastating, for a time. Even when relationships evolve naturally and change is expected, the transformation in a relationship may not be easy. Parents die. Children grow up and move away from home. Siblings get new jobs on the other side of the country.

In the aftermath of a failed relationship, there are things you can do to ease the pain. The first is simple: Do *something.* Mow the lawn, clean out the closets, go for a run, see a movie. It won't completely get your mind off your loss, but it beats languishing on your bed, thinking about what you might have done differently or what could have been. Also, accept that you feel bad. If you're not experiencing unhappiness over the end of a relationship, it means that the relationship wasn't terribly meaningful in the first place. Understand that unhappiness normally accompanies the end of a relationship, and allow yourself your natural emotional response. Finally, and perhaps most important, talk about your sadness. Seek out a friend or a relative. Discussing your feelings will help you deal with them better. If your sadness over a relationship feels totally overwhelming or continues for what you perceive to be too long a time, talk to a counselor or other professional. He or she can help you gain a better understanding of the situation and perhaps help you understand why you are taking it so hard.

Remember, there is one sure cure for the heartache of a lost relationship: time. The pain will disappear eventually. As the saying goes, Time does heal virtually all wounds.

Speaking of **Success**

NAME: **Dr. Nicole R. Edwards**

SCHOOL: **B.A., Jackson State University;**

M.A and Ph.D., The University of Southern Mississippi, Hattiesburg, Mississippi;

Lane College, Jackson, Tennessee

Nicole Edwards teaches incoming first-year students at Lane College how to adjust to college life. Her inspiration for her teaching: her own personal life experience. Her academic career started off like any other student's, until her daughter Jalysa Monique was born during her sophomore year. Being a single parent was hard enough. But coupled with her daughter's numerous medical problems, Edwards faced a tough academic road.

"Previously I had only been responsible for myself," she noted. "I wasn't sure if I could work, go to school, and take care of a sick baby. It was overwhelming but I knew there wasn't another option."

Determined and committed, Edwards cited an undergraduate course on the introduction to university life at Jackson State University as providing her with the key to not only complete her undergraduate program, but to go on to earn a doctoral degree at the age of 27.

"The portion of the course geared toward time management was by far the most beneficial," she said. "I took full advantage of my day planner. I used it to account for every awakening moment during the day. I scheduled activities from the time I got up in the morning to the time I went to bed at night. This included work, school, time set aside for studying, as well as time designated for personal and social activities. This taught me self-discipline. I learned to stick with my schedule and I still practice this today in my professional career.

In addition to time management, it is also very important to stay on top of required academic work, and avoid waiting until the last minute. "I see so many students who wait until the last minute to work on projects and papers that may count for a significant share of their grade in a course," Edwards said.

"As a student, I would see upcoming projects and begin to work on them immediately. I would submit them early and ask my instructor for feedback. This allowed me sufficient time to make necessary modifications to my work and still meet the deadline. I found this to increases the quality of my work and decrease my level of stress. This is also a tactic that has stayed with me over the years."

Looking Back

Why is the increasing racial, ethnic, and cultural diversity of society important to me?

▶ The diversity of the United States is increasing rapidly, and the world is becoming smaller as television, radio, the Internet, the Web, and international commerce bring people and cultures closer together.

▶ Being aware of diversity can allow you to accept the challenge and opportunity of living and working with others who are very different.

How can I become more at ease with differences and diversity?

▶ Cultural competence begins with accepting diversity by seeking out others who are different, as well as exploring your own prejudices and stereotypes.

▶ You can learn about other cultures by traveling to other countries and geographic areas. It also helps to accept differences simply as differences.

How can I build lasting relationships and deal with conflict?

▶ Relationships not only provide social support and companionship, but they also help people understand themselves.

▶ The central components of good relationships are trust, honesty, mutual support, loyalty, acceptance, and a willingness to embrace change.

▶ Listening is an important skill for relationship building, demonstrating that the listener really cares about the other person.

▶ Conflict is inevitable in relationships, and sometimes it is useful because it permits us to clear up misconceptions and miscommunications before they escalate.

▶ Although the end of a relationship can be very painful, the pain does subside over time.

[KEY TERMS AND CONCEPTS]

Race (p. 214)

Ethnicity (p. 214)

Culture (p. 214)

Cultural competence (p. 215)

Prejudice (p. 217)

Stereotypes (p. 218)

Reflective feedback (p. 225)

Loneliness (p. 226)

"I" statements (p. 226)

Zero-sum game (p. 230)

[RESOURCES]

AT SCHOOL

Anyone who feels he or she is facing discrimination based on race, gender, ethnic status, sexual orientation, or national origin should contact a college official *immediately*. Often there is a specific office that handles such complaints. If you don't know which campus official to contact, speak to your academic adviser or someone in the dean's office and you'll be directed to the appropriate person. The important thing is to act and not to suffer in silence. Discrimination is not only immoral, but it is against the law.

IN PRINT

Beverly Tatum's *"Why Are All the Black Kids Sitting Together in the Cafeteria?" And Other Conversations about Race* (HarperCollins, 2003 rev. ed.) explores race, racism, and the everyday impact of prejudice.

In *Affirming Diversity* (Allyn & Bacon, 2004), Sonia Nieto examines how ethnic and cultural factors affect student success.

Finally, Joseph Folger, Marshall Poole, and Randall Stutman's *Working through Conflict: Strategies for Relationships, Groups, and Organizations* (Allyn & Bacon, 2004) suggests a variety of practical approaches to resolving conflict.

ON THE WEB

The following sites on the Web provide the opportunity to extend your learning about the material in this chapter. (Although the Web addresses were accurate at the time the book was printed, check the *P.O.W.E.R. Learning* Web site [**www.mhhe.com/power**] for any changes that may have occurred.)

▸ "Communication Improvement" (**www.colorado.edu/conflict/peace/treatment/commimp.htm**) is an outline posted by Confliction Research Consortium at the University of Colorado. It includes a lengthy section on improving communications, with added links to improving listening skills and conflict resolution.

▸ "Language and Culture" (**www.ncela.gwu.edu/resabout/culture/**), a site from George Washington University's National Clearinghouse for English Language Acquisition & Language Instruction Educational Programs, provides links dealing with culture, diversity, and multiculturalism, connecting to everything from the American Folk Life Center to worldwide ethnology resources.

▸ Understanding "Race Relations" (**racerelations.about.com**), a comprehensive site on About.com, discusses topics ranging from affirmative action to white privilege. Hundreds of links are provided for more in-depth discussions and background on a variety of subjects, including race relations, hate crimes, gay/lesbian issues, and many other topics.

TAKING IT TO THE NET

1 Explore cultural differences using the Internet. Go to Yahoo! (**dir.yahoo.com**), choose "Society and Culture," and then "Cultures and Groups." Click on "Cultures" and type a topic that you find interesting into the search field. Make sure to limit your search to just this category. How many pages did you find? Read and compare the information from different cultural groups.

2 Use the Internet to help find a volunteer organization that sounds interesting to you. Using either Yahoo! (**www.yahoo.com**) or AltaVista (**www.altavista.com**), enter "volunteer organizations" into the search field. Examine the volunteer organizations listed and write down the ones that you find interesting. Consider contacting one or more to explore possibilities of participating in the organization that will mesh with your other responsibilities.

The Case of . . .
Keeping Your Mouth Shut

Jorge Azar had immigrated with his parents to the United States from the Dominican Republic when he was eleven years old. Although Jorge had become fluent in English, he still spoke with an accent. Jorge had never felt self-conscious about it before. He'd lived most of his life in America in New York City, surrounded by dozens of different accents.

Now, though, Jorge had relocated with his wife out of New York. He'd enrolled in college to earn his degree in software engineering, and sitting in a classroom in which he was the only Hispanic, Jorge suddenly felt nervous to open his mouth. He was sure that no matter what he said, his fellow classmates would disregard it because of his accent. Despite graduating from high school in the top of his class, Jorge was struck dumb at the idea of answering the questions his instructors asked.

One day, Jorge couldn't avoid the problem anymore. In one of his programming classes, his instructor called on him by name to explain a technical term. Jorge knew what the term meant and how to explain it . . . but he was afraid that as soon as he spoke, he'd be laughed at. As the moments ticked by and the class waited for Jorge's response, he started to wonder why he'd enrolled in college in the first place.

1. Can you identify with Jorge's situation? Are there aspects of yourself that you feel self-conscious about?

2. What assumptions does Jorge fear his classmates will make?

3. What assumptions about his classmates is Jorge making?

4. What advice would you give Jorge to help him feel more comfortable not just speaking in class, but also in college in general?

5. Have you ever judged someone based not on what they say, but how they say it? What did you learn from this incident, and how could you avoid it in the future?

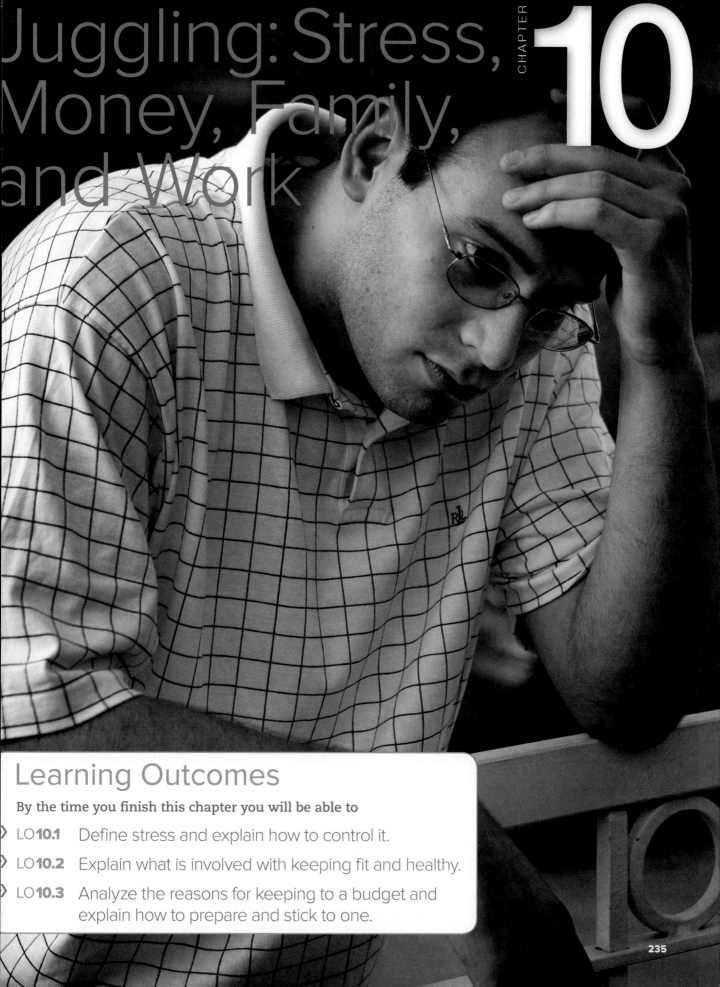

10

Juggling: Stress, Money, Family, and Work

Learning Outcomes

By the time you finish this chapter you will be able to

› LO**10.1**   Define stress and explain how to control it.

› LO**10.2**   Explain what is involved with keeping fit and healthy.

› LO**10.3**   Analyze the reasons for keeping to a budget and explain how to prepare and stick to one.

It had been a long day for Diana Michaels—and now, lying in bed, she couldn't fall asleep.

The many stresses and worries of her day kept repeating in her mind. The babysitter she relied on to watch her children in the afternoon when she went to nursing classes had told her she wanted a raise. Diana, a single mother, wasn't sure she could afford to pay more and still pay all the other bills: utilities, rent, car insurance, tuition, and the rest. Her paycheck from her job as an administrative assistant at a hospital was already stretched thin. And given that she worked full-time and was going to college, she didn't think she could find time to take on a new job or even additional shifts.

Diana reassured herself that she could figure out a way to save a little more money. She told herself that at the moment what she really needed was sleep. She had to get up at 5:00 a.m. to exercise, then get her children to school, then go to work, then go to class. But all she could do was toss and turn, stressing about all the many challenges she had to face in the morning.

Looking Ahead

Do you ever feel like Diana? Do you ever stay awake wondering how you'll meet the demands of family, bills, college, and work? Then you're no stranger to stress. It's something that all of us experience from time to time, but that college can often exacerbate. It isn't easy to be a student on top of being a parent, a spouse, an employee, and so forth. Almost a third of first-year college students report feeling frequently overwhelmed with all they need to do.[1]

Coping with stress is one of the challenges that college students face. The many demands on your time can make you feel that you'll never finish what needs to get done. This pressure produces wear and tear on your body and mind, and it's easy to fall prey to ill health as a result.

However, stress and poor health are not inevitable outcomes. In fact, by following simple guidelines and deciding to make health a conscious priority, you can maintain good physical and mental health. It's not easy to balance the many responsibilities of study and work and family, but it is possible.

Perhaps the greatest source of stress for college students, if not for most people in general, is money. Even under the best of circumstances, our finances present us with many challenges. But money stress is not inevitable, either. This chapter will show you how to manage your money. It begins by discussing the process of preparing a budget and identifying your financial goals—the basis for money management. The chapter goes on to examine ways you can keep track of your spending and estimate your financial needs and resources, and discusses ways to control your spending habits and save money.

» LO 10.1 Living with Stress

Stressed out? Tests, papers, job demands, family problems, volunteer activities . . . It's no surprise that these can produce stress. But it may be a surprise to know that so can graduating from high school, starting your dream job, falling in love, getting married, and even winning the lottery.

Virtually *anything*—good or bad—is capable of producing stress if it presents us with a challenge. **Stress** is the physical and emotional response we have to events that threaten or challenge us. It is rooted in the primitive "fight or flight" response wired into all animals—human and nonhuman. You see it in cats, for instance, when confronted by a dog or other threat: Their backs go up, their fur stands on end, their eyes widen, and, ultimately, they either take off or attack. The challenge stimulating this revved-up response is called a *stressor*. For humans, stressors can range from a first date to losing our wallet to facing a flash flood.

Stress
The physical and emotional response to events that threaten or challenge us

Because our everyday lives are filled with events that can be interpreted as threatening or challenging, stress is commonplace in most people's lives. There are three main types of stressors:

1. **Cataclysmic events** are events that occur suddenly and affect many people simultaneously. Tornadoes, hurricanes, and plane crashes are examples of cataclysmic events.

2. **Personal stressors** are major life events that produce a negative physical and psychological reaction. Failing a course, losing a job, and ending a relationship are all examples of personal stressors. Sometimes positive events—such as getting married or starting a new job—can act as personal stressors. Although the short-term impact of a personal stressor can be difficult, the long-term consequences may decline as people learn to adapt to the situation.

3. **Daily hassles** are the minor irritants of life that, singly, produce relatively little stress. Waiting in a traffic jam, receiving a tuition bill riddled with mistakes, and being interrupted by noises of major construction while trying to study are examples of such minor irritants. However, daily hassles add up, and cumulatively they can produce even more stress than a single larger-scale event. (**Figure 10.1** indicates the most common daily hassles in people's lives.[2])

Cataclysmic events
Sudden, powerful events that occur quickly and affect many people simultaneously

Personal stressors
Major life events that produce stress

Daily hassles
The minor irritants of life that, by themselves, produce little stress, but which can add up and produce more stress than a single, larger-scale event

What Is Happening When We Are Stressed?

Stress does more than make us feel anxious, upset, and fearful. Beneath those responses, we are experiencing many different physical reactions, each placing a high demand on our body's resources. Our hearts beat faster, our breathing becomes more rapid and shallow, and we produce more sweat. Our internal organs churn out a variety of hormones. In the long run, these physical responses wear down our immune system, our body's defense against disease. We become more susceptible to a variety of diseases, ranging from the common cold and headaches to strokes and heart disease. In fact, surveys have found that the greater the number of stressful events a person experiences over the course of a year, the more likely it is that he or she will have a major illness (see **Try It 1** on page 238, "Assess Your Susceptibility to Stress-Related Illness").

figure 10.1
Daily Hassles

Try It!

Assess Your Susceptibility to Stress-Related Illness

Are you susceptible to a stress-related illness? The more stress in your life, the more likely it is that you will experience a major illness.

To determine the stress in your life, take the stressor value given beside each event you have experienced and multiply it by the number of occurrences over the past year (up to a maximum of four), and then add up these scores.[3]

87 Experienced the death of a spouse

77 Got married

77 Experienced the death of a close family member

76 Were divorced

74 Experienced a marital separation

68 Experienced the death of a close friend

68 Experienced pregnancy or fathered a pregnancy

65 Had a major personal injury or illness

62 Were fired from work

60 Ended a marital engagement or a steady relationship

58 Had sexual difficulties

58 Experienced a marital reconciliation

57 Had a major change in self-concept or self-awareness

56 Experienced a major change in the health or behavior of a family member

54 Became engaged to be married

53 Had a major change in financial status

52 Took on a mortgage or loan of more than $10,000

52 Had a major change in use of drugs

50 Had a major conflict or change in values

50 Had a major change in the number of arguments with your spouse

50 Gained a new family member

50 Entered college

50 Changed to a new school

50 Changed to a different line of work

49 Had a major change in amount of independence and responsibility

Handling Stress

Stress is an inevitable part of life. In fact, a life with no stress at all would be so boring, so uneventful, that you'd quickly miss the stress that had been removed.

That doesn't mean, though, that we have to sit back and accept stress when it does arise. **Coping** is the effort to control, reduce, or tolerate the threats that lead to stress. There are many tactics you can employ to cope with the stress in your life, regardless of its cause or intensity.

Being in good physical condition is one excellent way to prepare for future stress. Stress takes its toll on your body, so it makes sense that the stronger and fitter you are, the less negative impact stress will have on you. For example, a regular

Coping

The effort to control, reduce, or learn to tolerate the threats that lead to stress

47 Had a major change in responsibilities at work

46 Experienced a major change in use of alcohol

45 Revised personal habits

44 Had trouble with school administration

43 Held a job while attending school

43 Had a major change in social activities

42 Had trouble with in-laws

42 Had a major change in working hours or conditions

42 Changed residence or living conditions

41 Had your spouse begin or cease work outside the home

41 Changed your choice of major field of study

41 Changed dating habits

40 Had an outstanding personal achievement

38 Had trouble with your boss

38 Had a major change in amount of participation in school activities

37 Had a major change in type and/or amount of recreation

36 Had a major change in religious activities

34 Had a major change of sleeping habits

33 Took a trip or vacation

30 Had a major change in eating habits

26 Had a major change in the number of family get-togethers

22 Were found guilty of minor violations of the law

Scoring: If your total score is above 1,435, you are in a high-stress category and therefore more at risk for experiencing a stress-related illness.

But keep in mind the limitations of this questionnaire. There may be factors in your life that produce high stress that are not listed. In addition, a high score does not mean that you are sure to get sick. Many other factors determine ill health, and high stress is only one cause. Other positive factors in your life, such as getting enough sleep and exercise, may prevent illness.

Still, having an unusually high amount of stress in your life is a cause for concern. If you do score high, you may want to take steps to reduce it.

To Try It online, go to www.mhhe.com/power.

exercise program reduces heart rate, respiration rate, and blood pressure at times when the body is at rest—making us better able to withstand the negative consequences of stress.

If you now drink a lot of coffee or soda, a change in your diet may be enough to bring about a reduction in stress. Coffee, soda, chocolate, and a surprising number of other foods contain caffeine, which can make you feel jittery and anxious even without stress; add a stressor, and the reaction can be very intense and unpleasant.

Eating right can alleviate another problem: obesity. Being overweight can bring on stress for several reasons. For one thing, the extra pounds drag down the functioning of the body. This can lead to fatigue and a reduced ability to bounce back when we encounter challenges to our well-being. In addition, feeling heavy in a society that acclaims the virtues of slimness can be stressful in and of itself.

Of course, stress is not just a question of diet and exercise. To cope with stress, you need to understand what causes it. In some cases, it's obvious—a series of bad test grades in a course, a family problem that keeps getting worse, a job supervisor who seems to delight in making things difficult. In other cases, however, the causes of stress may be more subtle. Perhaps your relationship with your wife or husband is rocky, and you have a nagging feeling that something is wrong.

Whatever the source of stress, you need to pinpoint it. To organize your assault on stress, then, take a piece of paper and list the major circumstances that are causing you stress. Just listing them will help put you in control, and you'll be better able to figure out strategies for coping with them.

Sources of Stress
1. Psychology professor talks so fast that notetaking is nearly impossible
2. Difficulty paying rent this month.
3. Not enough time to study for Tuesday's accounting test

Developing Effective Coping Strategies

A wide variety of tactics can help you deal with stress once you've identified its sources. In addition to lifestyle changes outlined above, among the most effective approaches to coping are these:

> **Take charge of the situation.** Stress is most apt to arise when we are faced with situations over which we have little or no control. If you take charge of the situation, you'll reduce the experience of stress. For example, if several work assignments are given to you all on the same day, you might try recruiting a coworker to help lighten your load.

> **Don't waste energy trying to change the unchangeable.** There are some situations that you simply can't control. You can't change the fact that you have come down with a case of the flu, and you can't change your performance on a test you took last week. Don't hit your head against a brick wall and try to modify things that can't be changed. Use your energy to improve the situation, not to rewrite history.

> **Look for the silver lining.** Stress arises when we perceive a situation as threatening. If we can change how we perceive that situation, we can change our reactions to it. For instance, if your computer science instructor requires you to learn a difficult spreadsheet program in a very short time, the saving grace is that you may be able to use the skill to your advantage in getting a high-paying job down the road. (You can practice finding the silver lining in **Try It 2.**)

Social support
Assistance and comfort supplied by others in times of stress

> **Talk to friends and family. Social support,** assistance and comfort supplied by others, can help us through stressful periods. Turning to our friends and family and simply talking about the stress we're under can help us tolerate

Look for the Silver Lining

Consider the following list of potentially stressful situations. Try to find something positive—a silver lining—in each of them. The first two are completed to get you started.

Situation	Silver Lining
1. Your car just broke down and repairing it is more than you can afford right now.	1. This is the perfect time to begin exercising by walking and using your bicycle.
2. Your boss just yelled at you and threatened to fire you.	2. Either this is a good time to open an honest discussion with your boss about your job situation, OR this is a good time to get a more interesting job.
3. You have two papers due on Monday and there's a great concert you wanted to go to on Saturday night.	3.
4. You just failed an important test.	4.
5. You're flat broke, you promised your friend you'd visit him, and you can't afford the tickets right now.	5.
6. Your last date went poorly and you think your girlfriend/boyfriend was hinting that it was time to break up.	6.
7. You just found out you missed the due date for your mortgage payment.	7.
8. You just got cut from a sports team or club activity you loved.	8.
9. Your best friend is starting to turn weird and seems not to enjoy being with you as much as before.	9.
10. You just realized you don't really want to pursue the career you're training for in college.	10.

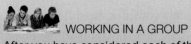 WORKING IN A GROUP

After you have considered each of these situations individually, discuss each of them in a group. What similarities and differences in others' responses did you find? Evaluate the different responses, and consider whether—and why—some ways of reframing the situations were better than others.

To Try It online, go to www.mhhe.com/power.

it more effectively. Even anonymous telephone hotlines can provide us with social support. (The U.S. Department of Health and Human Services maintains a master toll-free number that can provide telephone numbers and addresses of many national help lines and support groups. You can reach it by calling 1-800-336-4797.)

> **Relax.** Because stress produces constant wear and tear on the body, it seems possible that practices that lead to the relaxation of the body might lead to a reduction in stress. And that's just what happens. Using any one of several techniques for producing physical relaxation can prevent stress. Among the best relaxation techniques is *meditation.* Though often associated with its roots in the ancient Eastern religion of Zen Buddhism, meditation, a technique for refocusing attention and producing bodily relaxation, is practiced in some form by members of virtually every major religion. Meditation reduces blood pressure, slows respiration, and in general reduces bodily tension. You can learn about practicing meditation online, at the library, or at a meditation center in your area.

> **Remember that wimping out doesn't work—so keep your commitments.** Suppose you've promised a friend that you'll help him move, and you've promised yourself that you'll spend more time with your children. You've also started work building a porch on the front of your house. Now you are facing all the demands connected to these commitments and feeling stressed.

> You may be tempted to cope with the feeling by breaking some or all of your commitments, thinking, "I just need to sit at home and relax in front of the television!" This is not coping. It is escaping, and it doesn't reduce stress. Ducking out of commitments, whether to yourself or to others, will make you feel guilty and anxious and will be another source

From the perspective of . . .

A STUDENT The educational process can be stressful. When you consider your future career path, what are the areas of stress you may need to address?

of stress—one without the satisfaction of having accomplished what you set out to do. Find ways to keep your promises.

Placing Stress in Perspective

It's easy to think of stress as an enemy. In fact, most approaches to coping are geared to overcoming its negative consequences. But consider the following two principles, which in the end may help you more than any others in dealing with stress:

> **Don't sweat the small stuff . . . and it's all small stuff.** Stress expert Richard Carlson[4] emphasizes the importance of putting the circumstances

we encounter into the proper perspective. He argues that we frequently let ourselves get upset about situations that are actually minor.

So what if someone cuts us off in traffic, or does less than his or her share on a group project, or unfairly criticizes us? It's hardly the end of the world. If an unpleasant event has no long-term consequences, it's often best to let it go. One of the best ways to reduce stress, consequently, is to maintain an appropriate perspective on the events of your life.

› **Make peace with stress.** Think of what it would be like to have no stress—none at all—in your life. Would you really be happier, better adjusted, and more successful? The answer is "probably not." A life that presented no challenges would probably be, in a word, boring. So think about stress as an exciting, although admittedly sometimes difficult, friend. Welcome it, because its presence indicates that your life is stimulating, challenging, and exciting—and who would want it any other way?

» LO 10.2 Keeping Well

Eat right. Exercise. Get plenty of sleep.

Pretty simple, isn't it? We learn the fundamentals of fitness and health in the first years of elementary school.

Yet for millions of us, wellness is an elusive goal. We eat on the fly, stopping for a bite at the drive-in window of a fast-food restaurant. Most of us don't exercise enough either, because we feel we don't have enough time or because it's not much fun for us. And as for sleep, we're a nation in which getting by with as little sleep as possible is seen as a badge of honor.

For many college students, the bad habits are only made worse by the need to manage so many different sets of responsibilities. It is hard to concentrate on keeping well when you also need to keep your children cared for, your boss happy, your schoolwork complete, your household managed. Personal health can easily get lost in the shuffle of all these competing demands. At the end of the day, too many students feel as if they've run themselves ragged just trying to do the minimum to meet their many obligations.

> "The first wealth is health."
> Ralph Waldo Emerson, author and poet

Yet your health is too important to just ignore. There are strategies you can use to balance your commitments, and you can begin to eat more properly, exercise effectively, and sleep better. Approaches to accomplishing these goals include the following.

Juggling Your Responsibilities

› **Identify your priorities.** Taking your child to the dentist or studying for a final exam are examples of tasks that absolutely have to be accomplished. Updating your blog or cleaning out your garage are things that can be left to another day. This distinction seems obvious, yet too often we allow lower-priority tasks to crowd out the high-priority ones. Identify what is most important for you to achieve, and use your time and energy to accomplish these high-priority goals.

› **Use proven time management techniques.** There are only 24 hours in a day. Often, though, it can seem there is 25 hours' worth of work to do—or more.

To get a handle on your schedule, use the strategies outlined in Chapter 2. Creating daily to-do lists, calendars, and so forth will be a huge help in effectively meeting your many responsibilities.

> **Communicate with others about your obligations.** Remember that the people in your life—bosses, family members, instructors, fellow students—can't know you are managing a wide set of responsibilities unless you *tell them*. And while you can't expect special treatment just because you have a child at home or a second job to go to, you'll be surprised at how understanding others will be of such circumstances. Additionally, by communicating with those around you, you can work with them to find solutions when your life starts to feel overwhelming.

> **Multitask.** Don't draw strict limits regarding what you do and when. If you have a free 20 minutes at your job, use it to catch up on reading for classes. When your children are napping, see if there is work for your job you can accomplish at home. You don't want to fill every spare minute with work, but you want to take advantage of the gaps in your hectic day.

> **Don't put your own needs last.** It's easy to cut corners in your schedule by giving yourself the least attention—sleeping less, skipping leisure activities, eating on the go. But this sort of lifestyle is not sustainable. You need to treat yourself well if you are going to be an effective parent, student, and employee.

Eating Right

> **Eat a variety of "whole" foods, including fruits, vegetables, and grain products.** Strive to eat a range of different foods. If you make variety your goal, you will end up eating the right foods. You can learn more about maintaining variety in your diet by visiting the government Web site (**www.mypyramid .gov**) that describes the food guide "pyramid" and allows you to construct a personalized eating plan.

> > **Avoid processed foods.** Make an effort to choose "whole" foods, or foods in a state as close as possible to their natural state: brown rice is better than white rice, and both are better than a preservative-filled, packaged "rice casserole" mix.

> > **Avoid foods that are high in sugar and salt content.** Read labels on product packages carefully and beware of hidden sugars and salts. Many ingredients that end in *-ose* (such as dextrose, sucrose, maltose, and fructose) are actually sugars; salt can lurk within any number of compounds beginning with the word *sodium.*

> > **Seek a diet low in fat and cholesterol.** The fat that is to be especially avoided is saturated fat—the most difficult for your body to rid itself of.

> **Remember: Less is more.** You don't need to walk away stuffed from every meal. Moderation is the key. To be sure you don't eat more than your body is telling you to eat, pay attention to internal hunger cues.

> **Schedule three regular meals a day.** Eating should be a priority—a definite part of your daily schedule. Avoid skipping any meals. Breakfast is particularly important; get up early enough to eat a full meal.

- **Be sensitive to the hidden contents of various foods.** Soda and chocolate can contain substantial quantities of caffeine, which can disrupt your sleep and, along with coffee, become addictive. Many cereals—even those labeled "low fat"—contain a considerable amount of sugar or salt. Pay attention to labels. And watch out for fast foods: Research finds that eating fast foods just a few times a week leads to significant weight gains over the long run.[5]

- **If you want to lose weight, follow a sensible diet.** There's really only one proven way to lose weight: control your food portions, eat a well-balanced diet, and increase the amount of exercise you get. Fad, quick-fix diets are ineffective.

Making Exercise a Part of Your Life

Exercise produces a variety of benefits. Your body will run more efficiently, you'll have more energy, your heart and circulatory system will run more smoothly, and you'll be able to bounce back from stress and illness more quickly.

- **Choose a type of exercise that you like.** Exercising will be a chore you end up avoiding if you don't enjoy what you're doing.

- **Incorporate exercise into your life.** Take the stairs instead of elevators. Leave your car at home and walk to campus or work. When you're on campus, take the longer way to reach your destination.

- **Make exercise a group activity.** Exercising with others brings you social support and turns exercise into a social activity. You'll be more likely to stick to a program if you have a regular "exercise date" with a friend.

- **Vary your routine.** You don't need to do the same kind of exercise day after day. Choose different sorts of activities that will involve different parts of your body and keep you from getting bored. For example, for cardiovascular fitness, you might alternate between running, swimming, biking, or using a cardio training machine.

One note of caution: Before you begin an exercise program, it is a good idea to have a physical checkup, even if you feel you're in the peak of health. This is especially true if you're starting an exercise program after years of inactivity. You also might consult a personal trainer at the gym to set up a program that gradually builds you up to more vigorous exercise.

Getting a Good Night's Sleep

Do you feel as if you don't get enough sleep? You probably don't. Most college students are sleep-deprived, a condition that causes them to feel fatigued, short-tempered, and tense. Sleep deprivation makes staying alert in class nearly impossible (see the **Course Connections** feature on page 246).

Ultimately, insufficient sleep leads to declines in academic, work, and physical performance. You can't do your best at anything if you're exhausted—or even tired.

Often the solution to the problem is simply to allow yourself more time to sleep. Most people need around eight hours of sleep each night, although there are wide individual differences. In addition to sleeping more, there are also some relatively simple changes you can make in your behavior that will help you to sleep better. They include the following:

➤ **Exercise more.** Regular exercise will help you sleep more soundly at night, as well as help you cope with stress that might otherwise keep you awake.

➤ **Have a regular bedtime.** By going to bed at pretty much the same time each night, you give your body a regular rhythm and make sleep a habit.

➤ **Use your bed for sleeping and not as an all-purpose area.** Don't use your bed as a place to study, read, eat, or watch TV. Let your bed be a trigger for sleep.

➤ **Avoid caffeine after lunch.** The stimulant effects of caffeine (found in coffee, tea, and some soft drinks) may last as long as 8 to 12 hours after it's consumed.

➤ **Drink a glass of milk at bedtime.** Your mom was right: Drinking a glass of milk before you go to bed will help you get to sleep. The reason: Milk contains a natural chemical that makes you drowsy.

➤ **Avoid sleeping pills.** Steer clear of sleeping pills. Although they may be temporarily effective, in the long run they impair your ability to sleep because they disrupt your natural sleep cycles.

When we have more responsibilities than time, sleep is often the first thing to suffer. Getting an appropriate amount of sleep can actually help you get more done in the time you do have.

➤ **Don't try to force sleep on yourself.** Although this advice sounds odd, it turns out that one of the reasons that we have trouble sleeping is that we try too hard. Consequently, when you go to bed, just relax, and don't even attempt to go to sleep. If you're awake after 10 minutes or so, get up and do something else. Only go back to bed when you feel tired. Do this as often as necessary. If you follow this regimen for several weeks—and don't take naps or rest during the day—eventually getting into your bed will trigger sleep.

» LO 10.3 Managing Your Money

When it comes to addressing the stress in our lives, it's probably hard to overstate the impact of money. Few things command the attention—and worry—that money does. That's why it's essential to manage your money appropriately. Not only are many of your choices and opportunities influenced by money, but so too is your mental well-being.

Do you know where your money goes? Do you spend more than you think you should? Do you never have quite enough cash to buy the things you want?

Answering these questions and understanding the role money plays in your life is the first step of wise money management. To begin getting a grip on your finances, answer the questions in the **Journal Reflections** exercise on page 248.

If you have money problems—and there's virtually no one who doesn't have some concerns about finances—the solution is to develop a budget. A **budget** is a formal plan that accounts and plans for expenditures and income. Taking your goals into account, a budget helps determine how much money you should be spending each month, based on your income and your other financial resources. Budgets also help prepare for the unexpected, such as the loss of a job or an illness that would reduce your income, or for sudden, unanticipated expenses, such as a major car repair.

Budget
A formal plan that accounts for expenditures and income

Although all budgets are based on an uncomplicated premise—expenditures should not exceed income—budgeting is not simple. There are several times during the year that require especially large expenditures, such as the start of a semester, when you must pay your tuition and purchase books. Furthermore, your income can be erratic; it can rise and fall depending on overtime, whether another member of your family starts or stops working, and so forth. But a budget will help you deal with the ups and downs in your finances, smoothing the curves and extending your view toward the horizon. Learning budgeting skills can also help you at work, as discussed in this chapter's **Career Connections** on page 249.

> "There was a time when a fool and his money were soon parted, but now it happens to everybody."
> **Adlai Stevenson, politician**

Most of all, a budget provides security. It will let you take control of your money, permitting you to spend it as you need to without guilt, because you have planned for the expenditure. It also makes it easier to put money aside because you know that your current financial sacrifice will be rewarded later, when you can make a purchase that you've been planning for.

Budgeting is very personal: What is appropriate for one person doesn't work for another. For a few people, keeping track of their spending comes naturally; they enjoy accounting for every dollar that passes through their hands. For most people, though, developing a budget—and sticking to it—does not come easily.

However, if you follow several basic steps—illustrated in the P.O.W.E.R. Plan—the process of budgeting is straightforward.

P Prepare
Identify financial goals

O Organize
Determine expenditures and income

W Work
Make a budget that adds up

E Evaluate
Review the budget

R Rethink
Rethink financial options

P.O.W.E.R. Plan

P Prepare   Identifying Your Financial Goals

Your first reaction when asked to identify your financial goals may be that the question is a no-brainer: You want to have more money to spend. But it's not that simple. You need to ask yourself *why* you want more money. What would you spend it on? What would bring you the most satisfaction? Purchasing a DVD player? Paying off your debt? Saving money for a vacation? Starting a business? Paying for college rather than taking out loans?

Journal Reflections

My Sense of Cents

Answer the following questions about your financial sense.

1. How much money do you now have in your pockets and wallet? (Guess first, then look.) How close did you come?

2. Do you know how much money you typically spend in a month, including money spent on food, lodging, and other items?

3. How good a sense of your finances do you think you have? How secure do you feel in your understanding of where your money goes?

4. How important is money to you? Why?

5. Research shows that although winning the lottery or other large sums of money brings an initial surge in happiness, a year later the winners' level of happiness returns to what it was before.[6] Why do you think this is true in general, and would it be true for you?

You won't be able to develop a budget that will work for you until you determine your short- and long-term financial goals. To determine them, use **Try It 3,** "Identify Your Financial Goals" on page 250.

 Determining Your Expenditures and Income

Do you open your wallet for the $10 that was there yesterday and find only a dollar? Spending money without realizing it is a common affliction.

There's only one way to get a handle on where your money is going: Keep track of it. To get an overview of your expenditures, go through any records you've kept to identify where you've spent money for the last year—old checks, rent and utility receipts, and previous college bills can help you.

Budgeting on the Job

If you've ever held a job, the salary you received was determined, in part, by your employer's budget.

Although they may not always be accessible to every employee, budgets are part of the world of work. Regardless of who the employer is—be it a small dry cleaning business or the massive federal government—there is a budget outlining anticipated income and expenditures. Managers are expected to keep to the budget, and if their expenditures exceed what is budgeted, they are held accountable.

For this reason, the ability to create and live within a budget is an important skill to acquire. Not only will it help keep your own finances under control, but it will also prepare you to be financially responsible and savvy on the job—qualities that are highly valued by employers.

In addition, keep track of everything you spend for a week. *Everything.* When you spend 75 cents for a candy bar from a vending machine, write it down. When you buy lunch for $4.99 at a fast-food restaurant, write it down. When you buy a 44-cent stamp, write it down.

Record your expenditures in a small notebook that you carry with you all the time. It may be tedious, but you're doing it for only a week. And it will be eye-opening: People are usually surprised at how much they spend on little items without thinking about it.

From the perspective of . . .

A RECENT GRADUATE Have you considered how your new career may impact your personal budget? What preparations might you need to make to ensure that a higher monthly income results in a better standard of living?

Make a list of everything you think you'll need to spend over the next year. Some items are easy to think of, such as rent and tuition payments, because they occur regularly and the amount you pay is fixed. Others are harder to budget for because they can vary substantially. For example, the price of gasoline changes frequently. If you have a long commute, the changing price of gasoline can cause substantial variation in what you pay each month. (Use **Table 10.1** on page 252 to estimate your expenditures for the coming year. You can also prepare a monthly budget online at the *P.O.W.E.R. Learning* Web site at **www.mhhe.com/power**.)

When you are listing your upcoming expenditures, be sure to include an amount that you will routinely put aside into a savings account that pays you interest.

Try It!

3

Identify Your Financial Goals

Determining your financial goals will help set you on the path to securing your financial future. Use this **Try It** to get started.

Step 1. Use the planning tool below to identify and organize your financial goals.

Short-Term Goals

What would you like to have money for in the short term (over the next 3 months)? Consider these categories:

Personal necessities (such as food, lodging, clothes, household supplies, transportation, loan and credit card payments, medical and child-care expenses):

Educational necessities (such as tuition, fees, books, school supplies, computer expenses):

Social needs (e.g., getting together with family, friends, and others; clubs and teams; charitable contributions):

Entertainment (e.g., movies and shows, trips, recreation and sports):

Other:

Mid-Range Goals

What would you like to have money for soon (3 months from now to a year from now), but not immediately? Use the same categories:

Personal necessities:

Educational necessities:

Social needs:

Entertainment:

Other:

Long-Range Goals

What would you like to have money for 1 to 3 years from now? Use the same categories:

Personal necessities:

Educational necessities:

Social needs:

Entertainment:

Other:

Step 2. Now put each of your lists in *priority* order.

Short-Term Priorities:

Mid-Range Priorities:

Long-Range Priorities:

What does the list tell you about what is important to you? Did you find any surprises? Would you classify yourself as a financial risk taker or someone who values financial security?

 WORKING IN A GROUP

Consider these questions: Compare your priorities with those of your classmates. What similarities and differences do you find, and what can you learn from others' priorities?

To Try It online, go to **www.mhhe.com/power.**

table 10.1 Estimated Expenditures, Next 12 Months

Category	Now to 3 Months from now	3–6 Months from now	6–9 Months from now	9–12 months from now
Personal Necessities				
Food				
Shelter (rent, utilities, etc.)				
Clothing				
Household supplies				
Transportation (car payments, gas, car repairs, bus tickets, etc.)				
Loan and credit card payments				
Medical expenses				
Child-care expenses				
Other				
Educational Necessities				
Tuition and fees				
Books				
School supplies				
Computer expenses				
Other				
Social Needs				
Relationships				
Clubs and teams				
Charitable contributions				
Other				
Entertainment				
Movies and shows				
Trips				
Recreation and sports				
Other				
TOTAL				

It's important to get into the habit of saving money. Even if you start off small—putting aside just a few dollars a week—the practice of regularly putting aside some amount of your income is central to good financial management.

Determine Your Income Sources

You probably have a pretty good idea of how much money you have each month. But it's as important to list each source of income as it is to account for everything you spend.

Add up what you make from any jobs you hold. Also list any support you receive from family members, including occasional gifts you might get from relatives. Finally, include any financial aid (such as tuition reductions, loan payments, or scholarships) you receive from your college. Use **Table 10.2** to record this information. When you do, be sure to list the amounts you receive in terms of after-tax income.

 Work

Making a Budget That Adds Up

If you've prepared and organized your budget, actually constructing your budget is as easy as adding 2 + 2. Well, not exactly; the numbers will be larger. But all you need to do is add up your list of expenses, and then add up your sources of income. In a perfect world, the two numbers will be equal.

But most of the time, the world is not perfect: Most of us find that expenditures are larger than our income. After all, if we had plenty of excess cash, we probably wouldn't be bothering to make a budget in the first place.

If you find you spend more than you make, there are only two things to do: decrease your spending or increase your income. It's often

table 10.2 Estimated Income, Next 12 Months				
Category	Now to 3 Months from now	3–6 Months from now	6–9 Months from now	9–12 months from now
Wages				
Family Support				
Financial Aid				
Tuition reductions				
Loan income				
Scholarship payments				
Other				
Interest and Dividends				
Gifts				
Other				
TOTAL				

easiest to decrease expenditures, because your expenses tend to be more under your control. For instance, you can do many things to save money, including the following:

- **Control impulse buying.** If you shop for your groceries, always take a list with you, and don't shop when you're hungry.
- **Make and take your own lunch.** Brown-bag lunches can save you a substantial amount of money over purchasing your lunches, even if you go to a fast-food restaurant or snack bar.
- **Read the daily newspaper and magazines at the library or online.** Not only do college libraries subscribe to many daily newspapers and magazines, but major newspapers and magazines are also online.
- **Check bills for errors.** Computers make mistakes, and so do the people who enter the data into them. So make sure that your charges on any bill are accurate.
- **Cut up your credit cards and pay cash.** Using a credit card is seductive; when you take out your plastic, it's easy to feel as if you're not really spending money. If you use cash for purchases instead, you'll see the money going out.
- **Make major purchases only during sales.** Plan major purchases so they coincide with sales.
- **Share and trade.** Pool your resources with friends. Carpool, share resources such as computers, and trade clothes.
- **Live more simply.** Is cable TV an absolute necessity? Is it really necessary to eat out once a week? Do you buy clothes because you need them or because you want them? Do you really need to send so many text messages?

There are as many ways to save money as there are people looking to save it. But keep in mind that saving money should not necessarily be an end in itself. Don't spend hours thinking of ways to save a dime, and don't get upset about situations where you are forced to spend money. The goal is to bring your budget into balance, not to become a tightwad who keeps track of every penny and feels that spending money is a personal failure. To help you get started, get a sense of your current style of saving money in **Try It 4.**

Finally, it's important to remember that budgets may be brought into balance not only by decreasing expenditures, but also by increasing income. The most direct way to increase income is to get a job if you don't already have one, or to work more at the job you have.

 ## Reviewing Your Budget

Budgets are not meant to be set in stone. You should review where you stand financially each month. Only by monitoring how closely actual expenditures and income match your budget projections will you be able to maintain control of your finances.

You don't need to continually keep track of every penny you spend to evaluate your success in budgeting. As you gain more experience with your budget, you'll begin to get a better sense of your finances. You'll know when it may be possible to consider splurging on a gift for a friend, and when you need to operate in penny-pinching mode.

Try It! POWER

Determine Your Saving Style

4

Read each of the following statements and rate how well it describes you, using this scale:

  1 = That's me

  2 = Sometimes

  3 = That's not me

	1	2	3
1. I count the change I'm given by cashiers in stores and restaurants.			
2. I always pick up all the change I receive from a transaction in a store, even if it's only a few cents.			
3. I don't buy something right away if I'm pretty sure it will go on sale soon.			
4. I feel a real sense of accomplishment if I buy something on sale.			
5. I always remember how much I paid for something.			
6. If something goes on sale soon after I've bought it, I feel cheated.			
7. I have money in at least one interest-bearing bank account.			
8. I rarely lend people money.			
9. If I lend money to someone repeatedly without getting it back, I stop lending it to that person.			
10. I share resources (e.g., CDs, books, magazines) with other people to save money.			
11. I'm good at putting money away for big items that I really want.			
12. I believe most generic or off-brand items are just as good as name brands.			

Add up your ratings. Interpret your total score according to this informal guide:

  12–15: Very aggressive saving style

  16–20: Careful saving style

  21–27: Fairly loose saving style

  28–32: Loose saving style

  33–36: Nonexistent saving style

What are the advantages and disadvantages of your saving style? How do you think your saving style would affect your ability to keep to a budget? If you are dissatisfied with your saving style, how might you be able to change it?

To Try It online, go to www.mhhe.com/power.

The important thing is to keep your expenditures under control. Review, and if necessary revise, your budget to fit any changes in circumstances. Maybe you receive a raise at your job. Maybe the cost of gas goes down. Or maybe you face a reduction in income. Whatever the change in circumstances, evaluate how it affects your budget, and revise the budget accordingly.

R Rethink — Reconsidering Your Financial Options

If all goes well, the process of budgeting will put you in control of your financial life. Your expenditures will match your income, and you won't face major money worries.

In the real world, of course, events have a way of inflicting disaster on even the best-laid plans:

› You lose your job and can't afford to pay next month's mortgage.

› Your car breaks down and needs a $300 repair. You don't have $300.

› Your parents run into financial difficulties and you feel you need to help support them.

› Your dishwasher breaks, and repairing it will cost $500. If you pay for repairs, you can't afford tuition.

All of us face financial difficulties at one time or another. Sometimes it happens suddenly and without warning. Other times people sink more gradually into financial problems, each month accumulating more debt until they reach a point at which they can't pay their bills.

However it happens, finding yourself with too little money to pay your bills requires action. You need to confront the situation and take steps to solve the problem. The worst thing to do is nothing. Hiding from those to whom you owe money makes the situation worse. Your creditors—the institutions and people to whom you owe money—will assume that you don't care, and they'll be spurred on to take harsher actions.

These are the steps to take if you do find yourself with financial difficulties (also see **Table 10.3**):

table 10.3 Steps in Dealing with Financial Difficulties	
Assess the Problem	Make a list of what you owe and to whom. Figure out a reasonable amount you can put toward each debt. Work out a specific plan.
Contact Each of Your Creditors	Start with your bank, credit card companies, and landlord. Explain the situation. Show them your plan to pay off debt.
See a Credit Counselor	If you cannot work out a repayment plan on your own, visit a credit counseling service.
Stick to the Plan	Once you have a plan, make a commitment to stick to it. Your bank or creditor can help you identify a credit counselor.

- **Assess the problem.** Make a list of what you owe and to whom. Look at the bottom line and figure out a reasonable amount you can put toward each debt. Work out a specific plan that can lead you out of the situation.

- **Contact each of your creditors.** Start with your bank, credit card companies, and landlord, and continue through each creditor. It's best to visit personally, but a phone call will do.

  When you speak with them, explain the situation. If the problem is due to illness or unemployment, let them know. If it's due to overspending, let them know that. Tell them what you plan to do to pay off your debt, and show them your plan. The fact that you have a plan demonstrates not only what you intend to do, but also that you are serious about your situation and capable of financial planning.

  If you've had a clean financial record in the past, your creditors may be willing to agree to your plan. Ultimately, it is cheaper for them to accept smaller payments over a longer time than to hire a collection agency.

- **See a credit counselor.** If you can't work out a repayment plan on your own, visit a credit counseling service. These are nonprofit organizations that help people who find themselves in financial trouble. Your bank or a creditor can help you identify one, or you can call the National Foundation for Credit Counseling at 1–800–388–2227 or visit their Web site at **www.nfcc.org**.

- **Stick to the plan.** Once you have a plan to get yourself out of debt, follow it. Unless you diligently make the payments you commit to, you'll find your debt spiraling out of control once again. It's essential, then, to regard your plan as a firm commitment and stick to it.

HINDS
COMMUNITY COLLEGE

NAME: **Gustavus Dampier**

SCHOOL: **Hinds Community College, Jackson, Mississippi; Mississippi College, Clinton, Mississippi**

HOME: **Atlanta, Georgia**

When Gustavus Dampier first started classes he was confronted with two of the most challenging aspects of going to college: getting organized and managing his time. It wasn't long before he realized he needed to do something.

"I found it difficult to study my notes, primarily because they weren't organized. I wouldn't date my notes and would tend to lose them," he said. "I started by getting a folder for each of my courses and used them to keep my notes. I would label the notes with the chapters they covered and dated them. Once I did that I started doing much better."

As his notes became more organized, Dampier often rewrote them. By rewriting his notes, he was able to better remember and retain the material, and this in turn made him prepared for exams.

At the same time he was organizing his notes, Dampier, who belonged to the track team, realized he needed to better manage his time between his studies and athletic activities.

"I found running track and studying was difficult. I just wasn't managing my time," he said. "So I just started studying earlier in the day instead of waiting until the last minute. And when I had time, I would take advantage of it."

Dampier improved his grades as well as his study habits, eventually moving on to a four-year college.

"But the transition was difficult for me," he explained, "because it took me out of my comfort zone at Hinds. There I knew the instructors, knew the school, and had friends. When I entered Mississippi College, it was like starting over again.

"But I made an effort to visit my professors in their office and whenever I would see them I would greet them with 'good morning' or 'good afternoon,' so after awhile they remembered me just by being polite to them."

Looking Back

What is stress and how can I control it?

▸ Stress is a common experience, appearing in three main forms: cataclysmic events, personal stressors, and daily hassles. Excessive stress is not only unpleasant and upsetting, but it also has negative effects on the body and mind.

▸ Coping with stress involves becoming prepared for future stress through proper diet and exercise, identifying the causes of stress in one's life, taking control of stress, seeking social support, practicing relaxation techniques, training oneself to redefine and reinterpret stressful situations, and keeping one's promises.

What is involved in keeping fit and healthy, and why is it important for me to do so?

▸ For all people, keeping fit and healthy is both essential and challenging. Balance your responsibilities by identifying your priorities and using time management techniques.

▸ It is vital to learn to eat properly, especially by eating a variety of foods on a regular schedule and by restricting your intake of fat, cholesterol, and salt.

▸ Exercise is valuable because it improves health and well-being. Choosing exercises that we like, making everyday activities a part of exercise, and exercising with others can help form the habit of exercise.

▸ The third key element of good health is sleeping properly. Good exercise and eating habits can contribute to sound sleep, as can the development of regular sleeping habits and the use of sleep-assisting practices.

What are reasons for keeping to a budget and how can I prepare and stick to one?

▸ Concerns about money can be significantly reduced through the creation of a budget by which spending and income can be planned, accounted for, and aligned with your goals.

▸ Budgets provide security by helping you control your finances and avoid surprises.

▸ The process of budgeting involves identifying your financial goals, keeping track of current expenses and estimating future expenses, and making the necessary adjustments to keep income and spending in balance.

▸ If financial difficulties arise, contact your creditors and arrange a plan for paying off the debt. If you need help in designing a repayment plan, nonprofit credit counselors can help.

[KEY TERMS AND CONCEPTS]

Stress (p. 236)

Cataclysmic events (p. 237)

Personal stressors (p. 237)

Daily hassles (p. 237)

Coping (p. 238)

Social support (p. 240)

Budget (p. 247)

[RESOURCES]

AT SCHOOL

Many colleges have mental health counselors who can help you deal with emotional problems. If you are depressed, have trouble sleeping, or have other problems coping with the problems of life, speaking with a counselor can be extremely helpful. Check with your school's counseling center or health center to identify someone appropriate with whom to speak.

The bursar's or treasurer's office handles money affairs. Not only does it collect money owed for tuition, but it also may perform other services such as cashing checks.

If you are receiving financial aid, there is usually a particular office devoted to the complexities of scholarships, loan processing, and other forms of aid. The personnel in the office can be very helpful in maximizing your financial aid package as well as in solving financial problems related to your schooling. If you have a problem with your finances, see them sooner rather than later.

IN PRINT

10 Simple Solutions to Stress: How to Tame Tension and Start Enjoying Your Life (New Harbinger Publications, 2007) provides 10 simple techniques for coping with stress and its effects on your health and your life.

YOU: The Owner's Manual, Updated and Expanded Edition: An Insider's Guide to the Body That Will Make You Healthier and Younger (Collins Living, 2008) is an engaging and comprehensive book that not only provides practical information on how the body works, but also offers hundreds of pointers on how to live healthier, resist disease, and maintain a high quality of life.

Fred Rewey's *Winning the Cash Flow War* (Wiley, 2005) offers a clear path to getting all your finances under control.

ON THE WEB

The following sites on the Web provide the opportunity to extend your learning about stress, health, and wellness. (Although the Web addresses were accurate at the time the book was printed, check the *P.O.W.E.R. Learning* Web site [**www.mhhe.com/power**] for any changes that may have occurred.)

> The American Dietetic Association's Web site not only provides information for its professional members, but it also includes updated consumer tips and articles (**www.eatright.org/Public/**). Features include strategies for smart grocery shopping, discussion of the latest fad diets, and guidelines for healthy eating.

> "Stress Management" (**stress.about.com/od/copingskills/**), on About.com, offers in-depth and comprehensive information on coping with stress. Dozens of links cover teens through the elderly, self-assessment, psychotherapy, and relaxation techniques.

> "FinAid: The SmartStudent Guide to College Financial Aid" (**www.finaid.org**) provides a free, comprehensive, independent, and objective guide to student financial aid. It was created by Mark Kantrowitz, author of *The Prentice Hall Guide to Scholarships and Fellowships for Math and Science Students*. The site's "calculators" page (**www.finaid.org/calculators/**) offers loads of online calculators including: College Cost Projector, Savings Plan Designer, Expected Family Contribution and Financial Aid Calculator, Loan Payment Calculator, and Student Loan Advisor (undergraduate).

> "Managing Your Money" (**www.nd.edu/%7Efinaid/managing_money/**), sponsored by the Office of Financial Aid at Notre Dame University, offers eight links covering everything from responsible borrowing to tips on developing credit card smarts.

1. Find two stress reduction techniques. One possible strategy: Go to AltaVista (**www.altavista.com**) and enter the phrase "stress reduction techniques" into the search field. Examine the sites located until you find two stress reduction techniques. Try each of the techniques. Do you feel less stressed and more relaxed? Which of the techniques works best for you?

2. Discover three new ways to save money. Possible strategy: Using the search engine of your choice, enter the phrase "saving money." Examine the sites for tips and tricks to help you hold on to what you earn.

The Case of . . .
The Breaking Point

Staring at the balance in his checking account on his computer screen, Antonio Butler thought to himself, *It is all over.*

"It" was his college career. For three semesters Antonio had worked two jobs to pay his way through school. He'd been careful with his money, only rarely indulging in major new purchases such as a new computer and a refurbished car stereo.

Now, though, financial events beyond his control had taken their toll. His brother had broken his leg on a construction site and couldn't return to work for months. While details of compensation were being worked out, Antonio had helped support his brother and his young niece.

Staring at his checking account, Antonio realized that supporting his brother had added up to a lot more than he thought. Now his tuition was due—and Antonio simply did not have the money. Antonio had never felt the sinking sensation he now experienced: After everything he'd done, he believed his college career was finished.

1. Is Antonio's college career really over? What should his next steps be if he wants to stay in college?

2. What can Antonio do in the long term to make sure he doesn't face a similar crisis down the road?

3. Is there anything Antonio could have done to have avoided this situation in the first place?

4. Do you think Antonio was right to support his brother while he was injured? Would you have done the same thing in a similar circumstance in your own life?

5. Have you ever had a moment when you thought your financial plans had been ruined? In the end, was the situation as bad as it first appeared?

A Final Word

Throughout this book you've seen how the principles of P.O.W.E.R. Learning can be applied to a variety of situations, ranging from reading and writing to coping with stress. You can use the framework in any situation where you need to organize your thinking and behavior in a systematic way. It's a tool you can call on throughout your lifetime.

College is the beginning of a journey that leads to your future. This book has been designed to help you with the demands and challenges of college, but at the same time to prepare you for life after school. It has tried to show you that it is *you* who must make things happen to fulfill your goals and aspirations.

Ultimately, however, there are some key ingredients to success that no book can teach you and that only you can provide: integrity and honesty, intellectual curiosity, and love. I hope this book will help you as you consider what your contribution to the world will be and as you work to make that contribution.

Glossary

Academic honesty: Completing and turning in only one's own work under one's own name.

Acronym: A word or phrase formed by the first letters of a series of terms.

Acrostic: A sentence in which the first letters of the words correspond to material that is to be remembered.

Active listening: The voluntary act of focusing on what is being said, making sense of it, and thinking about it in a way that permits it to be recalled accurately.

Advance organizers: Broad, general ideas related to material that is to be read or heard, which pave the way for subsequent learning.

Analogy: A comparison between concepts or objects that are alike in some respects, but dissimilar in most others.

Attention span: The length of time that attention is typically sustained.

Auditory/verbal learning style A style that favors listening as the best approach to learning.

Blended (or hybrid) courses: Instruction is a combination of the traditional face-to-face classroom interaction and a significant amount of online learning.

Blog: A Web-based public diary in which a writer provides commentary, ideas, thoughts, and short essays.

Browser: A program that provides a way of navigating around the information on the Web.

Budget: A formal plan that accounts for expenditures and income.

Call number: A unique classification number assigned to every book (or other resource) in a library. Call numbers are used for ease of location.

Career Portfolio: A dynamic record that documents your skills, capabilities, achievements, and goals, as well as provides a place to keep notes, ideas, and research findings related to careers.

Cataclysmic events: Sudden, powerful events that occur quickly and affect many people simultaneously.

Concept mapping: A method of structuring written material by graphically grouping and connecting key ideas and themes.

Coping: The effort to control, reduce, or learn to tolerate the threats that lead to stress.

Cramming: Hurried, last-minute studying.

Critical thinking: A process involving reanalysis, questioning, and challenge of underlying assumptions.

Cultural competence: Knowledge and understanding about other races, ethnic groups, cultures, and minority groups.

Culture: The learned behaviors, beliefs, and attitudes that are characteristic of an individual society or population, and the products that people create.

Daily hassles: The minor irritants of life that, by themselves, produce little stress, but which can add up and produce more stress than a single larger-scale event.

Daily to-do list: A schedule showing the tasks, activities, and appointments due to occur during the day.

Decision making: The process of deciding among various alternatives.

Distance learning: The teaching of courses at another institution, with student participation via video technology or the Web.

Educated guessing: The practice of eliminating obviously false multiple-choice answers and selecting the most likely answer from the remaining choices.

E-mail: Electronic mail, a system of communication that permits users to send and receive messages via the Internet.

Emoticons (or smileys): Symbols used in e-mail messages that provide information on the emotion that the writer is trying to convey. Emoticons usually look like faces on their side, with facial expressions related to the intended emotion or tone.

Ethnicity: Shared national origins or cultural patterns.

Evaluation: An assessment of the match between a product or activity and the goals it was intended to meet.

Flash cards: Index cards that contain key pieces of information to be remembered.

Freewriting: A technique involving continuous, nonstop writing, without self-criticism, for a fixed period of time.

Frontmatter: The preface, introduction, and table of contents of a book.

Hearing: The involuntary act of sensing sounds.

"I" statements: Statements that cast responses in terms of oneself and one's individual interpretation.

Information competency: The ability to determine what information is necessary, and then to locate, evaluate, and effectively use that information.

Instant messaging: A system that allows one to use a computer to communicate in real time with friends and instructors.

Interlibrary loan: A system by which libraries share resources, making them available to patrons of different libraries.

Internet: A vast network of interconnected computers that share information around the world.

Learning disabilities: Difficulties in processing information when listening, speaking, reading, or writing, characterized by a discrepancy between learning potential and actual academic achievement.

Learning style: One's preferred manner of acquiring, using, and thinking about knowledge.

Left-brain processing: Information processing primarily performed by the left hemisphere of the brain, focusing on tasks requiring verbal competence, such as speaking, reading, thinking, and reasoning; information is processed sequentially, one bit at a time.

Link: A means of "jumping" automatically from one Web page to another.

Listserv: A subscription service through which members can post and receive messages via e-mail on general topics of shared interest.

Loneliness: A subjective state in which people do not experience the level of connection with others that they desire.

Long-term goals: Aims relating to major accomplishments that take some time to achieve.

Master calendar: A schedule showing the weeks of a longer time period, such as a college term, with all assignments and important activities noted on it.

Meta-message: The underlying main ideas that a speaker is seeking to convey; the meaning behind the overt message.

Mnemonics: Formal techniques used to make material more readily remembered.

Motivation: The inner power and psychological energy that directs and fuels behavior.

Online database: An index in electronic form composed of an organized body of information on a related topic.

Overlearning: Studying and rehearsing material past the point of initial mastery to the point at which recall becomes automatic.

Personal stressors: Major life events that produce stress.

Plagiarism: Taking credit for someone else's words, thoughts, or ideas.

Podcast: An audio or video recording that can be accessed on the Internet and viewed on a computer or downloaded to a mobile device.

P.O.W.E.R . Learning: A system designed to help people achieve their goals, based on five steps: *Prepare, Organize, Work, Evaluate,* and *Rethink.*

Prejudice: Evaluations or judgments of members of a group that are based primarily on membership in the group and not on the particular characteristics of individuals.

Priorities: The tasks and activities that one needs and wants to do, rank-ordered from most important to least important.

Problem solving: The process of generating alternatives to work on.

Procrastination: The habit of putting off and delaying tasks that need to be accomplished.

Race: Traditionally, biologically determined physical characteristics that set one group apart from others.

Read/write learning style: A style that involves a preference for written material, favoring reading over hearing and touching.

Recall: A way to request library materials from another person who has them.

Receptive learning style: The way in which we initially receive information.

Reflective feedback: A technique of verbal listening in which a listener rephrases what a speaker has said, trying to echo the speaker's meaning.

Rehearsal: The process of practicing and learning material.

Right-brain processing: Information processing primarily performed by the right hemisphere of the brain, focusing on information in nonverbal domains, such as the understanding of spatial relationships and recognition of patterns and drawings, music, and emotional expression.

Search engine: A computerized index to information on the Web.

Short-term goals: Relatively limited steps toward the accomplishment of long-term goals.

Social support: Assistance and comfort supplied by others in times of stress.

Stacks: The shelves on which books and other materials are stored in a library.

Stereotypes: Beliefs and expectations about members of a group that are held simply because of their membership in the group.

Stress: The physical and emotional response to events that threaten or challenge us.

Study groups: Small, informal groups of students whose purpose is to help members work together and study for a test.

Study notes: Notes taken for the purpose of reviewing material.

Tactile/kinesthetic learning style: A style that involves learning by touching, manipulating objects, and doing things.

Test anxiety: A temporary condition characterized by fears and concerns about test-taking.

Text messaging (texting): This communication method permits you to send short messages from mobile phones to other phones or e-mail accounts.

Time log: A record of how one spends one's time.

Visual/graphic learning style: A style that favors material presented visually in a diagram or picture.

Visualization: A memory technique by which images are formed to help recall material.

Web: A highly graphical interface between users and the Internet that permits users to transmit and receive not only text but also pictorial, video, and audio information.

Web page: A location (or site) on the Web housing information from a single source and (typically) links to other pages.

Weekly timetable: A schedule showing all regular, prescheduled activities due to occur in the week, together with one-time events and commitments.

Working backward: The strategy of starting at the desired solution or goal and working toward the starting point of the problem.

Zero-sum game: A situation in which when one person wins, the other person automatically loses.

Endnotes

Chapter 1

1. Gottesman, G. (1994). *College survival.* New York: Macmillan. P. 70.
2. "The American Freshman: National Norms for 2006," published by American Council on Education and University of California at Los Angeles Higher Education Research Institute.
3. Gottesman, G. (1994). *College survival.* New York: Macmillan. P. 70.
4. Adapted from Lazear, D. (1999). *The intelligent curriculum: Using MI to develop your students' full potential.* Tucson, AZ: Zephyr Press.

Chapter 2

1. National Survey of Student Engagement: 2004 Annual Report.
2. Adapted from Ferner, J.D. (1980). *Successful time management.* New York: Wiley. P. 33.

Chapter 3

1. Tyler, S. (1997). *Been there, should've done that.* Haslett, MI: Front Porch Press. P. 117.
2. Adapted from Johnson, G. (2000). *The living world* (2nd ed.). New York: McGraw-Hill.
3. Tyler, S. (1997). *Been there, should've done that.* Haslett, MI: Front Porch Press. P. 114.

Chapter 4

1. Tobias, S. (1995). *Overcoming math anxiety.* New York: W. W. Norton & Company.
2. Tyler, S. (1997). *Been there, should've done that.* Haslett, MI: Front Porch Press. P. 128.

Chapter 5

1. Bransford, J. D., & Johnson, M. K. (1972). Contextual prerequisites for understanding: Some investigations of comprehension and recall. *Journal of Verbal Learning and Verbal Behavior,* 11, p. 722.
2. Gold, P. E., Cahill, L., & Wenk, G.L. (2003, April) The low-down on ginkgo biloba. *Scientific American,* pp. 86–91.

Chapter 6

1. Farquharson, L. (2003, September 15). Find a job. *The Wall Street Journal,* p. R8.
2. Combs, P. (1998). *Major success.* Berkeley, CA: Ten Speed Press, p. 103.
3. *21st century lives: Neurosurgeon Ben Carson* (Accessed September 8, 2000). **www.abcnews.go.com/onair/WorldNewsTonight/wnt000908_21st_carson_feature.html.** ABC News.
4. Ibid.

Chapter 7

1. Liebovich, L. (2000, August 10). Choosing quick hits over the card catalog. *The New York Times,* pp. 1, 6. Based on material from Eliot Soloway, University of Michigan, School of Education.

Chapter 8

1. Adapted from Haplern, D. F. (1996). *Thought and knowledge: An introduction to critical thinking* (3rd ed.). Mahwah, NJ: Erlbaum; and Bransford, J. D., & Stein, B. S. (1993). *The ideal problem solver* (2nd ed.). New York: W. H. Freeman.
2. Forer, B. (1949). The fallacy of personal validation: A classroom demonstration of gullibility. *Journal of Abnormal and Social Psychology,* 44, pp. 118–123.
3. Byrne, D., & Kelley, L. (1981). *An introduction to personality* (3rd ed.). Englewood Cliffs, NJ: Prentice Hall. P. 304.

Chapter 9

1. Nolan, M.F. (1997, April 26). Tiger's racial multiplicity. *The Boston Globe,* p. A11.
2. Tatum, B. D. (1997). *"Why are all the black kids sitting together in the cafeteria?" And other conversations about race.* New York: Basic Books.
3. Malone, M. S. (1993, July 18). Translating diversity into high-tech gains. *The New York Times,* p. B2.
4. Sponholz, M., & Sponholz, J. (1996). *The Princeton Review college companion.* New York: Random House. P. 24.

Chapter 10

1. Sax, L. J., Astin, A. W., Korn, W. S., & Mahoney, K. (1999). *The American freshman: National norms for fall 1999.* Los Angeles: Higher Education Research Institute, UCLA.
2. Chamberlain, K., & Zika, S. (1990). The minor events approach to stress: Support for use of daily hassles. *British Journal of Psychology,* 81, pp. 469–481.
3. Source of table: Marx, M. B., Garrity, T. F., & Bowers, F. R. (1975). The influence of recent life experience on the health of college freshman. *Journal of Psychosomatic Research,* 19, pp. 87–98.
4. Carlson, R. (1997). Don't sweat the small stuff . . . and it's *all small stuff.* New York: Hyperion.
5. Pereira, M., Kartashov, A. I., Ebbeling, C. B., Van Horn, L., Slattery, M. L., Jacobs, Jr., D. R., & Ludwig, D. S. (2005, January 1.) Fast-food habits, weight gain, and insulin resistance (The CARDIA Study): 15-year prospective analysis. *The Lancet,* 365, pp. 36–42.
6. Diener, E., & Biswas-Diener, R. (2002). Will money increase subjective well-being? *Social Indicators Research,* 57, pp. 119–169.

Credits

Photo Credits

Page 1, Mel Yates/Stone+/Getty Images

Page 6, (l) Commercial Eye/Iconica/Getty Images, (r) Nick White/Digital Vision/Getty Images

Page 7, Comstock/Getty Images

Page 12, Jupiterimages/Workbook Stock/Getty Images

Page 17, Photos 12/Alamy

Page 18, Mike Kemp/Rubberball Productions/Getty Images

Page 19, Digital Vision

Page 25, (l) Courtesy of Robert S. Feldman, (r) Logo of South Seattle Community College. Reprinted with permission.

Page 30, curved-light/Alamy

Page 32, Comstock/Getty Images

Page 38, Brand X Pictures/PunchStock

Page 41, Image Source/Getty Images

Page 43, George Doyle & Ciaran Griffin/Stockbyte/Getty Images

Page 45, George Doyle & Ciaran Griffin/Stockbyte/Getty Images

Page 50, (l) Courtesy of Robert S. Feldman, (r) Logo of Fort Berthold Community College. Reprinted with permission.

Page 54, PhotoAlto/Sigrid Olsson/Getty Images

Page 56, Simon Jarratt/CORBIS

Page 58, Juice Images/Alamy

Page 61, Tom Grill/CORBIS

Page 64, Photodisc/Alamy

Page 72, (l) Courtesy of Robert S. Feldman, (r) Logo of Thomas Nelson Community College. Reprinted by permission of Thomas Nelson Community College.

Page 76, Simon Jarratt/CORBIS

Page 81, Comstock Select/CORBIS

Page 85, Dennis MacDonald/Alamy

Page 86, Andersen Ross/Stockbyte/Getty Images

Page 92, Red Chopsticks/Getty Images

Page 94, Thinkstock/CORBIS

Page 98, Getty Images

Page 103, Ken Banks/CORBIS

Page 112, Ian Shaw/Alamy

Page 113, CMCD/Getty Images

Page 117, Sonda Dawes/Image Works

Page 121, Library of Congress, Prints and Photographs Division

Page 122, Ryan McVay/Getty Images

Page 125, (l) Courtesy of Robert S. Feldman, (r) Logo of Art Institute of Houston. Reprinted with permission.

Page 129, Digital Vision

Page 133, (bl) Jeff Cadge/Photographer's Choice/Getty Images, (bc) Brand X Pictures/PunchStock, (br) UpperCut Images/Getty Images, (t) Mark Andersen/Rubberball Productions/Getty Images

Page 147, Jack Hollingsworth/Getty Images

Page 151, Zia Soleil/Iconica/Getty Images

Page 154, (l) Courtesy of Robert S. Feldman, (r) Logo of Yale University. Reprinted with permission.

Page 158, Royalty-Free/CORBIS

Page 161, Rubberball Productions/Getty Images

Page 176, BananaStock/Jupiterimages

Page 177, Photodisc/Getty Images

Page 184, (l) Courtesy of Robert S. Feldman, (r) Logo of Surry Community College. Reprinted with permission.

Page 189, Satchan/CORBIS

Page 192, The McGraw-Hill Companies/Gary He Photographer

Page 193, Rubberball Productions

Page 195, Eyebyte/Alamy

Page 201, Design Pics Inc./Alamy

Page 208, (l) Courtesy of Robert S. Feldman, (r) Logo of Lehman College. Reprinted with permission.

Page 212, BananaStock/Jupiterimages

Page 215, Ryan McVay/Getty Images

Page 216, PictureNet Corporation/Alamy

Page 219, Roy Hsu/UpperCut Images/Getty Images

Page 224, John Giustina/Iconica/Getty Images

Page 227, Burke/Triolo Productions/Brand X/CORBIS

Page 231, (l) Courtesy of Robert S. Feldman, (r) Logo of Lane College. Reprinted with permission.

Page 235, The McGraw-Hill Companies, Inc./Gary He, photographer

Page 242, Jose Luis Pelaez Inc/Blend Images/Getty Images

Page 244, CORBIS Premium Collection/Alamy

Page 246, Rob Melnychuk/Getty Images

Page 249, Jose Luis Pelaez, Inc./Blend Images/CORBIS

Page 253, ukscapes/Alamy

Page 258, (l) Courtesy of Robert S. Feldman, (r) Logo of Hinds Community College. Reprinted by permission of Hinds Community College.

Text Credits

Page 4, Figure 1.1: © 2008 The Regents of the University of California. All Rights Reserved.

Page 90, Peanuts cartoon—is life a multiple choice test?: Peanuts by Charles Schultz © United Feature Syndicate, Inc. Reprinted by permission.

Page 112, Peanuts cartoon—about this book: Peanuts by Charles Schultz © United Feature Syndicate, Inc. Reprinted by permission.

Page 134, Table 6.1: Source: U.S. Bureau of Labor Statistics

Page 180, Cartoon—First they do an Online Search: © The New Yorker Collection 1998 Arnie Levin from cartoonbank.com. All Rights Reserved.

Page 178, Cartoon—Ask Your Search Engine: © The New Yorker Collection 2000 John Caldwell from cartoonbank.com. All Rights Reserved.

Page 182, Cartoon—Nobody Knows You're a Dog: © The New Yorker Collection 1993 Peter Steiner from cartoonbank.com. All Rights Reserved.

Page 196, Cartoon—No, Yes, Maybe: © 2009 Charles Barsotti from cartoonbank.com. All Rights Reserved.

Page 199, Cartoon—FoxTrot: FoxTrot © 2009 Bill Armend. Reprinted by permission of Universal Press Syndicate. All Rights Reserved.

Page 214, Figure 9.1, Diversity Wheel: Loden: *Implementing Diversity, Best Practices for Making Diversity Work in Your Organization.* Used by permission of The McGraw-Hill Co., Inc.

Page 238, Try It #1: Reprinted from *Journal of Psychosomatic Research*, Volume 19, Issue 1, Martin B. Marx, Thomas F. Garrity and Frank R. Bowers, *The influence of recent life experience on the health of college freshmen*, pp. 87–98. Used with permission from Elsevier, Inc.

Index

WELCOME TO YOUR FRESHMAN EXPERIENCE

We would like to welcome you as you begin your educational experience at your new college. As a freshman we encourage you to familiarize yourself with your college's philosophy and commitment to you as a new member of their community. We have provided you with activities that will help you become acquainted with your college and reach your full learning potential. Your ability to deal with change, your personal motivating forces, and your views on diversity and tolerance will be examined. You will be asked to assess your values, sense of self, and your belief system as they pertain to your future success. You will learn how to monitor your time and spending habits, in hopes that you will best be able to reach important life goals. Ultimately, you will gain an understanding of yourself and your future goals, which will prepare you for a meaningful and productive life as an educated member of our society.

We wish you success in your educational journey.

Nancy A. Gerli, MS

Freshman Seminar Coordinator

Professor

Suffolk Community College

Kristen Cosentino, CSW

Adjunct Representitive for

Freshman Seminar

Instructor

Suffolk Community College

The transition from High School to College- PREPARING FOR & DEALING WITH CHANGE

EXERCISE 1.1:

Your transition into college may depend on whether you are a recent high school graduate or a returning student. Compare and contrast the similarities and differences between high school and/or your prior experiences and college.

       <u>High School</u>   <u>College</u>

<u>Similarities:</u>

_____   _____

_____   _____

_____   _____

_____   _____

_____   _____

_____   _____

_____   _____

<u>Differences:</u>

_____   _____

_____   _____

_____   _____

_____   _____

_____   _____

PREPARING FOR & DEALING WITH CHANGE

EXERCISE 1.2:
This exercise will help you determine and clarify your goals for a college education.

1. List your favorite activities/hobbies_____

    _____

    _____

2. List your interests_____

    _____

3. What are your reasons for attending this particular college?
    _____

    _____

4. What are your college expectations?_____

    _____

    _____

5. How can you get the most from your college experience?

    _____

    _____

6. What are some areas of study that are of interest to
    you?_____

    _____

7. What career do you feel will best suit you? Why?

    _____

    _____

PREPARING FOR & DEALING WITH CHANGE

EXERCISE 1.3:

As you make your transition into college, you need to be aware of the reasons you are attending. This exercise will help you evaluate these reasons. Are you in college for the right reasons?

I'm attending college because:

_____A college education will help me get a better job
_____My parents say I have to go
_____My friends are all at college, some here
_____I need a degree for my future career goals
_____I want to learn new things
_____I want to make a lot of money
_____I want to have fun & experience the college life
_____I want to meet new people
_____I want to prove that I can do it
_____It can help me gain valuable knowledge
_____I want to be a role model for my family and friends
_____I don't know what I want to do with the rest of my life
        yet, college is a good way to find out what my
        interests are
_____It was either go to school or get a job

Evaluate your responses. Are you here to gain the most out of your academic future? Do you think you will continue on the path you have chosen or do you need to reevaluate your current decisions? Explain.

_____

_____

_____

_____

_____

_____

PREPARING FOR & DEALING WITH CHANGE

EXERCISE 1.4:
This exercise will help you to determine and evaluate your personality as it applies to your personal, academic, career, relationship and learning styles goals. Check the appropriate line following each statement. Give each check a point value of (1). Add up the points in each column to obtain your **TOTAL**.

	Often	Sometimes	Seldom

Auditory Learner

		Often	Sometimes	Seldom
1.	I learn best by class lectures, explanations and discussions	____	____	____
2.	I learn by listening to tapes	____	____	____
3.	I learn better by repeating things out loud	____	____	____
4.	I follow oral directions better than written ones	____	____	____
5.	I would rather listen to a news broadcast than read about it in a newspaper	____	____	____
	TOTAL	____	____	____

Visual Learner

		Often	Sometimes	Seldom
1.	I learn best by notes written on the chalkboard	____	____	____
2.	I prefer reading textbooks rather than listening to lectures	____	____	____
3.	I learn by using charts, diagrams or pictures	____	____	____
4.	I remember things best by picturing them in my mind	____	____	____
5.	I can understand and follow directions on maps	____	____	____
	TOTAL	____	____	____

Tactile Learner

		Often	Sometimes	Seldom
1.	I tend to hold objects while learning or studying	____	____	____

2.	I enjoy working with my hands	____ ____ ____
3.	I play with keys or objects in my pockets	____ ____ ____
4.	I smoke, snack or chew gum while studying	____ ____ ____
5.	I am comfortable hugging, handshaking or touching	____ ____ ____

TOTAL   ____   ____   ____

Score: Your highest score indicates your particular learning style. Your learning style influences your sensory preference for obtaining useful information. Furthermore, it examines how you learn in academic situations.

Auditory Learners: If you scored highest in the auditory learning section, then you learn best by listening to lectures. You can absorb a lecture with little effort. You tend to concentrate on what the instructor is saying, rather than on the visual aids presented.

Visual Learners: If you scored highest in the visual learning section, then you tend to learn more with visual components such as diagrams and demonstrations. As a visual learner you benefit from charts, diagrams, notes and overhead projections. You retain more information when you utilize flash cards or index cards. You can become easily distracted when professors use lectures alone. In general, visual learners tend to tune out auditory information and focus on visual details.

Tactile Learners: If you scored highest in the tactile learning section, then you are more likely to learn by "hands on" experience. You learn not by lectures or visual presentations, but by engaging in the activity at hand. You are most likely to excel in art, recreation and technical classes. Overall, tactile learners learn best by doing, by applying their knowledge into fieldwork, labs and projects. You will excel in science, math, nursing, and business oriented classes.

Your learning style can help you succeed in college. You can use your learning profile when choosing your major and planning your goals. Focus on courses or jobs that best match your learning preferences. Although, it is ideal that you master all learning styles, the ones that you most identified with will help you recognize your strengths and weaknesses for your stage of learning.

JOURNAL ENTRY
Preparing for and dealing with change

Write about your transition into college. Was this a difficult change?

Why or why not?

_____

_____

_____

_____

_____

_____

_____

_____

_____

_____

_____

_____

_____

_____

_____

_____

_____

_____

_____

_____

_____

_____

SELF ESTEEM & MOTIVATION

EXERCISE 1.1:

Self esteem or your self image plays a major role in your success as a college student. Self esteem is your sense of personal worth that is derived more from how you feel about yourself than from recognition or praise from others. Understanding the importance of a positive self esteem, causes of poor self worth and developing a positive outlook will be incorporated in the following exercises. Complete the following self assessment to evaluate your self esteem.

Place a check under "Agree" or "Disagree" as each statement applies to you.

		Agree	Disagree
1.	Overall, I am satisfied with myself and my accomplishments	___	___
2.	I constantly question my decisions and feel I should have done things differently	___	___
3.	I feel I have several bad qualities that interfere with my goals	___	___
4.	In general, I feel I am as capable as others	___	___
5.	I don't have much respect for myself or my decisions	___	___
6.	I do things impulsively rather than thinking things through	___	___
7.	I feel I have not accomplished much in my life	___	___
8.	I don't worry too much about what other people think of me and my life style	___	___
9.	I feel that I have many positive qualities	___	___
10.	I feel that I am more of a leader than a follower	___	___

SCORE: For items 1,4,8,9 and 10, give yourself a point each time you checked "Agree." For items 2,3,5,6 and 7, give yourself a point each time you checked "Disagree." This highest possible score is ten, the lowest is zero. The higher your score, the higher your self esteem. The lower your score, the lower your self esteem. Those with high self esteems are likely to score between 8-10. Those with low self esteems are likely to score below 3.

Evaluate your score. Do you feel your score accurately reflects how you feel about yourself?_____

SELF ESTEEM & MOTIVATION

EXERCISE 1.2:
Rather than focus on problems, you should focus on possibilities.
The key is to empower yourself and embrace your strengths,
talents, knowledge and capabilities. The following exercise will
help you recognize these qualities in order for you to build on
them.

**1.   List at least five things you are currently doing for
yourself that you feel good about:**

1._____

2._____

3._____

4._____

5._____

2.   What are some things you enjoy doing? Name at least five:

1._____

2._____

3._____

4._____

5._____

**3.   Are you currently engaged in any of those activities you
listed in question 2? If so, what are they? If not, what is
preventing you from doing the things you enjoy?**

4.   What are some things that you normally do for yourself that
     you are now neglecting?

     _____

     _____

     _____

     _____

5.   What are you going to do to improve on the neglected areas of
     your life?

     _____

     _____

     _____

     _____

6.   How do you see these changes impacting on your self worth in
     regard to your academic and personal life?

     _____

     _____

     _____

     _____

SELF ESTEEM & MOTIVATION

EXERCISE 1.3:

What do you want? What do you need? How do you view your life currently? By answering these questions, you will gain a deeper appreciation of your distinctive attributes, abilities and competencies. The following exercise will help you recognize your positive strengths and qualities.

1.   Reflect on your strengths and abilities.   List at least five.

1._____

2._____

3._____

4._____

5._____

2.   Reflect on a time you were critical of yourself. Describe the circumstances surrounding your experience.

_____

_____

_____

_____

_____

3.   Reflect on a time you achieved something that you worked hard to accomplish. Explain how this experience made you feel.

_____

_____

_____

_____

_____

4. Reflect on a time when your thoughts and/or opinions were criticized. Did this experience discourage you or make you more determined to voice your opinion? Explain.

    _____

    _____

    _____

    _____

    _____

5. What qualities do you possess that make you special and unique? List at least five.

    1._____

    2._____

    3._____

    4._____

    5._____

6. Do you think that your qualities listed in question 5 exemplify positive self esteem? Why or why not?

    _____

    _____

    _____

    _____

    _____

SELF ESTEEM & MOTIVATION

EXERCISE 1.4:

Now that you have evaluated your self esteem and self worth as well as reflected on your strength and abilities, you need to overcome any discouragement you may be feeling. The following exercise will allow you to replace pessimistic thoughts with optimistic action. Optimism is a skill essential for overcoming setbacks and difficulties in college and in life.

The following exercise will help you to recognize and replace your pessimistic thoughts with more beneficial optimistic ones.

1.   List 5 pessimistic statements you could make about yourself every day:

    1._____

    2._____

    3._____

    4._____

    5._____

2.   List 5 optimistic statements that you can say about yourself every day:

    1._____

    2._____

    3._____

    4._____

    5._____

3.   List 5 pessimistic statements that others had said about you:

    1._____

    2._____

    3._____

    4._____

    5._____

    Do you agree or disagree with these statements? Explain.

    _____

    _____

    _____

    _____

    _____

4.   List 5 optimistic statements others have said about you:

    1._____

    2._____

    3._____

    4._____

    5._____

    Do you agree or disagree with these statements? Explain.

    _____

    _____

    _____

    _____

    _____

JOURNAL ENTRY

Self Esteem and Motivation

Discuss a time when you felt your self esteem was very low or very high. What or whom do you think attributed to your feeling this way? After reading the chapter on self esteem and completing the exercises, what important steps do you think you need to take to improve the way you feel about yourself. Explain.

_____

_____

_____

_____

_____

_____

_____

_____

_____

_____

_____

_____

_____

_____

_____

_____

_____

_____

_____

_____

_____

VALUES

EXERCISE 1.1:

Values are our beliefs and attitudes about things. Values are derived from a combination of family, society or individual ideology. Your values make you unique because they are based on your own personal experiences and background. It is important to identify what is important to you as your motivation and goals are greatly influenced by your beliefs. The following exercises will allow you to clarify your values and help you gain a greater understanding of those that are most important to you.

Assess your current values. Rank the following values on a scale from 1-25; 1 being the most important to you, 25 being the least important.

_____Sense of self (self esteem and self worth)
_____Relationship with family
_____Relationship with friends (including boyfriends and girlfriends)
_____Respect for self and others
_____Honesty and integrity
_____Life (yours and others)
_____Job
_____Happiness
_____Possessions (house and car)
_____Love
_____Personality (include sense of humor)
_____Considerate of others, caring
_____Being reliable, dependable
_____Physical appearance
_____Wealth (money)
_____Education
_____Nature (includes animals)
_____Drugs/alcohol
_____Religious beliefs
_____Having fun (includes sports)
_____Kindness
_____Loyalty
_____Responsibility
_____Health
_____Intimacy

List any other values that are important to you:

_____

_____

_____

_____

After reviewing your selections, think about how you obtained these values. Are you living up to your beliefs? Do they truly reflect who you are? Explain.

_____

_____

_____

_____

_____

_____

VALUES

EXERCISE 1.2:

Imagine that you are traveling in a small passenger plane and it has just crashed in the Andes Mountains. It is 2:30 in the afternoon on January 15th. A light snowfall has begun and all of the communication equipment on board has been destroyed. Of the ten passengers on board, only eight survived the crash. The pilot and co-pilot were killed in the fire that engulfed and destroyed the plane. No one else was seriously injured. The plane was traveling from Florida and all passengers were dressed in light weight clothing.

Before the plane was destroyed, the passengers were able to salvage the 15 items listed below. Rank these items from 1-15 according to their importance to your survival; 1 being the most important and 15 being the least.

_____Five wool blankets
_____First Aid Kit
_____Map of the area
_____A woman's compact with mirror
_____A dozen packages of crackers
_____Bottled water
_____Battery operated flashlight
_____A Swiss army knife
_____Five crumpled magazines
_____A bottle of whiskey
_____A pair of skis with poles
_____Two pairs of sunglasses
_____A cell phone
_____A book of matches
_____A pack of cigarettes

Briefly explain why your top five choices are of the utmost importance for survival.

_____

_____

_____

_____

_____

_____

_____

VALUES

EXERCISE 1.3:

You have a value system which is derived from family, friends, society and individual beliefs. Everyday your value system is challenged. You are forced to make choices based on these governing factors. Do you adhere to your value system, do you conform to the norm of the group or do you acquiesce to society's expectations? How do you decide? How strong are your beliefs? Are you able to take responsibility for your decisions, even though you may be criticized for them? The following exercise will test your individual values.

Drawbridge Exercise:

Read the story below; then follow the instructions at the end of the story.

As he left for a visit to his outlying districts, the jealous baron warned his pretty wife; "Do not leave the castle while I am gone, or I will punish you severely when I return!"

As the hours passed, the young baroness grew lonely, and despite her husband's warning, decided to visit her lover, who lived in the countryside nearby.

The castle was located on an island surrounded by a wide, fast-flowing river. A drawbridge linked the island and the land at the narrowest point in the river.

"Surely my husband will not return before dawn," she thought, and she ordered her servants to lower the drawbridge and leave it down until she returned.

After spending several hours with her lover, the baroness returned to the drawbridge, only to find it blocked by a madman wildly waving a knife. "Do not attempt to cross this bridge, baroness, or I will kill you," he raved.

Fearing for her life, the baroness returned to her lover and asked him to help.

"Our relationship is only a romantic one," he said. "So I will not help."

The baroness then sought out a boatman on the river, explained her plight to him, and asked him to take her across the river in his boat.

"I will do it, but only if you can pay me a fee of five marks."

"But I have no money with me!" cried the baroness. "That is too bad replied the boatman, no money, no ride."

Her fears growing, the baroness ran crying to the home of a friend, and after explaining her situation, she begged for enough money to pay the boatman his fee.

"If you had not disobeyed your husband, this would not have happened," the friend said. "I will give you no money."

With dawn approaching, and her last resource exhausted, the baroness returned to the bridge in desperation, attempted to cross to the castle, and was slain by the madman.

Directions: In the preceding story there are six characters. They are in alphabetical order:

_____the baron
_____the baroness
_____the boatman
_____the friend
_____the lover
_____the madman

Using the list above, rank each character according to how responsible he or she was for the baroness's death. Rank the characters from 1 to 6, with 1 being the most responsible and 6 being the least responsible. Now, work with the other members of your group, and decide as a group on a rank order for the six characters.

Discuss how your rankings were similar or different from the group rankings. After discussion, did you find yourself questioning your answers? Explain.

_____

_____

_____

_____

_____

_____

_____

_____

_____

VALUES

EXERCISE 1.4:

Thus far you have defined your values. You were asked to challenge your values and to question your conformity. Your values are constantly imposed on your decision making process. The outcomes of your decisions not only have a great impact on your life, but they also affect others. The following exercise will ask you to impose your values on others and to take responsibility for your choices.

The enrollment management committee has been instructed to cut back on student enrollment for the following semester. There are 10 students that will be affected by these cut backs. The committee must rank students according to who should continue, number 1 being the most deserving, 10 being the least deserving.

Listed below are the student's achievements thus far. Factors to consider include:

1. Potential for success, and capabilities.
2. Student's goals and motivation.
3. Ability to overcome adverse situations.
4. Reasons for wanting a college degree.
5. The likelihood of completing a college education.

The Students:

1. ____**Mary:** Honors student involved in many college clubs and community services. She has a full college scholarship and has an accumulative GPA of 4.0. She lacks social skills and does not get along well with her classmates and professors. She is having difficulty adjusting to college life away from her family.

2. ____**Jim:** An all state quarterback in high school. He plans to play football at the college level. He was given a full athletic scholarship to this college. He was an average high school student who placed into developmental classes when he took the college placement test. He is undeclared in his major, however, he would like to become a coach. His class attendance is poor.

3. ____**Sandie:** Average high school student. Passing grades in math and science. She has declared a major in biology, at the insistence of her parents. However, she is doing poorly at the college level in these subjects. Her study habits are good and she has excelled in her English classes. She lives at home and her parents are in the process of a divorce.

4. _____**Helen**: A divorced mother of three. She is a 30 year old returning student who graduated high school 12 years ago. She has no prior college experience. She is applying for the nursing program in the Fall after meeting basic college education requirements. She pays for college by working part time and receiving financial aid.

5. _____**Pierre**: An exchange student from France. Already has a college degree in physical therapy from his country. Although visiting for only a year, he has already been accepted into the college's Honor's Society. He is paying for his education and is here solely to experience our culture. He is seriously involved with another student who he hopes to someday marry.

6. _____**Billy**: Barely passed high school, and his college grades are poor. He is on academic probation, but is very well liked and respected by his peers and professors. His parents are paying for his education. He is undecided regarding his major and future. He enjoys the social aspect of college and is a natural leader.

7. _____**Ernie**: Graduated in the top five percent of his high school class. His parents are very influential in the community. He is uninvolved in campus life, and has below average grades. He is not working up to his full potential. Although he was extremely popular in high school, he finds himself lonely and unfulfilled in the college environment.

8. _____**Beth**: Very active in her college life. Accepted into a sorority and is very active in their cause. Her parents pay for her education and her uncle is on the college's Board of Trustees. She is constantly absent from classes and is on the verge of being dismissed from the college.

9. _____**Isabelle**: A 55 year old LPN who has worked for the past 12 years in a nursing home. She has been a dedicated house wife and mother of 3 who has decided to further enrich her life. She is working towards a degree in psychiatric nursing and is receiving financial aid for returning students. She is an exemplary student who is excelling both academically and socially.

10. _____**Will**: An average college student who works 35 hours a week to pay for his college education. He is aiming for a degree in automotive technology. His schedule does not allow for him to become involved with campus activities. He is a hard worker who is aiming for a degree in order to one day have his own automotive repair business.

Only the top 5 students will be able to remain enrolled at the college.
Choose the 5 students who you feel are the most deserving. List the
students and explain the reasons for your decisions.

1. _____

   _____

   _____

2. _____

   _____

   _____

3. _____

   _____

   _____

4. _____

   _____

   _____

5. _____

   _____

   _____

JOURNAL ENTRY
Values

Has college impacted your current values? If so, how, if not, why not?

_____

_____

_____

_____

_____

_____

_____

_____

_____

_____

_____

_____

_____

_____

_____

_____

_____

_____

_____

_____

_____

GOAL SETTING

EXERCISE 1.1

Goal setting is a relatively simple process. It is the implementation of this process that may prove difficult. Goals may include short term and long term, as well as, personal and academic. It is important to recognize these different types of goals in order to set realistic expectations with reasonable time lines. The following exercises will allow you to examine your current goals and decide on future objectives.

List 5 of your short term goals (include all aspects of your life)

1. _____

2. _____

3. _____

4. _____

5. _____

List 5 of your long term goals (include all aspects of your life)

1. _____

2. _____

3. _____

4. _____

5. _____

List 5 personal goals that are most important to you

1. _____

2. _____

3. _____

4. _____

5. _____

List 5 of your current academic goals.

1. _____

2. _____

3. _____

4. _____

5. _____

Assess the academic goals you listed above. What classes are required
in order for you to achieve these goals? What is the curriculum needed
for completion of your academic career? How many credits are required
in your field of interest? Will you be able to achieve these goals at
this college or will you need to further your education elsewhere?
Explain your answers.

_____

_____

_____

_____

_____

_____

_____

_____

_____

_____

_____

_____

_____

_____

_____

_____

GOAL SETTING

EXERCISE 1.2:

The following exercise will ask you to evaluate your "current skill level." A skill is something you have mastered but can also be developed through practice, thus providing you with the ability to do something well. Put a check mark (%) next to the skills you currently possess. Identify your top 5 skills by placing an asterisk (*) to the right of them. Then, circle those remaining skills you would like to develop I the course of your life.

____being organized
____taking chances
____working with your hands, constructing and/or repairing things
____creativity
____working well with others
____helping others
____communicating
____open mindedness
____sensitivity
____looking at things objectively
____budgeting money
____outgoing
____compromising
____being assertive
____responsible
____completing tasks
____public speaking
____motivated
____meticulous
____analytical
____setting and accomplishing goals
____honesty
____innovative, developing new ideas
____competitive
____being persuasive
____articulating thoughts and feelings
____writing
____dependable and loyal
____learning and applying knowledge
____teaching others
____active listening
____planning events
____problem solving
____gathering information
____other: _____
____other: _____

GOAL SETTING

EXERCISE 1.3:

Now that you have defined and evaluated your skills, this exercise will help you discover your aptitudes. An aptitude is an inner strength that may be biologically inherited, or learned through education, motivation and hard work. For example, if your parents are both athletic, you have a higher biological probability of also being athletic by genetics alone. The following exercise will help you discover your aptitudes. Place a check (%) next to the aptitudes that you feel you possess.

1. _____**Theoretical reasoning**. Individuals who possess this quality have the ability to solve complex problems, interpret literature and think logically.

2. _____**Linguistic reasoning**. Individuals with this ability have strong verbal skills and can better solve problems when they hear them described rather than by visual presentations.

3. _____**Spatial connections**. Individuals who possess this quality are able to write and communicate effectively.

4. _____**Grammar usage**. Individuals who possess this quality are able to write and communicate effectively.

5. _____**Technical ability**. Individuals who have strong technical ability are able to easily manipulate machinery and technical equipment.

6. _____**Clerical ability**. Individuals with clerical capabilities are able to work effectively in an office or business setting.

7. _____**Mathematical ability**. Individuals possessing this ability can easily solve mathematical equations.

8. _____**Spelling ability**. Individuals who possess this quality do well with memorization, and understanding patterns and details.

After reviewing the aptitudes you have checked, explain how these may be beneficial to you when planning your life goals.

_____

_____

_____

GOAL SETTING

EXERCISE 1.4:
This exercise will help you begin to think about the goals that you would like to achieve in your lifetime. Rank the following goals from 1-5 in the order that you would like to achieve them, 1 for the highest priority and 5 being of importance, but not of the utmost priority.

1. ____health
2. ____good marriage
3. ____nice house
4. ____fame and fortune
5. ____attractiveness
6. ____job security
7. ____financial security
8. ____love
9. ____politically influential
10. ____education
11. ____freedom
12. ____spirituality
13. ____self-confidence
14. ____popularity
15. ____entrepreneur/self employment
16. ____family
17. ____friendship
18. ____understanding life's purpose

Discuss your reasons for choosing the goals you selected. What do you think the likelihood is of you achieving these goals I your lifetime? Do you think the goals you didn't choose may eventually end up on your list of priorities? Why or why not?

_____

_____

_____

_____

_____

_____

_____

_____

JOURNAL ENTRY

Goal Setting

Based on the previous evaluations of your aptitudes, qualities and goals, do you feel you are on a path to success, based on your own definition of success? Explain.

_____

_____

_____

_____

_____

_____

_____

_____

_____

If you were to die today, what could be written about your accomplishments thus far on your epitaph. Write how you feel you will be remembered.

_____

_____

_____

_____

_____

_____

_____

_____

_____

_____

TIME MANAGEMENT

EXERCISE 1.1:

Monitoring your time offers you the opportunity to discover how you spend your time, your lives. When you know how your time is spent, you can better find ways to adjust and manage it, doing those things that are most important to you. The purpose of time management is to help you manage your time so you can better incorporate and plan out your goals. It is important that you do not lose sight of your goals, what you want academically, personally and financially. The following exercise will ask you to monitor how you spend your time for 7 days.

Monitor your time 24 hrs. a day for 7 days. Write down each time you engage in a particular activity. Note the time you started and ended. Include:

1. waking up each morning
2. time spent getting ready
3. time spent eating
4. travel time
5. class time
6. work time
7. study time
8. exercise
9. watching television

10. talking on the phone
11. time on computer/Internet
12. domestic chores (laundry/cleaning)
13. going to church
14. shopping
15. hanging out with friends
16. partying
17. any other activities:

_____

_____

_____

For example:

Monday

```
 8:00am: wake up
 8:15:   get into the shower
 8:45:   eat breakfast
 9:00:   go to school
 9:30:   in class
10:45:   class ends
```
(include the rest of your daily activities until the time you went to bed)

MONDAY: Date_____

TIME   ACTIVITY

TUESDAY: Date_____

TIME   ACTIVITY

WEDNESDAY: Date_____

TIME   ACTIVITY

THURSDAY: Date_____

TIME   ACTIVITY

<u>FRIDAY</u>: Date_____

TIME   ACTIVITY

<u>SATURDAY</u>: Date_____

TIME   ACTIVITY

<u>SUNDAY</u>: Date_____

TIME   **ACTIVITY**

Now that you've monitored your time, add up how much time you spent in each activity. The total for the 7 days should add up to 168 hours (24 hours a day x 7 days = 168 hours).

ACTIVITY   **HOURS SPENT**

  1. sleeping   _____
  2. time spent getting ready   _____
  3. time spent eating   _____
  4. travel time   _____
  5. class time   _____
  6. work time   _____
  7. study time   _____
  8. exercise   _____
  9. watching television   _____
10. talking on the phone   _____
11. time on computer/Internet   _____
12. domestic chores (laundry/cleaning) _____
13. going to church   _____
14. shopping   _____
15. hanging out with friends   _____
16. partying   _____
17. any other activities:

    _____   _____
    _____   _____
    _____   _____

TOTAL (168 HOURS)   _____

TIME MANAGEMENT

EXERCISE 1.2:

In order to achieve your goals, you need a plan. You've monitored and evaluated how you've spent your time, so you can better plan for your present and future goals. Plan for your future, take control. The following exercise will ask that you incorporate a calendar, planner, or student handbook into your daily routine. A calendar or some form of it is a great time management technique, college success depends on it. You can not remember, nor are you expected to remember all class assignments, due dates, job schedules and other significant obligations you may have.

Include in your calendars the following:

1. class assignments and due dates for each class (refer to class syllabus)
2. your job schedule
3. doctor appointments
4. birthdays
5. any other dates or obligations to remember

TIME MANAGEMENT

EXERCISE 1.3

You've been asked to plan and schedule your daily activities. How do you decide how to prioritize your busy day? The following exercise will ask you to make decisions concerning everyday occurrences. How would you schedule your time? Rank these options in the order of importance to you, 1 being a major priority, 7 being of least importance.

____get gas for the car, almost on empty
____pick up food, your friends are coming for dinner
____get cigarettes, you have 1 left
____you don't have any money, pick up your pay check
____bank closes at 5pm
____pick up mom at work at 5pm
____get dry cleaning for work tomorrow, closes at 5pm

JOURNAL ENTRY
Time Management

What discoveries did you make after completing your time monitor exercise?

I discovered that I spent most of my time on _____

_____

_____

I discovered that I spent the least amount of time on _____

_____

_____

I would like to spend more of my time on _____

_____

_____

I do not want to spend so much time on _____

_____

_____

How did you feel monitoring your time? Did you find it cumbersome or useful? Explain.

_____

_____

_____

_____

_____

_____

_____

_____

_____

_____

_____

MONEY MANAGEMENT

EXERCISE 1.1:

Managing money can be stressful. The key to financial freedom is to develop a budget that will enable you to live within your means. As a college student, you are often faced with difficult financial decisions, such as paying for tuition, books and finding extra money for social or recreational enjoyment. The following exercise will ask you to monitor your spending for 7 days and will give you an idea about how much money you spend compared to how much you make.

Monitor how much money you spend everyday for 7 days. Write down every item you purchase and how much it costs for the next 7 days. For example, if you purchase a soda, list "soda" in the item column and the money you spend on it, "$1.00." Remember to include all purchases such as gas, good, clothes and cigarettes.

MONDAY: Date_____

ITEM   **COST**

TUESDAY: Date_____

ITEM   COST

WEDNESDAY: Date_____

ITEM   COST

THURSDAY: Date_____

ITEM   COST

FRIDAY: Date_____

ITEM   COST

SATURDAY: Date_____

ITEM   COST

SUNDAY: Date_____

ITEM   COST

TOTAL SPENT FOR THE WEEK: _____

MONEY MANAGEMENT

EXERCISE 1.2:

Now that you've monitored your spending for 7 days, this exercise will ask you to list all your monthly expenses in order to assess how much money you have left over at the end of each month for the "extras" like entertainment.

Review your current **monthly** expenses. List how much you spend in each of the following categories as they apply to you. You can estimate your monthly expense by your weekly money monitor. For example, if you spent $40 during your money monitor, you would estimate that you spend $160 a month on food ($40 x 4 weeks = $160).

Monthly Expenses	Money Spent
HOUSING:	
Rent	_____
Utilities	
Gas/oil	_____
Electricity	_____
Telephone (cell phone)	_____
Total Utilities	_____
Mortgage Payments	_____
Total for other household expenses	
(decorating, maintenance/repair, yard work	
and other domestic help)	_____
FOOD/CLOTHING/TRANSPORTATION:	
Food/groceries	_____
Clothing/laundry	
Clothing purchases	_____
Coin laundry/dry cleaning	_____
Total clothing/laundry	_____
AUTO MAINTENANCE:	
Gas and oil	_____
Repairs	_____
Insurance	_____
Loan payments	_____
Other form of transportation (bus/cab)	_____
Total for auto maintenance	_____

TOTAL FOR HOUSING, FOOD, CLOTHING AND TRANSPORTATION   _____

**TOTAL FOR HOUSING, FOOD, CLOTHING
AND TRANSPORTATION**   _____
(from the previous page)

EDUCATION
(if you are responsible for your tuition, how
 much does it cost you per month)   _____

PERSONAL CARE
Toiletries
Vitamins/nonprescription drugs   _____
Make-up   _____
Haircuts/beauty salon   _____
Total personal care   _____

MEDICAL CARE
Prescription drugs
Doctor visits   _____
Dentist visits   _____
Optician and glasses/contact lenses   _____
Total medical care   _____

ANY OTHER LOAN PAYMENTS: TOTAL   _____

CHARGE ACCOUNT PAYMENTS: TOTAL   _____

                 _____

MEDICAL INSURANCE: TOTAL   _____

OTHER EXPENSES   _____
legal
Miscellaneous expenses

Total other expenses   _____
                                                  _____

TOTAL COMMITTED EXPENSES   _____
(total for housing, food/clothing/transportation
 and other committed expenses)

CURRENT MONTHLY INCOME AND INCOME NEEDS

MONTHLY INCOME
Employment _____
Self employment _____
Other income _____
Total income _____

DISCRETIONARY INCOME

Monthly income – Expenses = Discretionary Income

1)   Take your total monthly income and subtract your expenses from it
     to find your **discretionary income**. Your discretionary income is
     how much money you have left over at the end of each month for
     the "extras" like entertainment.

2)   Divide your discretionary income by 4 to get how much extra
     money you have per week.

3)   Divide this number by 7 to get how much money you have to spend
     each day.

4)   Compare your weekly discretionary income #2 to how much you
     actually spent during your weekly money monitoring. Are they
     consistent? Did you spend more than you were able to spend or
     did you spend according to your budget? Why or why not?

_____

_____

_____

_____

_____

_____

JOURNAL ENTRY
Money Management

What discoveries did you make after completing your money monitor exercise?

I discovered that I spent most of my money on _____

_____

_____

I discovered that I spent the least amount of money on _____

_____

_____

I would like to spend less money on _____

_____

_____

I would like to save money for _____

_____

_____

How did your weekly spending compare to how much you were actually allowed to spend according to your discretionary income analysis? Are you spending more than you make? If so, how much more weekly? Monthly?

_____

_____

_____

_____

_____

_____

_____

_____

_____

DIVERSITY

EXERCISE 1.1:

Following are some terms used to describe groups of people. In the
space provided, write down stereotypes that come to mind when others
refer to these groups. Stereotypes are fixed ideas about an individual
or social status based on superficial characteristics and observable
traits which are generalized to the entire group.

Blonde Female:

_____

_____

Computer Analyst:

_____

_____

Priest:

_____

_____

Housewife:

_____

_____

Football Player:

_____

_____

Fraternity Brother:

_____

_____

DIVERSITY

EXERCISE 1.2:

This exercise will ask you to reexamine your current stereotypes and prejudices. Interview someone of a different ethic background that you feel is often prejudged against or stereotyped.

1)   Who did you interview? _____

2)   What is their ethnic background?_____

3)   Were they born in this country? _____
     If not, where were they born?   _____

4)   What conflicts or challenges have they had to endure living as a member of a different ethnic group in America?

     _____

     _____

     _____

5)   Have they had to sacrifice their belief system in order to conform to the norm of our culture? Explain.

     _____

     _____

     _____

6)   How did they maintain their cultural background while living in our culture? Do they still adhere to their cultural traditions (for example, holiday celebrations, memorable occasions, etc.)? Explain.

     _____

     _____

     _____

7)   How have your views about this individual's ethnicity changed after this interview? Or has it?

     _____

     _____

     _____

8)   Did you begin your interview having preconceived judgments? Explain.

_____

_____

_____

9)   What were some of the things you discovered about yourself after this interview?

_____

_____

_____

10)   What are your intentions to change your preconceived thoughts regarding this ethnic group? Or do you still feel that same way prior to the interview?

_____

_____

_____

JOURNAL ENTRY
Diversity

Discrimination is defined as mistreating people because of differences based on age, race, ethnicity, etc. Describe a time in your life when you felt discriminated against because you were different in some way. The differences could be as insignificant as your hair color, clothes, religious affiliation, age, economic status or accent.

_____

_____

_____

_____

_____

_____

_____

_____

_____

_____

_____

_____

_____

_____

_____

_____

_____

_____

_____

_____

RELATIONSHIPS

EXERCISE 1.1:

In our lifetime we are involved in many different relationships. How
we are perceived in these relationships, and how we get along depends
on our attitudes and willingness to compromise. It is our willingness
to communicate our thoughts, feelings and ideas that help formulate
meaningful relationships. The following exercises will help you
recognize and examine the way you perceive your relationships.

1.   You are shopping with a friend or girlfriend, and she tries on
     a dress and asks you if it makes her look fat and it does, what
     would you say? Why?

     _____

     _____

     _____

2.   You are interested in your friends ex-boyfriend/girlfriend and
     would like to start dating him/her. Would you be honest with
     your friend or secretly date, hoping that your friend would not
     find out?

     _____

     _____

     _____

3.   Your parents have been divorced for a number of years. Your
     mother has now told you that she wants to remarry. You have
     always hoped for a reconciliation between your parents. What
     would you say to your mother about this situation?

     _____

     _____

     _____

     _____

RELATIONSHIPS

EXERCISE 1.2:

If you can master the art of communication, which includes both verbal communication and active listening, you can form more meaningful and fulfilling relationships. The way you say things, through your tone or gestures is often more important than what you say. Take responsibility for your feelings and verbalize how you feel in order to get your point across. The following exercise will ask that you take responsibility for your feelings. Create "I" statements based on the scenarios below. "I" messages allow you to clearly communicate how you feel regarding a particular situation without placing blame.

Example:

As always, you were late and now we missed the movie.

Rephrase ("I" Message):

I feel that when you are late, it means you don't care about our plans and that upsets me.

1) My professors give me bad grades because they think I'm stupid.
   Rephrase ("I" Message):

   _____

   _____

2) You never help me. You are never there for me.
   Rephrase ("I" Message):

   _____

   _____

3) My boyfriend/girlfriend never listens to me.
   Rephrase ("I" Message):

   _____

   _____

4) My friends don't take me seriously.
   Rephrase ("I" Message):

   _____

   _____

5) My parents constantly put down my ideas.
   Rephrase ("I" Message):

   _____

   _____

RELATIONSHIPS

EXERCISE 1.3:

When faced with a conflicting situation, how do you react? Do you respond aggressively, assertively, passively or manipulatively. **Aggressive** people are often insensitive to the rights and feelings of others. They are demanding, hostile and malicious. **Assertive** people are open and direct about their views and stand up for what they believe in. **Passive** people let others influence their thoughts and decisions. They don't express how they feel or what their needs are. **Manipulative** people play the role of a victim to get others to do what they want. They are non assertive, submissive and don't take responsibility for their actions. The following exercise will ask you to examine how you would react in various situations. Write down what style you would tend to use in each situation, whether it be aggressive, assertive, passive or manipulative and explain what you would do and why.

1)   A telemarketing person is trying to get you to buy a product. They are very persistent and will not let you get off the phone. How would you react?

_____

_____

_____

2)   Someone sitting next to you is smoking, and the smoke bothers you. How would you react?

_____

_____

_____

3)   You are at a movie and the people behind you are talking loudly. How would you react?

_____

_____

_____

4)   Your doctor keeps you waiting more than 30 minutes. How would you react?

_____

_____

_____

5) You're standing in line at a movie that you've been waiting months to see. Tickets are limited and someone moves in front of you. How do you react?

_____

_____

6) Your friend owes you money and now you really need it for overdue bills. How do you react?

_____

_____

7) You are at a very exclusive restaurant. The food that you received is not what you have ordered. How would you react?

_____

_____

8) Your friends want to set you up on a blind date after you just broke up with your boyfriend/girlfriend. You have no interest in pursuing another relationship at this time. How would you react?

_____

_____

9) You receive unjust criticism from someone who just met you. How would you react?

_____

_____

10) You want to start a conversation with someone who you have been trying to meet. You are at a party and you see that person there. How do you react?

_____

_____

JOURNAL ENTRY
Relationships

Think about one of your current relationships (boyfriend/girlfriend, parent, spouse, or friend). Write about some things that are not working or that you find un-fulfilling. Examine the role you play in the dilemma. How can you resolve these issues and find fulfillment in this relationship?

HEALTH & WELLNESS

EXERCISE 1:1:

At times, college can prove to be very stressful. Being physically and mentally healthy will help you stay focused and ultimately allow you to reach your academic goals. Poor health habits linked to college students may include skipping meals, eating quick, convenient snacks or fast food, overeating, smoking, abusing alcohol and drugs, not exercising or getting enough sleep. It is important to take care of your health. Your body fuels your mind. The following exercises will ask you to evaluate your current "health" style.

The Public Health Service developed the following test. Its purpose is to help you determine how well you are doing in your attempt to stay healthy. The behaviors covered in the test are recommended for most people, although some of them may not apply to people with chronic disease, disabilities, or to pregnant women.

For each statement, check "A" for always, "S" for sometimes or "N" for almost never

EXERCISE/FITNESS

		A	S	N
1.	I maintain a desired weight, avoiding overweight and underweight	3	1	0
2.	I do vigorous exercise for 15 to 30 minutes at least 3 times a week (e.g. running, swimming, brisk walk).	3	1	0
3.	I do exercises that enhance my muscle tone for 15 to 30 minutes at least 3 times a week (e.g. yoga & calisthenics).	2	1	0
4.	I use part of my leisure time participating in individual, family, or team activities that increase my level of fitness (e.g. gardening, bowling, golf and baseball).	2	1	0

Exercise/Fitness Total Score: _____

EATING HABITS

		A	**S**	**N**
1.	I eat a variety of foods each day, such as fruits and vegetables, whole-grain breads and cereals, lean meats, dairy products, dry peas and beans, and nuts and seeds.	4	1	0
2.	I limit the amount of fat, saturated fat, and cholesterol I eat (including fat in meats, eggs, butter, cream, shortenings, and organ meats such as liver).	2	1	0
3.	I limit the amount of salt I eat by cooking with only small amounts, not adding salt at the table, and avoiding salty snacks.	2	1	0
4.	I avoid eating too much sugar (especially frequent snacks of candy or soft drinks).	2	1	0

Eating Habits Total Score: _____

ALCOHOL & DRUGS

		A	**S**	**N**
1.	I avoid drinking alcoholic beverages or I drink no more than one or two drinks a day.	4	1	0
2.	I avoid using alcohol beverages or other drugs (especially illegal drugs) as a way of handling stressful situations or the problems in my life.	2	1	0
3.	I am careful not to drink alcohol when taking certain medications (for example, medicine for sleeping, pain, colds, and allergies), or when pregnant.	2	1	0
4.	I read and follow the label directions when using prescribed and over-the-counter.	2	1	0

Alcohol and Drug Total Score: _____

CIGARETTE SMOKING

If you never smoke, enter a score of 10
for this section and go to the next section
on stress control.

	A	S	N

1. I smoke only low-tar and low-nicotine
    cigarettes or I smoke a pipe or cigars.

	2	1	0

Smoking Total Score: _____

STRESS CONTROL

	A	S	N

1. I have a job or do other work that I enjoy.

	2	1	0

2. I find it easy to relax and express my
    feelings freely.

	2	1	0

3. I recognize early and prepare for events or
    situations likely to be stressful for me.

	2	1	0

4. I have close friends, relatives, or others
    whom I can talk to about personal matters
    and call on for help when needed.

	2	1	0

5. I participate in group activities (such as
    church and community organizations) or
    hobbies that I enjoy.

	2	1	0

Stress Control Total Score: _____

SAFETY

	A	S	N

1. I wear a seat belt while riding in a car.

	2	1	0

2. I avoid driving while under the influence
    of alcohol or other drugs.

	2	1	0

3. I obey traffic rules and the speech limit
    when driving.

	2	1	0

			A	**S**	**N**

4. I am careful when using potentially harmful
    products or substances (such as household
    cleaners, poisons, and electrical devices).

                                                            2   1   0

5. I avoid smoking in bed.

                                                            2   1   0

Safety Total Score: _____

Total your score separately for each of the six health styles and then evaluate your scores as follows:

9-10 Your health style in this area is excellent. You not only are
aware of the importance of this area to your health but also are
practicing good habits in this area.

6-8 Your health style in this area is good but you have room for
improvement. Look at the items you answered "Sometimes" or
"Almost Never." What changes can you make in this area to
improve your health style?

3-5 Your health is at risk in this area. Seek help for your health
problems in this area.

0-2 Your health is at serious risk in this area. You need to change
your health-compromising behaviors. Go to your health
counseling center for help.

HEALTH & WELLNESS

EXERCISE 1.2:
This exercise will help assess your current habits and attitudes concerning health. Complete the following sentences:

EATING:
1.   I eat when I am…

_____

2.   One thing I would like to change about my die is…

_____

3.   My eating habits are…

_____

4.   Sometimes I eat unhealthy food because…

_____

EXERCISE:
1.   I usually exercise…

_____

2.   The last time I did cardio/aerobic exercise was…

_____

3.   It would be easier for me to exercise if…

_____

4.   As a result of my physical activity I feel…

_____

5.   Some physical improvements that I would like to make are…

_____

HARMFUL SUBSTANCES:
1.   I smoke cigarettes…

_____

2.   I consider my use of alcohol…

_____

3.   The illegal drugs that I have abused in the past are…

4. When it comes to my use of drugs and alcohol, I am concerned that…

    _____

5. I would describe my use of cola, coffee and other caffeinated
    drinks as…

    _____

SLEEP:
1. Every night I sleep at least…
    _____ hours

2. On weekends I normally sleep…
    _____ hours

3. Sometimes I have trouble sleeping when…
    _____

4. When I wake up in the morning I feel…
    _____

5. When I went to sleep last night I…
    _____

RELATIONSHIPS:
1. My alcohol and drug use has been an issue with…
    _____

2. The way I feel about myself has affected my relationships…
    _____

3. My friends would say that emotionally I am…
    _____

4. Most of the time, I feel that my relationships are…
    _____

5. My relationships can be improved if I…
    _____

My overall concerns regarding my health and wellness are…

_____

_____

_____

_____

HEALTH & WELLNESS

EXERCISE 1.3:

The following exercise will help you assess your use of drugs and
alcohol. Respond to the following statements by checking **Yes** or **No**.

		YES	NO
1.	I drink or use drugs to relieve tension	___	___
2.	I fell I am a normal drug/alcohol user	___	___
3.	I crave drugs/alcohol	___	___
4.	Drug/alcohol use is jeopardizing my academic performance	___	___
5.	My parents/friends worry about my drug/alcohol use	___	___
6.	My alcohol/drug use has gotten me into trouble at work and/or school	___	___
7.	I often regret my use of drugs/alcohol	___	___
8.	I sometimes do not remember what happened the night before during an alcohol/drug binge	___	___
9.	Alcohol/drug use is affecting my reputation	___	___
10.	I have gotten into legal trouble as a result of my alcohol/drug use	___	___
11.	I have attended AA or NA meetings.	___	___
12.	Parties I attend often include drugs/alcohol	___	___
13.	I sometimes drink or use drugs when I am alone	___	___
14.	I cannot stop drinking after one or two drinks	___	___
15.	I have used drugs/alcohol when driving or operating machinery	___	___
16.	I have medical problems related to alcohol/drug use	___	___
17.	I engage in risky behavior as a result of alcohol/ drugs	___	___
18.	I often drink or use drugs before noon	___	___
19.	Drinking/drug use has affected by sleeping	___	___
20.	I spend a great deal of time trying to obtain alcohol or drugs	___	___
21.	I need to increase my use of alcohol/drugs to achieve the desired effect	___	___
22.	I spend a lot of money on drugs/alcohol	___	___
23.	I need more alcohol/drugs the next morning	___	___
24.	I feel I can quit anytime	___	___
25.	I feel the need to justify my drinking/drugging	___	___

26. I envy people who can have a good time without using drugs or alcohol   ___ ___

27. I have missed school or work because of a hangover   ___ ___

28. I have promised myself to quit using drugs/ alcohol and then have changed my mind   ___ ___

29. I do things while using drugs/alcohol that I would not do while sober   ___ ___

30. I worry about my drug/alcohol use   ___ ___

SCORING

Now count the number of questions you answered "yes." If you answered "yes" to 5 or more questions, it is recommended that you speak to a professional drug or alcohol counselor. It may not mean that you have a serious problem, however, it is possible that drugs or alcohol can be adversely affecting your life.

HEALTH & WELLNESS

EXERCISE 1.4:

Stress is detrimental to your physical and mental well-being. Many college students feel tremendous pressure and stress. They tend to deal with this stress either by internalizing it, medicating it by alcohol or drug use or acting out, usually I anger. Anger is symptomatic of stress, frustration and pain. The following exercise will help you assess your level of anger and your reactions to it. It is important to vent your anger in a positive way, it is okay to be angry, but it is not okay to hurt others in the process. Read each of the following statements and circle the response that best describes you.

1. I am easily angered

Almost never	Sometimes	Often	Almost always
1	2	3	4

2. I have a heated temper

Almost never	Sometimes	Often	Almost always
1	2	3	4

3. I am stubborn during arguments

Almost never	Sometimes	Often	Almost always
1	2	3	4

4. I am angered by other's simple-mindedness

Almost never	Sometimes	Often	Almost always
1	2	3	4

5. I am angered when people do no recognize or appreciate my hard work

Almost never	Sometimes	Often	Almost always
1	2	3	4

6. I easily fly off the handle and lose control

Almost never	Sometimes	Often	Almost always
1	2	3	4

7. When I get angry, I often say things that I later regret

Almost never	Sometimes	Often	Almost always
1	2	3	4

8. I do not handle criticism well

Almost never	Sometimes	Often	Almost always
1	2	3	4

9. When I am angry, I feel like hitting someone
    Almost never   Sometimes   Often   Almost always
            1   2   3   4

10. I am angered when I am humiliated in front of others
    Almost never   Sometimes   Often   Almost always
            1   2   3   4

Scoring:

Add up the total of all the numbers you circled. The higher your
total, the more anger tends to dominate your life.

    If you scored 16 or below, your anger is not of concern.
    If you scored 17-20, your anger level is average.
    If you scored 21-24, your anger level is high.
    If you scored 25 or over, you may benefit from anger management
    intervention.

JOURNAL Entry

Health and Wellness

Write about what changes you can make in the next month regarding your physical and mental health in order to improve your overall well being.

_____

_____

_____

_____

_____

_____

_____

_____

_____

_____

_____

_____

_____

_____

_____

_____

_____

_____

_____

_____

_____

PLANNING FOR YOUR FUTURE

EXERCISE 1.1:

When deciding on a career, one of the questions you need to ask yourself is, "Do I want a career or a job?" A job is something you do so that you have financial security. A career is something that helps define who you are, as well as provides financial independence. The following exercise will assist you in determining what path is right for you.

Put a check mark next to the following values you consider important in a career.

1. Having plenty of time to spend with my family   ____
2. Being mentally challenging   ____
3. Working in an environment where moral issues are important   ____
4. Being emotionally and intellectually satisfied   ____
5. Contributing to the welfare of others   ____
6. Having a sense of self-fulfillment   ____
7. Working close to home   ____
8. Happiness   ____
9. Creative freedom   ____
10. Making a lot of money   ____
11. Having opportunities for promotions   ____
12. Having authority/power   ____
13. Making your own job schedule   ____
14. Working with people similar to me   ____
15. Having vacation time and holidays off   ____
16. Having a sense of accomplishment   ____
17. Other _____   ____
18. Other _____   ____
19. Other _____   ____

Based on the values you checked off, what types of careers do you feel will serve you best. Explain.

_____

_____

_____

_____

_____

_____

_____

PLANNING FOR YOUR FUTURE

EXERCISE 1.2:
The following exercise will help you to explore your self-management skills. Place a check mark next to the following skills and qualities you feel you possess.

1. Following directions _____
2. Completing assignments on time _____
3. Getting along with others _____
4. Learning quickly _____
5. Taking pride in work _____
6. Good attendance/being on time _____
7. Good sense of humor _____
8. Hard working _____
9. Positive attitude _____
10. Motivated _____
11. Trustworthy _____
12. Organized _____
13. Good time management skills _____
14. Optimistic _____
15. Assertiveness _____
16. Creative _____
17. Honest _____
18. Fair _____
19. Confident _____
20. Responsible _____
21. Easy going _____
22. Imaginative _____
23. Determined _____
24. Patient _____
25. Self starter _____
26. Task oriented _____
27. Reliable _____
28. Flexible _____
29. Knowledgeable _____
30. Realistic _____
31. Being on time _____
32. High energy _____
33. Other _____ _____
34. Other _____ _____
35. Other _____ _____

Review the items you checked off, selected your 5 strongest skills sand number them 1-5. 1 being the strongest, 5 being the weakest. Based on these skills selected, what careers do you think you may be successful at and why?

1. _____

2. _____

3. _____

4. _____

5. _____

Review your list again. Take a moment to reflect on the items you did not choose. Are there any skills that you would like to develop that you feel will be beneficial to your career choice? How would you go about developing these abilities?

_____

_____

_____

_____

_____

_____

_____

PLANNING FOR YOUR FUTURE

EXERCISE 1.3:

This exercise will ask that you look beyond your own lives and explore the changes you would like to make relating to different situations. It asks that you take control of your lives and responsibilities for your choices.

List what changes you would make in regard to the following situations if possible.

1. **College:** _____

    _____

    _____

    If I could, I would _____

    _____

    _____

2. **Family:** _____

    _____

    _____

    If I could, I would _____

    _____

    _____

3. **Friends:** _____

    _____

    _____

    If I could, I would _____

    _____

    _____

4.   **Relationships:**_____

_____

_____

If I could, I would _____

_____

_____

5.   **World events:**_____

_____

_____

If I could, I would _____

_____

_____

6.   **Education:**_____

_____

_____

If I could, I would _____

_____

_____

7.   **Drugs/alcohol:**_____

_____

_____

If I could, I would _____

_____

_____

JOURNAL ENTRY
Planning for your future

Imagine money was not an issue, and you could do anything you wanted to
do and be anything you wanted to be. What would be your aspirations?
What career path would you take? What would make you feel the most
fulfilled, and the happiest?